OXFORD MONOGRAPHS IN INTERNATIONAL LAW

Neutrality in Contemporary International Law

OXFORD MONOGRAPHS IN INTERNATIONAL LAW

The aim of this series is to publish important and original pieces of research on all aspects of international law. Topics that are given particular prominence are those which, while of interest to the academic lawyer, also have important bearing on issues which touch the actual conduct of international relations. Nonetheless the series is wide in scope and includes monographs on the history and philosophical foundations of international law.

General Editors

PROFESSOR CATHERINE REDGWELL
Chichele Professor of Public International Law at the University of Oxford and Fellow of All Souls College, Oxford

PROFESSOR ROGER O'KEEFE
Professor of International Law at Bocconi University, Milan

RECENT TITLES IN THE SERIES

Geographical Change and the Law of the Sea
Kate Purcell

Statehood and the State-Like in International Law
Rowan Nicholson

Confronting the Shadow State
An International Law Perspective on State Organized Crime
Henri Decœur

Irresolvable Norm Conflicts in International Law
The Concept of a Legal Dilemma
Valentin Jeutner

Institutionalizing State Responsibility
Global Security and UN Organs
Vincent-Joël Proulx

Neutrality in Contemporary International Law

JAMES UPCHER

OXFORD
UNIVERSITY PRESS

OXFORD
UNIVERSITY PRESS

Great Clarendon Street, Oxford, OX2 6DP,
United Kingdom

Oxford University Press is a department of the University of Oxford.
It furthers the University's objective of excellence in research, scholarship,
and education by publishing worldwide. Oxford is a registered trade mark of
Oxford University Press in the UK and in certain other countries

First Edition published in 2020

Impression: 1

Published in the United States of America by Oxford University Press
198 Madison Avenue, New York, NY 10016, United States of America

British Library Cataloguing in Publication Data
Data available

Library of Congress Control Number: 2019955822

ISBN 978–0–19–873976–0

Printed and bound in Great Britain by
Clays Ltd, Elcograf S.p.A.

Foreword

Dr James Edward Upcher was born in Hobart, Tasmania, Australia, in 1979. He attended The Friends' School, a Quaker school in Hobart, and the humanist ideals of Quakerism infused his character and his outlook on the world. He obtained his Bachelor of Arts with First Class Honours and a Bachelor of Laws with First Class Honours at the University of Tasmania, winning the University Medal. He continued his studies at Oxford's Merton College, where he obtained, in 2011, his DPhil (public international law) under a Sir Robert Menzies Memorial Scholarship in Law and a Commonwealth Scholarship. His thesis, entitled 'Neutrality in International Law', was supervised by Professor Stefan Talmon.

Having qualified as a Barrister and Solicitor of the Supreme Court of Victoria, Australia, he practised public international law at leading law firms in London. In 2014, he joined Newcastle Law School (Newcastle University, United Kingdom) as Lecturer in Law, where he taught mainly public international law, international human rights law, and international investment law. His research interests revolved around international dispute settlement, the history and theory of international law, and the law of armed conflict.

James died as the result of an accident on 18 May 2017, aged 37. With his death, we lost a colleague, a mentor, a friend.

Modest, Discerning, and a Loyal Friend

James was a man of integrity, modesty, and intellect. He was meticulous and passionate, a deep thinker and empathetic. He was independent and discerning, always trustworthy and a true confidant. He was engaged with people, asking questions, keen to learn about what their thoughts and opinions were about law, politics, the world, people, and arts.

James was quiet about his own accomplishments and ambitions. Indeed, you had a difficult task on your hands persuading him to say anything about them. He hardly spoke about the awards and scholarships he had received. I first learned through a press article that he was awarded (as co-author) the Smit-Lowenfeld Prize for the best article in the field of international arbitration in 2013 ('Public International Law, Investment Treaties and Commercial Arbitration: an Emerging System of Complementarity?', published in *Arbitration International*).

James consciously focused on supporting the people he cared about. He was a devoted friend, trying to inspire people to pursue their dreams and do what they love. He had a real and positive influence on the lives of many people. He had a beautiful soul. His boundless curiosity and enthusiasm were contagious. Having worked, taught, and travelled with him, I have been one of the fortunate beneficiaries of James' virtues.

A Charismatic Scholar

When I first met James in 2011, I was curious to know why he decided to specialize in international law. After completing his undergraduate studies at the University of Tasmania, he was awarded the Tim Hawkins Memorial Scholarship. This scholarship provided him with the extraordinary opportunity to spend some time in The Hague, where he interned with the International Criminal Tribunal for the former Yugoslavia and discovered the practice of international criminal law. That experience played an instrumental role in his career in international law. In his own words: 'I have always had an academic interest in international law and was particularly drawn to international humanitarian law from the beginning of my studies. The legal regulation of armed conflict presents issues of moral philosophy in an acutely practical context; these very difficult issues have to be translated into a legal framework that is clear and effective. The events of 11 September 2001 and subsequent acts of global terrorism —one of which tragically took Tim Hawkins' life—have given rise to new and urgent questions of international humanitarian law.' An armed conflict, in James' mind, resembled a Greek tragedy: a situation where tensions and dilemmas emerge, leading human beings to their destiny.

Following his stay in the Dutch capital, he moved back to Australia where he worked for a major law firm. In 2005, he moved to Oxford for his doctoral studies. As a researcher and academic, he was characterized by an undogmatic approach to law. He was uninterested in schools of thought and defied *taxonomic delimitations*. Although he refused to understand the rationale behind the schism between *privatistes* and *publicistes*, he would admit that *publicistes* have a better sense of humour!

James was an author in the truest sense of that word. He understood that writers write; they don't just have a book or an article in them one day. He mastered the subtleties and secrets of the English language and paid attention to every single detail. His intellectual rigour and humanity have always permeated his work. The majority of his writings, including this book, focus on international humanitarian law and international arbitration. That said, James excelled in all aspects of international law. He had an in-depth knowledge of the sources and the subjects of international law, the law of State responsibility, and international procedural law. His deep understanding of the principles underpinning international law made him a charismatic author and teacher.

Prior to joining Newcastle Law School, James occasionally lectured on international investment law at University College London, and presented papers in numerous conferences around the world. From 2011 to 2013, he taught international law to government officials in the Middle East. I had the pleasure of co-teaching with him a plethora of modules. His teaching skills never ceased to impress me.

A Committed Practitioner

In 2011, following the successful completion of his doctoral studies, James teamed up with prominent public international law practitioners in London. His tremendous work ethic and meticulous nature became readily apparent. He was also warm and refreshingly modest in a legal profession not necessarily renowned for that quality. James was a mentor to many who sought out his advice.

From 2011 to 2017, he advised States and private entities on public international law issues. He advised in connection with disputes heard, *inter alia*, at the International Court of Justice and the International Centre for Settlement of Investment Disputes. He was involved as counsel in cases before the Permanent Court of Arbitration. He had the opportunity to collaborate with States in Latin America, Europe, and Asia. Despite his busy schedule, James never stopped doing *pro bono* work. He was genuinely committed to a project supporting the United Nations Arms Trade Treaty—a multilateral legally binding agreement that regulates the international trade of conventional weapons through the lens of existing human rights and humanitarian law. He treated his work with the utmost dedication, seriousness, and professionalism. Colleagues and clients describe him as a selfless team player and a relentless battler. He was a role model for all of us.

James' parents and brother, partner, and friends know that James was, of course, much more than just a scholar and a lawyer. He found interest in every aspect of the human condition. While international law was often at the centre of discussions with his *entourage*, music, poetry, philosophy, and literature were indispensable components. In this context, James managed to create a broader family. With his vibrant and multifaceted personality, he wanted to fight injustice.

In order to carry his legacy forward to future generations of students, Janet and John Upcher , their son, Will, and his Law School friends, Peter Haig, Tom Warner, and Jonathan Kelp, have established, in partnership with the University of Tasmania, the James Upcher Prize. The University of Oxford, thanks to the generosity of James' colleagues in London, offers the James Upcher Memorial Scholarship.

As Joachim Du Bellay put it: *Heureux qui, comme Ulysse, a fait un beau voyage.*

Dr Ioannis Konstantinidis
Doha

General Editors' Preface

James Upcher's *Neutrality in Contemporary International Law* persuasively makes the case for the continuing vitality and practical significance of what might be mistaken for the fusty clutter of the nineteenth-century law of nations. Dr Upcher maintains that the law of neutrality, that curious corpus of international rules straddling the *jus ad bellum* and the *jus in bello* and classically pertaining to a formal state of war between States, continues to apply by operation of law, and not simply on a voluntary basis, in the present era of the conventional and customary prohibitions on the use of interstate force and of the concept in international humanitarian law of 'armed conflict'. Its application, he continues, is triggered by the simple existence of an armed conflict of an international character. Precisely what, however, the rules of the law of neutrality permit or require today is a further question, on which Dr Upcher elaborates by reference to a rich body of State practice. Moreover, the application of these rules, he explains, is subject to the obligations and rights of Member States under the Charter of the United Nations.

Neutrality in Contemporary International Law is the fascinating product of extensive research, detailed and creative analysis and argumentation, and panoramic vision. It is a worthy testament to its author, as well as to the esteem in which he was held and the fondness with which he is remembered by his loyal peers.

RO'K, CR

Milan and Oxford
December 2019

Note from the Publisher

The sad circumstances in which this book was produced presented a number of challenges. James Upcher was in the process of updating the text, which was adapted from his PhD thesis, when he passed away in 2017. This means that references to newer developments, cases, or sources are missing from this volume. The chapter on the historical development of neutrality was a new addition to the text, and in a less finished state than the other chapters. It has therefore been included here as an annex rather than the first chapter it was meant to be.

We would not have been able to publish the book without the invaluable work of Associate Professor Veronika Bilkova, who edited the text left behind by James to ensure it was suitable for publication. Her sensitive, thoughtful approach meant that as little as possible was changed while ensuring that the book reads well, its sources are fully cited, and the analysis remains accurate. Professor Robert Kolb also provided important feedback and support.

My sincere thanks go to Lucía Pérez, our Senior Production Editor, for her stellar work in getting this book to publication; to Anthea Davey, for her careful copy-edit; and to Yvonne Dixon and Deborah Shelley for their work on the index and tables.

I am profoundly grateful to Janet and John Upcher, James' parents, and Helena Anderson, his partner, for their support and advice, as well as their help during the book's production process.

Merel Alstein

Oxford
January 2020

Contents

Table of Cases

List of Abbreviations

AAAPSS	*Annals of the American Academy of Political and Social Science*
AFDI	*Annuaire français de droit international*
AFLR	*Air Force Law Review*
AILN	*Australian International Law News*
AJICL	*African Journal of International and Comparative Law*
AJIL	*American Journal of International Law*
AJILS	*American Journal of International Law Supplement*
AJILSS	*American Journal of International Law Special Supplement*
ALRC	*Australian Law Review Commission*
Annuaire	*Annuaire de l'Institut de Droit International*
AP	*Associated Press*
AP I	Geneva Protocol I Additional to the Geneva Conventions of 12 August 1949, and Relating to the Protection of Victims of International Armed Conflicts
APSR	*American Political Science Review*
ARIEL	*Austrian Review of International and European Law*
AdV	*Archiv des Völkerrechts*
AYIL	*Australian Yearbook of International Law*
Australia *Air Operations Law Manual*	Australia *Operations Law for RAAF Commanders* (AAP 1003) (2nd edn 2004)
Australia *LOAC Commander's Guide*	Australia *Law of Armed Conflict Commander's Guide* (ADFP 37 Supp 1 – Interim Edition (1994))
BBC	*British Broadcasting Corporation*
BCICLR	*Boston College International and Comparative Law Review*
BFSP	*British Foreign and State Papers*
BYBIL	*British Yearbook of International Law*
Cal Western ILJ	*California Western International Law Journal*
Canada *LOAC Manual*	Canada *Law of Armed Conflict at the Operational and Tactical Levels* (2nd edn 2003)
Castrén *Neutrality*	E Castrén *The Present Law of War and Neutrality* (1954)
CC	*Cooperation and Conflict*
CJTL	*Columbia Journal of Transnational Law*
Col LR	*Columbia Law Review*
CTS	*Consolidated Treaty Series*
CUP	*Cambridge University Press*
CWRJIL	*Case Western Reserve Journal of International Law*
CYIL	*Canadian Yearbook of International Law*
DJCIL	*Duke Journal of Comparative and International Law*
DJILP	*Denver Journal of International Law and Policy*

DRC	Democratic Republic of the Congo
DSB	*United States Department of State Bulletin*
East JIL	*Eastern Journal of International Law*
EH Rev	*English Historical Review*
EILR	*Emory International Law Review*
EJIL	*European Journal of International Law*
France *Manuel de droit des conflits armés*	France Ministry of Defence *Manuel de droit des conflits armés* (Ministère de la Defense, Paris 2001)
FRY	Federal Republic of Yugoslavia
GB	*The Green Bag*
GC I	Geneva Convention for the Amelioration of the Condition of the Wounded and Sick in Armed Forces in the Field
GC II	Geneva Convention II for the Amelioration of the Condition of Wounded, Sick and Shipwrecked Members of Armed Forces at Sea
GC III	Geneva Convention III Relative to the Treatment of Prisoners of War
GC IV	Geneva Convention IV Relative to the Protection of Civilian Persons in Time of War
Ger LJ	*German Law Journal*
Germany *Humanitarian Law Manual*	Germany Federal Ministry of Defence *Humanitarian Law in Armed Conflict Manual* (English Edition) (Triservice Manual ZDv 15/2) (1992)
GG	*Global Governance*
GLJ	*Georgetown Law Journal*
GYIL	*German Yearbook of International Law*
Hague Air Rules	*Hague Draft Rules of Aerial Warfare* (1923) 'General Report of the Commission of Jurists at The Hague Part II: Rules of Aerial Warfare' (1923) 17 AJILS 245
Hague Conference Proceedings	*The Proceedings of the Hague Peace Conferences: The Conference of 1907* 5 Vols (1920–1921)
HC III	Hague Convention III Relative to the Opening of Hostilities
HC V	Hague Convention V Respecting the Rights and Duties of Neutral Powers and Persons in Case of War on Land
HC XIII	Hague Convention XIII Concerning the Rights and Duties of Neutral Powers in Naval War
Helsinki Principles	Committee on Maritime Neutrality 'Final Report' International Law Association Report of the Sixty-Eighth Conference (Taipei 1998) (International Law Association, Taipei 1998) (*Helsinki Principles on the Law of Maritime Neutrality*)
HILJ	*Harvard International Law Journal*
HJLPP	*Harvard Journal of Law and Public Policy*
HPCR Manual	Program on Humanitarian Policy and Conflict Research *Manual on International Law Applicable to Air and Missile Warfare* (2009)
How LJ	*Howard Law Journal*

IA	*International Affairs*
ICLQ	*International and Comparative Law Quarterly*
ICRC	International Committee of the Red Cross
IDFLR	*Israel Defence Force Law Review*
IEHC	High Court of Ireland Decisions
ILC	International Law Commission
ILM	*International Legal Materials*
ILQ	*International Law Quarterly*
Int Conc	*International Conciliation*
Int Relations	*International Relations*
Int Spectator	*The International Spectator*
IO	*International Organization*
IP	*International Peacekeeping*
IR	*Irish Reports*
Irish YIL	*Irish Yearbook of International Law*
IRRC	*International Review of the Red Cross/Revue internationale de la Croix-Rouge*
IS	*International Security*
ISIA	*Irish Studies in International Affairs*
IYHR	*Israel Yearbook on Human Rights*
IYIA	*Indian Yearbook of International Affairs*
IYIL	*Italian Yearbook of International Law*
JAGJ	*Judge Advocate General Journal of the United States Navy*
JAIL	*Japanese Annual of International Law*
JCH	*Journal of Contemporary History*
JEH	*Journal of Economic History*
JOP	*Journal of Politics*
JPR	*Journal of Peace Research*
Keesing's	*Keesing's Contemporary Archives/Keesing's Record of World Events*
LJIL	*Leiden Journal of International Law*
LNOJ	*League of Nations Official Journal*
LNTS	*League of Nations Treaty Series*
LOAC	*Law of Armed Conflict*
LOSB	*Law of the Sea Bulletin*
LOSC	United Nations Convention on the Law of the Sea
Louisiana LR	*Louisiana Law Review*
MEZ	Maritime Exclusion Zone
Mich LR	*Michigan Law Review*
Mil LR	*Military Law Review*
Minn LR	*Minnesota Law Review*
MP	*Marine Policy*
MPYBUNL	*Max Planck Yearbook of United Nations Law*
NATO	North Atlantic Treaty Organisation
Naval LR	*Naval Law Review*
NDLR	*Notre Dame Law Review*

New Zealand *Interim LOAC Manual*	New Zealand *Interim Law of Armed Conflict Manual* (DM 112) (1992)
NILR	*Netherlands International Law Review*
NJIL	*Nordic Journal of International Law*
Northwestern ULR	*Northwestern University Law Review*
NT	*Nordisk Tidsskrift for International Ret*
NYIL	*Netherlands Yearbook of International Law*
NYUJILP	*New York University Journal of International Law and Politics*
ODIL	*Ocean Development and International Law*
OJLS	*Oxford Journal of Legal Studies*
ONUC	United Nations Operation in the Congo
Oppenheim	L Oppenheim *International Law—A Treatise* (vol II, 1st edn 1906; vol II, 3rd edn 1921 (ed R F Roxburgh); vol II, 7th edn 1952 (ed H Lauterpacht))
OUP	Oxford University Press
PAS	*Proceedings of the American Society of International Law*
PW	*Problems of the War* (Transactions of the Grotius Society vols 1–3)
QLR	*Quinnipiac Law Review*
RBDI	*Revue belge de droit international*
RCADI	*Revue de cours de l'académie de droit international*
RDI	*Rivista di diritto internazionale*
RDPM	*Revue de droit pénal militaire et de droit de la guerre*
REDI	*Revue égyptien de droit international*
RGDIP	*Revue général de droit international public*
RIAA	*United Nations Reports of International Arbitral Awards* 1948-
RIS	*Review of International Studies*
ROP	*Review of Politics*
San Remo Manual	Institute of International Humanitarian Law *San Remo Manual on International Law Applicable to Armed Conflicts at Sea* (1994)
SJIL	*Stanford Journal of International Law*
SJILC	*Syracuse Journal of International Law and Commerce*
SWB	*BBC Summary of World Broadcasts*
Sweden *IHL Manual*	Sweden *International Humanitarian Law in Armed Conflict with Reference to the Swedish Total Defence System* (1991)
Syd LR	*Sydney Law Review*
SZIER	*Schweizerische Zeitschrift für internationales und europäisches Recht/Revue suisse de droit international et de droit européen*
TEZ	Total Exclusion Zone
TGS	*Transactions of the Grotius Society*
Tucker	*Neutrality at Sea* R W Tucker *The Law of War and Neutrality at Sea* (1957)
UK	United Kingdom of Great Britain and Northern Ireland
UK	*Manual of the Law of Armed Conflict*UK *Manual of the Law of Armed Conflict* (2004)

UK *The Law of War on Land*	UK *The Law of War on Land, being Part III of the Manual of Military Law* (1958)
UN Charter	*Charter of the United Nations* (1945)
UNCIO	*United Nations, Documents of the United Nations Conference on International Organisation, San Francisco 1945* 22 vols (United Nations, New York 1945-1955)
UNDPKO	*United Nations Department of Peacekeeping Operations*
UNPROFOR	United Nations Peacekeeping Force
UNSC	United Nations Security Council
UNTS	*United Nations Treaty Series*
US	*United States of America*
USAFAJLS	*United States Air Force Academy Journal of Legal Studies*
US *Law of Naval Warfare Manual*	US *Law of Naval Warfare Manual* (1955)
US *Land Warfare Manual*	US *Manual on the Law of Land Warfare* (FM 27-10) (1956)
US *Naval Commander's Handbook*	US *Naval Commander's Handbook* (NWP 1-14M) (2007)
US *Operational Law Handbook*	US *Operational Law Handbook* (2009)
VJIL	*Virginia Journal of International Law*
VTJL	*Vanderbilt Journal of Transnational Law*
YBIHL	*Yearbook of International Humanitarian Law*
YBILC	*Yearbook of the International Law Commission*
YJIL	*Yale Journal of International Law*
ZaöRV	*Zeitschrift für ausländisches öffentliches Recht und Völkerrecht*

Introduction

1. Neutrality Yesterday and Today

In 1952, Hersch Lauterpacht famously noted that the laws of war existed at the 'vanishing point' of international law.[1] At the time Lauterpacht was writing, the rules for the conduct of hostilities appeared outdated in light of both their widespread violation in World War II and by the comprehensive regulation of recourse to force under the UN Charter. There was every reason to doubt whether the laws of armed conflict could or would continue to exist, at least as they had traditionally been understood and applied. It soon became apparent, however, that the system of collective security could not function as intended; there were considerable practical and political difficulties associated with the identification of, and effective sanctions against, an aggressor. As a matter of practical necessity, the law of armed conflict rapidly began to enjoy renewed importance.[2] And that importance continues today; no one interested in contemporary international affairs could deny the vital role of the law of armed conflict in the restraint of hostilities. In no sense does it exist at the margins of international law.

If any area could be identified as one that exists at the 'vanishing point' of international law today, a strong case could be advanced that the law of neutrality occupies that precarious ground. The law of neutrality governs the relationship between States which are engaged in hostilities and those States which are not engaged in hostilities—between belligerents and neutrals, to use the traditional terminology. It strikes many today as outmoded and obsolete, of a different era of international law: its rules the unstable product of compromise;[3] in its essence incompatible, indeed utterly irreconcilable, with the prohibition on recourse to force and the development of collective security.[4] In 1968, Sir Ian Brownlie remarked in a book review that the law of neutrality was a topic on which

[1] H Lauterpacht 'The Problem of the Revision of the Law of War' (1952) 29 BYBIL 360, 382.

[2] On this point see H Lauterpacht 'The Limits of the Operation of the Law of War' (1953) 30 BYBIL 206, 207–8; R Sloane 'The Cost of Conflation: Preserving the Dualism of *Jus ad Bellum* and *Jus in Bello* in the Contemporary Law of War' (2009) 34 YJIL 47, 64–5.

[3] M Janis 'Neutrality' in H B Robertson Jr (ed) *The Law of Naval Operations* (International Law Studies 64, US Naval War College, Newport 1991) 148, 153.

[4] For a powerful argument along these lines, see H Lauterpacht 'The Future of Neutrality, December 1941' in E Lauterpacht (ed) *International Law: Being the Collected Papers of Hersch Lauterpacht* vol V (CUP, Cambridge 2004) 675.

international lawyers had been in recent years 'rather reticent.'[5] International lawyers have, by and large, remained reticent on the topic of neutrality in the decades since.[6]

This reluctance is entirely understandable. The applicability and content of the law of neutrality—indeed, its very existence—is radically uncertain, and has been for a considerable period of time. Indeed, at the International Law Association's 1932 meeting in Oxford, Lord McNair contended that:

> There are two basic factors in the development of International Law at the present moment: (1) that the whole conception of neutrality is in the melting-pot, and (2) that the whole conception of what is meant by a state of war is in the melting-pot. I think that most of us have to take this line: I cannot tell you what the law of neutrality is to-day, I can tell you where to find what was the law of neutrality in 1914, but I cannot conscientiously tell you what it is to-day.[7]

No international lawyer today is likely to say that the law of neutrality is one of the key factors in the development of international law. Yet it would be equally unrealistic today to say that neutrality—or, at least, non-participation in hostilities by non-belligerent States—has disappeared entirely. Evidence confirms that it is rarely invoked explicitly in contemporary international armed conflicts. Yet armed conflicts continue to occur and the machinery of collective security does not respond adequately to every illegal use of force. What, then, of the relationship between the States participating in hostilities and those which are not participating in hostilities—between belligerents and neutrals? Is that relationship now governed solely by the law of peace? Or does the law of neutrality continue to live on, either in its traditional mode or in modified form?

Perhaps surprisingly, there has been little extended consideration in the academic literature of these and other questions concerning the position and content of neutrality in contemporary international law.[8] Indeed, since 1945 there has been no detailed treatment of the way in which the law of neutrality has developed, disappeared, or been modified by other areas of international law. It is the purpose of this monograph to examine in detail the development of the law of neutrality and its contemporary content and application.

[5] I Brownlie 'Review of S R Chowdhury, *Military Alliances and Neutrality in War and Peace*' (1968) 16 ICLQ 832, 833.

[6] V Lowe *International Law* (OUP, Oxford 2007) 287.

[7] Neutrality Committee 'Report of the Neutrality Committee' in International Law Association Report of the Thirty-Seventh Conference (International Law Association, Oxford 1932) 159, 185.

[8] The law of neutrality has been recently examined in a general historical perspective: S Neff *The Rights and Duties of Neutrals: A General History* (Manchester University Press, Manchester 2000); K Wani *Neutrality in International Law: From the Sixteenth Century to 1945* (Routledge 2017).

2. Types of Neutrality in International Law Distinguished

One of the principal difficulties in addressing the subject matter with adequate precision is the definitional difficulty with the term 'neutrality.' It has been said—not very helpfully—that 'neutrality' is, itself, a 'neutral' term, 'in the sense that it lacks, even in the legal field, a well-defined meaning and has many connotations.'[9] This view has been frequently accompanied by the argument that the law of neutrality reflects the relative bargaining power of the parties at any given time.[10] The law of neutrality must be grasped historically, as considered in detail in the Annex to this book. Neutrality may be used to denote a course of foreign policy as well as a legal status. The political concept of neutrality is distinct from the legal one and will not be considered. But there are also certain types of legal neutrality that cannot be considered in detail in the course of this study.

a. Permanent Neutrality and Neutralization

The concept of neutrality under examination in this book differs in part from the concept of permanent neutrality or neutralization. Neutralization was a product of the nineteenth century concern with the maintenance of a balance of power, and it was hoped that the preservation of the neutralization of territory would act as a *cordon sanitaire* that could prevent the enlargement of the theatre of battle.[11] Although it has been claimed that examples of neutralization may be found much earlier,[12] the most significant examples of neutralization occurred at the Congress of Vienna, in an attempt to secure a lasting European balance of power.[13] At the

[9] J H W Verzijl *International Law in Historical Perspective: Part IX-B The Law of Neutrality* (Sijthoff & Noordhoff, Alphen Aan Den Rijn 1979) 12. The *New Shorter Oxford English Dictionary* defines neutrality as an 'intermediate state or condition, a neutral position, middle ground.' It defines the adjective 'neutral' as meaning '[n]ot assisting or actively taking the side of either of two belligerent States or groups of States in a war; taking neither side or view in a dispute, disagreement, or controversy.' *The New Shorter Oxford English Dictionary* vol II (Clarendon Press, Oxford 1993) 1911.

[10] N Ørvik *The Decline of Neutrality 1914–1941* (2nd edn Frank Cass, London 1971) 13; Castrén *Neutrality* 427.

[11] See W Grewe, *The Epochs of International Law* (M Byers (ed and tr)) (Walter de Grutyer 2000) 434. The first edition of Oppenheim doubted whether neutralization would survive beyond the nineteenth century: 'neutralised States ... are a product of the nineteenth century only and it remains to be seen whether neutralisation can stand the test of history.' (L Oppenheim *International Law: Volume I* (Longman's, London 1905) 144).

[12] There is an argument that a status of permanent neutrality was created much earlier than the nineteenth century. Verzijl suggests that the first permanent neutrality was in the thirteenth century, while Grewe suggests that permanent neutrality dates from the neutralization of the principality of Liege in 1478. See Grewe (n 11) 371.

[13] There had been an intention to neutralize Malta under the Treaty of Amiens in 1802, but it did not eventuate. For a discussion of the balance of power at the Congress of Vienna, see A Osiander *The States System of Europe, 1640–1990: Peacemaking and the Conditions of International Stability* (Clarendon Press, Oxford 1994) chapter 4.

Congress of Vienna, Switzerland was declared permanently neutral.[14] The Free City of Cracow was established under the joint protection of Russia, Austria, and Prussia, according to which the City was to be 'libre, indépendente, et strictement neutre.'[15] Other cases of neutralization followed in the nineteenth century. In 1839, the Netherlands, Great Britain, Russia, France, Prussia, and Austria signed the Treaty of London, which formed the Kingdom of Belgium (it had been united with the Netherlands at the Congress of Vienna but the two had been effectively separated by 1830).[16] The Treaty of London neutralized the Kingdom of Belgium, as part of a strategy to create a 'buffer State' between Germany and France.[17] In 1867, Luxembourg was neutralized as a Free City. There are a number of other examples of neutralizations throughout the nineteenth century.[18]

In these examples, the process of creation of neutral status is profoundly different from the production of neutrality by States upon the outbreak of hostilities. The status of permanent neutrality is one created primarily, but not always, by treaty.[19] The nineteenth century form of neutralization was a form of 'conventional neutrality'; it differs—to use Wheaton's terminology—from the 'natural neutrality' every State has a right to observe upon the outbreak of hostilities.[20] While the obligations of natural neutrality arise only upon the outbreak of hostilities, a permanently neutral State is obliged in peacetime to avoid every engagement that might compromise its neutrality during a situation of armed conflict or war.[21] A permanently neutral State is forbidden from entering into alliances or treaties of guarantee that may involve it in war not involving defence of its own territory.[22]

[14] Act of the Congress of Vienna 9 June 1815 2 BSFP 7 Article 34, Annex XIA; see H J Morgenthau 'The End of Switzerland's "Differential" Neutrality' (1938) 32 AJIL 558; D Vagts 'Switzerland, International Law and World War II' (1997) 91 AJIL 466. The Swiss maintain that the permanent neutrality of Switzerland is based on the Déclaration du Congrès de Vienne of 20 March 1815, the Acte d'accession de la confédération de la Suisse of 27 May 1815 and the Acte portant reconnaissance et garantie de la neutralité perpétuelle de la Suisse et de l'inviolabilité de son territoire signed in Paris on 27 November 1815. Grewe (n 11) 434.

[15] Act of the Congress of Vienna, 9 June 1815 2 BFSP 7 Article VI. Cracow lost its independence in 1846 when it was annexed by Austria. See Treaty of Vienna 3 November 1846, de Martens, 9 NRG 575; E Winslow 'Neutralisation' (1908) 2 AJIL 366, 372.

[16] Winslow 'Neutralisation' (1908) 2 AJIL 366, 369.

[17] Ibid. Prussia hoped that the neutralization of Belgium would serve to maintain the 'peace, repose and good order of Europe.' H J Tobin 'Is Belgium Still Neutralised?' (1932) 26 AJIL 514, 523.

[18] For example, the Ionian Islands were neutralized by the Great Powers when the group was transferred to Greece in 1864. See Winslow 'Neutralisation' 372.

[19] Hence there is a subtle difference between 'permanent neutrality' and 'neutralization.' While States or territories that are 'neutralized' by treaties are designated as 'permanently neutral', a State can declare itself 'permanently neutral' without that neutrality being imposed or guaranteed by other States pursuant to a treaty; 'neutralization' refers to a status of neutrality imposed from without: C F Wicker *Neutralisation* (OUP, London 1911) 1.

[20] *Wheaton's International Law* (Dana (ed)) (8th edn Little, Brown, Boston 1866) 516.

[21] Ibid 516.

[22] F Greene 'Neutralisation and the Balance of Power' (1953) 47 APSR 1041, 1047. Wicker suggested that a permanently neutral State could enter into defensive alliances. See Wicker (n 19) 57–8.

The concept of permanent neutrality or neutralization differs from the concept of neutrality considered here, both in terms of its method of creation and in terms of the amplitude of its content. The State practice of permanently neutral States will be considered in the following pages only to the extent that it illuminates the general practice of States with regard to the operation of neutrality during hostilities. The book does not attempt a more detailed enquiry into the ambit of permanent neutrality.

b. Neutrality in Non-International Armed Conflict: Recognition of Belligerency

The second type of neutrality that cannot be considered in this monograph is the application of neutrality to a specific situation of non-international armed conflict: a recognition of belligerency. It is necessary briefly to describe the concept.

The doctrine of recognition of belligerency was the means by which the law of neutrality was applicable to non-international conflicts.[23] According to this doctrine, the intensity of the conflict determined the rights and duties of the contestants and the extent to which third States were permitted to intervene to influence the outcome.[24] Three different levels of conflict were contemplated: rebellion, insurgency, and belligerency.[25] A rebellion denoted a conflict of low intensity, short duration, and local character.[26] If the conflict developed in intensity such that the rebel movement achieved control of a substantial portion of territory, the rebellion was deemed an 'insurgency.' It was frequently the case that third States recognized, on an ad hoc basis, the insurgents for the purposes of regularizing intercourse with the insurgents.[27] Insurgency was, therefore, a 'catch-all designation' that left third States substantially free to calibrate their legal relations with insurgents.[28]

Recognition of belligerency indicated that the insurgents had acquired a degree of effective control of territory such that they openly challenged the government's

[23] See A Cullen, 'Key developments affecting the scope of internal armed conflict in international humanitarian law' (2005) 183 Mil LR 69; R Bartels 'Timelines, Borderlines and Conflicts: The Historical Evolution of the Legal Divide between International and Non-international Armed Conflicts' (2009) 91 IRRC 35, 48–56.

[24] Recognition of belligerency did not involve questions of claims to governmental authority, and hence is more related to the law of neutrality than to recognition of governments. D P O'Connell *International Law: Volume 1* (2nd edn Stevens & Sons, London 1970) 148. On recognition of governments, see S Talmon *Recognition of Governments in International Law: With Particular Reference to Governments in Exile* (Clarendon Press, Oxford 1998)

[25] See H A Wilson, *International Law and the Use of Force by National Liberation Movements* (Clarendon Press, Oxford 1988) 22–9; R Higgins 'International Law and Civil Conflict' in E Luard (ed) *The International Regulation of Civil Wars* (Thames and Hudson, London 1972) 169.

[26] E Castrén *Civil War* (Suomalainen Tiedeakatemia, Helsinki 1966) 30.

[27] H Lauterpacht *Recognition in International Law* (CUP, Cambridge 1957) 270–1.

[28] R A Falk *Legal Order in a Violent World* (PUP, Princeton 1968) 119.

claim to represent the State.[29] To recognize the insurgents as belligerents was to acknowledge that the conflict had reached such a pitch of intensity that the situation should be treated analogously to an inter-State war.[30]

Recognition of belligerency was therefore constitutive in character: the act of recognition provided each side with the rights and duties they would have in an inter-State war. Such recognition brought into operation the law of neutrality.[31] This process differs from the way neutral status is produced in international armed conflict. In non-international armed conflict that reaches the level at which recognition of belligerency would usually be accorded, it is the non-participant States which engage in the act of recognition and deem the contending parties as belligerents, and thereby bind themselves to the law of neutrality; there was no sense of legal obligation as in the sense in which neutral status was created in international armed conflict. In non-international armed conflict, third States therefore had considerable discretion whether to apply the law of neutrality or not. Since the metropolitan or parent government for obvious reasons would frequently be reluctant to accord recognition to a rebel force operating on its territory, third States could recognize the belligerency of the non-governmental force and apply the law of neutrality without the metropolitan government's consent.[32] In practice these circumstances were restricted to situations in which the third State's interests were materially affected, such as when warfare was occurring at sea that affected the shipping of third States; otherwise, if premature, the third State's recognition of belligerency would amount to intervention in the metropolitan government's domestic affairs.[33]

Hence there was a need to develop criteria that could govern when recognition of belligerency could lawfully be accorded, commonly thought to be the following: the existence of an armed conflict of a general character within a State; the occupation and administration by the rebels of a substantial portion of the national territory; the conduct of hostilities through organized armed forces according to the laws and customs of war under a responsible authority; and the existence of other circumstances necessitating third States to indicate their attitude towards the situation.[34] However, although these criteria were indications that recognition of belligerency was to be determined as a matter of fact rather

[29] The distinction between recognition of insurgency and recognition of belligerency is not always clear. See R Jennings and A Watts (eds) *Oppenheim's International Law: Volume 1 Peace* (9th edn Longman, Harlow 1992) 165; O'Connell International Law: Vol I (n 24) 151–2.

[30] L Moir *The Law of Internal Armed Conflict* (CUP, Cambridge 2002) 5.

[31] Castrén *Civil War* (n 26) 138–9; *The Ambrose Light* (1885) 25 Fed 408. However, cf O'Connell's view that recognition acts as acknowledgement of a situation created by international law.

[32] Moir (n 30) 8–10.

[33] J Crawford *The Creation of States in International Law in International Law* (2nd edn OUP, Oxford 2006) 381.

[34] H Lauterpacht *Recognition in International Law* (CUP, Cambridge 1947) 176; M N Shaw *International Law* (6th edn CUP, Cambridge 2008) 1149–50.

than political preference,[35] these criteria did not ever gain widespread acceptance as preconditions to recognition of belligerency and the process largely remained discretionary.[36]

The doctrine gained acceptance in the early nineteenth century in various conflicts in the Spanish-American colonies, when the United States granted recognition to the South American States in 1815.[37] The most well-known example of recognition of belligerency was the United Kingdom's declaration of neutrality in the US Civil War, which constituted implicit recognition of belligerency of the Confederate States.[38] The shortcomings of the doctrine became increasingly apparent throughout the nineteenth century; third States were reluctant to accord recognition of belligerency when the metropolitan government had not done so.[39] The difficulties associated with it were perhaps most clearly exposed after the Spanish Civil War broke out in 1936.[40] In that conflict, recognition of belligerency was not granted by any State, despite the magnitude and intensity of the conflict clearly meriting such recognition. Rather than according recognition of belligerency, outside powers focused on the status of the government. One group of States recognized the nationalists as the *de jure* government of Spain and furnished it with substantial military assistance.[41] Other States concluded an agreement stipulating non-intervention in the conflict.[42] The degree of foreign State involvement in the armed conflict was so extensive that it was considered doubtful whether the doctrine of recognition of belligerency was applicable at all.[43]

The operation of the doctrine of recognition of belligerency was not clear following the Spanish Civil War and in other conflicts throughout the twentieth century, leading to speculation by a number of publicists that the doctrine had fallen into desuetude. It is not necessary to examine the correctness of this view here; the doctrine's operation is sufficiently distinct from the application of

[35] Moir (n 30), 14–15. [36] Ibid 17. Cf McNair *International Law Opinions: Volume I* 141.

[37] See J B Moore *A Digest of International Law: Volume I* (US Government Printing Office, Washington 1906); H A Smith (ed) *Great Britain and the Law of Nations: Volume I* (P S King & Son, London 1932) 261–333.

[38] J B Moore *History and Digest of International Arbitrations: Volume I* 595.

[39] As in the Greek revolt against the Ottoman Empire (1821–1829), the Hungarian Civil War (1848–1849), and the Cuban Wars of Liberation against Spain (1868–1878 and 1895–1898).

[40] E C Stowell 'Spain and the Nations' (1936) 30 AJIL 675; J W Garner 'Questions of International Law in the Spanish Civil War' (1937) 31 AJIL 66; A D McNair 'The Law Relating to the Civil War in Spain' (1937) 53 LQR 471; N J Padelford 'International Law and the Spanish Civil War' (1937) 31 AJIL 226; E Borchard '"Neutrality" and Civil Wars' (1937) 31 AJIL 304; V A O'Rourke 'Recognition of Belligerency and the Spanish War' (1937) 31 AJIL 398; H A Smith 'Some Problems of the Spanish Civil War' (1937) 18 BYBIL 17; W L Walker 'Recognition of Belligerency and Grant of Belligerent Rights' (1937) 23 TGS 177; N J Padelford 'Foreign Shipping During the Spanish Civil War' (1938) 32 AJIL 264; C G Fenrick 'Can Civil Wars Be Brought Under the Control of International Law?' (1938) 32 AJIL 538.

[41] Garner 'Questions of International Law' above n 40.

[42] See N J Padelford 'The Non-Intervention Agreement and the Spanish Civil War' (1937) 31 AJIL 578; J W Garner 'Recognition of Belligerency' (1938) 32 AJIL 106.

[43] Lauterpacht *Recognition in International Law* 252.

neutrality in international armed conflict that recognition of belligerency will not be considered further in this study.

3. Outline of the Book

The monograph proceeds in five chapters. Chapter 1 addresses the challenges to neutrality of the prohibition of the threat or use of force in international law. After considering the way in which neutral status was created in traditional international law, the chapter considers the argument that the twentieth and twenty-first centuries have seen the development of a concept of 'optional neutrality' and the possibility of a position of non-belligerency. Having concluded that this argument does not accurately describe the way in which neutrality is invoked in contemporary international law, Chapter 2 proceeds to consider the thresholds for the application and termination of neutrality.

Chapter 3 turns to an investigation of the rights and duties of neutrality that result from the creation of the status of neutrality, in an effort to understand the contemporary content of neutrality. Chapter 4 then considers how these neutral rights and duties are modified when the UN Security Council takes action under Chapter VII of the UN Charter. Chapter 5 turns from a consideration of the rights and duties of neutrals to an examination of the rights of belligerents against neutrals. Although it is the case that neutral duties correspond to belligerent rights, and vice versa, the chapter examines the way in which recourse by belligerents to the law of contraband, the law of blockade, and war zones against neutrals has been affected by the UN Charter. The development of neutrality up to the early twentieth century is described in the Annex to this book.

Chapter 1
Neutrality, Non-Belligerency, and the Prohibition of the Use of Force

The law of neutrality exists today in an uncertain state principally because of the vast changes to the law on the use of force that have challenged neutrality's very place in the corpus of international law. Indeed, the prohibition on the threat or use of force in international law throws into doubt the entire edifice on which the law of neutrality is built: the distinction between a state of belligerency and a state of neutrality, and the legality (or extra-legality) of war. As the Prime Minister of Japan remarked in 2002, regarding Hague Convention V and XIII, concerning neutrality in land and naval warfare respectively,

> ...these Conventions were adopted when war was not generally considered to be illegal under international law...The provisions relating to neutral States in these Conventions cannot be applied currently as they were in the past.[1]

In the past—at least in the nineteenth century—the formalism of international law distinguished sharply between different statuses—peace and war, neutrality and belligerency—and States were free to move between these categories (or, as often as not, were forced to move between these categories), unconstrained by restrictions stemming from the delictual character of war.

However, States are now restricted by the prohibition on the threat or use of force. Much of the difficulty that surrounds any attempt to understand the operation of neutrality in contemporary international law is an attempt to grasp the implications for it of the prohibition on aggressive war. Indeed, the problems determining how the law of neutrality is invoked in contemporary international law have led to the view that the law of neutrality is in a 'chaotic' state.[2] If the unrestricted right to go to war was the foundation of neutrality, and if that right has now been abolished, it may signal vast changes in the creation of neutral status in contemporary international law.

One prominent view is that those changes have been very profound, and have altered the way in which neutrality is invoked. That view suggests that the

[1] (2002) 45 JAIL 107.

[2] A Gioia 'Neutrality and Non-Belligerency' in H H G Post (ed) *International Economic Law and Armed Conflict* (Martinus Nijhoff, Dordrecht 1994) 51, 51.

prohibition of the use of force in international law means that there is now no basis for adhering to the view that non-participating States may have the duties of neutrality foisted upon them. Instead, these writers suggest, neutrality has been transformed into an optional legal status that States are free to take up or decline as they see fit, subject to those rules being displaced by the UN Charter. Those States that choose not to take up the status of neutrality upon an armed conflict breaking out occupy a position of non-belligerency; and they are free, in that status, to deviate from the substantive rules of neutrality.

This chapter undertakes to determine whether this argument finds support in the developments surrounding neutrality in the twentieth and twenty-first centuries. It suggests that this argument, although initially attractive, in fact creates certain difficulties and does not reflect the state of the law. Before moving to an engagement with this argument in detail, it is first necessary to sketch the way in which the status of neutrality was created in nineteenth century international law.

1. The 'State of War' Doctrine and Recognition

a. War in Nineteenth Century International Law

Legal doctrine on war in the nineteenth century possessed a rationalistic character.[3] The existence of war brought into operation a different legal order and set of rules.[4] States could occupy only two possible statuses when war was declared: '[a]ll, who take part in the war, are Belligerents; all, who stand aloof from the contention of the Belligerents, are neutral.'[5]

Neutrality was therefore a legal status resulting from, and dependent upon, the existence of war, as an 1862 opinion of the Law Officers of the Crown made plain:

> The international obligation to which the Minister of Ecuador refers in his despatch, and which he appears to think ought regulate the conduct of England at the present moment in its relations with the States of Peru and Ecuador, is that of neutrality; but neutrality, both according to the law of nations and the municipal law of this country, means the neutrality of one State, as between two or more States who are at war between themselves; and has no bearing upon a state

[3] S Neff *War and the Law of Nations: A General History* (CUP, Cambridge 2005) 168.

[4] A D McNair 'The Legal Meaning of War, and the Relation of War to Reprisals' (1925) 11 TGS 29, 33.

[5] T Twiss *The Law of Nations Considered as Independent Political Communities: On the Rights and Duties of Nations in Time of War* (2nd edn Clarendon Press, Oxford 1875) 436.

of peace, however probable a future war may be, or however much, or however reasonably, war may be apprehended.[6]

Because of its far-reaching effects the state of war was not simply a matter between the duelling belligerents, however much the analogy between wars and duels prevailed in the nineteenth century; the existence of war 'inevitably and automatically affected the entire world.'[7] Determining whether a state of war actually existed, however, was not a straightforward matter. The existence of war was not a factual assessment but an indication of intention on the part of the belligerent States. A state of war existed when one or more of the belligerents decided that war existed; non-participant States were not competent to assess the character of hostilities.[8]

It followed that the state of war doctrine was highly artificial because it could be both under- and over-inclusive.[9] Dependent on belligerent caprice, a war could exist between parties without the presence of any force or hostilities; alternatively, belligerents could withhold the imprimatur of war to a large-scale conflict if it was in their interests to do so.[10] By characterizing a use of force as a reprisal rather than an act of war, belligerents could avoid the application of all doctrine associated with war, and non-participant States were then not deemed to be neutrals.[11]

Nevertheless, despite its inherent unpredictability, the state of war doctrine gained considerable adherence in State practice in the course of the nineteenth and early twentieth centuries.[12] Certain belligerent activities could implicitly indicate the existence of a state of war: for example, the exercise of traditional belligerent rights, such as the visit and search of neutral ships or the setting up of a blockade.[13] In the dispute between China and France in 1884–1885, during which France enacted blockade measures but refused to admit the existence of war, Britain stated that the enforcement of the blockade against neutrals would be an acknowledgement that the conflict was war and not a series of reprisals.[14]

[6] A D McNair (ed) *International Law Opinions* vol III (CUP, Cambridge 1956) 152.

[7] Neff (n 3) 191.

[8] See I Brownlie *International Law and the Use of Force by States* (Clarendon Press, Oxford 1963) 26–7.

[9] N Berman 'Privileging Combat? Contemporary Conflict and the Legal Construction of War' (2004–2005) 43 CJTL 1, 16.

[10] J B Moore *Digest of International Law* vol VII (US Government Printing Office, Washington DC 1907) 153.

[11] E Nys *Le droit international, les principes, les théories, les faits* vol II(1st edn A Castaigne, Brussels 1906) 587.

[12] Brownlie (n 8) 26–40; F Grob *The Relativity of War and Peace: A Study in Law, History and Politics* (Yale University Press, New Haven 1949).

[13] Q Wright 'When Does War Exist?' (1932) 26 AJIL 362, 364.

[14] 'Letter from Earl Granville to M Waddington' (1884–1885) 76 BFSP 426–7.

b. Recognition of Neutrality

Non-participants did not have a legal right to adopt the *status* of neutrality in the way that belligerents could invoke the state of war. A State's ability to remain neutral in a particular conflict was, more often than not, reduced to a question of the relative power and strategic importance of the belligerents and neutrals involved. The decision to permit a State to claim neutrality was political rather than legal—a matter of sovereign prerogative.[15] Neutral status was granted only to non-participant States if the belligerents chose to treat them as such, by the mechanism of recognition. According to James Lorimer, neutrality 'spring[s] from and depend[s] on recognition.'[16]

Recognition of neutrality by belligerents in the nineteenth century may be regarded as constitutive in character.[17] The process of recognition transformed the *de facto* neutral position of non-participants into *de jure* neutrals bound by the law of neutrality. As with recognition of States in nineteenth century international law, recognition of neutrality functioned as a 'juristic baptism' that brought into existence the rights and duties of neutrality.[18] Such recognition was typically brought about through belligerent acquiescence in the exercise of neutral rights.[19] A belligerent that refused to recognize neutrality did not violate international law, because the status of neutrality did not come into existence unless and until belligerents accepted it.[20] A State's declaration of neutrality therefore served no legal purpose and had no legal effect; it signalled merely the neutral State's intention to comply with the duties of neutrality and to remain aloof rather than to become a party to the conflict.[21]

A belligerent could refuse to recognize a State's claims to neutrality, which led to certain results. A refusal to recognize could result in the severance of diplomatic relations between the two States; alternatively, a belligerent could choose to extend and broaden the conflict by declaring war against the State whose neutrality it refused to recognize. If a belligerent did choose to grant recognition of neutrality, that recognition could be accompanied by the imposition of certain conditions on the neutral State.[22]

[15] D Kennedy 'International Law and the Nineteenth Century: History of an Illusion' (1997–1998) 17 QLR 99, 129–30.

[16] J Lorimer *Institutes of the Law of Nations: A Treatise of the Jural Relations of Separate Political Communities* vol II (William Blackwood and Sons, Edinburgh 1884) 130.

[17] In non-international armed conflicts that achieved the characteristics of an international war, the situation was reversed: the recognition of insurgents as belligerents created the legal relationship of neutrality between third States and the duelling belligerent parties.

[18] J Crawford *The Creation of States in International Law* (2nd edn OUP, Oxford 2006) 16.

[19] Oppenheim (1st edn) vol II 406. [20] Ibid.

[21] F Deák and P Jessup (eds) *A Collection of Neutrality Laws, Regulations and Treaties of Various Countries* vol I (Greenport Press, Westport 1974) 26 (Argentina); 36 (Austria-Hungary).

[22] During the Russo-Japanese war of 1904–1905 belligerent acceptance of China's neutrality was made dependent on China's fulfillment of certain stipulations. See A S Hershey 'Some Questions of

Once established through belligerent recognition, the rights and duties of neutrality came into existence in law. However, a State's status of neutrality was exchangeable for the status of belligerency at any stage in the hostilities.[23] Such an exchange of status could occur in one of two ways. The neutral could become a belligerent simply by abandoning its neutral position and voluntarily entering the war on the side of one of the belligerents. Alternatively, since the ability to initiate war had primacy over any claim to territorial inviolability, the neutral State could become a belligerent through a declaration of war issued against it, or through invasion of its territory by a belligerent. Absent a treaty relationship, a State possessed neither the right nor the duty to remain neutral.[24]

It has been suggested that the traditional relationship between war and neutrality should be seen in contractual terms: the duty to remain impartial was the *quid pro quo* for a belligerent's tolerance of neutral trade with the enemy.[25] This is true, but it does not disguise the fact that the status of neutrality was subservient to the intentions of belligerents, who could choose to declare war at any time.

2. The State of War Doctrine in The Early Twentieth Century

a. The Attempt to Codify the State of War Doctrine

The state of war doctrine led to frequent confusion and much uncertainty, as belligerent intention was notoriously difficult to discern. It was the purpose of Hague Convention III Relative to the Opening of Hostilities to define when the law of neutrality was applicable. It was hoped that Hague Convention III would complement Hague Conventions V and XIII on neutrality in land and maritime warfare, respectively.

The intention of Hague Convention III was to ensure that the obligations of neutrality arose at a certain definable point in time: when neutral States received notification, official or otherwise, as to the opening of hostilities in accordance with Article 2.[26] According to Article 2, neutral obligations begin upon a declaration of war.[27] The language of Article 2, however, is frustratingly ambiguous, as it

International Law Arising from the Russo-Japanese War II: The Hay Note and Chinese Neutrality' (1904) 16 GB 375.

[23] A Vandenbosch 'Neutrality and Problems of Peaceful Change' (1936) 30 PAS 129, 136.

[24] Q Wright 'Project of the American Institute of International Law on Maritime Neutrality (No 26)' (1927) 21 AJIL 127, 128.

[25] W L Williams 'Neutrality in Modern Armed Conflicts: A Survey of the Developing Law' (1980) 90 Mil LR 9, 21.

[26] HC III art 2. J B Scott *The Hague Peace Conferences of 1899 and 1907* vol I (Johns Hopkins Press, Baltimore 1909) 518–20.

[27] HC III art 2. Carl Schmitt has noted that the declaration of war was based on 'the desire for juridical form, and on the premise that there is no third party in matters of war and peace: *Tertium*

speaks unhelpfully of notification of a state of war to 'neutral' powers. To designate a neutral State as one that has not yet to receive notification confuses the very purpose of Hague Convention III, which seeks to make neutral status contingent on notification of the existence of a state of war. The language of the Convention appears to suggest that all non-participating States are *deemed* neutral upon the outbreak of hostilities, whether or not they are aware of the war's existence. But Hague Convention III did not prevent belligerents from carrying out large-scale hostilities without a declaration of war, thereby precluding the application of neutrality to the conflict by non-participants. In light of its poor drafting and many uncertainties it is unlikely that Hague Convention III was declaratory of customary international law at the time of its signature.[28]

b. Further Uncertainties About War

Hague Convention III did nothing to relieve the difficulties of the state of war doctrine which, despite its uncertainties, continued to attract significant adherence in the early twentieth century.[29] The difficulties of ascertaining when war existed became more pronounced following the adoption of the Covenant of the League of Nations and the Pact of Paris.[30] The Covenant of the League of Nations permitted war only in circumscribed circumstances. The Pact of Paris deemed resort to war an international delict amongst its signatories.[31] Pursuant to these instruments, war was no longer treated as a legitimate expression of sovereign competence.[32]

These developments prefigured significant restraints on the use of force. However, the attempts to regulate war in the League Covenant and the Pact of Paris remained wedded to the 'state of war' doctrine, and States intent on belligerent ambitions could circumvent formal classification of their actions as war. Simply by declining to declare war or expressing an *animus belligerendi*, a State could achieve numerous warlike objectives without attracting the increasing international opprobrium associated with war.[33] This meant that, in many instances in which hostilities undoubtedly reached the level of war in a material

non datur.' C Schmitt *The* Nomos *of the Earth in the International Law of the* Jus Publicum Europaeum (G L Ulmen (tr)) (Telos Press, New York 2003) 259.

[28] Y Dinstein *War, Aggression and Self-Defence* (4th edn CUP, Cambridge 2005) 32.
[29] Brownlie (n 8) 26–40.
[30] G Schwarzenberger '*Jus Pacis ac Belli?* Prolegomena to a Sociology of International Law' (1943) 37 AJIL 460, 477.
[31] Treaty Providing for the Renunciation of War as an Instrument of National Policy (adopted 27 August 1928, entered into force 24 July 1929) 94 LNTS 57.
[32] See generally Q Wright 'The Outlawry of War' (1925) 19 AJIL 76; Q Wright 'Neutrality and Neutral Rights Following the Pact of Paris for the Renunciation of War' (1930) 24 PAS 79.
[33] See generally T Baty 'Abuse of Terms: "Recognition"; "War"' (1936) 30 AJIL 377.

sense, the law of neutrality was not applied by non-participant States because of the absence of belligerent intention to treat the situation as war. There emerged in State practice a trend towards recourse to non-war forcible action such as reprisals or 'self-help' measures in order to avoid sanction under the League Covenant or a breach of the Pact.[34] These various 'twilight zones' between war and peace complicated the application of rules attendant on a state of war, particularly the law of neutrality.[35] Japan's invasion of Manchuria, for example, was not seen as a 'resort to war' under the League Covenant.[36] As Sir Gerald Fitzmaurice noted in a Foreign Office minute:

> ...what is occurring in the Far East, although it bears all the ordinary marks of war, is not in fact a war. It has as a matter of fact been in the interests of both parties, for reasons I need not enter into here, to take this view of what is happening. It would be open to the Chinese at any time to convert what is going on into a war by declaring that they considered themselves to be at war with Japan.[37]

In practice, the lack of formal classification of the conflict suited all parties, who 'actively connived in maintaining the fiction that war did not exist.'[38]

c. The Emergence of Voluntary Neutrality

The increasing opprobrium attaching to war in legal doctrine and public policy, as well as the blurring of war and peace in practice, created considerable difficulties for the law of neutrality. The view began to emerge that, given the problematic status of war in international law, the automatic application of neutrality upon the outbreak of hostilities should be rethought. In 1919, Cavaglieri expressed unease that the existence of a state of war could have the effect of subjecting non-participants automatically to the law of neutrality.[39]

In State practice there was some support for the view that the law of neutrality could not be relied upon at all in light of the prohibition on force. In a memorandum that it issued upon signature of the Optional Clause of the Statute of the Permanent Court of International Justice, the United Kingdom included a

[34] Ibid 395.

[35] J L Kunz 'Neutrality and the European War 1939–1940' (1941) 39 Mich LR 719, 722, 728.

[36] J L Brierly 'Sanctions' (1931) 17 TGS 67, 79; H Lauterpacht '"Resort to War" and the Interpretation of the Covenant During the Manchurian Dispute' (1934) 28 AJIL 43; C G Fenwick 'War Without a Declaration' (1937) 31 AJIL 694; E Borchard 'Neutrality' (1938) 48 YLJ 37, 51.

[37] Cited in A Carty and R A Smith *Sir Gerald Fitzmaurice and the World Crisis: A Legal Adviser in the Foreign Office, 1932–1945* (Kluwer Law International, The Hague 2000) 32.

[38] Brownlie (n 8) 60; Grob (n 12) 143.

[39] A Cavaglieri 'Belligeranza, Neutralità e Posizioni Giuridiche Intermedie' (1919) 13 RDI 58.

discussion of the effect of the Covenant of the League of Nations and the Pact of Paris on the law of neutrality:

> The effect of those instruments [i.e. the Covenant of the League of Nations and the Pact of Paris], taken together, is to deprive nations of the rights to employ war as an instrument of national policy, and to forbid the States which have signed them to give aid or comfort to an offender. As between such States, there has been in consequence a fundamental change in the whole question of belligerent and neutral rights. The whole policy of His Majesty's present Government (and, it would appear, of any alternative government) is based upon a determination to comply with their obligations under the Covenant of the League and the Peace Pact. This being so, the situation which we have to envisage in the event of a war in which we were engaged is not one in which the rights and duties of belligerents and neutrals will depend upon the old rules of war and neutrality, but one in which the position of the members of the League will be determined by the Covenant and the Pact.[40]

This policy was soon put into practice. Following the invasion of Ethiopia (then Abyssinia) by Italy in 1935, the Minister for League of Nations Affairs, Anthony Eden, stated that the law of neutrality did not automatically apply to the conflict, since the Italian action was contrary to the Covenant:

> If His Majesty's Government had regarded themselves as neutrals they would have taken the regular step of issuing a proclamation of neutrality. No such step has been taken... We do not consider that any Covenant-breaking State has any legal right to require the observance by other members of the League of any of the laws of neutrality... In the present case there has been, as yet, no collective decision and Members of the League have therefore the right to apply the rules of the Hague Convention on a purely *de facto* basis. To do less would be to treat the Covenant-breaking State more favourably than if no breaking of the Covenant had taken place. We found that immediate instructions had to be given to our authorities to guide their actions, and for the reason I have given no other course seemed to be possible except to instruct them to apply the Hague Convention rule on a *de facto* basis.[41]

Other attempts to reconcile the law of neutrality with the prohibition of aggression sought to hedge their bets. Reflecting the uncertainty of the age, the Harvard

[40] 'Memorandum on the Signature by his Majesty's Government in the United Kingdom of the Optional Clause of the Statute' (1931) 25 AJILS 82, 89–90.

[41] Hansard HC vol 305 cols 218–219 (23 October 1935). On the League of Nations response to the Italian invasion see Q Wright, 'The Test of Aggression in the Italo-Ethiopian War' (1936) 30 AJIL 45.

Research Project on International Law prepared two sets of draft articles that dealt with the law of neutrality. One set of rules applied when a state of war was in existence.[42] Another set, which envisaged considerable discrimination by non-participants against the law-breaker, was to apply in the event of international aggression.[43] This uncertainty was to continue into the era of the UN Charter.

3. The Application of Neutrality and the Prohibition of War

The debates throughout the 1920s and 1930s, concerning the invocation of the law of neutrality in circumstances in which the position of war in international law was undergoing profound change, prefigured a number of debates that continue in the contemporary era. It was the creation of the UN Charter, however, that has led to fundamental challenges to the way in which the status of neutrality may be created in international law.

a. Article 2(4) of the UN Charter and the Rejection of War

The aim of the founders of the UN was to prohibit the unilateral use of force by States except in self-defence.[44] The 'cornerstone' of the UN Charter is Article 2(4).[45] It provides that:

> All Members shall refrain in their international relations from the threat or use of force against the territorial integrity or political independence of any state, or in any other manner inconsistent with the Purposes of the United Nations.[46]

The capacious language used by Article 2(4) represents an attempt to circumvent the uncertainties associated with the language of war. As Stürchler writes, '[t]he new wording in the UN Charter was created to overcome the deficiency that governments could deny the existence of a state of war by simply omitting to attribute that word to their military actions.'[47] The term 'force' does not cover every

[42] 'Draft Convention on Rights and Duties of Neutral States in Naval and Aerial War' (1939) 33 AJILS 167.

[43] 'Draft Convention on Rights and Duties of States in Case of Aggression' (1939) 33 AJILS 819.

[44] C Gray 'The Charter Limitations on the Use of Force: Theory and Practice' in V Lowe et al (eds) *The United Nations Security Council and War: The Evolution of Thought and Practice Since 1945* (OUP, Oxford 2008) 86.

[45] *Armed Activities on the Territory of the Congo (Democratic Republic of the Congo v Uganda)* 2005 <http://www.icj-cij.org/docket/index.php?p1=3&p2=3&k=51&case=116&code=co&p3=4> accessed 20 December 2007 [148].

[46] UN Charter art 2(4).

[47] N Stürchler *The Threat of Force in International Law* (CUP, Cambridge 2007) 2, 34.

imaginable type of pressure, such as political or economic force, but is limited to armed force.[48]

There are two exceptions under the UN Charter to the prohibition on the threat or use of force in Article 2(4). The first is enforcement action ordered or authorized by the UN Security Council acting pursuant to Chapter VII of the Charter. The second is individual or collective self-defence against an armed attack pursuant to Article 51.

b. The Existence of Neutrality under the UN Charter

It is acknowledged that Article 2(4) of the Charter—in speaking of the prohibition of the threat or use of force rather than 'war'—constituted an important innovation in the law on the use of force.[49] Certain writers contended that by eradicating all reference to war or a state of war in the Charter, Article 2(4) had abolished not only the legal institution of war but also all legal doctrine associated with or attendant to it, such as the law of prize as well as the law of neutrality.[50]

However, this view does not accord with State practice. There is general acceptance that the rules on the conduct of hostilities, drawn up at a time when war was not prohibited, continue to apply despite the prohibition of force. In 1975, for example, the Japanese government expressed doubt whether Hague Convention IV Respecting the Laws and Customs of War on Land was still in force.[51] It was noted that Hague Convention IV:

> ...was drawn up at a time when war in general was not outlawed in international law. For this reason there are at present different views about the applicability of the Convention to the present situation, where under Article 2, paragraph 4 of the UN Charter, the use of force against the territorial integrity or political independence of any state, or in any manner inconsistent with the Purposes of the United Nations is prohibited.[52]

As the Japanese government acknowledged, however, there existed compelling reasons to uphold the applicability of the Convention.[53] Upon the ratification of the Protocol for the Prohibition of the Use in War of Asphyxiating, Poisonous or

[48] A Randelzhofer 'Article 2(4)' in B Simma et al (eds) *The Charter of the United Nations: A Commentary I* (2nd edn OUP, Oxford 2002) 112, 117–21.

[49] *Military and Paramilitary Activities in and against Nicaragua (Nicaragua v United States of America)* [1986] ICJ Rep 14 (Dissenting Opinion of Judge Sir Robert Jennings 528, 530).

[50] E Lauterpacht 'The Legal Irrelevance of the "State of War"' (1968) 62 PAS 58; C G Fenwick 'Is Neutrality Still a Term of Present Law?' (1969) 63 AJIL 100, 101–2.

[51] Hague Convention IV Respecting the Laws and Customs of War on Land (adopted 18 October 1907, entered into force 26 January 1910) 205 CTS 277.

[52] (1984) 27 JAIL 113–14.

[53] Ibid.

Other Gases, and of Bacteriological Methods of Warfare,[54] the Japanese government stated that there existed a 'consensus interpretation' that 'those international conventions on what are called laws of war which have been concluded in the past and which will be concluded in future will be applicable to such wars in the *de facto* sense, irrespective of the question whether it is called the use of force or otherwise.'[55] The International Court of Justice has also accepted the applicability of the law on the conduct of hostilities without regard to whether hostilities amount to the technical condition of 'war'.[56]

Nor has the UN Charter abolished the status of neutrality. It has, however, had a significant effect on the way in which the status of neutrality operates. In Michael Bothe's words, the UN Charter 'constitutes a kind of overlay network of norms under which the old law still exists, but may, to a certain extent, take on a different shape or be deprived of some of its traditional effects.'[57] With regard to the status of neutrality, the UN Charter now regulates the way in which a State's neutral status may be overridden and the circumstances in which neutral status may be abandoned.

First, it is argued that a State's neutral status may be overridden in circumstances in which the UN Security Council decides on enforcement measures under Chapter VII of the Charter. Depending on the measures adopted by the Security Council, a State may be prevented from remaining neutral or its ability to comply with neutral duties may be heavily qualified.

Secondly, it is suggested that the law on the use of force now regulates a State's ability to move between the statuses of 'belligerent' and 'neutral.' In the nineteenth century, a State's movement between these statuses was unregulated by international law. A neutral State was entirely free to abandon its neutral status for belligerency on the side of either belligerent party during the course of hostilities. Now, the UN Charter determines the circumstances in which a State may exchange a position of neutrality for one of belligerency. While a State may abandon neutrality to participate in enforcement action authorized by the UN Security Council acting under Chapter VII of the Charter, it may not abandon its neutrality for belligerency on the side of the State against which the Security Council is

[54] Protocol for the Prohibition of the Use in War of Asphyxiating, Poisonous or Other Gases, and of Bacteriological Methods of Warfare (adopted 17 June 1925, entered into force 8 February 1928) 94 LNTS 65.

[55] See (1975) 19 JAIL 176–7. The UN Security Council has acknowledged the continued application of the 1925 Geneva Protocol for the Prohibition of the Use in War of Asphyxiating, Poisonous or Other Gases, and of Bacteriological Methods of Warfare in the era of the UN Charter: See UNSC Res 612 (9 May 1988) SCOR Resolutions and Decisions [1].

[56] *Nicaragua* (n 49) [215]; *Legality of the Threat or Use of Nuclear Weapons* (Advisory Opinion) [1996] ICJ Rep 226 [54]; [78]; *Legal Consequences of the Construction of a Wall in the Occupied Palestinian Territory* (Advisory Opinion) [2004] ICJ Rep 136 [78]; [89]; *Case Concerning Armed Activities on the Territory of the Congo* (n 45) [172]; [217].

[57] M Bothe 'Comments' in H H G Post (ed) *International Economic Law and Armed Conflict* (Martinus Nijhoff, Dordrecht 1994) 35, 36.

taking action. Similarly, in situations of self-defence, a State may abandon its status of neutrality to assist the victim of an armed attack (provided the conditions for the exercise of collective self-defence are fulfilled) but it may not exchange its neutral status for belligerency on the side of the aggressor.[58]

A further aspect of neutral status modified by the UN Charter's prohibition on the threat or use of force is the concept of recognition of neutrality. The importance of belligerent recognition of neutrality made sense in an era where the intentions of belligerents played a fundamental role in determining whether a state of war existed. However, the importance of recognition of neutrality had already been challenged by the development of the view that neutrality was an aspect of State sovereignty.[59] The one context in which it retained some relevance was in relation to the devolution of the British Commonwealth.[60] The traditional view was that a declaration of war by Great Britain bound the Dominions to a common belligerency; a declaration of neutrality by a Dominion in such a context would imply secession from the British Empire.[61] The question therefore arose whether a British dominion could declare its neutrality independently of the British Crown, whether such a declaration of neutrality would be valid absent recognition by the Crown.[62] The question arose with regard to recognition of Ireland's neutrality in World War II, when it remained formally a member of the Commonwealth.[63]

However, recognition of neutrality no longer has the significance it possessed in nineteenth century international law, and its importance seems to be limited to the creation of a State's permanent neutrality.[64] With regard to temporary

[58] H Meyrowitz *Le principe de l'égalité des belligerants devant Le droit de la Guerre* (Éditions A Pedone, Paris 1970) 312–13.

[59] Scott (n 26) 544.

[60] For a discussion of devolution within the British Commonwealth see Crawford (n 18) 358–72.

[61] P J Noel Baker *The Present Juridical Status of the British Dominions in International Law* (Longmans, Green and Co, London 1929) 330–42; M M Lewis 'International Legal Status of the British Self-Governing Dominions' (1922–1923) 3 BYBIL 21, 38.

[62] C D Allin 'The Neutrality of British Dominions' (1922) 20 Mich LR 819; C D Allin 'Proposals for the Neutrality of the British Colonies' (1922) 37 PSQ 415; H McD Clokie 'The British Dominions and Neutrality' (1940) 34 APSR 737; Kunz (n 35) 730–2; A Stewart 'The British Government and the South African Neutrality Crisis, 1938-39' (2008) 123 EH Rev 947. An earlier question had arisen with respect to the possibility of a protectorate remaining neutral when the protecting power is at war: *The Ionian Ships* 164 ER 394; H A Smith (ed) *Great Britain and the Law of Nations: Volume I—States* (P S King & Son, London 1932) 67–76.

[63] See 'Memorandum by the Secretary of State for Dominion Affairs: The Neutrality of Eire' Cab/66/1/34. For discussion see R Fisk *In Time of War: Ireland, Ulster and the Price of Neutrality 1939–1945* (Paladin, London 1983) 110–11.

[64] It may be that recognition continues to have a role in the creation of a State's permanent neutrality. See, for example, UNSC 'Note Verbale dated 1 March 1982 from the Permanent Mission of France to the United Nations addressed to the Security Council: Annex Declaration by the French Republic Concerning the Neutrality of Malta' (3 March 1982) UN Doc S/14892 (calling on other States to recognize Malta's neutrality); UNSC 'Letter dated 26 July 1989 from the Permanent Representative of the Lao People's Democratic Republic to the United Nations addressed to the Security Council' (26 July 1989) UN Doc S/20751.

neutrality, however, a refusal to recognize neutrality could not, for example, have the effect of forcing the neutral State to 'resort to war' and join the hostilities.

Hence, while the prohibition on the threat or use of force has had a profound effect on the application of neutral status, certain writers insist that the concept of neutrality has been transformed by international law into an entirely optional status.

4. Neutrality as an Optional Status

a. The Argument for Optional Neutrality

Since recognition of neutrality is no longer of importance in determining whether a non-participant State will be entitled to rely upon the law of neutrality, the question has arisen whether there exists any obligation to apply the law of neutrality at all. A prominent thesis suggests that, following the developments in the law on the use of force, neutrality has become a 'purely optional' legal relationship that non-participant States are free to take up if they wish.[65]

Since Article 2(4) now provides to all Member States the right to territorial inviolability, this argument contends, States that are not participating in hostilities cannot be obligated to adopt the law of neutrality upon the outbreak of war or even armed conflict. States are free, under the UN Charter, to remain non-participants without assuming the duties of neutrality.[66] Andrea Gioia argues that 'it is now difficult to maintain, as before, that third States' peacetime rights should be limited in exchange for the mere non-involvement in the armed conflict, which is already guaranteed by a peremptory norm of international law.'[67] Since neutrality in contemporary law does not bestow additional rights beyond those available in peacetime, and involves only a series of duties imposed upon non-participant States, there is little, if any, benefit to States in being accorded the status of neutrals.[68] This makes it difficult, as a matter of principle, to sustain the view that the outbreak of armed conflict or war foists the status of neutrality on non-participant States.[69]

This view also relies on the greater flexibility permitted to States under Article 51. According to Dietrich Schindler's influential argument, it is Article 51 of the

[65] D Schindler 'Transformations in the Law of Neutrality Since 1945' in A J M Delissen and G J Tanja (eds) *Humanitarian Law of Armed Conflict: Challenges Ahead* (Martinus Nijhoff, Dordrecht 1991) 367, 373.

[66] Ibid 378–80; Gioia (n 2) 57, 78–9; A Gioia 'Neutrality in Air Warfare' in N Ronzitti and G Venturini (eds) *The Law of Air Warfare: Contemporary Issues* (Eleven International Publishing, Utrecht 2006) 181, 183.

[67] Gioia (n 2) 64. [68] Schindler (n 65) 380.

[69] Gioia (n 2) 64; C Greenwood 'The Concept of War in International Law' (1987) 36 ICLQ 283, 300.

Charter that has affected the law of neutrality to a greater extent than the other provisions of the Charter.[70] Because Article 51 permits States to take various intermediate positions along the spectrum of non-belligerency, Schindler suggests that the traditional dichotomy between neutrality and belligerency has been abolished.[71] Article 51 of the Charter is said to have the following sweeping consequences for the application of neutrality:

> States not wishing to take part in the armed conflict on the victim's side are no longer obliged to apply the law of neutrality. Benevolent neutrality or non-belligerency have become legally admitted attitudes. Neutrality has become purely optional.[72]

Thus in the event of an armed attack against another State, Schindler argues that a State which does not wish to involve itself in hostilities is not bound by the law of neutrality. Instead, it may choose to do any of the following: it may participate in collective self-defence when the conditions which govern it have been satisfied; it may provide non-belligerent assistance to the victim of the armed attack; or it may choose to issue a declaration of neutrality or otherwise to signal its assumption of neutral status.

b. Objections to the Optional Approach

It is suggested that a number of objections may be mounted against the view that neutrality is purely voluntary.

i. Neutrality as a policy position

If neutrality is purely an optional status it is not clear what circumstances would compel a State voluntarily to subject itself to its obligations. Indeed, on this approach it is unclear whether it would be appropriate to describe the obligations of neutrality as 'obligations' at all, as the decision to adhere to impartiality and abstention would be transformed into a political option rather than a legal obligation.[73] A more consistent position may be to argue that Article 2(4) has not merely altered the way in which neutrality becomes applicable to situations of

[70] Schindler (n 65) 373; see also D Schindler 'State of War, Belligerency, Armed Conflict' in A Cassese (ed) *The New Humanitarian Law of Armed Conflict* (Editoriale Scientifica, Naples 1979) 3, 15.

[71] Schindler (n 65) 373. [72] Ibid.

[73] W H von Heinegg '"Benevolent" Third States in International Armed Conflicts: The Myth of the Irrelevance of the Law of Neutrality' in M N Schmitt and J Pejic (eds) *International Law and Armed Conflict: Exploring the Faultlines* (Martinus Nijhoff, Leiden 2007) 543, 567.

armed conflict, but has eliminated neutrality altogether and replaced it with non-participation under the Charter.[74]

ii. Acceptance of war

The view that neutrality arises automatically upon an armed conflict reaching a certain threshold of fighting does not accept the concept of war or provide succour to an aggressor, as certain writers have claimed.[75] A position of neutrality accepts the institution of war (or, more accurately, it accepts the existence of hostilities) only to the same extent as does the law of armed conflict. A corollary of this argument is that since a belligerent may no longer establish a state of war, it may no longer presume that third States are required to comply with neutrality.[76] This view misses the fact that neutrality is not an ironclad position that is fixed until the end of hostilities but is a status that may be changed or displaced in certain circumstances. For example, when the UN Security Council decides on binding enforcement action under Chapter VII of the UN Charter, every State will be required to comply with that action.[77] Similarly, a State may choose to support the victim of an armed attack in collective self-defence. The law of neutrality accepts war only to the extent that it attempts to regulate its effects and to prevent its extension to States not directly involved.

iii. Problems of self-defence

A further difficulty in accepting the voluntary approach concerns the status of the State engaging in discrimination against an aggressor State. A number of writers contend that the concept of self-defence in the Charter strengthens the traditional law of neutrality by carefully circumscribing its ambit and by depriving all but those immediately affected of the pretence of intervention.[78] Hence to permit discrimination by neutrals under the law of self-defence would potentially undermine the purpose animating the law of self-defence, as well as opening the door to an aggrieved belligerent to take countermeasures under the law of neutrality.[79] It is radically unclear whether a neutral State discriminating in favour of a victim

[74] For this view see O Corten *Le droit contre la guerre: l'interdiction du recours à la force en droit international contemporain* (Pedone, Paris 2008) 265–6. At one point Schindler appears to come close to this position, stating that neutrality could be considered to be obsolete except for the fact that 'in certain cases governments nevertheless refer to it.' Schindler (n 65) 370.

[75] P M Norton 'Between the Ideology and the Reality: The Shadow of the Law of Neutrality' (1976) 17 HILJ 249, 308; C Chinkin *Third Parties in International Law* (Clarendon Press, Oxford 1993) 300.

[76] Q Wright 'The Present Status of Neutrality' (1940) 34 AJIL 391, 404; G Scelle 'Jus in Bello, Jus ad Bellum' in *Varia Juris Gentium: Liber Amicorum Presented to J P A François* (A W Sitjhoff, Leiden 1959) 292, 292 n 1.

[77] For a more detailed discussion of this point, see Chapter 4.

[78] See D P O'Connell (I A Shearer (ed)) *The International Law of the Sea: Volume II* (Clarendon Press, Oxford 1984) 1141; R R Baxter 'The Legal Consequences of the Unlawful Use of Force Under the Charter' (1968) 62 PAS 68, 73; Meyrowitz (n 58) 353–5.

[79] von Heinegg (n 73) 553.

State or against an aggressor in the circumstances of self-defence should retain its neutral status or whether it becomes, through its non-belligerent assistance, a State engaging in collective self-defence.

State practice provides little guidance in this area. This is despite the fact that self-defence has often been invoked in doctrine to support claims to discriminate against an aggressor.[80] Self-defence was offered as one ground for the United States' departure from impartiality by Attorney General Jackson prior to its entry into World War II.[81] Lauterpacht, in his memorandum of advice to the US government, noted that '[t]here is no practical limit to State action which may be made to rest on the broad shoulders of the doctrine of self-defence.'[82] There exists a danger, however, that such a wide interpretation of self-defence will serve to escalate and widen the hostilities, thereby defeating the purpose of the law of neutrality as well as the law of self-defence under the Charter.

iv. The principle of reciprocity

The view that neutrality is now voluntary also undermines the principle of reciprocity. Reciprocity means that 'bilateral relationships between at least formally equal parties are not unidirectional, but necessarily involve at least some element of *quid pro quo*.'[83] While the principle of reciprocity has been increasingly challenged as the basis of enforcement of the laws of war,[84] it continues to have an important role.[85] It has been generally acknowledged that the law of neutrality has its basis in the principle of reciprocity.[86] If there is no obligation to adhere to the status of neutrality then there is little to compel compliance with the duties of neutrality. The acute ambiguities associated with the voluntary approach render it highly likely that belligerents would consider the exchange of status as a breach of international obligations, and would seek to respond to that breach with

[80] For example, Oppenheim (7th edn) vol II 651; C Greenwood 'The Relationship Between *Ius ad Bellum* and *Ius in Bello*' (1983) 9 RIS 221, 230.

[81] 'Address by Robert H Jackson, Attorney General of the United States, Inter-American Bar Association, Havana, Cuba, March 27, 1941' (1941) 35 AJIL 348, 357. Cordell Hull, on the other hand, writing in support of the Lend-Lease Act, stated that the US 'faces a peril so deadly that the concept of neutrality and the niceties of international law must give way before the grim need of self-defence.' G Schwarzenberger 'The "Aid Britain" Bill and the Law of Neutrality' (1941) 27 TGS 1.

[82] H Lauterpacht 'Memorandum on the Principles of International Law Governing the Question of Aid to the Allies by the United States, 15 January 1941' in E Lauterpacht (ed) *International Law: Being the Collected Papers of Hersch Lauterpacht* vol V (CUP, Cambridge 2004) 645, 655.

[83] M Byers *Custom, Power and the Power of Rules* (CUP, Cambridge 1999) 89; M Virally 'Le principe de réciprocité dans le droit international contemporain' (1967) 122 RCADI 3.

[84] J de Preux 'The Geneva Conventions and Reciprocity' (1985) 244 IRRC 25; J-M Henckaerts and L Doswald-Beck (eds) *Customary International Humanitarian Law* vol I (CUP, Cambridge 2005) 498–9 (Rule 140).

[85] A Roberts 'The Equal Application of the Law of War: a Principle under Pressure' (2008) 90 IRRC 931, 944; K Ipsen 'Combatants and Non-Combatants' in D Fleck (ed) *The Handbook of International Humanitarian Law* (2nd edn OUP, Oxford 2008) 79, 94; F Hampson 'Belligerent Reprisals and the 1977 Protocols to the Geneva Conventions of 1949' (1988) 37 ICLQ 818, 829.

[86] H Lauterpacht 'The Limits of the Operation of the Law of War' (1953) 30 BYBIL 206, 238.

countermeasures.[87] This approach, therefore, has the potential to undermine the very purpose of the law of neutrality, which is to restrain the escalation and expansion of international armed conflicts.

v. The status categories in the law of armed conflict

The argument that neutrality is now an optional position disrupts the system of oppositional status categories, which have traditionally regulated the law of armed conflict.[88] It is received practice that a number of terms in the law of armed conflict are defined in opposition to one another. One example is the definition of 'civilian' which is defined in opposition to 'combatant' in Article 50 of Additional Protocol I: a civilian is 'any person who does not belong to one of the categories of persons referred to in Article 4A(1), (2), (3) and (6) of the Third Convention and in Article 43 of this Protocol.'[89] The ICRC Commentary notes that:

> This definition has the great advantage of being *ne varietur*. Its negative character is justified by the fact that the concepts of the civilian population and the armed forces are only conceived in opposition to each other, and that the latter constitutes a category of persons which is now clearly defined in international law and determined in an indisputable manner by the laws and regulations of States.[90]

The binary classifications fundamental to the law of armed conflict can, of course, be confounded by political reality; and a number of these categories have in recent times been placed under severe strain.[91] Thus in speaking of the distinction between combatants and civilians, Ipsen notes that '[r]egardless of this basic classification persons can be in closer proximity to one or the other primary status—either due to national law or administrative measures, or because of actual circumstances.'[92] A civilian who chooses to participate directly in hostilities loses his general protection from attack,[93] and if captured may be prosecuted under national laws.[94] However, by participating directly in hostilities, the civilian does

[87] See M Bothe 'The Law of Neutrality' in D Fleck (ed) *The Handbook of International Humanitarian Law* (2nd edn OUP, Oxford 2008) 571, 582.
[88] See generally D Jinks 'Protective Parity and the Laws of War' (2003–2004) 79 NDLR 1493, 1493–4.
[89] AP I art 50.
[90] Y Sandoz et al (eds) *Commentary on the Additional Protocols of 8 June 1977 to the Geneva Conventions of 12 August 1949* (Martinus Nijhoff, Geneva 1987) 610–11.
[91] See N Bhuta 'States of Exception: Regulating Targeted Killing in a "Global Civil War"' in P Alston and E MacDonald (eds) *Human Rights, Intervention and the Use of Force* (OUP, Oxford 2008) 243.
[92] Ipsen (n 85) 79.
[93] AP I art 51(3).
[94] See generally R R Baxter 'So-Called "Unprivileged Belligerency": Spies, Guerillas, and Saboteurs' (1951) 28 BYBIL 323.

not exchange his civilian status for that of a combatant.[95] Nor does he acquire an intermediate status between the two.[96]

vi. Additional Protocol I: States 'not a Party to the Conflict'

It could be suggested that the law of neutrality does not follow such binary status categories because of the language used in Additional Protocol I to the Geneva Conventions. Additional Protocol I distinguishes between 'neutral States', on the one hand, and 'States not Parties to the conflict', on the other.[97]

The phrase 'States not Parties to the conflict' is not defined in Additional Protocol I, and has been subjected to different interpretations. The phrase has been marshalled in support of the view that neutrality is a voluntary position.[98] Others have accepted that Additional Protocol I recognizes that the traditional dichotomy between belligerency and neutrality has been blurred.[99] This position, or a variation on it, appears to be the view taken in the ICRC Commentary on Additional Protocol I, which notes that the phrase reflects an acceptance of the view that 'other forms of non-participation in a conflict have been added to neutrality as defined by treaty and customary law.'[100]

The ICRC's interpretation has been sharply criticized, however.[101] Different interpretations of the phrase have been offered. Many writers suggest that the phrase is not intended to widen forms of non-participation in armed conflict, but is instead a reference to the threshold of applicability for neutrality. This interpretation suggests that, unlike the law of armed conflict, which applies whenever an armed conflict exists within the meaning of common Article 2 of the Geneva Conventions, the law of neutrality applies only to a declared war or large-scale armed conflict; hence in many armed conflicts the law of neutrality will not formally be applicable and non-participant States are better seen as 'States not Parties

[95] R Goodman 'The Detention of Civilians in Armed Conflict' (2009) 103 AJIL 48, 51; K Watkin 'Combatants, Unprivileged Belligerents and Conflicts in the 21st Century' (2003) 69 IDFLR 73, 74–5; K Dörmann 'The Legal Situation of "Unlawful/Unprivileged Combatants"' (2003) 85 IRRC 45, 48ff. Cf Y Dinstein 'Distinction and Loss of Civilian Protection in International Armed Conflicts' in M D Carsten (ed) *International Law and Military Operations* (International Law Studies 84, US Naval War College, Newport 2008) 183, 188–9.

[96] J S Pictet (ed) *Commentary IV: Geneva Convention Relative to the Protection of Civilian Persons in Time of War* (ICRC, Geneva 1958) 51 (emphasis in original); H-P Gasser 'Protection of the Civilian Population' in D Fleck (ed) *The Handbook of International Humanitarian Law* (2nd edn OUP, Oxford 2008) 237, 262–3.

[97] AP I art 2(c); art 9(2)(d); art 19; art 22(2)(a); art 30(3); art 31; art 37(1)(d); art 39(1); art 64(1) and (3).

[98] Gioia (n 2) 58.

[99] H S Levie *The Code of International Armed Conflict* vol II (Oceana Publications, London 1986) 790.

[100] *Commentary on the Additional Protocols* (n 90) 61 (footnote omitted). See also 60, where it is noted that the expression 'rules of international law applicable in armed conflict' is used to refer, *inter alia*, to treaty rules 'especially intended to apply in armed conflicts, including the law of neutrality.'

[101] E Kussbach 'Le protocole additionnel I et les états neutres' (1980) 62 IRRC 231.

to the conflict.'[102] The language recognizes that 'there are situations where a State not Party to the conflict is not neutral in a technical or traditional sense, but where the relevant provision of the Protocol should apply.'[103]

The Vienna Convention on the Law of Treaties cannot directly be applied to the provisions of Additional Protocol I, because Protocol I predates the entry into force of the Vienna Convention.[104] However, it is accepted in customary international law that, if the meaning of treaty language is clear when viewed in its context and in light of the treaty's object and purpose, reference to *travaux préparatoires* is unnecessary.[105] But since the meaning of the phrase 'States not Parties to the conflict' is open to radically different meanings, a good claim may be made that recourse to preparatory material is necessary.

The drafting history suggests an initial intention to replace the language of neutrality with a wider term. At the Conference of Government Experts in 1972, it was stated that the use of the term 'neutral States' should be replaced by '"States not party to the conflict" because the concept of neutrality was changing, and this new phraseology was broader and expressed better the position of such States.'[106] Following the Conference of Government Experts, a draft protocol was prepared, which replaced the term 'neutral' with 'State not engaged in the conflict' and 'State which is not a party to the conflict.'[107] In introducing the draft at the Diplomatic Conference on the Reaffirmation and Development of International Humanitarian Law Applicable in Armed Conflicts, held between 1974 and 1977, Jean Pictet argued that it was appropriate to use the term 'States not Parties to a conflict' 'since there were now varying degrees of neutrality, such as non-belligerence.'[108]

This view was rejected at the Diplomatic Conference. The proceedings indicate a division between those States which preferred the ICRC's draft, and those which preferred to preserve continuity in terminology between the Additional Protocols

[102] See, for example, the interpretation favoured by Bothe (n 87) 579: 'In those fields where the rules of international humanitarian law have a lower threshold of application than the law of neutrality, the use of the term "other state not party to a conflict" is the logical consequence of this situation.' See also M Bothe 'Neutrality in Naval Warfare: What is Left of Traditional International Law?' in A J M Delissen and G J Tanja (eds) *Humanitarian Law of Armed Conflict: Challenges Ahead: Essays in Honour of Frits Kalshoven* (Martinus Nijhoff, Dordrecht 1991) 387, 390; I A Shearer *Starke's International Law* (11th edn Butterworths, London 1994) 521.

[103] M Bothe, K J Partsch and W A Solf (eds) *New Rules for Victims of Armed Conflicts: Commentary on the Two 1977 Protocols Additional to the Geneva Conventions of 1949* (Martinus Nijhoff, The Hague 1982) 106.

[104] Vienna Convention on the Law of Treaties (adopted 23 May 1969, entered into force 27 January 1980) 1155 UNTS 331.

[105] *Article 3, Paragraph 2, of the Treaty of Lausanne (Frontier Between Turkey and Iraq)* PCIJ Rep Series B No 12, 22; *Case of the S S 'Lotus'* PCIJ Rep Series A No 10, 16.

[106] *Conference of Government Experts on the Reaffirmation and Development of International Humanitarian Law Applicable in Armed Conflicts: Second Session 3 May–3 June 1972: Report on the Work of the Conference* vol I (ICRC, Geneva 1972) 41.

[107] See *Draft Protocols to the Geneva Conventions of August 12, 1949* (ICRC, Geneva 1973) 3–27.

[108] *Official Records of the Diplomatic Conference on the Reaffirmation and Development of International Humanitarian Law Applicable in Armed Conflicts, Geneva 1974–1977* vol XI (Federal Political Department, Berne 1978) 195 (CDDH/II/SR.20).

and the Geneva Conventions. Those who argued for the phrase 'State not party to a conflict' did so for different reasons. Poland was concerned that use of the term 'neutral' could lead to confusion between permanent neutrality and temporary neutrality.[109] The United Kingdom was unsure whether elements of the Additional Protocols were compatible with strict neutrality.[110]

Those who sought the inclusion of the term 'neutral' argued for the need to maintain similar language across the Geneva Conventions and the Additional Protocols.[111] The German delegate noted that neutrality 'could play an important part in the settlement of international armed conflicts, and it was essential to avoid any impression that neutrality had become obsolete.'[112] The representative of Austria stated that:

> 38. If, however, the new term was intended to enlarge the field of application . . . her delegation could not accept such an idea. The introduction of a term not used in the Conventions would be contrary to the understanding that the rules decided on by the Conference should supplement, not supersede, existing regularions [sic]. Moreover, it would be confusing to have regulations directed to neutral States in the Conventions and additional regulations for States not parties to the conflict in the Protocols, and there would inevitably be difficulties in interpretation.
>
> 39. Furthermore, the term 'States not parties to the conflict' might endanger the very concept of neutrality. Neutral status, where States did not, and did not intend to, enter into armed conflict carried certain well-defined rights and duties. It implied a policy in wartime which was foreseeable and could be relied upon. The use of an ill-defined and vague term, with no legal protection, would weaken the concept of neutrality and upset international legal safety.[113]

What resulted was a compromise formula; under a proposal of the United Kingdom, Austria, Finland, Sweden, and Switzerland, the phrase 'States not Parties to a conflict' was replaced by 'Neutral or other States not Parties to a conflict.'[114]

It is difficult to derive a clear intention of the drafters from the *travaux préparatoires*. All that can be said with confidence is that the eventual wording of the Additional Protocols is the result of compromise. The language cannot be regarded as indicating an acceptance of certain forms of non-participation or non-belligerency in customary or treaty law, as the ICRC Commentary claims.

[109] Ibid 59 (CDDH/II/SR.8).
[110] Ibid 60 (CDDH/II/SR.8).
[111] Ibid 59 (CDDH/II/SR.8).
[112] Ibid 61 (CDDH/II/SR.8).
[113] Ibid 195–6 (CDDH/II/SR.20).
[114] *Official Records of the Diplomatic Conference on the Reaffirmation and Development of International Humanitarian Law Applicable in Armed Conflicts, Geneva 1974–1977* vol III (Federal Political Department, Berne 1978) 95 (CDDH/45).

Nor cannot it provide support for the view that neutrality has been transformed into an optional status.

Indeed, military manuals have not interpreted Additional Protocol I in this way. It has been acknowledged, with certain qualifications, that military manuals provide a form of *opinio juris*.[115] Review of a series of national military manuals suggests only limited support for the view that neutrality is a voluntary legal position.[116] Three manuals assert this view:

Australia (*Air Operations Law Manual*): 'A neutral State is defined as a State that has proclaimed its neutral status or otherwise assumed neutral status with respect to an ongoing conflict.'[117]

Sweden: 'The rules of the law of neutrality become applicable only on the outbreak of a war, both to states that have proclaimed neutrality and to the belligerents. If a conflict breaks out, any state wishing to remain neutral in that conflict should notify the belligerents and other states of this decision.'[118]

United States: 'Customary international law contemplates that all nations have the option to refrain from participation in an armed conflict by declaring or otherwise assuming neutral status.'[119]

A greater number of military manuals reject this approach and provide that neutrality is applicable upon a certain threshold of conflict being reached:

Australia (*LOAC Commander's Guide*): 'Under customary international law, all nations, in the absence of an international commitment to the contrary, have the right to refrain from participation in an armed conflict by adopting neutral

[115] See C Garraway 'The Use and Abuse of Military Manuals (2004) 7 YIHL 425, 431; H H G Post 'Some Curiosities in the Sources of the Law of Armed Conflict Conceived in a General International Legal Perspective' (1994) 25 NYIL 83, 97–101; L Doswald-Beck, 'The International Law of Naval Armed Conflicts: the Need for Reform' (1986–1987) 7 IYIL 251, 260; W M Reisman and W K Lietzau 'Moving International Law from Theory to Practice: The Role of Military Manuals in Effectuating the Law of Armed Conflict' in H B Robertson Jr (ed) *The Law of Naval Operations* (International Law Studies 64, US Naval War College, Newport 1991) 1, 7. For an expression of certain reservations concerning the use of military manuals, see 'Letter from John Bellinger III, Legal Adviser, US Dept. of State, and William J Haynes, General Counsel, US Dept. of Defense, to Dr Jakob Kellenberger, President, International Committee of the Red Cross, Regarding Customary International Law Study' (2007) 46 ILM 514.

[116] Certain other manuals are silent on the issue or leave it open: for example, the UK *Manual on the Law of Armed Conflict*. On the reluctance of the UK *Manual* to state its positions on various aspects of the law of armed conflict, see Garraway (n 115) 434–5. See also W H von Heinegg 'Manoeuvring in Rough Waters: The UK Manual of the Law of Armed Conflict and the Law of Naval Warfare' in A Fischer-Lescano et al (eds) *Frieden in Freiheit: Festschrift für Michael Bothe zum 70. Geburtstag* (Nomos Verlag, Baden-Baden 2008) 427. Other manuals, such as the Italian *Elementary Rules of Armed Conflict Manual (Regole Elementari di Diritto di Guerra)* (1991) simply reproduce ICRC materials, such as F de Mulinen *Handbook of the Law of War for Armed Forces* (ICRC, Geneva 1989).

[117] Australia *Air Operations Law Manual* § 12.2.

[118] Sweden *IHL Manual* § 5.1.

[119] US *Naval Commander's Handbook* § 7.2.

status. There is no requirement in international law for a "declaration of neutrality." However, all nations which do not expressly declare the contrary, by word or action, are neutral and the rights and duties of neutrality apply to them. Neutral status remains in effect unless and until the neutral nation abandons its neutral stance and enters into the conflict, or is itself the subject of an attack by a belligerent.'[120]

Canada: 'For most States neutrality is the result of their non-participation in an armed conflict.'[121]

France: 'Un Etat qui n'est pas partie à un conflit armé est un Etat neutre. Lorsqu'elle n'est pas formellement déclarée, la neutralité peut résulter du comportement effectif d'un Etat.'[122]

Germany: '**Neutrality** (from the Latin *ne-uter* = not either) is defined in international law as the **status** of a state which is not participating in an armed conflict between other states.'[123]

New Zealand: 'In the event of an armed conflict, international law imposes duties and confers rights upon those States which are not Parties to the conflict.'[124]

A greater number of military manuals promulgated since 1977 continue the binary approach to status categories, and have not interpreted the terminology of Additional Protocol I as a recognition of a third status between neutrality and belligerency. However, since it has been noted that military manuals 'cannot be a replacement for a meaningful assessment of operational State practice in connection with actual military operations'[125], it is necessary to turn to an assessment of whether optional neutrality is reflected in State practice.

c. Optional neutrality in practice

As evidence that customary international law now supports the view that neutrality has been transformed into an optional status and a position of non-belligerency is possible, Dietrich Schindler cites various instances when States departed from neutral duties in the Vietnam conflict, the 'Arab-Israeli Conflict' and the Iran-Iraq war.[126] Gioia has also argued that customary international law

[120] Australia *LOAC Commander's Guide* § 1103.
[121] Canada *LOAC Manual* § 1302(2).
[122] France *Manuel de droit des conflits armés* 88.
[123] Germany *Humanitarian Law Manual* § 1101.
[124] New Zealand *Interim LOAC Manual* § 1501(1).
[125] 'Letter from John Bellinger III and William J Haynes' (n 115) 515.
[126] Schindler (n 65) 373. It is unclear whether Schindler's undated reference to the 'Arab-Israeli Conflict' is a reflection of the view that the situation in Israel-Palestine since 1948 should be seen as a continuous state of hostilities with intermittent periods of cease-fires, as certain writers have contended, or whether he is referring to one particular armed conflict. His separate reference to the Yom

reflects the voluntary approach.[127] There are, however, a number of difficulties associated with their approach to the discovery and evaluation of customary international law.

i. The status and the duties of neutrality distinguished

First, Schindler nowhere indicates how neutrality in State practice is to be assessed. His principal evidence for the voluntary approach to neutrality is that States have in practice deviated from neutral duties.[128] This elides the distinction between the status of neutrality and the duties of neutrality. Since neutrality is not synonymous with impartiality, the distinction between the status of neutrality and the rights and duties of neutrals must be kept in mind. While it may be the case that States depart in a number of instances from full compliance with the duties of neutrality, this is not sufficient evidence that the status of neutrality is inapplicable *prima facie* to a particular armed conflict. Just because States may in reality discriminate in favour of a party to an armed conflict, this does not necessarily mean that it does not occupy the status of a neutral; a State may simply choose to act contrary to a duty that flows from that status.

To buttress his contention that non-belligerency is now a position recognized by international law, Gioia finds assistance in the review of practice undertaken by Titus Komarnicki in 1952.[129] Komarnicki controversially suggested that the position of 'non-belligerency' adopted by various States in World War II 'provide a proof that the rules of neutrality were no longer considered by some states as automatically binding upon the members of the international community.'[130]

This view cannot be accepted. 'Non-belligerency', a stance publicly pronounced by a small number of States in World War II, was not accompanied by corresponding *opinio juris* and did not meet with general acceptance. For example, in 1940, in reply to a question concerning the difference between non-belligerency and neutrality, the British Under-secretary of State for Foreign Affairs responded that:

> 'Non-belligerency' is a term which so far as I am aware has been used for the first time during the present war and does not as yet possess any definite meaning in international law. A declaration of non-belligerency has presumably to be regarded, amongst other things, as an indication of the political attitude which the State concerned desires to adopt towards the war. The question whether it

Kippur War of 1973 (ibid 369) suggests that he does not take the view that the conflict should be seen as an unbroken state of war.

[127] Gioia (n 2) 60. [128] Schindler (n 65) 373.
[129] T Komarnicki 'The Place of Neutrality in the Modern System of International Law' (1952–I) 80 RCADI 399.
[130] Ibid 456.

> also implies a legal status distinct from that of neutrality and involving certain legal consequences is not at present clear and may have to be decided in the light of the circumstances of a particular case.[131]

States that departed from the duties of neutrality either offered legal justification by arguing that neutrality (and not a separate status of non-belligerency) had developed following the Covenant of the League of Nations and the Pact of Paris and no longer required adherence to the duty of impartiality; or, much more commonly, they acted contrary to neutrality in a clandestine fashion and did not seek to justify their conduct legally.

The first approach was taken by the United States. The United States declared its neutrality in the European war in 1939.[132] The German attack on the Western front, however, led the United States to focus on the possibility of assisting the Allies without engaging in full belligerency.[133] On 23 September 1940, US President Roosevelt announced the transfer of destroyers to Great Britain in exchange for the leasing of certain naval bases in the Caribbean.[134] In March 1941, the Lend-Lease Act was passed by the United States' Congress, which gave the power to sell, transfer title to, exchange, lease, lend or otherwise dispose of any 'defence article' to a country the defence of which was deemed vital to the defence of the United States.[135]

Following the passage of the Lend-Lease Act, the 'near-belligerent' activities of the United States intensified to include, *inter alia*: the patrolling of the Atlantic to ensure supplies to Great Britain; the severance of diplomatic relations with Italy and Germany; the encouragement of US citizens to enlist in Allied armies; the training of Allied pilots on US territory; the detention of Axis ships; the freezing of Axis assets and the black-listing of Axis commercial interests; and the protection of Greenland and Iceland.[136]

The basis for this activity was discussed by the US Attorney General in 1941.[137] The principal justification advanced was that US non-belligerent assistance to the

[131] Hansard HC vol 367 cols 229–230 (27 November 1940 WA).

[132] (1939) 1 DSB 201.

[133] L Preuss 'The Concepts of Neutrality and Non-Belligerency' (1941) 218 AAAPSS 97, 106.

[134] 'United Kingdom-United States: Exchange of Naval and Air Bases for Over-Age Destroyers' (1940) 34 AJILS 183; 'United States Attorney General: Opinion on Exchange of Over-Age Destroyers for Naval and Air Bases' (1940) 34 AJIL 728. For debate on the 'destroyers for bases' agreement, see H W Briggs 'Neglected Aspects of the Destroyer Deal' (1940) 34 AJIL 569; Q Wright 'The Transfer of Destroyers to Great Britain' (1940) 34 AJIL 680; E Borchard 'The Attorney General's Opinion on the Exchange of Destroyers for Naval Bases' (1940) 34 AJIL 690.

[135] 'An Act to Promote the Defence of the United States' (1941) 35 AJILS 76.

[136] Preuss (n 133) 108; R Divine *The Reluctant Belligerent: American Entry Into World War II* (Wiley, New York 1965) 107–28.

[137] Jackson (n 81). The address was formulated with the assistance of Hersch Lauterpacht. For a discussion of Lauterpacht's involvement see E Lauterpacht 'Editor's Introduction to This Section' in E Lauterpacht (ed) *International Law: Being the Collected Papers of Hersch Lauterpacht* vol V (CUP, Cambridge 2004) 635.

Allies was consistent with the concept of neutrality as understood following the Pact of Paris.[138] The nineteenth century concept of neutrality that demanded impartiality had been superseded by developments in international organization.[139] Attorney General Jackson invoked Grotius as providing intellectual support for the concept of qualified neutrality, and asserted that 'the United States and other States are entitled to assert a right of discriminatory action by reason of the fact that, since 1928 so far as it is concerned, the place of war and with it the place of neutrality in the international legal system have no longer been the same as they were prior to that date.'[140]

But the United States, despite its own articulation of the permissibility of discrimination under the law of neutrality, did not indicate an acceptance of non-belligerency. It was hostile to the concept when Argentina raised the possibility of a collective declaration of non-belligerency.[141] Following the German invasions of Denmark and Norway, Argentina, which was formally neutral, sought to articulate a 'midway position' between belligerency and neutrality.'[142] In 1940, the Argentine Foreign Minister, Cantilo, informed the US ambassador that the US Republics should abandon the 'fiction of neutrality' and announce that they had become non-belligerents.[143] Concrete suggestions proposed by Argentina suggested non-belligerency would entail 'relaxation in the rules of neutrality under international law with special reference to the internment of belligerent nationals, the non-use of the ports of the Americas and territorial waters by belligerent submarines and the treatment of belligerent vessels used as auxiliary transports or warships.'[144]

US officials interpreted the proposal to mean 'abandonment of neutrality for something new and between neutrality and unneutrality, to be defined as a non-belligerent status, a role claimed by Italy.'[145] Cantilo's proposal would force the American republics to proceed 'helter-skelter along the unchartered road of "non-belligerency."'[146] Thus the US affirmed that its position was officially one of neutrality, 'regardless of how [the rules of neutrality] are being interpreted.'[147] Argentina eventually withdrew the proposal altogether.[148]

138 Jackson (n 81) 350. 139 Ibid 349–50.

140 Ibid 353–4. Cf H Lauterpacht 'Memorandum on the Principles of International Law Governing the Question of Aid to the Allies by the United States, 15 January 1941' in E Lauterpacht (ed) *International Law: Being the Collected Papers of Hersch Lauterpacht Volume 5: Disputes, War and Neutrality* (CUP, Cambridge 2004) 645.

141 See generally J S Tulchin 'The Argentine Proposal for Non-Belligerency, April 1940' (1969) 11 Journal of Inter-American Studies 571.

142 S E Hilton 'Argentine Neutrality, September, 1939 – June, 1940: A Re-Examination' (1966) 22 The Americas 227, 238.

143 'Strong War Stand Urged on Americas' *New York Times* (New York 13 May 1940) 1.

144 'Washington is Cool to New War Stand' *New York Times* (New York 14 May 1940) 12.

145 Ibid. 146 Tulchin (n 141) 575.

147 'Washington is Cool to New War Stand' (n 144) 12.

148 For Argentina's neutrality see J L Kunz 'The Position of Argentina' (1944) 38 AJIL 436.

Schindler's claim is that '[n]o State, since 1945, has ever considered itself bound by the law of neutrality in the case of a state of war recognized by parties to a conflict.'[149] However, his evidence for this appears to be based on the fact that not every non-participant State complies with neutral duties or issues a declaration of neutrality upon the outbreak of armed conflict or war.[150] His analysis attempts to show that actions contrary to neutral duties indicate evidence of an intermediate legal status between neutrality and belligerency. However, lack of compliance with a legal rule is not evidence for the formation of a new rule.[151] Nor is a declaration of neutrality determinative for the application of neutrality.[152]

ii. Evidence of optional neutrality

Secondly, the examples of State practice that Schindler invokes do not support his thesis. There is evidence that States have considered themselves bound by the law of neutrality in circumstances where a state of war exists. Upon the outbreak of the 1967 war between Israel and a number of Arab States, which was accompanied by numerous declarations of war,[153] France stated that: 'Le terme de *neutralité* s'applique très exactement à un cas déterminé, qui est celui de la guerre. Un pays neutre est un pays qui ne participe pas à une guerre.'[154] The conflict was one that it 'did not hesitate' to qualify as war.[155] Hence France's position towards the hostilities was one of neutrality.[156] Similarly, while somewhat reluctant to deploy the language of neutrality, the United States appeared to indicate that, since it was not a belligerent, it was in legal terms a neutral State:

> We are in a situation where several governments have declared war. We are not a belligerent. We do not have forces involved in this violence. Our citizens in the area are entitled to the treatment that is due to citizens of countries who are not belligerents. They are not enemy aliens...
>
> But this traditional word of international law, "neutrality," does not involve indifference...So there is the position at law that we are not a belligerent.[157]

[149] Schindler (n 65) 375. [150] Ibid 368–9.

[151] *Military and Paramilitary Activities in and Against Nicaragua* (n 49) [186].

[152] Castrén *Neutrality* 424; Kunz (n 35) 749.

[153] Declarations of war were issued on 5 June 1967. See *Keesing's* (1967–1968) 22135–22,136 (Algeria, Iraq, Kuwait, Sudan, Yemen). For a discussion of the conflict see R Higgins, 'The June War: the United Nations and Legal Background' (1968) 3 JCH 253.

[154] (1967) 13 AFDI 867, 892. [155] (1968) 14 AFDI 879, 900.

[156] (1967) 13 AFDI 892: 'Je crois que le terme dont il s'agit doit être utilisé pour caractériser la position du Gouvernement français et de la plupart des autres gouvernements du monde, en particulier des grandes puissances, pendant les quelques jours qu'a duré la guerre entre Israël et les pays arabes, et ce pour deux raisons: d'une part, nous n'avons pas participé à cette guerre, donc nous étions neutres, et personne n'a jamais émis l'opinion, dans cette Assemblée ou ailleurs, que nous devions y participer; d'autre part, nous n'avons pas pris parti dans la guerre, ce qui est une autre acception du terme de neutralité.'

[157] 'The Situation in the Near East: Statements by Secretary Rusk, News Briefing at the White House, 5 June 1967' (1967) 65 DSB 949–50. See also 'Israel Claims Land and Air Successes as Britain and US Declare Neutrality' *Guardian* (London 6 June 1967) <http://www.guardian.co.uk/

The evidence of the 1967 war suggests that non-participant States did consider themselves to occupy a status of neutrality. There is no evidence that States considered neutrality to be a purely optional response.

Schindler seeks to find support for the optional theory in the conflict in Vietnam. While the hostilities in Vietnam did not result in widespread adoption of neutral status by non-participant States, there is no evidence that this was because States viewed the status of neutrality to be voluntary. The Vietnam conflict instead demonstrates a reluctance to assume the status of neutrality because of the uncertain nature of the hostilities. In particular, the belligerents had refused to classify the conflict as a war.[158] In 1969 the Swedish Foreign Minister expressed the view that:

> The determination of what restraints based on international law we must observe in connexion with the Viet Nam conflict is complicated somewhat by the circumstance that in some measure the conflict is a civil war and by the fact that there may be different views as to the extent to which the traditional limitations of the law of neutrality concerning loans and credits to belligerent countries would be applicable to assistance for development. However one assesses these complicated elements, restraint may be advisable as long as the war lasts.[159]

In the absence of a determination by the belligerents as to the nature of the hostilities, non-participants are under no obligation to apply the law of neutrality. In circumstances where the belligerents have refused to classify the nature of the conflict, non-participants are free to adopt neutral status if they wish; however, they are under no legal obligation to do so and a declaration of neutrality does not affect the relationship between the belligerents and other non-participating States.[160]

Japan took a similar approach to the characterization of hostilities. Japan noted that, although an armed conflict was taking place, 'neither of the parties had treated it as a formal war under international law, which, as its legal consequence, would give rise to regulations concerning rights and duties of belligerents and neutrals.'[161] Nor had any non-participating State treated the situation as a war

fromthearchive/story/0,,1680910,00.html> accessed 3 March 2007; J W Finney 'US Seeks to Hold a Neutral Stance' *New York Times* (New York, 6 June 1967) 1.

[158] The United States characterized its action in Vietnam as collective self-defence of South Vietnam in accordance with Article 51 of the UN Charter: 'The Legality of US Participation in the Defence of Viet-Nam, 4 March 1966' (1966) 60 AJIL 565. In 1966, Australian Prime Minister Harold Holt stated that Australia 'was not technically in a state of war' with North Vietnam but was engaged instead 'in a number of limited operations with military forces': (1966) AYIL 149, 155.

[159] Cited in H Blix 'When are the Laws of War and Neutrality Applicable?' (1976) 32 REDI 125, 136.

[160] A D McNair and A Watts *The Legal Effects of War* (4th edn CUP, Cambridge 1966) 9–10.

[161] (1969) 13 JAIL 105.

under international law by declaring neutrality.[162] In this scenario there was no obligation on Japan to assume neutral status.

The UK view also supports Japan's understanding. In responding to protests by China that the UK had permitted belligerent use of Hong Kong in violation of the law of neutrality, the UK did not question that the law of neutrality would be applicable at a certain threshold. It questioned instead whether the law of neutrality was applicable due to the lack of clarity regarding the nature of the hostilities in Vietnam.[163]

There exist more recent examples that also provide strong evidence that neutrality has not been transformed into a voluntary position. During the conflict between Argentina and the UK over the Falkland Islands, for example, Ireland stated that it would remain neutral 'should war be formally declared between Britain and Argentina over the Falkland Islands.'[164]

Case law also rejects the optional theory. In *United States v List,* the Tribunal stated that:

> Whatever may be the cause of a war that has broken out, and whether or no the cause be a so-called just cause, the same rules of international law are valid as to what must not be done, may be done, and must be done by the belligerents themselves in making war against each other, and as between the belligerents and neutral States. This is so, even if the declaration of war is *ipso facto* a violation of international law…[165]

This is a strong argument for adherence to the traditional application of neutrality. More recently, in *Horgan v An Taoiseach et al,* Ireland sought to argue that the plaintiff had not demonstrated that there was a generally recognized principle of international law that obligated States to apply the law of neutrality upon the outbreak of hostilities.[166] The Court rejected this view; it was held that:

> …there does still exist in international law a legal concept of neutrality whereunder co-relative rights and duties arise for both belligerents and neutrals alike in times of war in circumstances where the use of force is not 'UN led'.[167]

[162] Ibid.

[163] (1966) 70 RGDIP 736, 743–5. China repeated the protest the following year: (1967) 71 RGDIP 717, 740.

[164] Cited in S P Subedi 'Neutrality in a Changing World: European Neutral States and the European Community' (1993) 42 ICLQ 238, 255.

[165] *Trials of War Criminals Before the Nuernberg Military Tribunals under Control Council Law No 10:* vol 11 (US Government Printing Office, Washington DC 1948) 1230, 1247.

[166] *Horgan v An Taoiseach et al* [2003] 2 IR 468, 496.

[167] Ibid 504 per Kearns J.

This practice is, to put it mildly, at odds with Schindler's thesis. It strongly suggests that the optional concept of neutrality cannot be accepted as a statement of positive international law.

5. Conclusion

The prohibition of the threat or use of force in international law has had profound effects on the status of neutrality. It has not, however, led to the acceptance of an optional theory of neutrality or of a concept of non-belligerency in international law.

Indeed, this chapter demonstrates that the view that neutrality is an obligatory legal status upon the hostilities reaching a certain threshold has not been replaced by another legal rule. Customary international law continues to support the view that neutrality becomes obligatory for States that are not parties to an international armed conflict. Therefore, the law of neutrality is *prima facie* applicable to non-participating States rather than an optional position that States are free to discard at will.

Chapter 2
The Application and Termination of Neutrality

The previous chapter has put forward the view that the concept of neutrality has not become optional for States in the era of the UN Charter, and that international law does not recognize a concept of 'non-belligerency' that exists somewhere in the shadowlands between strict neutrality and full participation in an international armed conflict. Based on an examination of State practice, international law appears to continue to recognize that the law of neutrality remains applicable upon a certain threshold of hostilities being reached.

A particularly difficult question that has been the subject of some debate concerns just where this threshold is. While it is now uncontroversial that the law of armed conflict is applicable upon the existence of an armed conflict, regardless of whether that armed conflict is also characterized as war,[1] whether a similar view holds true for the law of neutrality is considerably more controversial. Indeed, the prevailing view still appears to be that the law of neutrality is dependent for its application on the existence of war. For those who reject the institution of war in contemporary international law, there still remains a perception that neutrality has not developed alongside the rest of the law of armed conflict with regard to its applicability, but instead requires a higher threshold of fighting, either in scale, duration, or intensity, before its rules come into operation.

Claims for the law of neutrality's unique place in contemporary international law appear to be behind this approach. As Erik Castrén has pointed out, the law of neutrality sits apart from both the *jus ad bellum* and the *jus in bello*:

> The law of neutrality, to be sure, is not... part of the law of war if by the latter is meant rules of law relating to the mode of carrying on hostilities. But it is a body of law brought into being by war, and in this sense it may be included in the law of war in a broad sense. There is also a certain justification of the view that neutrality is the continuation of peace with certain exceptions and modifications caused by war, inasmuch as many rights belonging to both belligerent and neutral States are actually the same as during peacetime... It must therefore be

[1] GC I art 2; GC II art 2; GC III art 2; GCIV art 2.

> concluded that neutrality and the law of neutrality are to be regarded as forming an *independent institution.*[2]

The purpose of the present chapter is, first, to test this assumption by examining at what level of hostilities the law of neutrality is triggered in contemporary international law. Secondly, after having determined when neutrality is applicable, the chapter turns to an investigation of a much more neglected topic: the way in which the status of neutrality is terminated in international law.

1. The Threshold of Applicability of Neutrality

a. The Traditional Threshold: The State of War

While the existence of war previously conditioned the application of the entirety of the law of war, the comprehensive prohibition on the use of force in international law led to bifurcation in terminology between the *jus ad bellum* and the *jus in bello*. While the former prohibited the threat or use of 'force', the latter applies to situations of 'armed conflict' regardless of a declaration or other indication of war. Both the concepts of 'force' and 'armed conflict' capture situations below the threshold of 'war.'[3]

Nevertheless, it remains the predominant view in the legal literature that neutrality applies only in a situation of 'war'.[4] A Memorandum on the Legal Aspects of Neutrality presented to the Consultative Assembly of the Council of Europe in 1962 stated that:

> Occasional or temporary neutrality – often called simply neutrality – supposes a state of war in the formal or factual sense of the word. It describes the situation of a State which remains outside armed conflicts involving other States. When a state decides to adopt this attitude, its decision takes the form of a conditional

[2] Castrén *Neutrality* 424 (emphasis in original).

[3] D Kritsiotis 'Topographies of Force' in M N Schmitt and J Pejic (eds) *International Law and Armed Conflict: Exploring the Faultlines* (Maritnus Nijhoff, Leiden 2007) 29, 46–7.

[4] R Bindschedler 'Neutrality, Concept and General Rules' in R Bernhardt (ed) *Encyclopedia of Public International Law: Volume III* (Elsevier, Amsterdam 1997) 549, 559; K Zemanek 'Neutrality in Land Warfare' in R Bernhardt (ed) *Encyclopedia of Public International Law: Volume III* (Elsevier, Amsterdam 1997) 555; I A Shearer Starke's *International Law* (11th edn Butterworths, London 1994) 521; Y Dinstein 'The Laws of Neutrality' (1984) 14 IYHR 80; D Schindler 'State of War, Belligerency, Armed Conflict' in A Cassese (ed) *The New Humanitarian Law of Armed Conflict* (Editoriale Scientifica, Napoli 1979) 3; K Skubiszewski 'Use of Force by States. Collective Security. Law of War and Neutrality' in M Sørensen (ed) *Manual of Public International Law* (Macmillan, London 1968) 739; H Kelsen (R W Tucker (ed)) *Principles of International Law* (2nd edn Holt, Rinehart and Winston, New York 1967) 155; A D McNair and A Watts *The Legal Effects of War* (4th edn CUP, Cambridge 1966) 9; Castrén *Neutrality* 34–5; Tucker *Neutrality at Sea* 199–200; J L Kunz 'The Laws of War' (1956) 50 AJIL 313, 326; Oppenheim (7th edn) vol II 655.

> act which involves the application, for a time, of rules pre-determined and pre-arranged in international law. These rules involve a balance of rights and obligations and make up what is called the law of neutrality.[5]

There remains, however, significant uncertainty as to the contemporary meaning of war in international law.

i. The concept of war in contemporary international law

In modern international law the concept of 'war' would appear to be of marginal relevance.[6] Several developments have blurred what was previously a more distinct division between the concepts of war and peace, and armed conflict frequently exhibits elements of war and peace simultaneously.[7] This has made the task of distinguishing between belligerents and neutrals considerably more difficult.

A declaration of war no longer brings into being a self-contained regime of rules and no longer automatically results in the severance of diplomatic relations and the suspension of treaty relations.[8] The laws of peace, including international human rights law, remain applicable between belligerents subject to the principle of *lex specialis*.[9] The view that war brings about 'a complete rupture of international relations'[10] is no longer tenable as a statement of positive international law.

In 1970, Japan stated that 'there could be a question about whether what is called war, or war as a legal institution, can exist', while noting that 'it is thus conceivable that in future a war in the traditional sense which is initiated with the declaration of war or in some similar form will not be possible.'[11] Since 1970, however, there have been various instances of States issuing declarations of war or otherwise referring to the concept of war.[12]

[5] 'Report on the General Policy of the Council of Europe (Rapporteur: Mr M Macmillan) with a Memorandum on the Legal Aspects of Neutrality by Mr Struye, Chairman of the Political Committee' (9 May 1962 Doc 1420) (1962) 2 *Council of Europe Consultative Assembly* 14th Session 1, 37 [para 14] (footnotes omitted).

[6] See generally C Greenwood 'The Concept of War in International Law' (1987) 36 ICLQ 283.

[7] See G Schwarzenberger '*Jus Pacis ac Belli?* Prolegomena to a Sociology of International Law' (1943) 37 AJIL 460; M S McDougal 'Peace and War: Factual Continuum with Multiple Legal Consequences' (1955) 49 AJIL 63; P Jessup 'Should International Law Recognise an Intermediate Status Between Peace and War?' (1954) 48 AJIL 98.

[8] Y Dinstein *War, Aggression and Self-Defence* (4th edn CUP, Cambridge 2005) 19; ILC 'The Effect of Armed Conflict on Treaties: An Examination of Practice and Doctrine: Memorandum by the Secretariat' (1 February 2005) UN Doc A/CN.4/550; ILC 'First Report on the Effect of Armed Conflict on Treaties by Mr Ian Brownlie, Special Rapporteur' (25 April 2005) UN Doc A/CN.4/552.

[9] C Greenwood 'Scope of Application of Humanitarian Law' in D Fleck (ed) *The Handbook of International Humanitarian Law* (2nd edn OUP, Oxford 2008) 45, 73–4.

[10] *Dalmia Cement Ltd v National Bank of Pakistan* (1976) 67 ILR 611, 624.

[11] (1975) 19 JAIL 176–7.

[12] UNGA/UNSC 'Identical Letters Dated 12 July 2006 from the Permanent Representative of Israel to the United Nations addressed to the Secretary-General and the President of the Security Council'

If a distinction between war and armed conflict is to be recognized, there is a need to arrive at a suitable definition of war. It is apparent that the state of war doctrine, with its emphasis solely on the intentions of the belligerents, is entirely discredited. It has been described as 'almost completely a museum piece.'[13]

War must, therefore, be defined in objective terms. Historically, the search for a generally accepted definition of war has not been a fruitful one.[14] A comprehensive definition has been offered by Dinstein:

> War is a hostile interaction between two or more States, either in a technical or in a material sense. War in the technical sense is a formal status produced by a declaration of war. War in the material sense is generated by actual use of armed force, which must be comprehensive on the part of at least one party to the conflict.[15]

Even though it is still often referred to alongside 'armed conflict', it is questionable whether the concept of war continues to have any legal significance.[16] It is clear, for example, that a declaration of war has no effect on the application of the law of armed conflict, as the US made clear in a statement concerning a possible declaration of war on North Vietnam:

> There is nothing in modern international law which requires a state to declare war before engaging in hostilities against another state: nor would a formal declaration of war impose any obligations on an enemy by which he would not otherwise be bound...
>
> The legal rules of international law concerning the conduct of armed conflicts apply to all armed conflicts without regard to the presence or absence of declarations of war. All that is required is armed conflict between two or more international entities...The rules of war embodied in the Hague Conventions formulated in the early years of this century are considered, in general, to be

(12 July 2006) UN Doc A/60/937-S/2006/515; J Gettleman, 'Ethiopia Hits Somali Targets, Declaring War' *New York Times* (New York 25 December 2006) <http://www.nytimes.com/2006/12/25/world/africa/25somalia.html?ex=1324702800&en=76137f5021bdfbb8&ei=5088&partner=rssnyt&emc=rss> accessed 26 December 2006.

[13] C Greenwood 'Remarks' in A E Wall (ed) *Legal and Ethical Lessons of NATO's Kosovo Campaign* (International Law Studies 78, US Naval War College, Newport 2002) 127.

[14] A D McNair 'The Legal Meaning of War, and the Relation of War to Reprisals' (1925) 11 TGS 29; Q Wright 'When Does War Exist?' (1932) 26 AJIL 362; C Eagleton 'The Attempt to Define War' (1932–1933) 15 *Int Conc* 233; H Rumpf 'Is a Definition of War Necessary? (1938) 18 BULR 686; F Grob *The Relativity of War and Peace: A Study in Law, History and Politics* (Yale University Press, New Haven 1949); R W Tucker 'The Interpretation of War under Current International Law' (1951) 4 ILQ 11.

[15] Dinstein (n 8) 15.

[16] See Select Committee on the Constitution 'Waging War: Parliament's Role and Responsibility: Volume I' HL (2005–2006) 236-I [9].

> part of customary international law binding on all States, and their applicability is unrelated to declarations of war.[17]

It has been contended, however, that war continues to have certain legal consequences. One suggestion is that when hostilities cross the threshold from armed conflict to war, a State is released from compliance with the principle of proportionality under the *jus ad bellum*.[18] Thus when the United States was asked whether it would be desirable to seek a declaration of war in relation to the armed conflict in Vietnam, the US responded that:

> To declare war would add a new psychological element to the international situation, since in this century declarations of war have come to imply dedication to the total destruction of the enemy…[19]

The view that 'war' is regulated differently from other deployments of force seems difficult to sustain, and to hold that a State may be released from the constraints of proportionality because the conflict was treated as a state of war by one of the belligerents seems contrary to principle. There is no indication in the UN Charter (which mentions 'war' only in the preamble) that war is to be treated differently from other forms of force.[20] Moreover, as Dinstein admits, it is 'not always easy to determine whether resort to force in a particular situation amounts to war or is merely 'short of war.''[21] It seems problematic to base the application of the principle of proportionality on the drawing of what may be an illusory distinction.

State practice confirms that the principle of proportionality continues to apply even during a situation which is characterized as war. The hostilities between Argentina and the United Kingdom in 1982 following Argentina's invasion of the Falkland Islands have a firm claim to be considered as 'war.' After British forces recaptured the South Georgia Islands, the Argentine Foreign Minister announced on April 26 that Argentina was 'technically at war' with Britain.[22] The United

[17] 'Effects of a Formal Declaration of War: US Defense Department Statement' (1966) 5 ILM 791, 792. See also 'The Legality of US Participation in the Defence of Viet-Nam, 4 March 1966' (1966) 60 AJIL 565, 572–3.

[18] ILC 'Addendum to the Eighth Report on State Responsibility by Mr Roberto Ago' (1980) II(i) YBILC 13 [121]: '…the limits inherent in the requirement of proportionality are clearly meaningless where the armed attack and the likewise armed resistance to it lead to a state of war between two countries.' For a similar view see Dinstein (n 8) 237–42.

[19] 'Effects of a Formal Declaration of War' (n 17) 791.

[20] C Greenwood 'The Effects of the United Nations Charter on the Law of Naval Warfare' in W H von Heinegg (ed) *Visit, Search, Diversion and Capture: the Effect of the United Nations Charter on the Law of Naval Warfare* (Bochumer Shriften Band 24, Universität Brockmeyer, Bochum 1995) 133, 146.

[21] Dinstein (n 8) 230.

[22] *Keesing's* (1982) 31525.

Kingdom denied, however, that a state of war existed.[23] The UK justified its actions as self-defence under Article 51 of the UN Charter.[24]

While the parties differed as to how the hostilities should be characterized, under traditional law it takes only one belligerent to invoke the state of war doctrine. Therefore, even if the subjectivity associated with the state of war doctrine is rejected, a good case may be made that the hostilities constituted war 'in the material sense': diplomatic relations between Britain and Argentina ceased, Argentine assets in Britain were frozen, and imports from Argentina to Britain were prohibited.[25]

There was no suggestion, however, that the concept of proportionality was inapplicable to the hostilities. Indeed, one notable feature of the conflict was precisely the degree to which the belligerents were willing to justify their conduct according to the standards of necessity and proportionality in the *jus ad bellum*.[26]

The preferable view is that the characterization of a conflict as war has no effect on the application of proportionality; the principle of proportionality is relevant throughout the hostilities regardless of their formal classification.[27] An indication that a conflict constitutes 'war' may, however, have some factual significance in terms of the requirement of proportionality. As Greenwood points out, the larger the scale of the hostilities, the easier it will be for a State to demonstrate that it meets the requirements of necessity and proportionality under the *jus ad bellum*.[28]

ii. The relevance of war to neutrality

For purposes of the application of the law of armed conflict, of course, it is the fact of hostilities and not the intentions of belligerents which is the decisive issue. At first glance, this does not seem to be the case for the law of neutrality. Evidence suggests that a declaration of war will trigger the law of neutrality. In 1982, the Canadian Foreign Ministry stated that:

> There are valid reasons of policy for governments to avoid declaring a state of war. For example, if a state of war is declared, states not party to the conflict can demand observance of neutral rights.[29]

[23] See (1985) 56 BYBIL 526.

[24] See (1983) 54 BYBIL 542, 545–547, 549; (1984) 55 BYBIL 591–2; (1985) 56 BYBIL 526, 533; (1988) 59 BYBIL 581.

[25] A H Hudson 'Effect on Commercial law of Non-Declaration of War' in P Rowe (ed) *The Gulf War of 1990 in International and English Law* (Routledge, London 1993) 333, 334; see also M Evans 'The Restoration of Diplomatic Relations between Argentina and the United Kingdom' (1991) 40 ICLQ 473.

[26] Greenwood (n 20) 149–50.

[27] See also J G Gardam 'Proportionality and Force in International Law' (1993) 87 AJIL 391.

[28] Greenwood (n 20) 150.

[29] (1983) 21 CYIL 326.

Other State practice supports this position. The practice of States in the six-day war of 1967, and in the Vietnam conflict, supports the view that neutrality becomes applicable upon war being declared. Other examples reinforce this view. For example, in the 1971 war between India and Pakistan, Pakistan issued a declaration of war and noted that 'a state of war exists between Pakistan on the one hand and India on the other.'[30] The hostilities were very brief, so non-participant States were not required to indicate their position towards the hostilities; however, it was acknowledged that non-participants possessed the status of neutrals. The United States transmitted a warning to its shipping that '[n]eutral ships may be subject to visit and search on the high seas or in port of either belligerent country.'[31]

Declared wars are, however, relatively rare. The question therefore presents itself whether there is another form of war—war in the material sense—and how this type of war is to be distinguished from other forms of force, and who is to make that determination.[32]

States have occasionally used the language of 'de facto' war as a category separate from a legal state of war. While expressing some doubt whether war 'in the legal sense' could continue to co-exist with the UN Charter, Japan made reference to the concept of 'de facto' war as analogous to the state of war in traditional international law.[33] However, if 'de facto' war is simply used to express a comprehensive exercise of force on the part of at least one party to the conflict, it is unclear why the language of 'war' continues to be used instead of 'armed conflict.'[34] There is no evidence, for example, that a concept of 'de facto' war is regulated differently from other kinds of force.[35] As has been pointed out, de facto war is essentially a re-description of armed conflict.[36]

[30] See A K Pavithran 'The Indo-Pakistan War of 1971' (1972) 3 East JIL 247.

[31] 'Contemporary Practice of the United States Relating to International Law' (1972) 66 AJIL 378, 386.

[32] Greenwood (n 9) 54.

[33] (1975) 19 JAIL 176–7; (1982) 25 JAIL 157; (1984) 27 JAIL 113–14.

[34] Castrén *Neutrality* 35.

[35] Greenwood (n 20) 146.

[36] See Committee on the Use of Force 'Initial Report on the Meaning of Armed Conflict in International Law' International Law Association Report of the Seventy-Third Conference (Rio de Janeiro, 2008) (International Law Association, 2008) 814, 816; Committee on the Use of Force 'Draft Final Report on the Meaning of Armed Conflict in International Law' (The Hague 2010) (International Law Association, 2010) 1 < http://www.ila-hq.org/en/committees/draft-committee-reports-the-hague-2010.cfm> accessed 15 August 2010; Independent International Fact-Finding Mission on the Conflict in Georgia *Report: Volume II* (September 2009) 229 <http://www.ceiig.ch/Report.html> accessed 3 November 2009.

b. From War to Armed Conflict

i. The meaning of armed conflict

The Geneva Conventions of 1949 adopt the view that international humanitarian law should apply regardless of formal classification of an armed conflict as 'war.' Common Article 2 provides that the Geneva Conventions apply 'to all cases of declared or of any other armed conflict which may arise between two or more of the High Contracting Parties, even if the state of war is not recognized by one of them.'[37] The ICRC Commentary states that:

> This paragraph is entirely new. It fills the gap left in the earlier Conventions, and deprives the belligerents of the pretexts they might in theory invoke for evasion of their obligations. There is no longer any need for a formal declaration of war, or for recognition of the state of war, as preliminaries to the application of the Convention. The Convention becomes applicable as from the actual opening of hostilities. The existence of armed conflict between two or more Contracting Parties brings it automatically into operation.[38]

There are different views about when 'armed conflict' may be said to exist. The ICRC adopts a *de minimis* threshold and takes the view that there exists a situation of armed conflict whenever there is a resort to armed force between two or more States.[39] According to the ICRC Commentary, '[i]t makes no difference how long the conflict lasts, or how much slaughter takes place.'[40]

This view has been criticized for its focus on extending the protection of the Conventions rather than on strict analysis of what the law requires.[41] Determining the threshold at which the law of armed conflict does apply, however, is in many instances difficult.[42] It has been usefully suggested that two criteria may assist in determining whether an armed conflict exists: (i) the intensity of the hostilities; and (ii) the organization of the parties.[43]

[37] GC I art 2.

[38] J S Pictet (ed) *Commentary I: Geneva Convention for the Amelioration of the Condition of the Wounded and Sick in Armed Forces in the Field* (ICRC, Geneva 1952) 32.

[39] See ICRC *Violence and the Use of Force* (2008) <http://www.icrc.org/Web/Eng/siteeng0.nsf/htmlall/p0943/$FILE/ICRC_002_0943.pdf> (accessed 15 July 2008); ICRC 'How is the Term "Armed Conflict" Defined in International Humanitarian Law?' (March 2008) <http://www.icrc.org/web/eng/siteeng0.nsf/html/armed-conflict-article-170308?opendocument> (accessed 15 July 2008).

[40] *Commentary I* (n 38) 32.

[41] M E O'Connell 'Defining Armed Conflict' (2008) 13 JCSL 393, 397.

[42] UK *Manual on the Law of Armed Conflict* § 3.3.1.

[43] Committee on the Use of Force 'Initial Report' (n 36) 839–42. The criteria were originally proposed for non-international armed conflicts but are sometimes used to assess the existence of armed conflict as such.

ii. The requirements of organization and intensity

The concept of 'organization' is relatively straightforward: in order to constitute an international armed conflict there must be two entities capable of qualifying as 'parties' to an international armed conflict.[44] The requirement of 'intensity' is a more uncertain concept. The International Law Association has indicated that the concept of intensity requires 'more than a minor exchange of fire or an isolated or insignificant border clash.'[45] While this suggests that the duration of an armed conflict is not necessarily a determinate factor in deciding whether the requirement of intensity is met,[46] in practice, it is likely that the concepts of intensity and duration will be complementary. If a deployment of force is particularly extensive or devastating, a requirement that the conflict endure is significantly diminished; in hostilities where force is used at lower levels, it is more likely that the hostilities will need to be continuing in order to meet the requirement of intensity.

For an armed conflict to occur there is no requirement of belligerent intention to create an armed conflict.[47] The underlying rationale for the replacement of 'war' with 'armed conflict' was to ensure that the applicability of international humanitarian law did not depend on the will of governments.[48] In practice, an intention to prosecute an armed conflict will be evident but not determinative. Intention will be implicit in the requirement of intensity. Thus an accidental border skirmish would not lead to the application of the law of armed conflict because it would not satisfy the requirement of intensity, not because of the lack of intention.

c. Neutrality and Armed Conflict

The question of discerning the applicability of neutrality in international armed conflict presents certain difficulties. A review of State practice indicates significant inconsistencies and uncertainties in the application of neutrality and it is doubtful that a clear legal rule regarding applicability can be adequately determined.

The question of how to interpret this practice is therefore paramount. It is submitted that there are three possible interpretative positions. The first suggests that, absent a declaration of war, the status of neutrality is entirely optional. The second is that neutrality is applicable only in large-scale or 'extended' armed

[44] GC I art 2. [45] Committee on the Use of Force 'Interim Report' (n 36) 841. [46] Ibid.

[47] Cf N Melzer *Targeted Killing in International Law* (OUP, Oxford 2008) 250–1. It should be noted that Melzer understands the requirement of belligerent intent as a constructive test, which is presumed when there is armed interference with another State's 'sphere of sovereignty.'

[48] See D Schindler 'The Different Types of Armed Conflicts According to the Geneva Conventions and Protocols' (1979) 163 RCADI 131; S Vité 'Typology of Armed Conflicts in International Humanitarian Law: Legal Concepts and Actual Situations' (2009) 91 IRRC 69, 72.

conflicts. The third is that neutrality is applicable to all situations of international armed conflict.

i. Neutrality restricted to declared war

The first position holds that neutrality is obligatory only in situations where war is declared. In armed conflict that does not constitute declared war, the law of neutrality is available as an option for States that wish to take advantage of it.

This view can explain certain aspects of State practice. Adopting this view would explain the inconsistent application of the law of neutrality in armed conflicts that are not declared wars, and explains why only certain States appear to comply with neutral duties in various armed conflicts, even when it is disputed that an armed conflict is taking place. For example, following the invasion of Cambodia by Vietnam in December 1978, which Vietnam sought to describe as an internal dispute and not as an armed conflict, Thailand declared its 'strict neutrality' with regard to the 'armed conflict.'[49] While Thailand's compliance with the duties of neutrality was disputed, its ability to be neutral was not questioned.[50] Because no war was declared, other States had no need to adopt a position towards the hostilities.

Nevertheless, this view also presents certain difficulties and cannot be reconciled with some State practice. This view cannot explain why, for instance, in conflicts that are not declared wars, belligerent States seek to enforce compliance with the law of neutrality. No formal declaration of war was made during the Yom Kippur (October) War of 1973 between Israel and Egypt and Syria; yet this did not prevent Egypt and Syria from classifying States according to whether they were 'friendly', 'neutral', or 'supporting Israel', and from imposing economic countermeasures on States that were assisting Israel in violation of the law of neutrality.[51]

Similarly, in the conflict between Iran and Iraq, neither of the parties declared war during eight years of hostilities.[52] This did not prevent Iran from insisting that States comply with Hague Convention XIII and issuing frequent protests at what it perceived to be violations of neutral duties.[53] In the conflict between Eritrea and Ethiopia, between 1998 and 2000, which was not accompanied by a

[49] UNSC Verbatim Record (25 February 1979) SCOR Resolutions and Decisions 9; *Keesing's* (1979) 29615.

[50] *Keesing's* (1979) 29618–29619.

[51] See J J Paust and A P Blaustein 'The Arab Oil Weapon: A Threat to International Peace' (1974) 68 AJIL 410, 411; I F I Shihata 'Destination Embargo of Arab Oil: Its Legality Under International Law' (1974) 68 AJIL 591.

[52] F Mehr, 'Neutrality in the Gulf War' (1989) 20 ODIL 105.

[53] See, for example, UNSC 'Letter dated 19 July 1985 from the Permanent Representative of the Islamic Republic of Iran to the United Nations addressed to the Secretary-General' (22 July 1985) UN Doc S/17348; UNSC 'Letter dated 7 July 1988 from the Acting Permanent Representative of the Islamic Republic of Iran to the United Nations addressed to the Secretary-General' (11 July 1988) UN Doc S/20003.

declaration of war,[54] Eritrea protested against what it perceived to be Djibouti's unneutral assistance to Ethiopia.[55] It would seem, therefore, that this view fails to reflect international practice.

This view also presents certain difficulties with regard to the harmonization of the application of neutrality; in particular, it would create certain difficulties regarding the application of the provisions relating to neutrality contained in the Geneva Conventions. It has been noted that neutrality has an important place in the Geneva Conventions.[56] If neutrality is applicable only in war, however, the incoherent situation could arise in which, during an armed conflict that is not also 'war', a State could invoke the neutrality provisions of the 1949 Conventions but could not invoke the rules on neutrality contained in the 1907 Conventions. It would be anomalous if a State could claim neutral status under the 1949 Conventions but could not invoke the substantive rules on neutrality because a war has not formally been declared.[57]

For these reasons, the view that neutrality is applicable only in situations of declared war should be rejected.

ii. The applicability of neutrality to 'extended' international armed conflict

The second possibility is that neutrality is applicable in armed conflicts that are not declared wars, but it is not applicable to *all* situations of armed conflict: it is applicable only in armed conflicts of considerable intensity, scale, or duration. This view seems to have considerable explanatory power. This approach can account for why State practice indicates only widespread compliance with the duties of neutrality in international armed conflicts that are of significant scale and intensity. It explains why there are many conflicts in which the law of armed conflict is applied but the law of neutrality is not.

Theoretically, this approach could explain the distinction made by some writers between modern international humanitarian law and the *jus in bello* proper. The purpose of the former—the extension of humanitarian protections as widely as possible—explains its application at a lower level of conflict; the latter, because it does not concern 'humanitarian' rules of armed conflict but economic warfare

[54] The Eritrea-Ethiopia Claims Commission rejected the claim that a declaration of war had been issued: Eritrea-Ethiopia Claims Commission 'Partial Award – *Jus ad Bellum,* Ethiopia's Claims 1-8' (2006) 45 ILM 430 [17]. For critical discussion of the Award see C Gray 'The Eritrea/Ethiopia Claims Commission Oversteps its Boundaries: A Partial Award?' (2006) 17 EJIL 699.

[55] UNSC 'Letter dated 19 November 1998 from the Permanent Representative of Eritrea to the United Nations addressed to the President of the Security Council' (19 November 1998) UN Doc S/1998/1097.

[56] J L Kunz 'The Geneva Conventions of August 12, 1949' in G A Lipsky (ed) *Law and Politics in the World Community: Essays on Hans Kelsen's Pure Theory and Related Problems in International Law* (University of California Press, Berkeley 1953) 283, 288.

[57] P M Norton 'Between the Ideology and the Reality: The Shadow of the Law of Neutrality' (1976) 17 HILJ 249, 251.

that imposes significant burdens for non-participants, should be applicable at a higher threshold.[58]

This view has the added attraction of accounting for the language utilized in Additional Protocol I, which makes reference to both neutrals and States 'not Parties to the conflict.'[59] It has already been demonstrated, through examination of the *travaux préparatoires*, that this language is the result of compromise. However, one prominent interpretation of this language, on the basis of subsequent practice, is that it refers to the different threshold at which the law of neutrality comes into operation.[60]

If this interpretation is accepted, however, there exists a need to develop criteria that could signal the application of the law of neutrality to an armed conflict. Different proposals have been suggested. One proposal is that neutrality will apply when an armed conflict reaches a state of 'generalized hostilities.'[61] This is apparently distinct from armed conflict in its duration: a state of generalized hostilities 'is the *condition initiated and preserved* by persistent organized fighting—as distinct from the mere occurrence of fighting, which constitutes an armed conflict.'[62]

This seems to reflect international reality. It can account for the widespread adoption of the status of neutrality by non-participants during armed conflicts of considerable scale and duration, such as the Iran-Iraq war. It is also attuned to the thrust of the modern law of armed conflict, which seeks to regulate actual fighting, regardless of declarations of war.[63] It is able to explain why the law of neutrality is not observed in situations unaccompanied by actual fighting, regardless of whether a technical state of war is said to be in existence.[64]

As has been noted, however, a 'state of generalized hostilities' corresponds to the concept of war 'in the material sense.'[65] Like the latter concept, it is beset by all the difficulties that have plagued a definition of war. In particular, as with the concept of a material state of war, the concept of a state of generalized hostilities raises the question of which party is to determine whether such a state has come into existence.[66] If it is for the belligerents to determine, that is not too far removed from the state of war doctrine. If, conversely, the neutral States themselves are to determine that such a condition exists, this position is not far removed from the view that neutrality is an optional position.[67]

[58] For this view see Melzer (n 47) 244 n 9; Schindler (n 4) 5.
[59] For example, AP I art 31.
[60] M Bothe 'The Law of Neutrality' in D Fleck (ed) *The Handbook of International Humanitarian Law* (2nd edn OUP, Oxford 2008) 571, 579.
[61] G C Petrochilos 'The Relevance of the Concepts of War and Armed Conflict to the Law of Neutrality' (1998) VJTL 575, 605.
[62] Ibid (emphasis in original).
[63] GC I art 2.
[64] Petrochilos (n 61) 604.
[65] Ibid 605.
[66] Greenwood (n 9) 54.
[67] On this point in relation to an objective definition of war see Greenwood (n 6) 300–1.

Another suggestion is that it is the exercise of belligerent rights that triggers the application of neutrality. This can explain the widespread application of neutrality in predominantly naval conflicts such as the Iran-Iraq war, and why the application of neutrality has been frequently ignored in land-based conflict.[68] Since the exercise of belligerent rights at sea (and theoretically in the air) constitutes in practice the most intense interaction between belligerents and neutrals, this view would appear to be practically sound.[69] It also reflects the view that the application of neutrality is strongly dependent on its enforcement.

However, the view that neutrality becomes applicable upon the exercise of belligerent rights may amount to no more than a reaffirmation of the state of war doctrine in a different guise.[70] It would appear to be contrary to principle to hold that the status of neutrality is applicable to non-participants simply because a belligerent widens and escalates an armed conflict to encompass measures against neutral shipping. Moreover, it would also seem to be out of step with the development of the law of maritime warfare, which increasingly supports the view that any exercise of belligerent rights against neutrals must be compatible not only with the law of neutrality but also necessary and proportionate under the *jus ad bellum*.[71] Nor can reliance on the invocation of belligerent rights explain why neutral duties are applied consistently in armed conflicts that do not have a maritime component.

In light of the difficulty arriving at suitable criteria that can identify the existence of a protracted international armed conflict, it is difficult to disagree with the suggestion that it is 'impossible to establish this threshold in a general way. One can only say that there must be a conflict of a certain duration and intensity.'[72]

iii. The applicability of neutrality to all international armed conflict

In light of the uncertainties associated with the concept of 'extended armed conflict' a further possibility is that neutrality is applicable to all international armed conflict, regardless of whether that armed conflict is one of unusual intensity or scope.

[68] It has been suggested that, during the conflict between Eritrea and Ethiopia between 1998 and 2000, the law of neutrality played only a minor role because of the lack of extensive interference by the belligerents with third States, their nationals, or their aviation or shipping: W H von Heinegg 'International Economic Relations and Armed Conflict' in A de Guttry, H H G Post and G Venurini (eds) *The 1998–2000 War Between Eritrea and Ethiopia: An International Legal Perspective* (TMC Asser Press, The Hague 2009) 371, 385.

[69] It would also be in conformity with the traditional law regarding recognition of belligerency, according to which the exercise of belligerent rights against insurgents by the metropolitan government constituted an implicit recognition of belligerency and confirmation that the hostilities had reached the level of war. See J Crawford *The Creation of States in International Law* (2nd edn OUP, Oxford 2006) 380–1.

[70] For the view that belligerent rights are exercisable only during war, see D R Humphrey 'Belligerent Interdiction of Neutral Shipping in International Armed Conflict' (1997) 2 JCSL 23, 34.

[71] This argument is developed in detail in Chapter 5.

[72] Bothe (n 60) 578.

This approach has the appeal of coherence. According to this view, the law of neutrality is applicable at the same time as the law of armed conflict. From the perspective of harmonizing the application of the law of armed conflict and the law of neutrality, this view is attractive. It removes the artificiality associated with the position that the law of neutrality exists in a realm apart, subject to its own hermetic workings. More importantly, it has the practical benefit of removing many of the difficulties associated with determining the existence of war or protracted armed conflict.

Case law supports this view. In its Advisory Opinion on the *Legality of the Threat or Use of Nuclear Weapons*, the International Court of Justice stated that:

> ...as in the case of the principles of humanitarian law applicable in armed conflict, international law leaves no doubt that the principle of neutrality, whatever its content, which is of a fundamental character similar to that of the humanitarian principles and rules, is applicable (subject to the relevant provisions of the United Nations Charter), to all international armed conflict, whatever type of weapons might be used.[73]

This view is supported by recent case law concerning the 2003 invasion of Iraq. In *Attorney of the Federal Armed Forces v Anonymous (a Major of the Armed Forces)* the German Federal Administrative Court stated that neutrality became applicable upon the outbreak of international armed conflict, and that Germany was therefore a neutral State upon the outbreak of hostilities between the US-led coalition and Iraq in 2003.[74]

There are some difficulties with this position, however. In the contemporary international order, it seems unreasonable, as well as contrary to State practice, that the outbreak of international armed conflict in one region of the world could have the effect of foisting neutral status upon every State that is not involved in the conflict.[75] Such a position smacks of unreality.

Yet this situation is not unique to the law of neutrality; a similar difficulty has arisen in the law of armed conflict. It is an accepted tenet that the law of armed conflict applies throughout the territory where an armed conflict is taking place. However, as Garraway has pointed out, this raises an anomalous situation that often does not appear to reflect State practice.[76] This is an issue that does not admit of easy answers. In the case of neutrality, however, geographical proximity

[73] *Legality of the Threat or Use of Nuclear Weapons* (Advisory Opinion) [1996] ICJ Rep 226 [89].

[74] BVerwG 2 WD 12.04 (21 June 2005). A translation of key parts of the judgment is available at *Oxford Reports on International Law in Domestic Courts* ILDC 483 (DE 2005). See I Baudisch 'Case Note' (2006) 100 AJIL 911; N Schultz 'Was the War on Iraq Illegal? The German Federal Administrative Court's Judgement of 21st June 2005' (2006) 7 Ger LJ 25.

[75] Trevor Salmon has described this as the 'far-off country phenomenon.' See T C Salmon *Unneutral Ireland: An Ambivalent and Unique Security Policy* (Clarendon Press, Oxford 1989) 14.

[76] C Garraway 'To Kill or Not to Kill? – Dilemmas on the Use of Force' (2010) 14 JCSL 499, 508–9.

will play a critical role in the intensity of the obligations upon a neutral State: the closer the State is to the theatre of hostilities, the more stringent will be the obligations of neutrality.

A greater difficulty with this position is that it amounts to an admission that neutrality is a body of law that manifests low levels of compliance. In numerous armed conflicts, States have frequently declined to comply with the duties that flow from neutral status. This is not necessarily unusual; on many—perhaps most—international legal issues, States choose not to take a position unless they are required to do so.[77] However, in the case of neutrality it is particularly widespread, and further complicated by the fact that, in situations where the UN Security Council takes enforcement action under Chapter VII of the UN Charter, States are relieved from complying with the law of neutrality and may be under a duty to co-operate with the UN, so there is more fluidity to the status of neutrality than in other areas of the law of armed conflict.[78]

The lack of compliance with neutral duties is less problematic when it is recalled that, unlike many of the rules of the law of armed conflict, the basis of the law of neutrality remains grounded in the principle of reciprocity for its enforcement. Hence in many situations of conflict it may suit a belligerent not to insist on the enforcement of the duties of neutrality, especially if it is receiving useful assistance from a non-participating State. Just because the duties of neutrality are not being complied with, however, does not mean that the status of neutrality is not applicable to a particular conflict. For the desuetude of a certain legal rule to take place, there has to be a new general State practice 'indicating a particular new direction.'[79] It is therefore simplistic to claim that '[t]he succession of deviations away from the old standards applicable to a neutral may now be sufficient to say that those old rules no longer apply.'[80]

Indeed, it is possible to see in the International Court of Justice's statement in the *Legality of the Threat or Use of Nuclear Weapons* Advisory Opinion a distinction between the status and the duties of neutrality. What is notable about the Court's statement is not only its affirmation of the application of neutrality to all armed conflict, but its reference to the 'principle' of neutrality. This is used pointedly in contrast to the 'principles and rules' of the law of armed conflict.[81] The

[77] This point is well made by the New Zealand *Interim LOAC Manual* § 1502: 'As, generally speaking, States do not commit themselves on major issues unless they are compelled to do so, and as the vast majority of international armed conflicts since World War II have not resulted in substantial interference with the rights of uninvolved States, there has been a decline in the importance of the law of neutrality.'

[78] The relationship between neutrality and the UN Charter is examined in detail in Chapter 4.

[79] Y Dinstein 'The Interaction Between Customary International Law and Treaties' (2006) 322 RCADI 243, 324.

[80] D Flint 'Neutrality and the Iraqui-Iran [sic] War' (1984) AILN 47.

[81] *Legality of the Threat or Use of Nuclear Weapons* (n 73) [78]–[87] (referring to the principles and rules of international humanitarian law).

reference only to 'principles' with regard to neutrality is left unexplained in the judgment.

One way to understand that language, it is suggested, is to see the 'principle' of neutrality referred to by the Court as a reference to the status of neutrality. The Court states that the principle of neutrality is applicable in all international armed conflict 'whatever its content.'[82] The distinction between the principle of neutrality and its content is a distinction similar to that between the status of neutrality and its duties. Hence the Court appears to suggest that, while the status of neutrality is applicable to all armed conflict, the duties of neutrality may not necessarily be.

This approach would suggest that, while the status of neutrality and perhaps the 'core' duties associated with it—such as the duty to abstain from the provision of military material, or the duty to prohibit belligerent forces from transiting neutral territory—will be applicable in all international armed conflict, the more burdensome duties attaching to neutral status will be applicable only when an armed conflict reaches a large-scale conflict and when the rights of neutrals are affected.[83] This is a position that is accepted even by writers who insist on the optional view of neutrality, although they do so on the basis that a 'core' of duties associated with the duties of abstention and prevention is applicable to neutrals and 'non-belligerents' alike.[84]

This approach has an attractive symmetry with the ability of the parties to exercise belligerent rights against neutrals. It is increasingly accepted that a belligerent does not have the ability to interfere with neutral shipping in every armed conflict, and that the exercise of traditional belligerent rights must be justified as necessary and proportionate under the *jus ad bellum* in order that the principle of freedom of navigation not be disturbed.[85] This means that belligerent rights against neutrals will probably not be justified in low-level armed conflicts, where the principle of freedom of navigation will 'trump' a belligerent's claim to exercise belligerent rights. But as an international armed conflict expands, the easier it will be for a belligerent to demonstrate that the requirements of necessity and proportionality under the *jus ad bellum* justify interference with neutral shipping.

[82] *Legality of the Threat or Use of Nuclear Weapons* (n 73) [89].

[83] Wolff Heintschel von Heinegg has similarly suggested that a core '*essentialia neutralitatis*' will be applicable to all international armed conflict. W H von Heinegg '"Benevolent" Third States in International Armed Conflicts: The Myth of the Irrelevance of the Law of Neutrality' in M N Schmitt and J Pejic (eds) *International Law and Armed Conflict: Exploring the Faultlines* (Martinus Nijhoff, Leiden 2007) 543, 565–7; W H von Heinegg 'The Current State of the Law of Naval Warfare: A Fresh Look at the *San Remo Manual*' in A M Helm (ed) *The Law of War in the 21st Century: Weaponry and the Use of Force* (International Law Studies 82, US Naval War College, Newport 2006) 269, 283.

[84] See A Gioia 'Neutrality and Non-Belligerency' in H H G Post (ed) *International Economic Law and Armed Conflict* (Martinus Nijhoff, Dordrecht 1994) 51, 83–4.

[85] For greater elaboration of this argument see Chapter 5.

From the opposite angle, it is in keeping with the purpose of the law of neutrality—namely, to prevent the escalation and spread of armed conflict—that the duties of neutrality should increase as an international armed conflict increases in intensity. Thus in the law of naval warfare, the principle of freedom of navigation is modified and increasingly restricted by the exercise of belligerent rights as an international armed conflict intensifies. As an international armed conflict expands in intensity and reach, in other words, the greater justification belligerents will have (because in accordance with the principle of proportionality) for taking action against neutral shipping. Equally, as an international armed conflict expands, the more onerous will be the duties of neutrality.

This view, it is suggested, best comports with modern State practice, national military manuals, and with the meaning and purpose of the law of neutrality.

2. The Termination of Neutrality

While the question of the applicability of neutrality has been debated extensively, the termination of neutral status has received much less attention. It is proposed to examine this question in three circumstances. The first is when a State terminates its own neutral status, either through direct participation in hostilities or in some other manner. The second concerns the termination of neutrality through the initiation of active hostilities against the neutral State. The third concerns the termination of neutrality through the cessation of hostilities.

a. Termination Through Agency of the Neutral State

i. Direct participation in hostilities

In 1870, when Britain was asked to take up a position of benevolent neutrality in the Franco-Prussian war, the British Foreign Secretary, Lord Granville, asked: 'Where could the line be drawn between a departure from the usual practice, in order to confer material advantages on one belligerent State to the exclusion of the other and a participation in hostilities?'[86]

The law of armed conflict contains reasonably detailed rules for the determination of when a civilian may be targeted in hostilities. In general terms, a civilian must not be the object of attack.[87] A civilian loses such protection, however, when he or she takes a 'direct part in hostilities.'[88] What is precisely encompassed by the

[86] (1870–1) 61 BFSP 759–60. [87] AP I art 51(2). [88] Ibid art 51(3).

phrase 'direct participation in hostilities' is an issue that has received recent judicial and academic attention.[89]

In contrast to the question of when an individual participates in hostilities, the question of when a neutral or non-participant State's violation of its neutral duties or assistance to a belligerent amounts to 'participation' in hostilities or 'co-belligerency' is one that has received almost no academic or judicial consideration. It is therefore necessary to examine if treaties and State practice provide any guidance as to when a State becomes a party to an armed conflict. It is to be hoped that this clarifies not only when a violation of the duty of non-participation leads to the loss of neutral status but also when a position of non-belligerency shades into participation.

The starting point of any consideration must be Article 4(2) of the Fourth Geneva Convention, which distinguishes between a neutral State, a belligerent State and a co-belligerent State:

> Nationals of a State which is not bound by the Convention are not protected by it. Nationals of a neutral State who find themselves in the territory of a belligerent State, and nationals of a co-belligerent State, shall not be regarded as protected persons while the State of which they are nationals has normal diplomatic representation in the State in whose hands they are.[90]

The Fourth Geneva Convention does not contain any discussion of how 'co-belligerency' is to be distinguished from neutrality. The ICRC Commentary notes that the meaning of 'co-belligerent' States is a synonym for 'allies.'[91] As an example of co-belligerency, it cites the example of Italy in World War II.[92] This reference is somewhat opaque: it is unclear whether the Commentary has in mind Italy's co-belligerency with Germany, or whether it refers to Italy's entry into the war on the side of the Allies. Given the existence of documentation announcing Italy's 'co-belligerency' on the side of the Allies, the Commentary's statement is presumed to be a reference to the latter.[93]

[89] See *Public Committee Against Torture in Israel v Israel* (2007) 46 ILM 375; N Melzer 'Interpretative Guidance on the Notion of Direct Participation in Hostilities under International Humanitarian Law' (ICRC 2009).

[90] GC IV art 4(2).

[91] J S Pictet (ed) *Commentary IV: Geneva Convention Relative to the Protection of Civilian Persons in Time of War* (ICRC, Geneva 1958) 49; M Bothe, K J Partsch and W A Solf (eds) *New Rules for Victims of Armed Conflicts: Commentary on the Two 1977 Protocols Additional to the Geneva Conventions of 1949* (Martinus Nijhoff, The Hague 1982) 440.

[92] *Commentary IV* (n 91) 49.

[93] Italy was acknowledged to be a 'co-belligerent' alongside the US, the Soviet Union, and the UK when it declared war against Germany in 1943. See 'Statement by the President of the United States, the Prime Minister of Great Britain, and the Premier of the Soviet Union on Italy's Declaration of War' (1943) *US Naval War College International Law Documents* (US Government Printing Office, Washington 1945) 92. It is notable that Italy was treated as a hostile destination for the purposes of prize law before it officially declared war in World War II, because of its stance of non-belligerency in

In any case, it would appear that examples of co-belligerency from before 1945 will be of only limited assistance, due not only to the scarcity of formal declarations of war in the era of the UN Charter, but also to the comprehensive prohibition of the threat or use of force in international law, which limits the situations in which co-belligerency will be possible. Unlike the situation in nineteenth century international law permitting recourse to war, under the UN Charter a belligerent can no longer legally 'create' another State's co-belligerency simply by declaring war on it. It is possible to identify a number of cases in which a neutral State will lose its neutrality.

One clear example is an invitation to a belligerent to enter neutral territory. When the US took action against Cambodia in 1970, justified on the grounds of self-defence and to prevent violations of Cambodia's neutrality, the US State Department's legal adviser stated that the 'advance, express request of the Government of Cambodia for our military activities on Cambodian territory' was not sought, because that would have 'compromised the neutrality of the Cambodian Government' and the United States 'did not wish to see Cambodia become a co-belligerent along with South Viet-Nam and the United States.'[94] This suggests that such an invitation will result in the loss of neutrality through the application of invited force on neutral territory.

Another example is when a neutral State directly engages in acts of war, and joins the hostilities through armed intervention.[95] In that situation, the neutral has clearly engaged in a use of force against another belligerent. It seems clear that a neutral State does not lose its neutrality by virtue of limited acts of military force in self-defence. At various stages of the Iran-Iraq war, the US used force putatively in self-defence. In September 1987, US army helicopters caught an Iranian landing craft, the *Iran Ajr*, laying mines in an international shipping lane used regularly by US ships in the central Persian Gulf. Helicopters strafed the Iranian vessel until it stopped laying mines. When the helicopters returned forty minutes later and discovered that the ship had resumed mine-laying activities, the *Iran Ajr* was again attacked.[96] In October 1987, a Silkworm missile fired by Iranian forces from Iranian-occupied, Iraqi territory on the Fao peninsula struck the *Sea Isle City*, a US-flagged tanker, in Kuwaiti territorial waters. In response, US naval forces destroyed Iran's Rashadat platform, a former oil drilling platform located in international waters, on the basis that the use of the platform to launch helicopter and small boat attacks against neutral shipping represented a

the war: *The Finland* (1945) (unreported). See S W D Rowson 'Prize Law During the Second World War' (1947) 24 BYBIL 160, 191–2; Whiteman *Digest* XI 164.

[94] 'Military Operations in Cambodia' (1970) 64 AJIL 932, 935. [95] Greenwood (n 9) 58.

[96] D L Peace 'Major Maritime Events in the Persian Gulf Between 1984 and 1991: A Juridical Analysis' (1990–1991) 31 VJIL 545, 555.

continuing threat to US commercial ships and naval forces.[97] There were other incidents in which the US Navy fired on other ships and aircraft.[98]

The legality of these actions as self-defence may be open to doubt. However, the US's status as a non-participant was not questioned; there was no suggestion that the US had become a 'co-belligerent' on the side of Iraq through these actions. Chinkin argues that a single response in self-defence most likely does not transform a neutral into a belligerent, but that 'continued actions of sufficient intensity over a long duration' could transform a neutral into a belligerent.[99]

ii. Indirect participation in hostilities

More difficult questions as to the termination of neutral status concern the considerable grey zone of activity that covers both a neutral's acquiescence in belligerent activity on neutral territory that the neutral State is powerless to prevent, as well as various forms of 'aid and assistance' rendered as an unneutral service.

Regarding the first scenario, mere powerlessness on the part of the neutral would not be enough for it to be converted into a belligerent. It is likely that the neutral State's mere sufferance or tolerance of belligerent action on its territory would not be sufficient to convert it into a belligerent itself; while it would violate the duty of prevention, such a violation would not, for instance, permit the opposing belligerent to treat targets on neutral territory as military objectives.

The more difficult area is when a neutral State provides substantial logistical or financial support to one belligerent in violation of the law of neutrality. The most detailed example is that of Kuwait and, to a lesser extent, Saudi Arabia during the Iran-Iraq war, and it is worth examining the issue in some detail.

During the Iran-Iraq war, Iran repeatedly protested at the conduct of Kuwait, which it believed to be assisting Iraq. In a letter to the Security Council on 25 May 1984, Iran stated that 'some States in the area and beyond' which 'pour extensive financial and material resources into Iraq' were encouraging Iraq to threaten international shipping. The letter went on to note that, while these States acting in support of Iraq 'wish to remain secure from the consequences of their obvious backing of the aggressor Iraq' they had contributed to the internationalization of the conflict 'from which they can hardly remain secure.'[100] In 1985, Iran noted that, 'contrary to the idea of friendly neighbourly relations', cargo ships heading for Kuwait had on board logistical goods and arms ultimately destined for Iraq.[101]

[97] Ibid 557–8. [98] Ibid 558–60.

[99] C Chinkin *Third Parties in International Law* (Clarendon Press, Oxford 1993) 308.

[100] UNSC 'Letter Dated 25 May 1984 from the Permanent Representative of the Islamic Republic of Iran to the United Nations Addressed to the Secretary-General' (25 May 1984) UN Doc S/16585.

[101] UNSC 'Letter Dated 25 September 1985 from the Permanent Representative of the Islamic Republic of Iran to the United Nations Addressed to the Secretary-General' (25 September 1985) UN Doc S/17496.

It noted that notification to Kuwait had been to no avail, and suggested that Kuwait's conduct contradicted its avowed position of neutrality in the hostilities.

In February 1987, Kuwait sought protection from the United States and from the Soviet Union for Kuwaiti-owned tankers.[102] Kuwait chartered three Soviet tankers and agreed to the reflagging of Kuwaiti ships by the US.[103] This reflagging operation was controversial and raised a number of important legal questions regarding whether there existed a genuine link between the State of nationality and the ship.[104] Nevertheless, the US began escorting reflagged Kuwaiti tankers through the Persian Gulf and the Strait of Hormuz in July 1987. The US claimed that its status as a neutral State in the conflict was not compromised by its reflagging operations, and that it was permitted to escort reflagged tankers.[105]

It was in 1987 that Iran appeared to view Kuwait's behaviour as amounting to participation in the armed conflict. In January 1987, it published the testimony of a captured Iraqi pilot, who stated that Kuwaiti airspace was used by Iraqi aircraft in the latter's attacks on neutral shipping.[106] The captured pilot stated that the use of Kuwaiti airspace was co-ordinated in advance.[107] Kuwait rejected these allegations and stated that it did not permit any party to use its airspace.[108] Citing the increasingly belligerent rhetoric of Iran regarding Kuwait's behaviour, in mid-1987 Kuwait asked the Security Council to take decisive action.[109]

In August 1987, Iran formally announced that it viewed Kuwait as having joined the war on the side of Iraq. In a letter of 14 August 1987, Iran stated that:

> The Government of the Islamic Republic of Iran has specifically called upon the State of Kuwait to maintain neutrality in the war. Regrettably, not only has Kuwait not observed the rules of neutrality by financially supporting Iraq but the officials of Kuwait have publicly acknowledged that their ports and other logistical facilities, including Kuwaiti airspace, are at the disposal of Iraq to fuel

[102] Peace (n 96) 553.

[103] 'The US Plan to Protect Kuwaiti Ships in the Gulf by Putting Them Under US Flags' (1987) 26 ILM 1429, 1430.

[104] On the reflagging generally see R Wolfrum 'Reflagging and Escort Operations in the Persian Gulf: an International Law Perspective' (1988–1989) 29 VJIL 387.

[105] 'United States: Secretary of Defence Report (Weinberger Report) to the Congress on Security Arrangements in the Persian Gulf' (1987) 26 ILM 1433, 1458.

[106] UNSC 'Letter Dated 5 January 1987 From the Charge D'Affaires A I of the Permanent Mission of the Islamic Republic of Iran to the United Nations Addressed to the Secretary-General' (5 January 1987) UN Doc S/18557.

[107] Ibid.

[108] UNSC 'Letter Dated 12 January 1987 From the Charge D'Affaires A I of the Permanent Mission of Kuwait to the United Nations Addressed to the Secretary-General' (12 January 1987) UN Doc S/18582.

[109] UNSC 'Letter Dated 29 July 1987 From the Charge D'Affaires A I of the Permanent Mission of Kuwait to the United Nations Addressed to the Secretary-General' (29 July 1987) UN Doc S/19005.

> its war machine and to support its military forces and to conduct aggressive operations against the Islamic Republic of Iran.[110]

Iran went on to note that it would 'respond appropriately' if Kuwait were to observe the rules of neutrality. However, as Kuwait had not indicated its intention to refrain from offering economic, logistical, and other assistance to Iraq, Kuwait would be regarded by Iran as a participant in the armed conflict:

> ...until the official announcement by Kuwait of its guaranteed withdrawal of financial, political and logistical support for Iraq and hence a position of complete neutrality, Kuwait will be regarded as a partner of Iraq in the war. The Islamic Republic of Iran will adjust its policies vis-à-vis Kuwait accordingly.[111]

This suggested that Iran viewed Kuwait as a co-belligerent, and it soon took forceful action against Kuwait. In August 1987, Kuwait reported that a Kuwaiti merchant vessel, the *Jabal Ali*, was struck by missiles en route to Dubai.[112] In October 1987, the *Sea Isle City*, a Kuwaiti-owned oil tanker (registered to the United States) anchored in Kuwaiti territorial waters, was hit by an Iranian missile.[113] Kuwait made further allegations of attacks by Iran on Kuwaiti territory.[114]

In late 1987, there were reports of Iraqi planes using Kuwaiti airspace. In one instance, an Iraqi fighter jet made an emergency landing on Bourbian Island, in Kuwait. Iran protested at this 'co-operation' between Kuwait and Iraq, and stated that to prove its neutrality the Government of Kuwait 'should take every measure to prevent further use of its facilities and airspace by Iraq.'[115] Kuwait rejected the allegations.[116]

On 22 December 1987, Iran protested again at the use of Kuwaiti airspace by Iraqi aircraft. It stated that '[T]he Government of Kuwait, by granting air corridor and flight permission to the Iraqi planes, has clearly co-operated with the Iraqi

[110] UNSC 'Letter Dated 14 August 1987 from the Permanent Representative of the Islamic Republic of Iran to the United Nations Addressed to the Secretary-General' (14 August 1987) UN Doc S/19041.

[111] Ibid.

[112] UNSC 'Letter Dated 1 September 1987 from the Permanent Representative of Kuwait to the United Nations Addressed to the Secretary-General' (1 September 1987) UN Doc S/19093.

[113] UNSC 'Letter Dated 16 October 1987 from the Permanent Representative of Kuwait to the United Nations Addressed to the Secretary-General' (16 October 1987) UN Doc S/19215.

[114] See, for example, UNSC 'Letter Dated 22 October 1987 from the Permanent Representative of Kuwait to the United Nations Addressed to the Secretary-General' (22 October 1987) UN Doc S/19227.

[115] UNSC 'Letter Dated 6 January 1988 from the Charge D'Affaires A I of the Permanent Mission of the Islamic Republic of Iran to the United Nations Addressed to the Secretary-General' (7 January 1988) UN Doc S/19409.

[116] UNSC 'Letter Dated 11 January 1988 from the Charge D'Affaires A I of the Permanent Mission of Kuwait to the United Nations Addressed to the Security Council' (11 January 1988) UN Doc S/19417.

regime.'[117] There were further allegations of violations of Kuwaiti airspace in January 1988, when Iraqi fighter jets allegedly flew through Kuwaiti airspace after having attacked the Resalat oil platform belonging to Iran.[118] Iran denounced what it called this act of 'co-operation' between Kuwait and Iraq and stated that it would hold Kuwait responsible for such co-operation.[119] Iran asked Kuwait to take 'immediate steps to stop making its territory available for all such future flights.'[120] As well as accusing Kuwait of 'co-operation' with Iraq, Iran also charged Kuwait with 'complicity' with Iraq.[121] On 20 April 1988, a Scud missile was fired into Kuwaiti territory.[122]

In light of Kuwait's undoubted breaches of the law of neutrality, other States provided mixed responses to the question whether Kuwait could be considered to be a 'co-belligerent' or a participant in the conflict. The US, while admitting that Kuwait was not strictly neutral and supported Iraq,[123] stated that it did not consider Kuwait to be a belligerent.[124] In July 1987, just before Iran's formal statement that Kuwait had become a belligerent in the war, the Netherlands approved the sale of mine-hunters to Kuwait. The Minister of Foreign Affairs sent a message to parliament detailing the foreign policy considerations that had influenced the decision to issue an export-licence to the firm selling the mine-hunters. An important consideration for the Dutch government was its view that:

[117] UNSC 'Letter Dated 7 July 1988 from the Acting Permanent Representative of the Islamic Republic of Iran to the United Nations Addressed to the Secretary-General' (11 July 1988) UN Doc S/20003. Kuwait again denied that it had permitted Iraq the use of its airspace. See UNSC 'Letter Dated 14 July 1988 from the Permanent Representative of Kuwait to the United Nations Addressed to the Secretary-General' (14 July 1988) UN Doc S/20015.

[118] UNSC 'Letter Dated 26 April 1988 from the Acting Permanent Representative of the Islamic Republic of Iran to the United Nations Addressed to the Secretary-General' (26 April 1988) UN Doc S/19841. For Kuwait's reply see UNSC 'Letter Dated 28 April 1988 From the Permanent Representative of Kuwait to the United Nations Addressed to the Secretary-General' (24 April 1988) UN Doc S/19849. Kuwait complained that Iran's statements amounted to a 'threat of force' within the meaning of Article 2(4) of the Charter. See UNSC 'Letter Dated 9 May 1988 from the Permanent Representative of Kuwait to the United Nations Addressed to the Secretary-General' (9 May 1988) S/19872.

[119] UNSC 'Letter Dated 26 April 1988 from the Acting Permanent Representative of the Islamic Republic of Iran to the United Nations Addressed to the Secretary-General' (26 April 1988) UN Doc S/19841.

[120] UNSC 'Letter Dated 26 April 1988 from the Acting Permanent Representative of the Islamic Republic of Iran to the United Nations Addressed to the Secretary-General' (26 April 1988) UN Doc S/19841.

[121] UNSC 'Letter Dated 18 April 1988 from the Acting Permanent Representative of the Islamic Republic of Iran to the United Nations Addressed to the Secretary-General' (18 April 1988) UN Doc S/19797; UNSC 'Letter Dated 4 May 1988 from the Charge D'Affaires A I of the Permanent Mission of the Islamic Republic of Iran to the United Nations Addressed to the Secretary-General' (5 May 1988) UN Doc S/19865.

[122] UNSC 'Letter Dated 20 April 1988 from the Permanent Representative of Kuwait to the United Nations Addressed to the Secretary-General (20 April 1988) UN Doc S/19811.

[123] 'The US Plan to Protect Kuwaiti Ships in the Gulf by Putting Them Under US Flags' (n 103) 1429.

[124] Ibid 1430.

> Kuwait is at present not directly involved in the armed conflict between Iraq and Iran in the region and there is no reason to suppose that it will become a belligerent of its own accord in the foreseeable future. Kuwait does not present a threat to neighbouring countries.[125]

Indeed, the Netherlands argued that, due to the presence of mines in the Gulf, Kuwait was entitled to rely on its right of self-defence under Article 51 of the Charter.[126]

According to this approach, financial assistance to one State, even on a massive scale and on repeated occasions, does not convert a breach of neutrality into participation as a belligerent. It is notable that Iran appeared to view Kuwait's behaviour as extreme. While it admitted that other States, such as the US, were deviating from their neutral duties, it did not go so far as to contend that the US was a participant, or a belligerent, in the armed conflict.

In its letter of 9 April 1987, for example, Iran stated that 'the Islamic Republic of Iran believes that United States military presence in the Persian Gulf and the strait of Hormuz, which is aimed at supporting the aggressor regime of Iraq, is the only source of instability and tension that would undoubtedly expand if the United States presence were to continue.'[127] Opinions differ regarding the extent of the US actions in favour of Iraq. It has been noted, for example that it would be 'difficult to conceive of those actions in terms other than those of active hostilities.'[128] At the time, the US continued to insist on its neutrality.[129]

Similarly, in June 1988, Iran accused Saudi Arabia of 'co-operation' with Iraq. It alleged that Iraqi jets made an emergency landing at Abu Jobil airport in Saudi Arabia, and that damaged parts of the Iraqi aircraft were later transported to Iraq, which Iran contended was an 'unequivocal violation of the principles of neutrality.'[130] It did not seek to suggest, however, that Saudi Arabia had become a party to the international armed conflict.

What this practice appears to demonstrate is that even massive financial and logistical support, and repeated violations of the law of neutrality, does not amount to co-belligerency or 'participation' in the hostilities. This approach

[125] R C R Siekmann 'Netherlands State Practice for the Parliamentary Year 1987-1988' (1988) 19 NYIL 249, 390.

[126] Ibid.

[127] UNSC 'Letter Dated 9 April 1987 from the Permanent Representative of the Islamic of Iran to the United Nations Addressed to the Secretary-General' (10 April 1987) UN Doc S/18794.

[128] G P Politakis 'From Action Stations to Action: US Naval Deployment, "Non-Belligerency," and "Defensive Reprisals" in the Final Year of the Iran-Iraq War' (1994) 25 ODIL 31, 39.

[129] (1988) DSB 61.

[130] UNSC 'Letter Dated 29 June 1988 From the Acting Permanent Representative of the Islamic Republic of Iran to the United Nations Addressed to the Secretary-General' (29 June 1988) UN Doc S/19971. Saudi Arabia rejected the allegation. UNSC 'Letter Dated 11 July 1988 From the Charge D'Affaires A I of the Permanent Mission of Saudi Arabia to the United Nations Addressed to the Secretary-General' (11 July 1988) UN Doc S/20007.

seems to be confirmed in recent case law, which has rejected the view that the granting of logistical facilities, in violation of the neutral duty of prevention, amounts to participation in hostilities. Thus in *Dubsky v Ireland*, the High Court of Ireland held that 'it cannot, in my view, follow either in logic or in law that there is a necessary equivalence between the loss of the status of neutrality for alleged failure to comply with norms of neutrality in international law and the establishment of participation in a war.'[131]

In recent State practice, the view is reaffirmed that the granting of logistical support, in violation of neutral duties, cannot amount to participation. Thus Italy contended with regard to the 2003 Iraq war that:

> We believe that the United States, the United Kingdom, the Netherlands, Denmark, quoting only some States which are members of NATO, are not operating outside international law, although I remind us that Italy, contrary to the past, does not participate with its own troops and means in military actions. Italy is not a co-belligerent country because, contrary to the past, we are not at war.
>
> Exactly like all the other European countries, including France and Germany – I think the only exception is Haider's Austria – and in accordance with our foreign policy's guidelines for conduct in the last fifty years, Italy guarantees logistic support and the right to overfly.[132]

In 2005, Italy reaffirmed this view. On 10 November 2005, the Minister for Defence stated that the Italian mission in Iraq did not amount to participation in war:

> Italy did not take part to war [sic]. Its position was clear from the very beginning: on 19 March 2003, the *Presidente del Consiglio* (President of the Council of Ministers) declared in Parliament, in an unambiguous and solemn way, the non-belligerency of Italy as expressed in the Supreme Council of Defence and sanction by the Parliament [sic]. All this absolutely excludes any active role of Italy in war. Rather, since the beginning of the Iraqi crisis Italy was strongly engaged in the search for solutions that could avoid the recourse to force, and this engagement was spent at all levels and carried out in all international contexts.[133]

[131] *Dubsky v The Government of Ireland & Ors* [2005] IEHC 442 per Macken J.

[132] (2003) 13 IYIL 288–9. The Minister then advanced various political reasons for the action, as 'confirming – I must state this – a relationship of political friendship with the United States, the United Kingdom, Denmark, the Netherlands, Spain, Poland, Bulgaria, Australia, New Zealand; to sum up, our friends and allies. We acted, exactly like France and Germany, which conceded the use of the bases and the right to overfly – France not having any base only gave the right to overfly – within the unity of the European views, which must be re-established in the future' (ibid at 289).

[133] (2005) 15 IYIL 376–7.

No State sought to challenge these statements. In light of this, it must be concluded that State practice does not yet support the view that action contrary to the neutral duties of abstention and prevention amounts to 'participation' in an armed conflict that would cause a neutral State to lose its neutrality. To constitute 'participation' or 'co-belligerency' it seems that direct military support must be given, or there must be some sort of direct, causal link between the neutral's action and an act of belligerency. There would therefore appear to be a significant 'gap' in present international law between the violation of neutral duties and the loss of neutral status.

b. Termination Through Hostilities Against the Neutral State

i. Hostilities against a neutral state

According to traditional doctrine, there is a fundamental difference between a valid repulsion of belligerent attempts to violate neutrality, and 'hostilities' against the neutral which create a state of war between the belligerent and the neutral.[134] Just as the state of war initiated by a belligerent created the factual relation of neutrality unless the non-participant chose to participate on the side of a belligerent, so an act of a belligerent—the initiation of war against a neutral—could unilaterally bring neutral status to an end.

According to James Brown Scott, the approach to neutrality in the Hague Conventions, which emphasizes various belligerent duties to respect neutral territory, marks an acceptance in international law that neutrals have 'acquired a standing in international law with rights of their own.'[135] But this is a considerable overstatement of the legal position. While it is true that belligerents had under the Hague Conventions certain duties to respect neutral rights, any right to immunity from interference was a limited one, as they were under no obligation to respect the status of neutrality. Once a State possessed the status of a neutral, there were certain rules that bound the belligerent in its relations with it; but there existed no 'right' of the neutral State to maintain that status in the absence of a prohibition on war. As Oppenheim noted in 1906, it was purely a question of policy, not of law, whether a State was able to retain its status of neutrality.[136]

In State practice this was demonstrated by Germany's invasion of Belgium and Luxembourg in World War I. The extinction of those States' neutrality by Germany was a matter on which the Hague Conventions were silent.[137] Certain

[134] Oppenheim (7th edn) vol II 684.

[135] J B Scott *The Hague Peace Conferences of 1899 and 1907* vol I (Johns Hopkins Press, Baltimore 1909) 543–4.

[136] Oppenheim (1st edn) vol II 317.

[137] 'The Hague Conventions and the Neutrality of Belgium and Luxemburg' (1915) 9 AJIL 959, 959.

authors sought to argue that this was not a tenable interpretation of the Hague Conventions. To argue that the Hague Conventions offered no protection against a belligerent invasion of neutral territory was, it was suggested, to rob the Hague Conventions of all practical utility.[138] However, this was to confuse a violation of neutrality with a termination of neutrality. While the Hague Conventions had much to say on the former, they were silent on the latter.[139] As a commentary on the invasion of Belgium and Luxembourg noted, the Hague Conventions:

> …do not, however, guarantee neutrality, nor do they prevent a state from declaring war against a state wishing to remain neutral, which thus becomes a belligerent and loses the benefit of the Convention.[140]

It was therefore only with the prohibition of the use of force that a State's claim to neutral status could be said to be protected by international law. This appears to be the thrust of the following statement in the third edition of *Oppenheim's International Law*, published in 1921 and edited by Richard Roxburgh:

> [T]he Law of Nations in its present development objects to a would-be neutral State being forced into war, and a belligerent who refuses to recognise it as neutral violates International Law, although not neutrality.[141]

Pursuant to the UN Charter, any termination of neutral status by a belligerent must be reconciled with the law on the use of force.[142] A State attempting to repel a violation of neutrality will retain its neutral status, until an armed conflict develops between it and the belligerent.

ii. Neutrality and belligerent occupation

A belligerent occupation of neutral territory will terminate that State's neutrality.[143] Thus the capture of a ship made in the territorial waters of neutral territory

[138] C de Visscher 'De la belligérance dans ses rapports avec la violation de la neutralité' (1916) 2 PW 93, 100. James Garner described as 'pure sophistry' the view that the law of neutrality was no longer relevant to the actions of Germany with regard to Belgium because of a supervening state of war between them: J W Garner *International Law and the World War* (Longmans, Green and Co, London 1920) 216.

[139] J D Falconbridge 'The Right of a Belligerent to Make War Upon a Neutral' (1918) 4 TGS 204, 209.

[140] 'The Hague Conventions and the Neutrality of Belgium and Luxemburg' (n 137) 969.

[141] Oppenheim (3rd edn) vol II 406. For a similar view see Q Wright 'Project of the American Institute of International Law on Maritime Neutrality (No 26)' (1927) 21 AJIL 127, 128.

[142] cf Castrén *Neutrality* 422–3: '[i]n a subjective sense, the right of neutrality would be the right to remain outside a war'; general international law does not, however, grant this right, with the possible exception of a permanently neutral State (such as Switzerland) the neutrality of which has been recognised or guaranteed by other Powers.'

[143] Oppenheim (7th edn) vol II 685; E H Feilchenfeld *The International Economic Law of Belligerent Occupation* (Carnegie Endowment for International Peace, Washington 1942) 8; G von Glahn *The*

under occupation is not unlawful as the capture is deemed to have occurred in enemy waters.[144] While the law is clear, in practice there has occasionally been some uncertainty. The German occupation of neutral Denmark in World War II raised some complicated questions. Germany invaded Denmark on 9 April 1940, and soon the territory and the most important Danish ports were occupied.[145] The Danish government, however, considered itself neutral during the occupation.[146] Alf Ross has suggested that in fact the Danish position was *sui generis*, neither belligerent nor neutral.[147] This argument was reliant on the fact that no state of war was formally said to exist between Germany and Denmark, and with the decline in the state of war doctrine the issue is of limited interest.[148]

c. Termination Through Cessation of Hostilities

If the neutrality of a State is not terminated by forcible action by a belligerent, or by the volition of the neutral State, the traditional position holds, in accordance with the view that neutrality is dependent on war, that neutral status ends with the termination of war, i.e. when a treaty of peace is concluded.[149]

Thus according to this view the fact that active hostilities have ceased is generally not sufficient to terminate a state of war.[150] As Sir Robert Jennings stated:

Occupation of Enemy Territory: A Commentary on the Law and Practice of Belligerent Occupation (University of Minnesota Press, Minneapolis 1957) 12. In minor instances, such as the repelling of a frontier incursion, a transformation of neutrality into belligerency will not occur and will instead be treated as a defence of neutral territory. See A Roberts 'What is a Military Occupation?' (1984) 55 BYBIL 249, 263.

[144] Thus in the case of *The Argun*, arising from the Russo-Japanese war of 1904–1905, a Japanese prize court determined that Korean territory, then under Japanese occupation, was 'not *de facto* neutral' and capture in its territorial waters was not unlawful. See S Takahashi *International Law Applied to the Russo-Japanese War* (Banks Law Publishing, New York 1908) 573–5; A S Hershey 'Some Questions of International Law Arising from the Russo-Japanese War I: Failure to Declare War and Alleged Violation of Korean Neutrality' (1904) 16 GB 306.

[145] R Lemkin *Axis Rule in Occupied Europe* (Carnegie Endowment for International Peace, Washington 1944) 157.

[146] H Kirchoff 'Denmark, September 1939-April 1940' in N Wylie (ed) *European Neutrals and Non-Belligerents in the Second World War* (CUP, Cambridge 2002) 34. See the proclamation to the Danish people issued by the Danish government on 9 April 1940: (1940) 11 NT 146.

[147] A Ross 'Denmark's Legal Status During the Occupation' (1949) 1 *Jus Gentium* 3. For a similar view see S Hurwitz 'Was Denmark at War?' (1945) 16 NT 49.

[148] There is some evidence from prize cases that Danish vessels were treated as enemy vessels: *The Prins Knud* 1 Ll PC (2nd) 57. The prize cases have been regarded as inconclusive: J L Kunz 'British Prize Cases, 1939-1941' (1942) 36 AJIL 204.

[149] Dinstein (n 8) 34–50; Dinstein (n 4) 80; H Levie 'The Nature and Scope of the Armistice Agreement' (1956) 50 AJIL 880, 884; G Schwarzenberger *International Law as Applied by International Courts and Tribunals* vol II (Stevens & Sons, London 1968) 575; Castrén *Neutrality* 423; J M Spaight *Air Power and War Rights* (3rd edn Longmans Green and Co, London 1947) 438.

[150] Dinstein (n 8) 25; Greenwood (n 9) 62.

> The mere cessation of hostilities... does not of itself end war; there must also be a cessation of the *animus belligerandi*, and where... a belligerent state issues a categorical assertion that the relationship of war persists between it and another state and acts on that assumption, there does not seem to be any real room for doubt that there is a continuing state of war in the technical sense.[151]

Termination of a war, therefore, comes about only in particular circumstances: by formal peace agreement; by *debellatio*; or some other definitive indication on the part of belligerents that they consider the state of war to have ceased.[152] According to traditional doctrine, armistice agreements, truces, and cease-fires, being temporary arrangements prior to conclusion of a treaty of peace, suspend, but do not terminate, a state of war.[153] Pursuant to this view, it would appear to follow that the rights and duties of neutrals remain applicable during these periods when hostilities are suspended and the rights of belligerents probably enforceable against them.[154]

Since the difficulties associated with the evaluation of State intention have been resolved by looking to the factual character of the hostilities, there would appear to be little support for adhering to the view that the status of neutrality remains applicable without actual fighting.[155] However, attempting to determine when hostilities have ended and neutrality ceases to apply is not without difficulty. The Geneva Conventions use different language to describe the end of hostilities.[156] The phrase 'general close of military operations' in Geneva Convention IV is intended to mean, according to the ICRC, 'the final end of all fighting between all those concerned.'[157] States have referred to compliance with neutral duties 'until the termination of hostilities.'[158]

It may be impossible to establish in the abstract when the status of neutrality will cease to apply and much will depend on the circumstances and whether the situation between the belligerents has normalized. State practice indicates, however, that the conclusion of a treaty of peace will not be required before the status of neutrality comes to an end. State practice suggests that some degree of permanence is required.

[151] R Y Jennings 'Government in Commission' (1946) 23 BYBIL 112, 124.

[152] See generally Q Wright 'How Hostilities have Ended: Peace Treaties and Alternatives' (1970) 392 AAAPSS 51; S D Bailey 'Cease-Fires, Truces, and Armistices in the Practice of the UN Security Council' (1977) 71 AJIL 461; W H von Heinegg, 'Factors in War to Peace Transitions' (2003–2004) 27 HJLPP 843, 848–55; C Bell 'Peace Agreements: Their Nature and Legal Status' (2006) 100 AJIL 373; McNair and Watts (n 4) 15.

[153] Jennings (n 151) 124.

[154] Oppenheim (7th edn) vol II 546–7; Castrén *Neutrality* 130; 423.

[155] Petrochilos (n 61) 604.

[156] GC IV art 6 ('general close of military operations'); cf GC III art 111 ('close of hostilities').

[157] Commentary IV (n 91) 62.

[158] UNSC 'Letter from the Permanent Representative of the Islamic Republic of Iran to the United Nations addressed to the Secretary-General' (28 January 1991) UN Doc S/22163.

i. Neutrality following an armistice

That much will depend on circumstances is confirmed by State practice with regard to armistices. Thus in the case of the *Attiliò Regolo,* Spain contended that the armistice agreement concluded after World War II between the US and Italy did not affect Spain's neutral duties.[159]

In other instances, States have ceased to comply with neutral duties in the absence of hostilities. In the aftermath of the 1948 war, various armistice agreements were concluded between Israel and the various Arab States.[160] Despite the existence of the armistice between it and Israel, Egypt continued to assert that a state of war continued to exist between it and Israel, and that it was entitled to exercise belligerent rights against enemy and neutral shipping in the Suez Canal.[161] Pursuant to this view, it published a contraband list and established a prize court.[162]

However, other States rejected this attempt to claim that a state of war continued to exist, and rejected the view that Egypt could continue to assert belligerent rights. In answer to the Egyptian explanation that, as a result of military events in Palestine, Egypt considered herself to be in a state of war, a French protest note of 1948 pointed out that Egypt's status as a belligerent had not been recognized.[163] The US asserted that the restraints on the sale of arms it had imposed at the outbreak of hostilities were no longer required.[164] The UN Security Council accepted that Egypt could not claim that it was actively a belligerent.[165] In this situation, therefore, neutrality was not generally applicable despite the lack of a binding treaty of peace.[166]

[159] *The Case of* Attiliò Regolo *and Other Vessels* (1945) 12 RIAA 1; P Leroy 'L'affaire de l'« Attiliò Regolo » et autres navires' (1965) 11 AFDI 278. The issue was not decided by the tribunal.

[160] General Armistice Agreement Between Israel and Egypt (1949) 42 UNTS 251; General Armistice Agreement Between Israel and Lebanon (1949) 42 UNTS 287; General Armistice Agreement Between Israel and Jordan (1949) 42 UNTS 303; General Armistice Agreement Between Israel and Syria (1949) 42 UNTS 327.

[161] R Higgins 'Legal Limits to the Use of Force by Sovereign States: United Nations Practice' (1961) 37 BYBIL 269, 311; T D Brown Jr 'World War Prize Law Applied in a Limited War Situation: Egyptian Restrictions on Neutral Shipping with Israel' (1965–1966) 50 Minn LR 849; L Gross 'Passage Through the Suez Canal of Israeli-Bound Cargo and Israeli Ships' (1957) 51 AJIL 530.

[162] S Dinitz 'The Legal Aspects of the Egyptian Blockade of the Suez Canal' (1956–1957) 45 Geo LJ 169, 171; J Trappe 'On the Jurisdiction of the Egyptian Prize Court, 1948-1960' (1959–60) 15–16 REDI 60.

[163] SWB (1948) Part III No 63 (12 August 1948) 65.

[164] UN Verbatim Record (4 August 1949) SCOR Resolutions and Decisions 26. Ralph Bunche, the acting UN mediator on Palestine, remarked that '...it would seem that the States of the Near East, as all others, would now be entitled to import such war materials as may be necessary to their national security' (ibid 22).

[165] UNSC Res 95 (1 September 1951) UN Doc S/2322.

[166] In the early 1950s, the Federal Republic of Germany (FRG) concluded an agreement with Israel to pay compensation for World War II. At various stages certain Arab States protested that this payment to Israel was a violation of the FRG's duties of neutrality. The FRG did not contest the view that it was subject to neutral duties, despite the lack of active hostilities in the Middle East. The situation is documented in Norton (n 57) 299 and Petrochilos (n 61) 584.

ii. Neutrality following a cease-fire

Similar issues regarding the exercise of belligerent rights arose again following the cessation of active hostilities in the 1967 war in the Middle East. In that situation, Egypt again argued that war continued to exist and that it was entitled to assert belligerent rights. Again the international community refused to accept the contention that a state of war existed or duties of neutrality were applicable.[167] France, which had imposed an arms embargo upon the outbreak of armed conflict, stated that the cessation of hostilities meant that the embargo no longer needed to be maintained.[168] The situation in the Middle East, it noted, could be qualified as 'a state which is not peace but which is without doubt not war.'[169] Other States, such as Belgium, rejected Egypt's attempt to exercise belligerent rights against merchant shipping, and emphasized the centrality of the principle of freedom of navigation.[170] In this situation, it appeared to be accepted that neutrality was not applicable in a situation of cease-fire.

A cease-fire came into effect between Iran and Iraq on 20 August 1988. On the same day, the commander of the Iranian Navy announced that Iranian forces would continue to exercise the right of visit, search, and seizure.[171] During peace talks on 25 August 25 1988, Iran insisted that under international law it possessed the right to search shipping because a formal state of belligerency existed.[172] A UK tanker was boarded and searched by Iran on 12 December 1988 – some five months after the cease-fire came into effect.[173]

This did not appear to affect neutral duties, however. During the course of active hostilities the UK had refused to sell military equipment to either side in line with its neutral or 'impartial' status.[174] Negotiations over a contract for the supply of military equipment to Iran, which had been suspended during active hostilities, were reopened in 1988 after the conclusion of the cease-fire.[175]

The above practice is varied and caution must be exercised in attempting to develop conclusions from it. The following thoughts may nevertheless be offered. First, the obligations associated with neutrality are generally regarded as extinguished by the end of active hostilities, particularly when accompanied by a stable cease-fire. Secondly, it appears that it is for the neutral State to make the assessment of when the obligations of neutrality may be relaxed.[176]

[167] See generally J E Fink 'The Gulf of Aqaba and the Strait of Tiran: The Practice of "Freedom of Navigation" After the Egyptian-Israeli Peace Treaty' (1995) 42 Nav LR 121, 127.

[168] (1968) 13 AFDI 897, 901. [169] (1972) 18 AFDI 1005. [170] See (1969) RBDI 306–7.

[171] D Momtaz 'Iran: Commentary' A De Guttry and N Ronzitti (eds) *The Iran-Iraq War (1980–1988) and the Law of Naval Warfare* (Grotius Publications, Cambridge 1993) 19, 28.

[172] *Keesing's* (1989) 36569. [173] Ibid 36570. [174] See (1987) 58 BYBIL 638.

[175] See I Anthony et al 'Appendix 6B: Register of the Trade in Major Conventional Weapons with Industrialised and Third World Countries, 1988' in *SIPRI Yearbook 1989* (OUP, Oxford 1989) 230, 252.

[176] This point is explicitly made by Switzerland with regard to the Iraq conflict. See Swiss Federal Department of Foreign Affairs 'Neutrality under Scrutiny in the Iraq Conflict: Summary of Switzerland's Neutrality Policy during the Iraq Conflict' (2 December 2005) <http://www.eda.admin.ch/eda/en/home/topics/intla/cintla/ref_neutr.html> accessed 21 January 2007.

3. Conclusion

This chapter has been devoted to an analysis of when precisely the law of neutrality becomes applicable in contemporary armed conflict. It has been suggested, after a consideration of legal doctrine and practice, that the most coherent approach to adopt, and one that is most practical for the conduct of military operations, is that the status of neutrality becomes applicable in an international armed conflict.

While States may, in many cases of hostilities, not be required to indicate their attitude towards the hostilities and will therefore find themselves released from scrutiny with regard to compliance, the status of neutrality will nevertheless be applicable. As an armed conflict escalates in tempo and scale, the role of non-participants in containing hostilities will increase and the duties of neutrality will in reality become more onerous, especially if the belligerents are able to insist on compliance.

Finally, the frequently overlooked question of when the status of neutrality ceases has been considered from three separate angles: first, when a neutral departs from neutral duties in such a way as to call into question its position of non-participation in the hostilities; secondly, when a neutral State is forced into hostilities by a belligerent; and thirdly, when an armed conflict between two belligerents comes to an end. While it is impossible to establish a general test for when the obligations of neutrality cease upon the cessation of hostilities between belligerents, it is apparent that it is the fact of the end of hostilities, not whether a treaty of peace or other formal conclusion of armed conflict has been concluded, which will be decisive.

Chapter 3
The Duties and Rights of Neutrals

The present chapter turns away from the question of when the status of neutrality is applicable in contemporary international law and turns to the question of the contemporary content of the law of neutrality. The precise content of the law of neutrality is an area—perhaps unsurprisingly—that continues to be plagued by uncertainty. In particular, this uncertainty surrounds whether it is possible to continue to refer to the rights and duties of neutrality at all.

This is because a prominent approach to the law of neutrality suggests that the substantive rules of neutrality contained in customary international law and in the two Hague Conventions of 1907 no longer exist as a matter of positive law; instead, this approach suggests, the content of the law of neutrality may be reduced to certain core principles, such as the principle that neutral territory is inviolable and that neutral States are required to abstain from participating in hostilities.

One might seek to find support for this view in the approach to neutrality seemingly adopted by the International Court of Justice in the *Legality of the Threat or Use of Nuclear Weapons* Advisory Opinion, where the Court referred to the 'principle' of neutrality instead of any specific duties reflected in the Hague Conventions.[1] The Court's treatment of neutrality was brief and oblique, however, and any attempt to extract sweeping conclusions concerning the corpus of neutral duties should be met with caution.

More recently, however, the UK *Manual of the Law of Armed Conflict* has exhibited this approach to neutrality. Unlike other prominent military manuals, the UK *Manual* contains no section devoted to neutral rights and duties but instead elucidates in two paragraphs the 'basic principles' that 'remain applicable' in that body of law.[2] Certain substantive rules that pertain to the relationship between belligerents and neutrals in aerial and naval warfare are contained in other parts of the text, however.

Unfortunately, the UK *Manual* nowhere indicates the methodology deployed in the reduction of neutrality to a set of basic principles rather than a body of interlocking rights and duties; and no evidence is advanced to demonstrate this development. Presumably, it is the failure of States explicitly to invoke the substantive duties of neutrality in contemporary international armed conflicts that informs the approach and that has implicitly repealed the substantive rules. It is

1 *Legality of the Threat or Use of Nuclear Weapons* (Advisory Opinion) [1996] ICJ Rep 226 [89].
2 UK *Manual of the Law of Armed Conflict* § 1.43.

mentioned in the UK *Manual* that the traditional law of neutrality has been, 'to a large extent, superseded' by the UN Charter.

This view is not only in direct conflict with the view held by various other prominent naval powers (most notably the US); as Chapter 4 will demonstrate, it also does not reflect entirely accurately the position of neutrality under the UN Charter when the Security Council takes enforcement action under Chapter VII.

Before examining in greater detail how the law of neutrality interacts with the UN Charter, however, it is necessary to consider whether the UK *Manual's* approach has any validity, and whether the content of the law of neutrality has in fact been reduced to certain core principles, or whether the rights and duties of neutrality as traditionally understood continue to exist.

1. The Concept of Impartiality

a. The Codification of Custom

It was in the nineteenth century that the law of neutrality experienced what has been termed its 'golden age.'[3] It was a period of steady advance in the acceptance of neutrality as a legal status with detailed rights and duties.[4] Even though the state of war doctrine led to considerable uncertainties in practice, the idea of a war as a duel between contestants brought into effect a 'realm of relative reason' (to use Carl Schmitt's phrase)[5] that apportioned defined rules to belligerents and non-participants alike.

Prior to 1907, however, there existed no convention that dealt comprehensively with matters of neutrality, either in conflict on land or at sea.[6] The Regulations annexed to Hague Convention II of 1899 contained various provisions relating to neutral States, but these dealt principally with the internment of belligerents in neutral territory.[7] It had been remarked at the 1899 Hague conference that there

[3] C de Visscher *Theory and Reality in Public International Law* (P E Corbett (tr)) (PUP, Princeton 1957) 297.

[4] E M Borchard 'Restatement of the Law of Neutrality in Maritime War' (1928) 22 AJIL 614, 616.

[5] C Schmitt *The* Nomos *of the Earth in the International Law of the* Jus Publicum Europaeum (G L Ulmen (tr)) (Telos Press, New York 2003) 142.

[6] The Declaration of Paris, signed in 1856, had touched on issues of importance to neutrality in naval warfare: Declaration of Paris (signed 16 April 1856) 115 CTS 1.

[7] Hague Convention II with Respect to the Laws and Customs of War on Land and its Annex: Regulations concerning the Laws and Customs of War on Land (signed 29 July 1899, entered into force 4 September 1900) 187 CTS 429 art 54; art 57–60. The Institute of International Law had also dealt with this issue in its manual on land warfare published in 1880. See Institut de droit international 'Les lois de la guerre sur terre. Manuel publié par l'Institut de droit international' (1881–1882) 5 *Annuaire* 157 art 79–83 (Oxford Manual on Land Warfare). An English translation may be found in J B Scott (ed) *Resolutions of the Institute of International Law* (Carnegie Endowment of International Peace, Washington D C 1916) 25.

was a need to define with greater precision the rights and duties of neutral States.[8] This was the purpose of Hague Conventions V and XIII, which deal with neutrality in, respectively, land and maritime warfare.[9]

While the two Hague Conventions have generally been regarded as a framework for the modern law of neutrality, it needs to be kept in mind that they exist side by side with customary international law.[10] Indeed, their principal importance has been as an expression of customary international law at the time of codification. The status of the Hague Conventions themselves is somewhat uncertain, for a number of reasons. First, the Conventions were ratified and have been acceded to by only a small number of States, and certain reservations have been entered.[11] Secondly, the Hague Conventions contain general participation clauses (*clausula si omnes*) and therefore apply only 'if all the belligerents are parties to the Convention.'[12] Hence, while the Hague Conventions offer important expressions of the content of neutrality at the time of adoption of the conventions, today customary international law is recognized as 'the decisive source of law for the contemporary law of neutrality.'[13]

A distinction is sometimes made between constitutive treaties creating new legal norms among the contracting parties, and declaratory treaties that reflect customary international law.[14] Hague Conventions V and XIII codify existing norms of customary international law.[15] The preamble to Hague Convention XIII notes that its purpose is directed 'to harmonizing the divergent views which, in the event of naval war, are still held on the relations between neutral Powers and belligerent Powers, and to anticipating the difficulties to which such divergence of views might give rise.'[16] Nevertheless, the purpose of Hague Convention XIII was not to cover the entire field of legal regulation between belligerents and neutrals; the preamble notes that 'in cases not covered by the present Convention, it is

[8] The representative of Luxembourg at the 1899 conference had emphasized the indefinite status of the rights and duties of neutral States in international law and asserted that a precise definition would assist legal certainty for both neutrals and belligerents. W I Hull *The Two Hague Conferences And Their Contributions to International Law* (Ginn & Company, Boston 1908) 199.

[9] HC V; HC XIII.

[10] See A Kiss (ed) *Répertoire de la pratique française en matière de droit international public vol VI* (Éditions CNRS, Paris 1969) § 1014.

[11] Hague Convention V has 34 State parties. Hague Convention XIII has 30 State parties.

[12] HC V art 20; HC XIII art 28. Its is considered that the clause was superseded by practice already before WWII. It was then formally abandonnes by Article 2, § 3, of Geneva Conventions I-IV of 1949 and related customary law. For more details, see P Gautier 'General Participation Clause (Clausula si omnes)' IV *MPEPIL* (2006) 368.

[13] Switzerland Federal Department of Foreign Affairs 'Swiss Neutrality in Practice Current Aspects: Report of the Interdepartmental Working Group of 30 August 2000' (30 August 2000) <http://www.eda.admin.ch/eda/en/home/topics/intla/cintla/ref_neutr.html> accessed 21 December 2006 [4.1].

[14] Y Dinstein 'The Interaction Between Customary International Law and Treaties' (2006) 322 RCADI 243, 346.

[15] On HC XIII, see *The Case of* Attiliò Regolo *and Other Vessels* (1945) 12 RIAA 1 [4]; for a discussion of the codification of HC V see W R Bisschop 'The *Altmark*' (1940) 26 TGS 67, 72.

[16] HC XIII preamble.

expedient to take into consideration the general principles of the law of nations.'[17] Indeed, what is *not* covered by Hague Convention XIII is at first glance surprising: noticeably, no attempt was made to codify the rules concerning contraband or blockade. The latter subject matter was left for a further codification effort at the 1908–1909 London Naval Conference, which led to the ill-fated Declaration of London, which set out various rules regarding blockade, contraband, and unneutral service, but which did not enter into force due to disagreement regarding the breadth of its rules.[18]

b. The Principle of Impartiality

Perhaps the most surprising absence from the Hague Conventions, however, is the lack of any specific duty of impartiality. The law of neutrality had frequently throughout history been identified with the concept of impartiality; a common view was that 'the character of neutrality was, that nothing should be granted to one party which was not allowed to the other.'[19]

This did not, however, reflect customary international law. The Hague Conventions do not contain a concrete duty of impartiality; instead, impartiality designates the way in which other neutral duties are discharged. Article 9 of Hague Convention V, for example, provides that:

> Every measure of restriction or prohibition taken by a neutral Power in regard to the matters referred to in Articles 7 and 8 must be impartially applied by it to both belligerents…[20]

Article 9 in Hague Convention XIII contains an obligation of a similar nature regarding non-discrimination in maritime warfare.[21] That this is an obligation of form and not of substance is supported by the authentic French text of Article 9 of Hague Convention V, which states that measures of restriction or prohibition should be 'uniformément appliquées.'[22]

[17] Ibid.

[18] This subject matter was to be formulated at the London Conference of 1909. The resulting Declaration Concerning the Laws of Naval War (signed 26 February 1909) 208 CTS 338 (Declaration of London) did not enter into force. The Declaration of London, however, has been seen as largely declaratory of customary international law at the time of its formulation. In a Preliminary Provision, the Signatory Powers indicated that 'the rules contained in the following Chapters correspond in substance with the generally recognised principles of international law.'

[19] (1819) 40 Parl Deb (HL) 1379 (Lord Bathurst). Lord Holland argued that 'impartiality constituted neutrality' (1391).

[20] HC V art 9. Article 7 of HC V provides that a neutral is not required to prevent the export or transport of arms and war material; Article 8 provides that the neutral State is not required to restrict or forbid the use of wireless telegraphy.

[21] HC XIII art 9.

[22] HC V art 9.

The French 'uniformément' is in many ways a more precise term than the English term 'impartiality'—a term that has generated a large amount of philosophical enquiry as to its ambit.[23] The term 'impartiality' may, in fact, be inclined to mislead, in suggesting a more capacious duty than that contained in Article 9 of Hague Convention V. Indeed, an alternative English translation of the first paragraph of Article 9, which is more accurate, has been rendered as follows:

> All restrictive or prohibitive measures taken by a neutral Power in regard to the matters mentioned in articles 7 and 8 must be applied uniformly by it to both the belligerents.[24]

The authentic French text of Article 9 of Hague Convention XIII, which refers to restrictions and prohibitions on the admission of belligerent warships and prizes into neutral ports, roadsteads, or territorial waters, uses the word 'également', which has been rendered as 'equally' in one English translation.[25]

This variation in language seems to have passed largely unnoticed. According to Higgins, Article 9 of Hague Convention XIII 'met with no difficulty in acceptance.'[26] Hyde notes simply '[t]hat impartiality should mark the conduct of the neutral in applying restrictions in the use of its own waters is too obvious to deserve comment.'[27] However, what Hyde refers to as a duty of impartiality is perhaps better described as a principle of impartiality, as the concept of impartiality refers only to the way in which other neutral duties are discharged; it is not itself a primary rule contained in the articles of either Hague Convention.

This view is strengthened by regard to the preamble to Hague Convention XIII, which states that neutral States have 'an admitted duty to apply these rules impartially to the several belligerents.'[28] In the authentic French, neutral States have 'un devoir reconnu d'appliquer impartialement aux divers belligérants les règles adoptées par elles.' The preamble refers only to a duty to apply 'these rules' (i.e. the rules of Hague Convention XIII) impartially; it does not refer to a general duty to maintain impartiality separate from the obligations listed in the Convention. This preambular statement refers to the way in which the other rules of neutrality are

[23] See J Raz *The Morality of Freedom* (Clarendon Press, Oxford 1986) 120–4; A Montefiore (ed) *Neutrality and Impartiality: The University and Political Commitment* (CUP, Cambridge 1975); D Kimel 'Neutrality, Autonomy and Freedom of Contract' (2001) 21 OJLS 473; D Kimel *From Promise to Contract: Towards a Liberal Theory of Contract* (Hart, Oxford 2003) 121; W Sadurski 'Neutrality of Law Towards Religion' (1989–1990) 12 Syd LR 420; W Sadurski 'Joseph Raz on Liberal Neutrality and the Harm Principle' (1990) 10 OJLS 122.

[24] 'Final Act and Conventions of the Second Peace Conference' (1908) 2 AJILS 1, 120.

[25] Ibid 206.

[26] A P Higgins *The Hague Peace Conferences and Other International Conferences Concerning the Laws and Usages of War: Texts of Conventions With Commentaries* (Cambridge University Press, Cambridge 1909) 466–7.

[27] C C Hyde 'The Hague Convention Respecting the Rights and Duties of Neutral Powers in Naval War' (1908) 2 AJIL 507, 514.

[28] HC XIII preamble.

applied; it does not indicate the existence of a separate duty extraneous to the Convention itself.[29]

James Brown Scott was one writer who did notice the absence of a general concept of impartiality in the Hague Conventions. He suggested that the absence of attention to the concept of impartiality contained in the Hague Conventions was deliberate because impartiality (in the more general sense of balancing between belligerents) represented an 'older conception of neutrality', which was being replaced by more stringent attention to the duties of abstention and prevention.[30] Hence the concept of impartiality in the Hague Conventions serves a more restricted role; it applies only when the neutral State seeks to take more restrictive measures than required by international law.

Given that the customary international law rules of neutrality exist alongside the rules of the Hague Conventions, the question arises whether a broader concept of impartiality (in particular, economic impartiality) exists in customary international law, or whether the approach of the Hague Conventions was declaratory of customary international law in this area at the time of codification.

The idea that neutrality required impartiality in the economic sphere is traceable to Vattel, who draws a sharp distinction between the supply of war material, captured by the duty of abstention, and other commercial transactions in wartime, governed by a duty of impartiality.[31] This idea of impartiality developed alongside a view that neutrality had to be 'perfect': during the nineteenth century, the view emerged that the law of neutrality could no longer be, as in earlier times, contracted out of and capable of modification by treaty. An example of the change in the conception of neutrality may be seen through an examination of Dana's revision of Wheaton's classic text. In his original work of 1836, Wheaton argued that the fulfilment of treaty obligations entered into before the outbreak of a war does not result in a forfeiture of neutrality, 'nor render [the neutral] the enemy of the other belligerent nation, because it does not render him the general associate of its enemy.'[32] Writing in 1866, Dana qualifies this statement heavily, noting in a footnote that:

> [t]he progress of modern times has been towards insisting on entire and impartial neutrality. It is difficult to conceive now of a State being permitted to continue a condition of limited and partial neutrality. A belligerent would be justified in treating any State as an enemy throughout, which rendered any aid

[29] It may therefore be compared to the preamble of Additional Protocol I, which may be read as emphasizing the principle of equal application of its provisions.

[30] J B Scott *The Hague Peace Conferences of 1899 and 1907* vol I (Johns Hopkins, Baltimore 1909) 546.

[31] E de Vattel *The Law of Nations* (J Chitty (tr)) (T & J Johnson & Co, Philadephia 1863) III [vii] § 104.

[32] H Wheaton *Elements of International Law* (Carey, Lea and Blanchard, Philadelphia 1836) 281.

> to its enemy, whether in pursuance of treaty obligations or not, or which gave or withheld belligerent privileges unequally.[33]

As the concept of 'perfect neutrality' developed, however, the emphasis on impartiality in the commercial sphere became increasingly important; writers began to document the difficulties that could arise when trading relationships were utilized by neutral States to affect the course of a war. Twiss documented the difficulty with particular clarity:

> ...a war may arise between the two countries, one of which in time of peace exports arms and imports provisions, whilst the other exports provisions and imports arms; in other words, between two countries, one of which is highly advanced in manufacturing industry, whilst the other is strictly agricultural. It is obvious that a Nation will not act with impartiality towards both Belligerents, if it should prohibit the exportation of arms and allow the exportation of provisions.[34]

To surmount this difficulty, the concept of the *courant normal* developed. This provided that the neutral State was entitled to maintain its existing trade relations upon the outbreak of war. Adherence to that principle 'cannot expose a Neutral Nation to any imputation of bad faith towards either of two Belligerent parties.'[35] A drastic change in trade relations upon the outbreak of armed conflict could, on the other hand, fuel the perception that a State was seeking to favour one belligerent over the other. The principle of *courant normal* operated on the assumption that 'impartial inaction' was more in keeping with the spirit of neutrality than 'impartial action.'[36]

Yet the concept of *courant normal* based on a concept of impartiality did not develop into a legal rule; it was a matter of policy for the neutral State only. In other words impartiality between belligerents was a mode of behaviour and not a specific duty; and there exists no case law citing a failure of impartiality sounding in a claim for damages.[37]

[33] H Wheaton (R H Dana (ed)) *Elements of International Law* (8th edn Little, Brown, Boston 1866) 518 n 203. By the time of the Boer War, customary international law suggested that the performance of the obligations of a pre-existing treaty was incompatible with neutrality: T Baty *International Law in South Africa* (Stevens and Haynes, London 1900) chapter 3; W E Hall *The Rights and Duties of Neutrals* (Longmans, Green and Co, London 1874) 49.

[34] T Twiss *The Law of Nations Considered as Independent Political Communities: On the Rights and Duties of Nations in Time of War* (2nd edn Clarendon Press, Oxford 1875) 473.

[35] Ibid 473–4.

[36] Cf L Preuss 'Some Effects of Governmental Controls on Neutral Duties' (1937) 31 PAS 108, 114.

[37] C Eagleton 'The Duty of Impartiality on the Part of a Neutral' (1940) 34 AJIL 99, 101.

Although certain draft rules of neutrality have proposed conceptions of neutrality that cast impartiality as a primary duty of neutrality,[38] it may be noted that this position does not reflect customary international law either at the time of the adoption of the Hague Conventions, or since. While States have occasionally adhered to positions of impartial neutrality,[39] such a course of conduct is not required by customary international law.[40]

The concept of impartiality in the law of neutrality is, therefore, closer to a principle than a specific rule. A principle is an underlying precept or assumption that conditions the application of a specific rule; in Fitzmaurice's account, a rule 'answers the question "what": a principle in effect answers the question "why"'.[41] Rules implement principles; principles serve to guide the application of specific rules. Applied to the law of neutrality, it is the principle of impartiality which guides the application of the duties of prevention and abstention. A neutral State is itself under no specific duty of impartiality in the conduct of its economic relations, however.

2. The Duty of Abstention from Hostilities

a. The Prohibition on the Supply of Military Material

i. The Division between the State and the Citizen

According to Article 6 of Hague Convention XIII, a neutral State may not supply, directly or indirectly, war ships, ammunition, or war material.[42] Under the traditional law, it may be said that this general norm exists in respect of any type of weapons, munitions, and war materials to the extent that the transaction is between governments.[43] To supply this material is a violation of a neutral duty, even if provided to belligerents on an equal basis.[44]

Traditionally this obligation exists only in relation to trade conducted by the State. Arms sales by private citizens were a different matter, as Articles 7 of Hague Conventions V and XIII provide.[45] The Conventions insist on a rigid division between the individual and the State because, as Smith writes, they:

[38] 'Harvard Draft Convention on Rights and Duties of Neutral States in Naval and Aerial War' (1939) 33 AJILS 167 art 4.

[39] See, for example, the joint statement of Denmark, Finland, Iceland, Norway and Sweden: (1939) 10 NT 136–7.

[40] See Switzerland Federal Department of Foreign Affairs 'White Paper on Neutrality: Annex to the Report on Swiss Foreign Policy for the Nineties' (29 November 1993) 21 <http://www.eda.admin.ch/eda/en/home/topics/peasec/sec/neutr.html> accessed 21 July 2007.

[41] G Fitzmaurice 'The General Principles of International Law Considered from the Standpoint of the Rule of Law' (1957-II) 92 RCADI 1, 7.

[42] HC XIII art 6.

[43] Y Dinstein 'The Laws of Neutrality' (1984) IYHR 80, 95.

[44] Hyde (n 27) 510.

[45] HC V art 7; HC XIII art 7.

> ...speak the language of nineteenth-century political institutions and of nineteenth-century war. The age of liberalism took a narrow view of the functions of the State... Sharp distinctions were drawn between the functions of the State and those of the individual, between State and individual property.[46]

Hence a neutral State was under an obligation to abstain from the provision of arms only in relation to direct provision of weaponry and had no duty to stop its citizens from engaging in the same industry. Pursuant to the 'commercial adventure' principle, citizens were free to sell and export arms to belligerents as they wished, subject to the ability of the belligerents to stop that trade.[47] They were also free to solicit loans to belligerents.[48] According to the perspective taken by the Hague Conventions, the restraint of the neutral citizen is the privilege of the belligerent rather than the duty of the neutral.[49]

Thus a belligerent was free to purchase, on the open market, such military material as it was able to obtain from neutral vendors. Geographical and economic factors could mean that one belligerent could obtain greater access than another to arms; this was the case, for example, with regard to the Boer War, when the UK was able to obtain large amounts of arms from Germany and Austria-Hungary; and in World War I, when the Allies were able to obtain large amounts of arms from the United States, while Austria-Hungary was prevented from doing so.[50] The US response reaffirmed the traditional law that citizens of neutral States were free to sell and export arms to belligerents.[51] Its rationale for this stance was that the sale of armaments should be free in time of war, because a general prohibition would escalate the purchase of arms during peacetime, encouraging policies of extreme militarism.[52]

[46] H A Smith 'The Government of Occupied Territory' (1944) 21 BYBIL 151, 151.

[47] Thomas Jefferson, when US Secretary of State, wrote to M Ternant, Minister Plenipotentiary of France, on 15 May 1793 that '[o]ur citizens have been always free to make, vend and export arms; that it is the constant occupation and livelihood of some of them. To suppress their callings, the only means, perhaps, of their subsistence, because a war exists in foreign and distant countries, in which we have no concern, would scarcely be expected.' W Lowrie and M St Clair Clarke (eds) *American State Papers: Documents, Legislative and Executive, of the Congress of the United States, from the First Session of the First to the Second Session of the Twenty-Second Congress, Inclusive* vol I (Gales and Seaton, Washington 1833) 147.

[48] Castrén *Neutrality* 478.

[49] Hyde (n 27) 512; see generally W C Morey 'The Sale of Munitions of War' (1916) 10 AJIL 467.

[50] See 'The German Minister for Foreign Affairs to Ambassador Gerard, 16 February 1915' (1915) 9 AJILSS 90; 'The German Ambassador to the Secretary of State, 4 April 1915' (1915) 9 AJILSS 125; 'The Austro-Hungarian Minister for Foreign Affairs to Ambassador Penfield, 29 June 1915' (1915) 9 AJILSS 146. See also 'The Sale of Munitions of War' (1915) 9 AJIL 927.

[51] 'The Secretary of State to the German Ambassador, 21 April 1915' (1915) 9 AJILSS 127; 'The Secretary of State to the Chairman of the Senate Committee on Foreign Relations' (1915) 9 AJILSS 255, 259–60. See also Commentary to Harvard Draft Convention on Neutrality in Naval and Aerial War (1939) 33 AJILS 167, 301–2 ('Commentary on Harvard Draft Convention on Neutrality').

[52] C N Gregory 'Neutrality and the Sale of Arms' (1916) 10 AJIL 543, 553–5; J W Garner 'Some True and False Conceptions Regarding the Duty of Neutrals in Respect to the Sale and Exportation of Arms and Munitions to Belligerents' (1916) 10 PAS 18, 26–7.

The distinction between the commercial acts of the citizen and the neutral State, fundamental to the traditional law, continued to find adherence following World War I. The Havana Convention on Maritime Neutrality of 1928 states, for example, that:

> Of the acts of assistance coming from the neutral states, and the acts of commerce on the part of individuals, only the first are contrary to neutrality.[53]

There is no question that the principle expressed in Articles 7 of Hague Convention V and XIII, according to which neutral States were not required to restrain the trade in arms by their citizens, represented a codification of customary international law at the time of adoption.[54]

It became increasingly recognized, however, that the sale of armaments by private citizens could have the effect of compromising a State's neutrality. Some unease had been expressed that the distinction between State and citizen in the sale of arms was an increasingly 'sophistical' practice.[55] The Harvard Draft Convention on the Rights and Duties of Neutral States in Naval and Aerial War, prepared in 1939, appeared to recognize this point, as it noted that a neutral State was permitted to place prohibitions upon the shipment of arms from its territory 'for the purposes of…safeguarding its neutrality.'[56]

Academic literature of the same period supported the view that the distinction between the State and the citizen no longer reflected principle or State practice.[57] Wolfgang Friedmann argued in 1938 that the consensus of State practice had eliminated the customary rule that a neutral State need not prevent the export of war materials to belligerents.[58] A more difficult question, he suggested, was whether there had emerged any rule to take its place:

> It is far more difficult to say what law, at the present stage, has replaced the old one. The new practice [of complete abstention from sale of armaments], which is developing through international treaties as above mentioned, has probably

[53] Convention on Maritime Neutrality (Signed on 20 February 1928, entered into Force 12 January 1931) 135 LNTS 187 art 15. On the Convention see E M Borchard 'Restatement of the Law of Neutrality in Maritime War' (1928) 22 AJIL 614, 616.

[54] Gregory (n 52).

[55] British Maritime Law Committee 'Report' in International Law Association Report of the Twenty-Ninth Conference (Portsmouth, 1920) (International Law Association, Portsmouth 1920) 165, 209–11 (remarks of J MacDonnell).

[56] Harvard Draft Convention on Neutrality (n 38) art 11.

[57] See also the comments made by Sir Gerard Fitzmaurice in a memorandum written in 1932 in A Carty and R A Smith (eds) *Sir Gerard Fitzmaurice and the World Crisis: A Legal Advisor in the Foreign Office* (Kluwer Law International, The Hague 2000) 98.

[58] W Friedmann 'The Growth of State Control over the Individual and its Effect upon the Rules of International State Responsibility' (1938) 19 BYBIL 118, 136.

> not yet hardened into a legal rule. All one can say is that a new customary rule is in the process of formation...[59]

The contemporary arms industry and its regulation by international law is a considerable topic of investigation.[60] In general terms, it is possible to state that arms manufacturing has, throughout the course of twentieth and twenty-first centuries, become a governmental rather than commercial enterprise. George Politakis has stated that:

> ...it is difficult to exaggerate the true meaning of arms export licensing, now a standard feature in the legislation of almost every arms-producing country. It may be said that the institutionalisation of a compulsory licensing procedure involving governmental decision-making has ended all discussion or doubt as to who is ultimately responsible for arms exports. The decision to bestow an export permit divests the transaction of any private character it might otherwise have had and transforms it into a governmental one...private arms exports proper are virtually non-existent.[61]

It is therefore necessary to investigate the effects of this development on the law of neutrality's treatment of the supply of military material.

ii. The prohibition on supply

If the nature of the arms industry has been transformed and is now predominantly controlled by the State, it is therefore necessary to enquire whether changes in the regulations of the arms industry have led to the crystallization of a legal rule regarding the supply of military material. It is possible to identify two broad perspectives. One view is that the State has been assimilated to the private trader, so that all neutral States are free to supply military material on the basis of *laissez faire* principles.[62] The opposing view suggests the reverse: that there now exists upon the neutral State an obligation to prohibit the sale of military material to belligerents.

State practice does not reflect the first view; it does indicate some support for the latter view. It was the latter view that appeared to take hold during World

[59] Ibid 137.

[60] For a recent discussion see Z Yihdego *The Arms Trade and International Law* (Hart, Oxford 2007).

[61] G P Politakis 'Variations on a Myth: Neutrality and the Arms Trade' (1992) 35 GYIL 435, 494; see also N Ronzitti 'International Supply of Conventional Armaments: Legal Aspects and Implications of the United Nations General Assembly Resolution 42/75 I' (1991) 26 *Int Spectator* 69, 74.

[62] J Stone *Legal Controls of International Conflict* (Maitland Publications, Sydney 1959) 413; M Greenspan *The Modern Law of Land Warfare* (University of California Press, Berkeley 1959) 551–2.

War II.[63] Practice since 1945 indicates some attempts by neutral States to prohibit the supply to belligerents of military material from their territory. During the 1948 war between Israel and the Arab States, Iran refused as a consequence of its neutrality to sell arms to Iraq or to permit its citizens to do so.[64] During the 1956 invasion of Suez, the United States took action to stop all shipments of arms to the region.[65] Several States imposed arms embargoes in the 1965 war between India and Pakistan,[66] as well as in the 1971 war between India and Pakistan.[67] In the 1967 war in the Middle East, France imposed an embargo on both belligerents immediately after war was declared.[68] Great Britain, which had followed a policy throughout the 1950s of balancing its supplies of military equipment between Israel and certain Arab States,[69] imposed an arms embargo on both belligerents that came into effect on 6 June 1967,[70] as did Canada and West Germany.[71] In the 1973 war in the Middle East, an arms embargo was imposed by a number of European States.[72] Whether these arms embargoes were imposed as a matter of legal obligation, however, is less clear.

The piecemeal practice indicating a trend towards prohibition of the provision of military material appeared to come under strain during the Iran-Iraq war. Each belligerent was able to obtain substantial amounts of military equipment from neutral States. Iraq received arms principally from the Soviet Union and France, but also from Italy, Spain, and Egypt.[73] Iran received arms principally from Libya, Syria, and North Korea.[74] As the war continued, Iran received increasingly large amounts of arms from China.[75] Both sides were also able to purchase armaments from private sources.[76]

[63] G Ginsburgs 'The Soviet Union, the Neutrals and International Law in World War II' (1962) 11 ICLQ 171, 184.

[64] SWB (1948) Part III No 55 (17 June 1948) 76.

[65] *Navios Corporation v The Ulysses II* (D Md 1958) 161 F Supp 932, 943.

[66] Belgium: (1968) RBDI 247; France: (1967) 71 RGDIP 198; Stockholm International Peace Research Institute (SIPRI) (F T Blackaby et al) (eds) *The Arms Trade with the Third World* (Almqvist & Wiksell, Stockholm 1971) 484–5. The US was accused by the Soviet Union of selling arms to Pakistan: SWB (1971) Part 1 Second Series SU/3864 (14 December 1971) (SU/3864/A3/2).

[67] H Mahajan *Arms Transfer to India, Pakistan and the Third World* (Young Asia Publications, New Delhi 1981) 208; (1971) 65 DSB 647, 652. The US resumed arms sales to both States only in 1975. See (1975) 79 RGDIP 1138. On France's policy see (1972) 18 AFDI 1026.

[68] (1967) 13 AFDI 895; see also (1971) 17 AFDI 1059–60.

[69] See R McNamara 'Britain, Nasser and the Outbreak of the Six Day War' (2000) 35 JCH 619, 620.

[70] L Dubouis 'L'embargo dans la pratique contemporaine' (1967) 13 AFDI 99, 115.

[71] P Norton 'Between the Ideology and the Reality: The Shadow of the Law of Neutrality' (1976) 17 HILJ 249, 299–300.

[72] Ibid 300. For Belgium see (1976) 12 RBDI 191.

[73] SIPRI 'Fact Sheet: The Iraq-Iran War and the Arms Trade' (March 1984) 3; E David 'La guerre du Golfe et le droit international' (1987) 23 RBDI 153, 170–1.

[74] (1981) 85 RGDIP 406.

[75] M Tran 'China Role in War Worries US/Reagan Administration Calls on Peking to Confirm Neutrality in Iran-Iraq Conflict' *Guardian* (London 27 August 1986). China eventually delivered Silkworm cruise missiles to both belligerents.

[76] SIPRI 'Fact Sheet' (n 73) 3–4. The report notes one example of an arms dealer who purchased captured Iranian military equipment from Iraq and then resold it to Iran.

However, there is evidence that such sales were viewed as incompatible with the law of neutrality, and the neutral States engaged in supplying Iran and Iraq either denied they were supplying arms to the belligerents and acted clandestinely, or they advanced other reasons—such as the existence of pre-existing contracts predating the armed conflict—for supplying arms.[77]

The States that were most emphatic in linking the law of neutrality to a prohibition on arms sales were the US and the UK. The US adopted the view that a position of neutrality was incompatible with the sale of arms to belligerents.[78] The US did in fact provide arms to the region (most infamously in the 'arms for hostages' arrangement with Iran, the so-called 'Iran-Contra' affair) but this assistance was provided covertly and was not asserted to be compatible with neutrality. In 1988, US Secretary of Defence Frank Carlucci affirmed that the US position 'has been and will continue to be one of strict neutrality.'[79]

The United Kingdom also repeatedly emphasized that it was not supplying either belligerent with armaments. It stated in 1982, for example, that:

> We are neutral in the war and we have not supplied arms or ammunition to either side. Sales of defence equipment are subject to customary licensing procedures. Applications are considered in the light of all relevant circumstances including our relations with the countries involved and, in the case of Iran and Iraq, our neutrality during the present state of hostilities.[80]

The British and US positions provide clear support for the view that neutrality requires abstention from the supply of certain forms of military material. Other neutral States during the Iran-Iraq war based their arms licensing practices on whether such weaponry was destined for a State engaged in armed conflict.[81]

In other conflicts, however, a prohibition on the supply of military material has been almost completely ignored. During the 2003 Iraq war Spain, Italy, Denmark, and the Netherlands all supplied arms or munitions to the coalition States.[82] These States did not refer to the law of neutrality in justifying their conduct, and instead cited political factors.[83]

[77] France, for example, on occasion argued that Iraq was the victim of Iranian aggression: (1983) 29 AFDI 909; (1984) 30 AFDI 1012–13. At other times France emphasized its impartiality towards the conflict: (1982) 28 AFDI 1094–5; (1983) 29 AFDI 854. President Mitterrand acknowledged the contradiction: (1984) 30 AFDI 951–2.

[78] (July 1981) 81 DSB 17; (July 1982) 82 DSB 45; (July 1983) 83 DSB 89; (April 1985) 85 DSB 57; (August 1987) 87 DSB 41; (July 1987) 87 DSB 59, 62, 66.

[79] (July 1988) 88 DSB 61.

[80] (1982) 53 BYBIL 559.

[81] See the position of the Netherlands: (1988) 19 NYIL 391. Belgium: (1971) 7 RBDI 220; (1984–1985) 18 RBDI 359, 367; (1989) 22 RBDI 402. Italy: (1986–1987) 7 IYIL 470–1.

[82] O Corten *Le droit contre la guerre: l'interdiction du recours à la force en droit international contemporain* (Pedone, Paris 2003) 279–80.

[83] Ibid.

This State practice indicates a somewhat chaotic range of positions, and reflects the fact that the regulation of the sale of military material is an area of considerable uncertainty. State practice suggests an increasing acceptance of the view that, to the extent that the arms industry is subject to the control or oversight of the State, the State, when neutral, is under a duty to prohibit sale to belligerents. Such sale would constitute a violation of the duty of abstention if permitted. This duty is limited somewhat, however, by a restricted view of what constitutes prohibited war materials, and any obligation actively to prevent the private supply of war materials would appear to be very loose. It is necessary to examine these issues in more detail.

iii. The extent of the prohibition on the supply of military material

It is necessary to consider what kind of material is covered by the prohibition. Article 6 of Hague Convention XIII prohibits supply of 'war-ships, ammunition, or war material of any kind.'[84] It has been noted, however, that this phrase was illustrative and not exhaustive, referring only to those items that the neutral State had, up to that time (i.e. 1907), attempted to trade.[85] Preuss argues that in theory 'war material of any kind' would include anything that a belligerent could deem to be contraband of war.[86] He suggests, with a degree of 'diffidence', that:

> A neutral government performs an unneutral act whenever it engages in commercial or financial intercourse with a belligerent which, if engaged in by a private individual, would legitimately expose such individual to belligerent penalties for trade in contraband, carriage of contraband, breach of blockade or unneutral service.[87]

Given increasingly expansive understandings of contraband in recent State practice,[88] which have all but eliminated the distinction between 'absolute' and 'conditional' contraband (i.e. between items used strictly for military purposes and items subject to dual use), it is unlikely that Preuss's interpretation would today find acceptance amongst States that are neutral in a given conflict.

The State practice reviewed above suggests that only material classifiable as 'absolute contraband' falls within the prohibition. During the Iran-Iraq war, for example, the UK stated that it prohibited the supply of what it deemed 'lethal equipment' to the belligerents.[89] Its policy towards the conflict was most fully set out in 1984:

> In order to reinforce our policy of doing everything possible to see this tragic conflict brought to the earliest possible end, we decided in December 1984 to

[84] HC XIII art 6. [85] Preuss (n 36) 116. [86] Ibid. [87] Ibid.
[88] For a fuller discussion of the law of contraband see Chapter 5.
[89] See (1983) 54 BYBIL 549; (1984) 55 BYBIL 597 ('lethal arms.').

> apply thereafter, the following set of guidelines to all deliveries of defence equipment to Iran and Iraq:
>
> (i) we should maintain our consistent refusal to supply any lethal equipment to either side;
>
> (ii) subject to that overriding consideration, we should attempt to fulfil existing contracts and obligations;
>
> (iii) we should not, in future, approve orders for any defence equipment which, in our view, would significantly enhance the capability of either side to prolong or exacerbate the conflict;
>
> (iv) in line with this policy, we should continue to scrutinise rigorously all applications for export licences for the supply of defence equipment to Iran and Iraq.[90]

It remains unclear what difference exists, if any, between 'lethal equipment' and 'defence equipment which…would significantly enhance the capability of either side to prolong or exacerbate the conflict.' The US has similarly referred to prohibitions on 'substantial' and 'major' military equipment.[91]

These statements indicate a desire to interpret the prohibition on the supply of military material as narrowly as possible, potentially restricting the prohibition to items such as chemical weaponry. It is suggested that the prohibition should extend beyond these items, to encompass major military equipment, which clearly includes items such as tanks, military helicopters, and fighter aircraft.

At the other end of the spectrum, it is possible to identify material which would not be covered by the prohibition; for example, the Netherlands indicated during the Iran-Iraq war that the sale of mine-hunting devices would not contravene the law of neutrality.[92] Between these two types of equipment there exists, however, a grey area of uncertainty. In the absence of a greater density of State practice, it is difficult to arrive at firm conclusions regarding the type of military material that is covered by the prohibition. State practice at present indicates an intention to limit the prohibition to significant items of military equipment, and not conventional weaponry.

The second question regarding the prohibition on military material relates to whether the prohibition on supply applies to arms transfers based on contracts pre-dating the outbreak of hostilities. The UK policy in the Persian Gulf aimed to 'fulfil existing contracts and obligations.'[93] France has also frequently sought to invoke pre-existing contracts as an exception to its general practice. In explaining

[90] (1985) 56 BYBIL 534.

[91] See (1971) 65 DSB 647, 652. In 1992, with regard to the UN-authorized action in Iraq, the US noted that it was prohibited for a neutral to furnish 'munitions' to a belligerent. See 'United States: Department of Defence Report to Congress on the Conduct of the Persian Gulf War – Appendix on The Role of the Law of War' (1992) 31 ILM 612, 638.

[92] (1988) 19 NYIL 359, 390.

[93] (1985) 56 BYBIL 534.

its massive transfers of arms to Iraq (and, to a lesser extent, Iran) France cited the existence of pre-existing contracts entered into before the international armed conflict broke out.[94] Similarly, Italy stated, with regard to the Iran-Iraq war, that it was following a 'restrictive policy' regarding new military supplies as well as 'previous commitments'; it nevertheless noted that it would 'tak[e] into account' the 'necessity to respect contracts that have already been signed, for obvious reasons of credibility and good faith at the international level.'[95] This does not appear always to have been accepted in previous conflicts, however. During the 1967 war, France prohibited the sale to Israel of fighter jets under the embargo it imposed at the outbreak of conflict, regardless of pre-existing contracts.[96] This practice suggests a degree of leniency in the fulfilment of contracts for weaponry that were entered into prior to the outbreak of armed conflict.

The third question concerns how far the prohibition on the sale of military material must extend in geographical terms. In other words, it is necessary to determine whether the prohibition on the provision of military material by the neutral State extends to all States situated in the region of hostilities or only those States which are directly involved in hostilities. The evidence would appear to support the latter interpretation. France used the phrase 'battlefield countries' ('pays de champ de bataille') in imposing an embargo after the outbreak of the 1967 war in the Middle East.[97] The UK also used a similar phrase during the 1973 Yom Kippur War.[98] In 1977, the Foreign Minister of Belgium was asked what was meant by the phrase 'impliqué dans un conflit' contained in Belgium's arms export policy. The Foreign Minister replied that it would refuse, suspend, or withdraw exportation licences for equipment destined for countries implicated in armed hostilities, meaning international armed conflict between two States.[99] A significant factor for the Netherlands in deciding to export mine-hunters to Kuwait included the fact that Kuwait was not 'directly involved' in the armed conflict between Iran and Iraq.[100]

It is likely that the prohibition extends only to direct provision of military materials, although there appears to be some support for the view that re-export provisions should be inserted into contracts for sale to States in the region of hostilities. Thus during the 1967 war, in selling military equipment to States in the region of hostilities, but not directly engaged in the fighting or bordering the

[94] (1981) 85 RGDIP 176–7; (1981) 27 AFDI 859; (1984) 30 AFDI 952; (1985) 31 AFDI 962–3; (1988) 34 AFDI 901; *Keesing's* (1983) 32595; see also R Koven 'French Jets Delivered to Iraqis' *Washington Post* (Washington DC 2 February 1981).

[95] (1986–1987) 7 IYIL 470–1. [96] (1972) 18 AFDI 1005. [97] (1970) 16 AFDI 962–3.

[98] Norton (n 71) 300.

[99] (1984–1985) 18 RBDI 367: 'Selon la pratique établie, le Gouvernement refuse, suspend ou retire les licences d'exportation à destination des pays impliqués dans des "hostilités armées." Par "hostilités armées" il faut entendre des hostilités internationales déclenchées entre deux Etats.'

[100] (1988) 19 NYIL 390. The Netherlands also considered it to be significant that Kuwait needed the mines for purposes of self-defence.

belligerents, France emphasized that it had taken measures to ensure that such military equipment was not re-exported to 'battlefield countries.'[101] The issue of the re-exporting of military materials arose again in the context of the Yom Kippur War in 1973, when it was alleged that military aircraft purchased by Libya from France had been utilized by Egypt during the conflict.[102] Belgium followed a similar policy of re-exportation.[103] In the absence of a greater density of practice, however, it is difficult to arrive at a firm conclusion.[104]

iv. Conclusion on the supply of military material

It is apparent that the question of a neutral State's duty of abstention with regard to the supply of military material is highly unclear; indeed, it may be said that the law is in a considerable state of disarray. While the State practice reviewed suggests support for the view that the neutral State itself is prohibited from supplying military material to belligerents, the extent of this prohibition is currently in a state of uncertainty. One area of uncertainty is what precisely is covered by the prohibition, in terms of an adequate definition of military material. Customary international law currently provides little guidance in this area.

Given the vast developments in the global armaments industry in the twentieth and twenty-first centuries, the extent of a neutral State's obligation to prevent its citizens from furnishing military assistance to belligerents is also unclear. If, indeed, the prohibition on the provision of military materials covers the provision of military materials by individuals (as certain aspects of current practice and academic opinion suggest), then it becomes necessary to enquire as to the standard a neutral State must comply with in preventing its citizens from furnishing such military assistance. Under the Hague Conventions, the duty to prohibit the supply of armaments is expressed in absolute terms, in contrast to other obligations which the neutral State is deemed to have discharged if it has employed the 'means at its disposal.'[105]

On the one hand, it could be suggested that, since the modern regulation of the armaments industries is subject to the control and supervision of national governments, the obligation to prohibit the supply of military material should be an absolute one.[106] Yet on the other hand, many of the other obligations of a neutral State are understood to be obligations of due diligence, and the existence of the

[101] For statements of the re-exportation policy see (1970) 16 AFDI 962–4; (1973) 19 AFDI 1028. See also the statements of Belgium: (1971) 7 RBDI 214–15; (1972) 8 RBDI 234.

[102] (1972) 18 AFDI 994; (1974) 20 AFDI 1029–30.

[103] (1987) 20 RBDI 340; (1991) 24 RBDI 273–88.

[104] In the conflict in Yemen, there was some speculation that Oman might have lost its status of a neutral state due to the smuggling of weaponry from Iran to the Yemeni rebels through Oman's territory. That would suggest that nowadays, States are expected not only to refrain from providing weapons themselves but also to prevent arms from being transported to belligerents through their territory. Yet, it is difficult to say whether such a rule has crystallized in customary international law.

[105] See, for example, HC XIII art 8.

[106] Politakis (n 61) 494.

law of contraband, which traditionally leaves it to the belligerent, rather than the neutral, to prevent the entry of contraband into belligerent territory through the right of visit and search, militates against the acceptance of an objective standard.

Whichever view is taken, it is apparent that this aspect of the duty of abstention is in urgent need of revision. The uncertainties that surround it have contributed to the considerable uncertainties pertaining to the duties of neutral States.

b. The Prohibition on Other Forms of Assistance: Economic Aid

The neutral State's duty of abstention has been said to cover other forms of assistance, as well as the furnishing of military material. In customary international law, there emerged in the nineteenth century a rule that prohibited the granting of credits or economic aid by the government or State organs of a neutral State to either belligerent.[107] The topic of State provision of economic assistance was not dealt with in the Hague Conventions, and it has been left for customary international law to deal with this area.

State practice during World War II demonstrates that any prohibition on economic assistance to belligerents was violated comprehensively. Almost every neutral State during World War II indulged in economic assistance to one or other of the belligerents.[108] Sweden, for example, issued public loans to Finland in the 'Winter War' against the Soviet Union.[109] Portugal exported significant amounts of Wolfram to Germany.[110] Spain also engaged in price discrimination between the Allies and the Axis with regard to the sale of Wolfram.[111] The US government provided loans to Great Britain and to Finland during the 'Winter War' between Finland and the Soviet Union.[112]

The Iran-Iraq War provides greater evidence that the provision of economic assistance may constitute a violation of neutrality. In that conflict, Iran protested on numerous occasions concerning the large amounts of financial assistance

[107] J Westlake *International Law* vol II (CUP, Cambridge 1907) 217.

[108] Ginsburgs (n 63) 191.

[109] J Degras (ed) *Soviet Documents on Foreign Policy* vol III (OUP, London 1953) 441; G Hägglöf 'A Test of Neutrality: Sweden in the Second World War' (1960) 36 IA 153, 157.

[110] See generally D L Wheeler 'The Price of Neutrality: Portugal, the Wolfram Question, and World War II' (1986) 23(1) *Luso-Brasilian Review* 107; D L Wheeler 'The Price of Neutrality: Portugal, the Wolfram Question, and World War II(II)' (1986) 23(2) *Luso-Brasilian Review* 97.

[111] L Caruana and H Rockoff 'A Wolfram in Sheep's Clothing: Economic Warfare in Spain, 1940-1944' (2003) 63 JEH 100; cf D Detwiler 'Spain and the Axis in World War II' (1971) 33 JOP 36, 51.

[112] (December 1939) DSB 609; (January 1940) DSB 19–20; (January 1940) DSB 55; (March 1940) DSB 295. The US government was at the time practising a form of non-belligerency, however. See 'Address by Robert H Jackson, Attorney General of the United States, Inter-American Bar Association, Havana, Cuba, March 27, 1941' (1941) 35 AJIL 348; H Lauterpacht 'Memorandum on the Principles of International Law Governing the Question of Aid to the Allies by the United States, 15 January 1941' in E Lauterpacht (ed) *International Law: Being the Collected Papers of Hersch Lauterpacht* vol V (CUP, Cambridge 2004) 645.

furnished by Kuwait to Iraq. As early as 1981, Iran protested against a multi-million dollar loan to Iraq by Kuwait.[113] In a letter to the Security Council on 25 May 1984, Iran stated that 'some States in the area and beyond' which 'pour extensive financial and material resources into Iraq' were encouraging Iraq to threaten international shipping. The letter went on to note that, while these States acting in support of Iraq 'wish to remain secure from the consequences of their obvious backing of the aggressor Iraq' they had contributed to the internationalization of the conflict 'from which they can hardly remain secure.'[114] In 1987, Iran contended that Kuwait's financial assistance to Iraq had led it into a situation of co-belligerency with Iraq.[115] As noted in Chapter 2, States did not accept that massive economic assistance by a neutral State constituted a form of co-belligerency; but it is clear that massive financial assistance would constitute non-neutral service in favour of one belligerent and is a violation of the neutral's duty of abstention.[116]

In this area, as with other aspects of the law of neutrality, a distinction has traditionally been made between the neutral State and the neutral citizen. Thus under Hague Convention V citizens of neutral States have been free to furnish 'supplies' or loans to one of the belligerents.[117] Whether this distinction remains applicable to contemporary international armed conflict is a matter that has received very little attention in State practice; when it is explicitly raised, it tends to be avoided.[118] The example of the Yom Kippur war of 1973 provides some evidence that the distinction is no longer recognized. One reason advanced for the nationalization of Dutch oil interests in Iraq and the enforcement of the oil embargo by Arab States against the Netherlands was the 'participation of various Dutch establishments and companies in collecting contributions for the Israeli war effort.'[119] This suggests that a neutral State is under a duty to prevent its citizens from soliciting loans for a belligerent, which is in accordance with the modern trend. As with the provision of military materials, however, there is a lack of practice in this area, and the matter must be regarded as uncertain.

Hence, it may be noted that the duty of abstention with regard to the provision of military materials and economic assistance to belligerents raises a number of

[113] 'Iran Calls Kuwaiti Attitude on Seized Ship Provocative' *AP* (5 May 1981). For its part, Kuwait complained of Iranian attacks on its territory in December 1980, in June 1981, and in December 1981. See *Keesing's* (1982) 31523.

[114] UNSC 'Letter Dated 25 May 1984 from the Permanent Representative of the Islamic Republic of Iran to the United Nations Addressed to the Secretary-General' (25 May 1984) UN Doc S/16585.

[115] UNSC 'Letter Dated 14 August 1987 from the Permanent Representative of the Islamic Republic of Iran to the United Nations Addressed to the Secretary-General' (14 August 1987) UN Doc S/19041.

[116] M Bothe 'The Law of Neutrality' in D Fleck (ed) *The Handbook of International Humanitarian Law* (2nd edn OUP, Oxford 2008) 571, 584.

[117] HC V art 18.

[118] During the 1967 war in the Middle East, US Secretary of State Dean Rusk refused to answer whether loans by private citizens would contravene the neutrality of the US. See (1967) 65 DSB 949–50.

[119] I F I Shihata 'Destination Embargo of Arab Oil: Its Legality under International Law' (1974) 68 AJIL 591, 594 n 15.

acute difficulties and uncertainties surrounding the ambit of the State's obligations. While the modern trend suggests that the State has a duty to prohibit its citizens from engaging in the provision of military materials and in economic assistance, the legacy of the traditional law's distinctions has permitted States to engage in what should properly be regarded as non-neutral service.

3. Duties of Prevention: General

As well as the obligation to abstain from certain actions, the neutral State is under a duty to prevent certain belligerent actions on its territory, as well as to restrain certain action taken by its neutral citizens abroad.

a. The Standard of Prevention

In traditional international law, the standard that a neutral State was required to exercise in order to discharge its obligation of prevention has traditionally been understood to be an obligation of 'due diligence.'[120] The Treaty of Washington of 1871 was concluded by the US and Great Britain to refer to arbitration claims which arose out of incidents during the American Civil War (and collectively known as the *Alabama* claims).[121] The Treaty outlined certain rules that the parties agreed were to govern the arbitration. The standard of prevention that the arbitral tribunal was to apply was one of 'due diligence.'[122]

The US and the UK had differed on what was required by the requirement of 'due diligence.' The United States had argued that due diligence was proportional to the subject and to the ability of the State attempting to exercise it:

> ...a diligence which shall, by the use of active vigilance, and of all the other means in the power of neutral, through all stages of the transaction, prevent its soil from being violated; a diligence that shall in like manner deter designing men from committing acts of war upon the soil of the neutral against its will,

[120] On the history of the concept of due diligence, see J A Hessbruegge 'The Historical Development of the Doctrines of Attribution and Due Diligence in International Law' (2004) 36 NYUJILP 265. On due diligence more generally see R Pisillo-Mazzeschi 'The Due Diligence Rule and the Nature of the International Responsibility of States' (1992) 35 GYIL 9.

[121] Treaty for an Amicable Settlement of All Causes of Differences between the United States and Great Britain (adopted 8 May 1871, entered into force 17 June 1871) 143 CTS 145 (Treaty of Washington) art 6.

[122] Ibid art 6. A meeting of the Institute of International Law in The Hague in 1875 adopted the view that the duty of prevention would be breached when the neutral demonstrated either a hostile intention (*dolus*) or manifest negligence (*culpa*). See J B Scott (ed) *Resolutions of the Institute of International Law* (Carnegie Endowment of International Peace, Washington D C 1916) 12, 13.

> and thus possibly dragging it into war which it would avoid; a diligence which prompts the neutral to the most energetic measures to discover any purpose of doing the acts forbidden by its good faith as a neutral, and imposes upon it the obligation, when it receives the knowledge of an intention to commit such acts, to use all the means in its power to prevent it.[123]

In contrast, the British argued that, in order to show a failure of due diligence, it had to be shown that there had been a failure to use such care as governments normally use in their domestic concerns.[124] The tribunal noted that the concept of due diligence was a duty arising 'in exact proportion to the risks to which either of the belligerents may be exposed from a failure to fulfil the obligations of neutrality on their part.'[125]

This left the term 'due diligence' in a state of some uncertainty.[126] Indeed, it was suggested at the 1907 Hague Conference that the phrase, 'due diligence' has 'become celebrated by its obscurity.'[127] To avoid the ambiguity associated with the phrase, the Hague Conventions preferred to use the term 'means at its disposal.'[128] More recent conventions have used similar language.[129] While it has been contended that the 'means at its disposal' indicates a more flexible understanding of the obligation than the requirement of 'due diligence',[130] this is not borne out in practice, and there is no indication that it was sought to introduce a more lenient standard by the use of this phrase; nor is there evidence that there exist different standards of liability under the Hague Conventions and in customary international law. The due diligence standard already imports a considerable amount of flexibility adaptable to a State's specific circumstances.[131] Both terms refer to an obligation of conduct rather than one of result. Hence the terms 'means at its disposal' and 'due diligence' will be used interchangeably in what follows.

The standard has two components. First, the neutral must have 'knowledge' of the violation of neutrality. Secondly, the neutral must employ the means at its disposal to respond to the violation. The requirement of knowledge emerges from Article 1 of Hague Convention XIII. That provides that belligerents are bound to abstain '...from any act which would, if knowingly permitted by any Power, constitute a violation of neutrality.'[132] The requirement of knowledge is consistent with the statement of the International Court of Justice in the *Corfu Channel Case*

[123] J B Moore *History and Digest of the International Arbitrations to which the United States has been a Party* vol I (Government Printing Office, Washington DC 1898) 572–3.
[124] Ibid. [125] Ibid 654. [126] Hyde (n 27) 513.
[127] *Hague Conference Proceedings* vol III 295. [128] For example, HC XIII art 25.
[129] See, for example, LOSC art 194(1).
[130] G Schwarzenberger *International Law as Applied by International Courts and Tribunals* vol II (Stevens & Sons, London 1968) 564.
[131] M N Shaw *International Law* (6th edn CUP, Cambridge 2008) 855. [132] HC XIII art 1.

that every State has an obligation 'not to allow knowingly its territory to be used for acts contrary to the rights of other States.'[133]

'Knowledge' in this context does not require actual knowledge. Instead, the State will be deemed to 'know' of the conduct against which it is necessary to take preventive measures when it has actual or constructive notice.[134] The due diligence standard is not, therefore, entirely subjective. In the context of the law of neutrality, it is not possible for a neutral State to turn a blind eye to activity in its territorial waters or in its territory; it will be deemed to have 'knowledge' of the belligerent conduct if it had actual knowledge or it was 'put on notice' that such conduct was likely to occur.

The neutral State must use the 'means at its disposal' to discharge the obligation of prevention. This has an objective and subjective element.[135] First, the State's capacity must be taken into account. Secondly, the State's use of that capacity in addressing the belligerent conduct must be evaluated. The 1928 Havana Convention on Maritime Neutrality describes this as a requirement that States use 'all the vigilance within their power' to prevent violations by belligerents.[136]

This might be thought to create an anomaly. The belligerent has an absolute duty not to use neutral territory, while the neutral is not under an absolute duty to prevent an infringement. Nevertheless, this position is consistent with the approach of the drafters of the Convention. It was noted at the Second Hague Conference that the neutral duty of prevention is not equivalent to the belligerent's duty to abstain from hostile action in neutral territory:

> An absolute obligation can be imposed upon a belligerent to refrain from certain acts in the waters of a neutral State: it is easy for it and in all cases possible to fulfil this obligation whether harbours or territorial waters are concerned. On the other hand, the neutral State cannot be obliged to prevent or check all the acts that a belligerent might do or wish to do, because very often the neutral State will not be in a position to fulfil such an obligation. It cannot know all that is happening in its waters and it cannot be in readiness to prevent it. The duty exists only to the degree that it can be known and discharged.[137]

The same requirement to use 'the means at its disposal' is used in relation to other provisions.[138]

[133] *The Corfu Channel Case* [1949] ICJ Rep 4, 22.

[134] T Becker *Terrorism and The State: Rethinking the Rules of State Responsibility* (Hart, Oxford 2006) 134.

[135] On this point see P Okowa *State Responsibility for Transboundary Air Pollution in International Law* (OUP, Oxford 2000) 79–81.

[136] Convention on Maritime Neutrality (n 53) art 26.

[137] *Hague Conference Proceedings* vol I 291.

[138] See for example, HCXIII art 21, imposing a duty on the neutral State to employ the means at its disposal to release it with its officers and crew and to intern the prize crew.

The concept of the 'means at its disposal' is used explicitly only in Hague Convention XIII, however. While the belligerent is under an absolute duty not to infringe neutral territory pursuant to Hague Convention V, it is left unclear, from the language of Article 5 of Hague Convention V, whether the neutral State is under an absolute duty to prevent such action, or whether it must, as with its duties in naval warfare, use the 'means at its disposal' to prevent such action.

On the face of it, it could be argued, from the language of Hague Convention V, that what is contemplated is an absolute standard of prevention; Article 5 states in categorical terms that 'A neutral Power must not allow any of the acts referred to in Articles 2 to 4 to occur on its territory.'[139] The proceedings of the 1907 Hague Conference make no reference to a standard of due diligence with regard to land warfare; and the comments extracted above, with regard to the duty on the neutral State to use the means at its disposal, refer to the seemingly special circumstances of territorial waters. In relation to its obligations on land, no such concession to a State's existing capacity is explicitly made. This interpretation is seemingly reinforced by the terms of Article 6 of Hague Convention V, which states that the responsibility of a neutral State is not engaged by the fact of persons crossing the frontier separately to offer their services. It was emphasized at the Hague Conference that the duty of a neutral State is 'limited by its frontiers', which suggests that this obligation is absolute within neutral jurisdiction.[140]

Even if the obligation contemplated at the 1907 Hague Conference was intended to be an absolute one (and it is not clear that it was), the better view, it is suggested, is that the neutral State's duty of prevention is judged according to whether it has exercised due diligence, both on land and with regard to its territorial waters. It is now accepted that the base of operations principle, formulated in the Treaty of Washington to refer to aspects of maritime neutrality, is equally applicable to war on land.[141] It would, in any case, create ambiguities and uncertainties if a neutral State were subject to different modes of liability depending on whether the belligerent conduct affected the neutral State's land or waters.

b. The Consequences of a Failure of Prevention

According to customary international law in the nineteenth century, a neutral State's failure to prevent the violation of its territorial integrity by a belligerent State entitled the opposing belligerent to enter neutral territory to address the

139 HC V art 5. 140 *Hague Conference Proceedings* vol I 140.

141 A recent reference to the concept of a 'base of operations' may be found in UNSC 'Letter dated 7 October 2001 from the Permanent Representative of the United States of America to the United Nations addressed to the President of the Security Council' (7 October 2001) UN Doc S/2001/946.

violation.[142] The traditional justification for this is that it is a manifestation of the neutral's failure to treat each belligerent on the basis of impartiality, and the aggrieved belligerent was therefore entitled to enter neutral jurisdiction to restore equilibrium.

The classic example is that of the *Altmark*. In 1940, the German naval auxiliary *Altmark*, carrying British prisoners of war, used Norwegian territorial waters to evade capture. Norway was unable to expel the vessel or to take action to put a stop to the violation of its neutrality. The *Cossack*, a British vessel, pursued the *Altmark* into Norwegian waters and boarded it.[143] Britain argued it was entitled to take action to end the violation of Norway's neutrality since Norway had failed in its duty of prevention.[144]

This approach to the failure to discharge the duty of prevention continues to be reflected in various military manuals. The UK *Manual of the Law of Armed Conflict*, for example, provides that if a neutral State is unable to terminate a violation of its neutral waters:

> ...the opposing belligerent must so notify the neutral State and give that neutral State a reasonable time to terminate the violation by the belligerent. If the violation of the neutrality of the State by the belligerent constitutes a serious and immediate threat to the security of the opposing belligerent and the violation is not terminated, then that belligerent may, in the absence of any feasible and timely alternative, use such force as is strictly necessary to respond to the threat posed by the violation.[145]

Other manuals are in similar terms.[146] There is no requirement that the violation of neutral territory amount to an armed attack before the opposing belligerent is entitled to take measures to put an end to the violation; the US *Naval Commander's Handbook* refers explicitly to 'self-help enforcement measures.'[147]

The question arises whether this expansive view of the rights of an opposing belligerent to take action against another belligerent in neutral territory is reconcilable with the UN Charter. The most implausible suggestion is that the thesis of aggressor discrimination, justified under the concept of *ex injuria jus non oritur*

[142] Castrén *Neutrality* 442; Anonymous 'International Law and Military Operations Against Insurgents in Neutral Territory' (1968) 68 Col LR 1127; Tucker *Neutrality at Sea* 262.

[143] For the correspondence between the British and Norwegian governments, see Cmd 8012 (1950). For discussion see C H M Waldock 'The Release of the *Altmark's* Prisoners' (1947) 24 BYBIL 216.

[144] See the exchange between the British and Norwegian governments contained in (1940) 11 NT 139–41.

[145] UK *Manual on the Law of Armed Conflict* § 13.9E.

[146] *San Remo Manual* § 22; Canada *LOAC Manual* § 811(2); Australia *Air Operations Law Manual* § 12.7; US *Naval Commander's Handbook* § 7.3.5, § 7.3.9(2); US *Operational Law Handbook* § XIV(A)(1); *Helsinki Principles* [2.1].

[147] US *Naval Commander's Handbook* § 7.3.9(2).

or a theory of *jus cogens*, would entitle a victim State to operate in neutral territory in order to enforce public order norms.[148] This view, however, is sweeping in its implications and seems to suggest that the enforcement of *jus cogens* would justify a violation of the prohibition on the use of force in neutral territory.

Another suggestion is that the law of neutrality is *lex specialis* with regard to the law on the use of force. This view is not convincing when robotically applied in an attempt to shear off the law of neutrality from the law on the use of force and other developments in international law. The difficulty with reliance on the concept of *lex specialis* is that it provides no basis for preference of one regime of rules over another. In this instance, given that the prohibition on the use of force constitutes a rule of *jus cogens* while the duties of neutrality do not, the theory of *lex specialis* holds little sway.[149] However, it could be argued that *lex specialis* applies to certain aspects surrounding a neutral State's duty of prevention in territorial waters, for example. Although there is no recent State practice regarding this, it could be argued that an exception is carved out with regard to the neutral's failure to prevent (impermissible) belligerent use of its territorial waters. The somewhat disparate views of various States on this make it difficult to reach strong conclusions.[150] As a matter of principle, it would appear to be undesirable to have different standards for the use of force against neutral territory on land and at sea.

A further justification offered is that the use of force against another belligerent operating in neutral territory is not a violation of the territorial integrity of the neutral State under Article 2(4) because it is directed only at the belligerent act and not at the neutral territory.[151] This view also seems difficult to sustain. An analogous argument has recently been put forward with regard to the use of force against terrorists overseas, in circumstances where there exists no attribution of terrorist acts to the State under the law of State responsibility. As Trapp has suggested, however:

[148] A Orakhelashvili 'Overlap and Convergence: The Interaction Between *Jus ad Bellum* and *Jus in Bello*' (2007) 12 JCSL 157, 193.

[149] On *lex specialis* as a problematic solution to norm conflict see M Milanović 'A Norm Conflict Perspective on the Relationship Between International Humanitarian Law and Human Rights Law' (2010) 14 JCSL 459, 473–6.

[150] See the survey of States on this question in 'Committee for the Protection of Human Life in Armed Conflicts: Law of Naval Warfare' 26 (1988) RDPM 11, 49–50. Sweden argued that an opposing belligerent was not permitted to take such action; belligerents were permitted in neutral waters for innocent passage only. Germany argued that a belligerent State was permitted to take action in neutral waters against another belligerent if there was a 'severe' violation of neutrality and self-defence permitted it. The US stated that a belligerent could take action against another belligerent in neutral waters if the neutral failed in its duty of prevention. Canada stated it could take action if it was 'absolutely required' and no alternative was feasible.

[151] J N Moore 'Legal Dimensions of the Decision to Intercede in Cambodia' (1971) 65 AJIL 38, 73.

> Using force against the base of operations of non-State terrorist actors within another State's territory surely amounts to a violation of that State's territorial integrity, even if the use of force is defensive and not targeted at the State's apparatus.[152]

In its decision in 1970 to take measures against North Vietnamese forces in Cambodian territory, the US demonstrated extreme reluctance to rely solely on the law of neutrality in justifying its conduct, and preferred to rely on the law of self-defence. Before the Security Council, the US stated that the measures were 'restricted in extent, purpose and time.'[153] In a further explanation, the US legal advisor stated that, while it could have sought the consent of the Cambodian government, it decided not to because of the risk that such an action would compromise Cambodia's neutrality.[154] While it was accepted that, under the traditional law, the US would have been entitled to take action directly on neutral territory against the opposing belligerent's violation, the US expressed considerable reluctance to do so absent justification under the law of self-defence. After reviewing a number of precedents in the traditional law, including the *Altmark*, the US legal adviser noted that those precedents no longer independently provided an adequate legal basis for belligerent action on neutral territory; instead, any such action had to be in accordance with the UN Charter.[155]

Whether the law of self-defence could provide an adequate justification for the US incursion into Cambodia is, however, a different issue. It is difficult to determine the 'armed attack' to which the United States was responding; and, even if there did exist an armed attack by the Viet Cong, it is unclear how US action in a third State was justified under the law of self-defence in light of a lack of attribution of the Viet Cong action to Cambodia.

It may be argued that the law of self-defence could not support such a wide interpretation, according to which activities by belligerent forces in neutral territory could, in the absence of attribution, permit an opposing State to take action in self-defence in the territory of the neutral State. An analogous question has arisen in the context of terrorist acts, or acts of armed bands, on the territory of a host State that is unable to control them, and the ability of States to respond to them under the law of self-defence.[156] A neutral State unable to prevent a

[152] K Trapp 'Back to Basics: Necessity, Proportionality, and the Right of Self-Defence against Non-State Terrorist Actors' (2007) 56 ICLQ 141, 145.

[153] UNSC 'Letter dated 5 May 1970 from the Permanent Representative of the United States of America to the United Nations addressed to the President of the Security Council' (5 May 1970) UN Doc S/9781.

[154] 'Contemporary Practice of the United States Relating to International Law' (1970) AJIL 928, 935.

[155] Ibid 939–40.

[156] This question has generated a large amount of literature. See generally C Gray *International Law and the Use of Force* (3rd edn, OUP Oxford 2008) chapter 6; C Tams 'The Use of Force Against Terrorists' (2009) 20 EJIL 359.

belligerent act on its territory is, it is submitted, in a similar situation to a State from whose territory rebel groups or armed bands are operating outside the host State's control.

The latter question was considered by the International Court of Justice in *Armed Activities on the Territory of the Congo*.[157] There, the Court was faced with a purported exercise of the right of self-defence against a State (the Democratic Republic of the Congo (DRC)) that had allegedly failed to control the activities of armed bands on its territory. It was argued on behalf of Uganda that:

> ...armed attacks by armed bands whose existence is tolerated by the territorial sovereign generate legal responsibility and therefore constitute armed attacks for the purpose of Article 51. And thus, there is a separate, a super-added standard of responsibility, according to which a failure to control the activities of armed bands, creates a susceptibility to action in self-defence...[158]

By contrast, counsel for the DRC argued that mere tolerance by the territorial sovereign could not amount to aggression and that, faced with the absence of any initial attack by the DRC, any countermeasure based on self-defence could only be disproportionate.[159] This encapsulates the difficulty that is faced by a neutral State unable to prevent its territory from belligerent infringement: mere tolerance does not amount to an armed attack which would justify the opposing belligerent from taking action in self-defence on the territory of the neutral State.

The Court found that Uganda had failed to demonstrate the necessary involvement of the DRC in the activities of the rebels.[160] The Court chose not to examine the question 'as to whether and under what conditions contemporary international law provides for a right of self-defence against large-scale attacks by irregular forces.'[161]

A more forthcoming approach was evident in the separate opinion of Judge Kooijmans, who noted that '[e]ven if one assumes...that mere failure to control the activities of armed bands cannot in itself be attributed to the territorial State as an unlawful act, that in my view does not necessarily mean that the victim State is under such circumstances not entitled to exercise the right of self-defence

[157] *Armed Activities on the Territory of the Congo (Democratic Republic of the Congo v Uganda)* [2005] ICJ Rep 168.

[158] *Armed Activities on the Territory of the Congo (Democratic Republic of the Congo v Uganda)* (2005) <http://www.icj-cij.org/docket/index.php?p1=3&p2=3&k=51&case=116&code=co&p3=2&PHPSESSID=f79d879d213ce5fdd2ab68570ba55f63> Oral Pleadings 18 April 2005 CR 2005/7 (Brownlie) [80].

[159] *Armed Activities on the Territory of the Congo (Democratic Republic of the Congo v Uganda* (2005) <http://www.icj-cij.org/docket/index.php?p1=3&p2=3&k=51&case=116&code=co&p3=2&PHPSESSID=f79d879d213ce5fdd2ab68570ba55f63> Oral Pleadings 25 April 2005 CR 2005/12 (Klein) [6].

[160] *Armed Activities on the Territory of the Congo* (n 157) [146].

[161] Ibid [147].

under Article 51.'[162] In light of the increasing acceptance of a right of self-defence against non-State actors without attribution to a particular State, he suggested that:

> If the activities of armed bands present on a State's territory cannot be attributed to that State, the victim State is not the object of an armed attack by it. But if the attacks by the irregulars would, because of their scale and effects, have had to be classified as an armed attack had they been carried out by regular armed forces, there is nothing in the language of Article 51 of the Charter that prevents the victim State from exercising its *inherent* right of self-defence.[163]

What is notable, in recent practice, is the increasing acceptance of, or acquiescence in, the use of force in self-defence against non-State actors on another State's territory, where attribution between the host State and the non-State actor is not immediately apparent.[164] Since Article 51 is an exception to the inter-State prohibition of the use of force in Article 2(4), however, there must be some connection between the State and the acts emanating from its territory for self-defence to be justified against the State territory. The law of neutrality cannot itself provide this connection.

One such argument is that the test of attribution has been relaxed such that mere tolerance of belligerent action (in the sense of an inability to prevent or repel such belligerent action) provides the necessary link with the host neutral State. In the context of the law of neutrality, it may be that a failure to prevent certain belligerent action bleeds into acquiescence, justifying a response by the aggrieved belligerent. Any response in self-defence would have to be calibrated strictly according to the principles of necessity and proportionality.[165] Article 21 of the International Law Commission's Articles on State Responsibility leaves open the question of the effect in self-defence on third States.[166]

It should be emphasized that such an exercise of self-defence against a belligerent on neutral territory could be justified only when the belligerent action amounted to an armed attack. This raises the question whether the aggrieved belligerent could take action against a belligerent on State territory when the belligerent has not committed an armed attack. It is submitted that much will depend on the circumstances; and the neutral State's failure to prevent a belligerent incursion may, in extreme circumstances, amount to co-belligerency.

[162] *Armed Activities on the Territory of the Congo* (n 157) Separate Opinion of Judge Kooijmans [26].

[163] Ibid [29]. See also *Armed Activities on the Territory of the Congo* (n 157) Separate Opinion of Judge Simma [12].

[164] See, for example, the review of State practice undertaken by Tams (n 156) 378–81.

[165] On this point see Trapp (n 152) 145–55.

[166] ILC 'Report of the International Law Commission on the Work of its 53rd Session' (23 April–10 August 2001) UN Doc A/56/10 art 21.

In the absence of further customary international law on the subject, it is submitted that this view should be preferred, and that a response to a violation of the law of neutrality must be justified both under the law of neutrality and in accordance with the law of self-defence. It is further suggested that no distinction should be made between the law of neutrality at sea and the law of neutrality on land or in the air; all such belligerent action against a violation must be justified under the law on the use of force.

4. Duties of Prevention in Naval Warfare

It is necessary to turn to the substantive duties of prevention. At sea, the neutral State is under a number of duties of prevention set out in Hague Convention XIII.

a. The Duty to Prevent the Establishment of a Base of Operations

Article 5 states that belligerents must not use neutral ports and waters as a base of naval operations against their adversaries.[167] The concept of a belligerent 'base of operations' arose in international law in the nineteenth century.[168] It proved to be a very uncertain concept in international law.

The term had been used in the Treaty of Washington.[169] According to the rule, the neutral was under an obligation to prevent a belligerent from using its territory as a launching point for hostile operations in a neighbouring territory. The presumption was that a belligerent warship would, if unrestrained, use a neutral port as a base. The obligation to prevent the use of a port as a base arose as soon as the warship entered neutral ports.[170] Private vessels entering neutral ports raised no such presumption.[171]

In the nineteenth century, there existed some debate as to what amounted to a 'base.'[172] There are conflicting views. Hall contended that it was the frequency of belligerent stays in neutral ports that provided evidence that the neutral port was being used as a base.[173] This was a popular view, particularly amongst British writers; but it became increasingly acknowledged in the late nineteenth century

[167] HC XIII art 5. [168] Tucker *Neutrality at Sea* 226.

[169] Treaty of Washington (n 121) art 6.

[170] US Naval War College *International Law Situations 1932* (US Government Printing Office, Washington DC 1934) 6.

[171] Ibid.

[172] For the arguments relating to scope of the base of operations principle during the *Alabama* claims, see US Department of State *Papers Relating to the Treaty of Washington* vol III (US Government Printing Office, Washington DC 1872–1874) 434; 513.

[173] W E Hall (A P Higgins (ed)) *International Law: A Treatise* (8th edn Clarendon Press Oxford 1924) 724.

and the early twentieth century that it was possible, without continuous use, for a neutral port to become a belligerent base if there was a direct connection between the use of the port and the hostile action.[174]

Article 5 of Hague Convention XIII specifies that it is the belligerent which must not use neutral ports and waters as a base of operations. The duty of a neutral State to prevent the belligerent use of neutral ports and waters as a base is derived from customary law and from Article 25 of Hague Convention XIII.[175]

The 'base of operations' principle remains a rule of neutrality that has been referred to in certain armed conflicts and is no longer limited to naval warfare. The example of Cambodia during the Vietnam conflict has been discussed already. The duty was also invoked by China against the UK during the conflict in Vietnam, where China accused the UK of permitting Hong Kong to be used as a base of operations for the US.[176] The UK denied that the law of neutrality was applicable because of the uncertain nature of the hostilities; however, it did not seek to contend that the base of operations principle was no longer part of the law.[177]

b. The Duty to Prevent Fitting Out and Arming in Neutral Jurisdiction

Article 8 provides that the neutral State must prevent the fitting out or arming of any vessel within its jurisdiction that it believes is bound for hostile operations against another belligerent, and also must prevent the departure from its jurisdiction of any vessel bound for hostile operations that was adapted entirely or partly within neutral jurisdiction.[178] This duty extends to preventing belligerent private vessels as well as warships from being fitted out or armed in neutral jurisdiction, and is therefore an exception to the distinction between State and private action that obtains throughout the Conventions.[179]

Like Article 5, Article 8 is a restatement of the rules contained in the Treaty of Washington. In the eventual arbitration of the claims arising from the American Civil War, Britain was found to have violated the duty to prevent the fitting out of

[174] The change may be seen by comparing the editions of Lawrence's text. Cf T J Lawrence *The Principles of International Law* (2nd edn Macmillan, London 1895) 504–5; T J Lawrence *The Principles of International Law* (5th edn D C Heath and Co, Boston 1910) 618–19.

[175] HC XIII art 25. [176] (1966) 70 RGDIP 743–5; (1967) 71 RGDIP 740.

[177] (1966) 70 RGDIP 745.

[178] HC XIII art 8. The principle has also been regarded as applicable to aerial warfare. See 'General Report of the Commission of Jurists at The Hague Part II: Rules of Aerial Warfare' (1923) 17 AJILS 245 (Hague Air Rules) art 46. J M Spaight argues that the duty in Article 46 of the Hague Air Rules is in some respects more onerous than the duty in HC XIII Article 8, as effective control of the preparation and supply of aircraft is more difficult than with regard to ships. See J M Spaight *Air Power and War Rights* (3rd edn Longmans, Green and Co, London 1947) 477.

[179] Tucker *Neutrality at Sea* 227–8.

vessels, including the *Alabama*, within its jurisdiction that subsequently cruised against Union shipping.[180] Article 8 is perhaps a product of its time, but its importance is to ensure that a State does not provide war material for use by a belligerent at sea. It has thereby been described as the corollary of the general prohibition on assisting parties to the conflict in their military effort.[181]

Since the specific prohibition of Article 8 has declined in importance, the obligation preventing the arming from neutral ports is invoked in contemporary State practice in a general way. Thus in the 1998–2000 armed conflict between Eritrea and Ethiopia, Eritrea protested against Djibouti's 'unwarranted cooperation with Ethiopia', and indicated that Djibouti's port was being used to equip Ethiopia with war material.[182] Djibouti responded by stating its neutrality towards the conflict and emphasizing the historical basis for Ethiopian usage of its port.[183]

c. The Twenty-Four Hour Rule

Hague Convention XIII provides in a number of instances that a belligerent warship is not permitted to remain in the ports, roadsteads, or territorial waters of the neutral State for a period of more than twenty-four hours.[184] It may only extend this period on account of damage or stress of weather.[185] If a belligerent warship does not leave a port where it is not entitled to remain, the neutral State is entitled to take such measures as it considers necessary to render the ship incapable of taking the sea during the war.[186]

The twenty-four hour rule has been questioned. The UK *Manual of the Law of Armed Conflict*, for example, states that:

> the United Kingdom takes the view that the old rule which prohibited belligerent warships from remaining in neutral ports for more than 24 hours except in unusual circumstances, is no longer applicable in view of modern State practice.[187]

[180] J B Moore *History and Digest of the International Arbitrations to which the United States has been a Party: Vol I* (Government Printing Office, Washington 1898) Chapter XIV 653; See generally T Bingham 'The Alabama Claims Arbitration' (2005) 54 ICLQ 1. For UK opinions concerning the *Alabama* see A D McNair (ed) *International Law Opinions* vol III (CUP, Cambridge 1956) 171–87.

[181] M Bothe 'The Law of Neutrality' in D Fleck (ed) *The Handbook of International Humanitarian Law* (2nd edn OUP, Oxford 2008) 571, 591.

[182] UNSC 'Letter dated 19 November 1998 from the Permanent Representative of Eritrea to the United Nations addressed to the President of the Security Council' (19 November 1998) UN Doc S/1998/1097.

[183] See UNSC 'Letter dated 11 November 1998 from the Permanent Representative of Djibouti to the United Nations addressed to the President of the Security Council' (11 November 1998) UN Doc S/1998/1062; UNSC 'Letter dated 20 November 1998 from the Permanent Representative of Djibouti to the United Nations addressed to the President of the Security Council' (20 November 1998) UN Doc S/1998/1107.

[184] HC XIII art 12; art 13; art 16. [185] Ibid art 14. [186] Ibid art 24.

[187] UK *Manual of the Law of Armed Conflict* § 13.4.

This is a minority view, however. Other military manuals continue to make reference to the twenty-four hour rule.[188]

d. Measures with Regard to Prize Law

The neutral State has, in Hague Convention XIII, a number of obligations with regard to the presence of prizes in neutral waters.[189] Adjudication in prize has not occurred for many years and the relevance of prize law to contemporary international law has been questioned.[190] The UK *Manual of the Law of Armed Conflict* states that 'the United Kingdom has not used prize courts for many years and is unlikely to do so in the future. Where a vessel or aircraft is captured by United Kingdom armed forces it may be deemed to be the property of Her Majesty's government.'[191] Nevertheless, there is little other evidence that prize adjudication has fallen into desuetude.[192]

Article 21 of Hague Convention XIII provides that a prize can be brought into a neutral port in three circumstances: unseaworthiness; stress of weather; or want of fuel or provisions. It must leave as soon as those circumstances are alleviated. If it does not, the neutral State must employ the means at its disposal to release the prize and to intern the prize crew.[193] Article 21 was invoked in 1939, when a US merchant vessel, the *City of Flint,* which had been captured by a German prize crew, was taken to the Soviet port of Murmansk.[194] The Soviet Union interned the crew, then reversed its decision and released the prize, claiming the reason for entering the port was distress under Article 21. The US protested that the circumstances under Article 21 were not met and the Soviet Union was under an obligation under Hague Convention XIII to release the prize in accordance with Article 22.[195]

188 US *Naval Commander's Handbook* § 7.3.2; Canada *LOAC Manual* § 810(1); *San Remo Manual* § 21; *Helsinki Principles* [2.2].

189 HC XIII art 21; art 22; art 23.

190 ALRC 'Criminal Admiralty Jurisdiction and Prize' (ALRC Report 48, Canberra 1990) 128: 'Although it can be argued that international law will continue to contain some form of prize law it is difficult to state with any precision what that prize law will be.' For a different view, W H von Heinegg 'The Current State of International Prize Law' in H H G Post (ed) *International Economic Law and Armed Conflict* (Martinus Nijhoff, Dordrecht 1994) 5.

191 UK *Manual of the Law of Armed Conflict* 367 n 103.

192 The UK Manual's statement has elicited strong criticism. See Y Dinstein *The Conduct of Hostilities under the Law of International Armed Conflict* (2nd edn CUP, Cambridge 2010) 248; W H von Heinegg 'The Current State of the Law of Naval Warfare: A Fresh Look at the San Remo Manual' in A M Helm (ed) *The Law of War in the 21st Century: Weaponry and the Use of Force* (International Law Studies 82, US Naval War College, Newport 2006) 269, 287. On prize adjudication generally see D J Bederman 'The Feigned Demise of Prize' (1995) 9 EILR 31.

193 HC XIII art 21.

194 See generally C C Hyde 'The *City of Flint*' (1940) 34 AJIL 89.

195 G Ginsburgs 'The Soviet Union as a Neutral 1939-1941' (1958) 10 *Soviet Studies* 12, 27–8.

Article 23, on sequestration of prize pending a decision of a prize court, has never been accepted as a rule of customary international law and has likely fallen into desuetude.[196]

The duties of prevention in naval warfare, although they have not recently been invoked, continue to be of relevance to the law of neutrality; and, although certain aspects of the Hague Conventions regarding naval warfare appear to have little relevance to contemporary armed conflict, the weight of academic opinion does not yet support the view that these provisions have fallen into desuetude.

5. Duties of Prevention on Land

a. The Duty to Prevent Movement of Troops or Convoys Across Neutral Territory

According to Hague Convention V, the neutral State must not permit belligerent troops from moving troops or convoys of munitions of war or supplies across its territory; it must not allow belligerents to set up communication devices on its territory; and it must not allow the forming of corps of combatants or the establishment of recruitment agencies on its territory.[197] These are duties on both belligerents and neutrals; while belligerents are under a duty not to take such action, neutrals are also under an obligation to prevent such action.

Each of these duties was consolidated in the nineteenth century. The question of the transit of belligerent troops across neutral territory had previously been a contested area in the law of neutrality. As the obligations of sovereignty became more strictly interpreted, debate turned to whether the granting of transit rights was compatible with neutrality. It became increasingly apparent that affording passage, even on the basis of impartiality, was out of step with the view of 'perfect neutrality' that prevailed in the nineteenth century. Hall, for example, viewed the grant of permission as an act done with 'the express object of furthering a warlike end...an interference in the war.'[198] By the end of the nineteenth century the privilege to grant passage across neutral territory was in decline.

Prohibition on belligerent passage is a fundamental duty reaffirmed in many recent conflicts. For example, during the Yom Kippur War of 1973, a number of States, including members of NATO, prohibited the US from using their territory for transit in order to provide supplies to Israel.[199] West Germany, for example, which emphasized its 'strict neutrality' in the conflict, prohibited arms shipments

[196] See Oppenheim (7th edn) vol II 561. [197] HC V art 5. [198] Hall (n 33) 52–3.

[199] L Gelb 'US Jets for Israel Took Route Around Some Allies' *New York Times* (New York, 25 October 1973) 1.

through its territory.[200] Arab States imposed an oil embargo on States that it concluded had breached the duties of neutrality.[201] The embargo was imposed on States such as the Netherlands and Portugal, which had permitted the US to move supplies across their territories.[202]

The 2003 Iraq War raised a number of questions concerning the movement of supplies and troops across neutral territory. Non-participating States took a wide range of positions on the use of their territory for transit. Permanently neutral States such as Switzerland and Austria closed their airspace entirely to coalition actions.[203] Other States, contrary to the duties of neutrality, rendered certain support to coalition States, including permission to refuel and overflight rights. Thus France, Germany, Italy, and Belgium permitted coalition States to use their territories for the transporting of troops.[204] These States did not seek to argue, however, that the law of neutrality was inapplicable; instead, they largely justified their conduct on the basis of alliance obligations under NATO.[205] Indeed, in *Horgan v An Taoiseach*, the Irish High Court upheld the rule prohibiting the granting of passage across a neutral State as a rule of customary international law.[206]

The prohibition on the transit of troops or supplies across neutral territory therefore continues to exist in contemporary international law.

b. The Duty to Prevent Erection of Communication Devices on Neutral Territory

According to Article 3, belligerents are forbidden to erect 'a wireless telegraphy station' or other apparatus for the purpose of communicating with belligerent forces on land or sea.[207] These rules obviously do not address the leaps in

200 'Bonn Bids US Halt Arms to Israel via Germany' *New York Times* (New York, 25 October 1973) 20; H Smith 'Moscow Exhibits Tension, But No Intent to Intervene' *New York Times* (New York, 26 October 1973) 1.

201 Shihata (n 119) 614–16.

202 A Shuster 'Europeans Irked by US Complaint' *New York Times* (New York, 30 October 1973) 14; Norton (n 71) 295.

203 (2004) 9 ARIEL 331, 402–4; Switzerland Federal Department of Foreign Affairs 'Neutrality Under Scrutiny in the Iraq Conflict: Summary of Switzerland's Neutrality Policy During the Iraq Conflict' (2 December 2005) [4.2.1]-[4.2.2] < http://www.eda.admin.ch/eda/en/home/topics/intla/cintla/ref_neutr.html> accessed 20 January 2007.

204 *Le Monde* (Paris, 26 March 2003) 12. On Belgium see O Corten 'Les arguments avancés par la Belgique pour justifier son soutien aux Etats-Unis dans le cadre de la guerre contre l'Irak' (2005) RBDI 417. On Italy see N Ronzitti 'Italy's Non-Belligerency During the Iraqi War' in M Ragazzi (ed) *International Responsibility Today: Essays in Memory of Oscar Schachter* (Martinus Nijhoff, Leiden 2005) 197.

205 Thus, see Chancellor Gerhard Schröder 'Policy State in the German Bundestag on the International Situation and on the Results of the Brussels European Council' (Berlin 3 April 2003) cited in N Ronzitti 'US Military Bases in Italy: In Keeping with International Law? Still Needed?' (2008) 43 *Int Spectator* 79, 87 n 14. See also Corten (n 82) 281–3.

206 *Horgan v An Taoiseach et al* [2003] 2 IR 468, 504–5 per Kearns J.

207 HC V art 2.

technology that have been made since 1907. With the emergence of modern communications in armed conflict and the increasing importance of cyberwarfare, there is a clear need to update the rules regarding the use of communication facilities that are based in neutral territory.[208]

The neutral State has an obligation to prevent the establishment of new communications devices in neutral territory; but it would not be considered a violation of neutrality, upon the outbreak of armed conflict, for the neutral State to take no action with regard to any communications devices already in existence and used by the belligerents. The neutral State would not be required to deviate from its peacetime standard.

c. The Duty to Prevent Corps of Combatants or Recruiting Agencies on Neutral Territory

The duty to prevent the recruitment of troops on neutral territory, which had gradually emerged in the eighteenth century, had become, by the nineteenth century the 'foundation of a duty'.[209] In Hague Convention V it is contained in Article 4.[210]

As in many other areas of neutrality, the distinction between public and private conduct creates certain difficulties, as there has proved in practice to be a fine line between the active recruitment of neutral nationals and the permission to volunteer.[211] To obviate the difficulties that may arise, national laws have frequently imposed much stricter standards than has been required under the law of neutrality.

Developments in international law have to some extent blurred and attenuated the distinction between volunteering and organized corps.[212] Thus the duty not to permit recruiting or the formation of corps of combatants has been supplemented by the duty to prevent the organization of armed bands, including mercenaries, from entering another State.[213] Nevertheless, neither the Declaration on Friendly Relations nor the General Assembly's Definition of Aggression impose on a State the obligation to prevent its nationals from volunteering or from joining a mercenary force.[214]

[208] On neutrality in cyberwarfare, see G K Walker 'Information Warfare and Neutrality' (2000) 33 VJTL 1079; J E Kastenberg 'Non-Intervention and Neutrality in Cyberspace: An Emerging Principle in the National Practice of International Law' (2009) 64 AFLR 43.

[209] Hall (n 33) 55.

[210] HC V art 4.

[211] See generally I Brownlie 'Volunteers and the Law of War and Neutrality' (1956) 5 ICLQ 570.

[212] H Burmester 'The Recruitment and Use of Mercenaries in Armed Conflict' (1978) 72 AJIL 37.

[213] UNGA Res 2625 (XXV) 'Annex: Declaration on Principles of International Law concerning Friendly Relations and Co-operation among States in Accordance with the Charter of the United Nations' (24 October 1970) UN Doc A/8028; UNGA Res 3314 (XXIX) 'Annex: Definition of Aggression' (14 December 1974) UN Doc A/9890 art 3(g).

[214] Burmester (n 212) 43.

The principal difficulty with Article 4 is the definitional ambit of the term 'recruiting agencies.' With the rise of private military and security companies, the question arises whether a neutral State has a duty to prevent, in time of armed conflict, the recruitment of citizens to take part in armed conflicts. It would be necessary to determine whether the prohibition on recruitment applies only to those who will be combatants or also encompasses those who might occupy a non-combat role that is related to the provision of security in a private military enterprise. If the latter, Article 18 (b) of Hague Convention V, which provides that '[s]ervices rendered in matters of police or civil administration are not to be considered as acts committed in favour of one belligerent', may provide an exemption.

d. Exceptions to the Duty of Prevention in Land Warfare

i. Humanitarian assistance

Under Article 14 of Hague Convention V, a neutral State may authorize the passage over its territory of the sick and wounded belonging to belligerent armies, on condition that the trains bringing them shall carry neither personnel nor war material.[215] In that case, the neutral State is bound to take 'whatever measures of safety and control are necessary for the purpose.'[216]

This duty is now supplemented by Article 23 of Geneva Convention IV, and by Article 70(1) of Additional Protocol I. Article 23 provides that:

> Each High Contracting Party shall allow the free passage of all consignments of medical and hospital stores and objects necessary for religious worship intended only for civilians of another High Contracting Party, even if the latter is its adversary. It shall likewise permit the free passage of all consignments of essential foodstuffs, clothing and tonics intended for children under fifteen, expectant mothers and maternity cases.[217]

According to Article 70(1) of Additional Protocol I, offers of humanitarian assistance will not be regarded as interference in the armed conflict or as unfriendly acts.[218]

Article 70(1) provides that humanitarian and impartial relief action 'shall be undertaken.'[219] It appears that, once there is agreement between the parties concerned in relief actions, there is an obligation on neutral States to accord access through their territory. Article 70(2), which provides that '...each High Contracting Party shall allow and facilitate rapid and unimpeded passage of all

[215] HC V art 14. [216] Ibid. [217] GC IV art 23. [218] AP I art 70(1).
[219] Ibid.

relief consignments, equipment, and personnel provided in accordance with this Section.'[220]

On various occasions, the Security Council has urged States proximate to humanitarian crises to facilitate the passage of humanitarian personnel. The Security Council has called on 'all parties concerned, including neighbouring States, to cooperate fully' in ensuring access for humanitarian personnel to civilians in armed conflict.[221] The Guiding Principles of Humanitarian Assistance, adopted by the UN General Assembly in 1991, state that 'States in proximity to emergencies are urged to participate closely with the affected countries in international efforts, with a view to facilitating, to the extent possible, the transit of humanitarian assistance.'[222]

ii. Volunteers

As already noted, along with the fundamental distinction between a State and its citizens, in the area of military recruitment a distinction was posited between the active recruitment of troops by a State, and the enlistment of those individuals acting under their own volition. Article 6 provides that the responsibility of a neutral State is not engaged by the fact of persons crossing the frontier separately to offer their services to one of the belligerents.[223]

It has already been noted that the distinction between volunteers and the prohibition in Article 4 has lost some of its import. Already in 1938, Friedmann argued that the doctrine of *rebus sic stantibus* now applies to the question of volunteers.[224] In World War II, however, the volunteer exception was utilized widely. Considerable numbers of putative volunteers fought in the 'Winter War' between the Soviet Union and Finland.[225] Following a request from Finland to Sweden to permit the passage of troops across its territory, Sweden replied that:

> With regard to troops consisting of volunteers it can probably be expected that an increase will take place during the immediate future in the size of the Swedish Volunteer Corps now active in Finland. Special efforts are being made to this end. It is, however, unfeasible to indicate the number of new volunteers.
>
> No prospect can be offered in the present situation of troops in any other form than volunteers or of permission for the passage of troop formations from belligerent countries.[226]

Following the outbreak of war between Germany and the Soviet Union, Spain dispatched 17,000 soldiers to the Eastern Front to fight alongside Germany.[227] It

220 Ibid art 70(2). 221 UNSC Res 1296 (19 April 2000) UN Doc S/RES/1296 [8].
222 UNGA Res 46/182 (19 December 1991) A/RES/46/182. 223 HC V art 6.
224 Friedmann (n 58) 137. 225 Ginsburgs (n 63) 213. 226 (1940) 11 NT 133.
227 On the operation see G R Kleinfeld and L A Tambs *Hitler's Spanish Legion: The Blue Division in Russia* (Southern Illinois University Press, London 1979).

was claimed by the Spanish government that the so-called 'Blue Division' was comprised of volunteers who had enlisted in the German regular forces entirely independently of State control.[228] In reality, a large number of these volunteers were regular soldiers of the Spanish army; the Blue Division itself was listed on the official rolls of the Spanish Military.[229]

Despite volunteering frequently shading into organized fighting, there is little evidence that States consider that they are under a duty to restrain neutral volunteers. In many instances, States have chosen to do so. For example, during Israel's War of Independence, the Greek government instructed consulates not to grant visas for travel for those volunteers intending to take part in the hostilities. The Greek government justified its conduct by noting that '[t]hus the Government intends to preserve absolute neutrality on the Palestine question.'[230] Volunteers have been evident in more recent conflicts.[231]

The difficulty is to distinguish genuine volunteers from those that are in fact organized by the State, such as the Blue Legion, or the Chinese volunteers that participated in the Korean War.[232] The crucial factor, it is suggested, is that of the degree of State involvement in transforming the private act into that of a State. The degree of State involvement and control necessary to transform what is purportedly a situation of volunteering into a forbidden corps of combatants will, it is submitted, be a lower standard than that required for attribution to be established under Article 8 of the International Law Commission's Articles on State Responsibility.[233]

6. Duties of Prevention in Aerial Warfare

Hague Conventions V and XIII set out the rights and duties of neutrality during war on land and at sea. Issues surrounding neutrality in aerial warfare (which arose as an issue for legal regulation only following World War I) were set out in

[228] E Hernàndez-Sandioca and E Moradiellos 'Spain and and the Second World War 1939-1945' in N Wylie (ed) *European Neutrals and Non-Belligerents During the Second World War* (CUP, Cambridge 2002) 246, 259–60.

[229] K Duff 'Spain Between the Allies and the Axis' in A Toynbee and V M Toynbee (eds) *Survey of International Affairs 1939–1946: the War and the Neutrals* (OUP, London 1956) 256, 285. Spain itself appeared to accept that the Blue Division was not a volunteer unit by proposing the 'theory of the two wars': while Spain was a neutral or non-belligerent State regarding the war between the UK and the Axis, it was a belligerent in the war between the Axis and the Soviet Union (see ibid 307).

[230] SWB (1948) Part III No 52 (27 May 1948) 37.

[231] See 'US Volunteers Join Kosovo Rebels' *BBC News* (London 20 April 1999) < http://news.bbc.co.uk/1/hi/world/europe/323739.stm> accessed 27 January 2007.

[232] See J G Verplaetse 'The *ius in bello* and Military Operations in Korea 1950-1953' (1963) 23 ZaöRV 679, 716; H J Taubenfeld, 'International Actions and Neutrality' (1953) 47 AJIL 377, 392–3.

[233] ILC 'Report of the International Law Commission on the Work of its 53rd Session' (23 April–10 August 2001) UN Doc A/56/10 art 8.

1923 in a report of the Commission of Jurists on the Rules of Aerial Warfare.[234] Those rules were never adopted in binding form.[235]

The status of the Hague Air Rules has been subjected to doubt and there is disagreement whether as a whole they reflect customary international law. According to some writers, State practice supporting the customary status of the Hague Air Rules is 'very meagre.'[236] Others contend that some of the rules have had a 'substantial influence' on the evolution of customary international law.[237] A number of the Hague Air Rules that deal with neutrality transpose the rights and duties of neutrality in maritime warfare to aerial warfare.[238]

It is not the purpose here to evaluate the status of the Hague Air Rules as a whole, or even to consider all of their provisions on neutrality, such as the rules on visit and search of neutral aircraft and aerial blockade.[239] What is considered are those rules that bear on the prevention of certain belligerent aerial conduct in neutral territory.

a. General Duty to Prevent Overflight of Neutral Territory

The basic rule is stated in Article 42 of the Hague Air Rules:

> A neutral government must use the means at its disposal to prevent the entry within its jurisdiction of belligerent military aircraft and to compel them to alight if they have entered such jurisdiction.
>
> A neutral government shall use the means at its disposal to intern any belligerent military aircraft which is within its jurisdiction after having alighted for any reason whatsoever, together with its crew and the passengers, if any.[240]

[234] 'General Report of the Commission of Jurists at The Hague Part II: Rules of Aerial Warfare' (1923) 17 AJILS 245 (Hague Air Rules).

[235] For general discussion see J W Garner 'Proposed Rules for the Regulation of Aerial Warfare' (1924) 18 AJIL 56.

[236] N Ronzitti 'The Codification of Air Warfare' in N Ronzitti and G Venturini (eds) *The Law of Air Warfare: Contemporary Issues* (Eleven International Publishing, Utrecht 2006) 3, 8; W H Parks 'Air War and the Law of War' (1990) 32 AFLR 1, 25–36.

[237] Y Dinstein 'Legitimate Military Objectives Under the Current *Jus in Bello*' in A E Wall (ed) *Legal and Ethical Lessons of NATO's Kosovo Campaign* (International Law Studies 78, US Naval War College, Newport 2002) 139, 169.

[238] For discussion see R Bierzanek 'Commentary to the 1923 Hague Rules for Aerial Warfare' in N Ronzitti (ed) *The Law of Naval Warfare: A Collection of Agreements and Documents with Commentaries* (Martinus Nijhoff, Dordrecht 1988) 396, 398. The analogy between aerial warfare and naval warfare has been criticized: S W D Rowson 'Prize Law During the Second World War' (1947) 24 BYBIL 160, 209–12.

[239] The most recent evaluation of the Hague Air Rules is contained in the study undertaken under the auspices of the Harvard Program on Humanitarian Policy and Conflict Research: see *HPCR Manual*. On aerial blockade see M N Schmitt 'Aerial Blockades in Historical, Legal and Practical Perspective' (1991) 2 USAFAJLS 21.

[240] Hague Air Rules art 42. The corresponding belligerent duty is contained in Article 39.

A rule in similar terms was quickly incorporated into other neutrality rules, such as the Havana Convention on Maritime Neutrality[241] and the Neutrality Rules promulgated by Scandinavian countries in 1938.[242] It has been contended that this rule was established in customary law by 1923, reflecting practice in World War I.[243] The general concept is now contained in a significant number of military manuals.[244]

The duty is a corollary to the duty to prevent the passage of troops and supplies across neutral territory in Article 2 of Hague Convention V.

b. Exceptions to the Duty of Prevention in Aerial Warfare

i. Hospital aircraft

An exception to the prohibition on belligerent aircraft in neutral jurisdiction exists with regard to hospital aircraft. According to Article 37 of the First Geneva Convention (as well as Article 40 of the Second Geneva Convention):

> medical aircraft of Parties to the conflict may fly over the territory of neutral Powers, land on it in case of necessity, or use it as a port of call.[245]

However, this is subject to a number of requirements. Medical aircraft must give the neutral State previous notice of their passage as well as obey all summons to alight, on land and on water.[246] The neutral State may place conditions or restrictions on the passage or landing of medical aircraft on their territory. Those conditions must be applied without discrimination between the belligerents.[247] Moreover, the wounded and sick who are disembarked must be detained by the neutral State.

The basic rule is reiterated in Article 31 of Additional Protocol I. Article 31 provides that, if a medical aircraft enters neutral territory in the absence of an agreement, and flies over the territory of a neutral State, either through error or emergency, it must make every effort to give notice of the flight and to

[241] Convention on Maritime Neutrality (n 53) art 14.

[242] See Declaration Regarding Similar Rules of Neutrality (signed 27 May 1938) 188 LNTS 294 art 8. On the declaration see N J Padelford 'The New Scandinavian Neutrality Rules' (1938) 32 AJIL 789; O Bring 'Commentary on the 1938 Stockholm Declaration' in N Ronzitti (ed) *The Law of Naval Warfare: A Collection of Agreements and Documents* (Martinus Nijhoff, Dordrecht 1988) 839. For Italian legislation incorporating the duty see H A Steiner 'Italian War and Neutrality Legislation' (1939) 33 AJIL 151.

[243] Spaight (n 178) 420; Bierzanek (n 238) 399.

[244] *San Remo Manual* § 18; UK *Manual of the Law of Armed Conflict* § 12.14A; Australia *Air Operations Law Manual* § 12.8; US *Naval Commander's Handbook* § 7.3.9. See also *HPCR Manual* § 168 (a).

[245] GC I art 37; GC II art 40. [246] Ibid. [247] Ibid.

identify itself. As soon as that medical aircraft is recognized, the neutral State must make all reasonable effort to give the order to land or alight, or to take other measures to safeguard its interests, and the medical aircraft must be given time to comply before it is attacked.[248] A medical aircraft that lands in neutral territory is subject to inspection as to its medical nature.[249] Like the provisions in Geneva Conventions I and II, Article 31 provides that the wounded, sick, and shipwrecked disembarked, other than temporarily, from a medical aircraft must be detained by that State where so required by the rules of international law applicable in armed conflict, in such a manner that they can no longer take part in the hostilities.[250] These rules have been reproduced in military manuals.[251]

ii. Overflight of straits passage

The right of passage through international straits extends to overflight over international straits.[252] Aircraft must proceed without delay over the strait; refrain from the threat or use of force against States bordering the strait; refrain from any activities other than those incident to their normal modes of continuous and expeditious transit unless rendered necessary by *force majeure* or by distress.[253] Aircraft exercising transit passage must also comply with certain obligations regarding compliance with the Rules of the Air established by the International Civil Aviation Organization as well as monitor the radio frequency assigned by the competent internationally designated air traffic control authority, or the appropriate international distress radio frequency.[254] A number of military manuals support the view that belligerent aircraft may utilize neutral straits for transit passage.[255]

The use of transit passage overflight rights has occasionally been a factor in armed conflicts. During the Yom Kippur War of 1973, for example, in which the US supported Israel with large amounts of military aid, US aircraft overflew the Strait of Gibraltar.[256] The ability to claim passage was of vital importance, since, as already discussed, most European States had refused to permit the US to transit over their neutral territories.[257]

[248] AP I art 31(2). [249] Ibid art 31(3). [250] Ibid art 31(4).

[251] UK *Manual of the Law of Armed Conflict* § 12.14A–12.14D; Canada *LOAC Manual* § 1308(1)–(4); *San Remo Manual* § 181–3.

[252] LOSC art 38. [253] Ibid art 39(1). [254] Ibid art 39(3).

[255] See, for example, UK *Manual of the Law of Armed Conflict* § 13.14–13.20; Canada *LOAC Manual* § 812; US *Naval Commander's Handbook* § 7.3.6.

[256] See J N Moore 'The Regime of Straits and the Third United Nations Conference on the Law of the Sea' (1980) 74 AJIL 77, 80–1.

[257] See L Gelb 'US Jets for Israel Took Route Around Some Allies' *New York Times* (New York 25 October 1973) 1.

7. Other Neutral Duties

The neutral State has a number of other duties that are not subsumable under other categories. Articles 11–15 of Hague Convention V substantially reproduce the provisions of Hague Convention II of 1899 relating to the internment of belligerents and wounded belligerents in neutral territory, with one addition.[258] If belligerent troops do pass into neutral territory, the neutral State is required to intern them, if possible, away from the theatre of war.[259] The innovation of Hague Convention V relates to escaped prisoners of war. Article 13 provides that escaped prisoners of war received on neutral territory are to be left at liberty.[260] The equivalent duty in naval war relates to the capture of prizes within neutral territorial waters: the neutral State 'must use the means at its disposal to release the prize with its officers and crew, and to intern the prize crew.'[261] If belligerent military aircraft enter the jurisdiction of a neutral State, the aircraft and its crew must be interned.[262]

8. The Rights Of Neutrals

a. The Inviolability of Neutral Territory

The Hague Conventions state that belligerents are under an obligation to respect the territory of neutral States. Article 1 of Hague Convention V states the general principle: 'The territory of neutral Powers is inviolable.'[263] According to Article 1 of Hague Convention XIII, 'belligerents are bound to respect the sovereign rights of neutral Powers and to abstain, in neutral territory or neutral waters, from any act which would, if knowingly permitted by any Power, constitute a violation of neutrality.'[264]

According to Articles 2 to 4 of Hague Convention V, belligerents are prohibited from taking certain actions on neutral territory.[265] Similarly, Article 2 of Hague Convention XIII provides that any belligerent act of hostility committed in the territorial waters of a neutral Power constitutes a violation of neutrality.[266] Articles 4 and 5 of Hague Convention XIII prohibit a belligerent from setting up a

258 Articles 11, 12, 14 and 15 are nearly identical to Articles 57–60 of Hague Convention II of 1899. Those provisions in turn have their basis in the Oxford Manual (n 7) art 79–83.

259 HC V art 11. According to Article 12 the neutral State must supply the interned troops with food, clothing and relief 'required by humanity.'

260 HC V art 13.

261 HC XIII art 3; art 24.

262 Hague Air Rules art 42.

263 HC V art 1.

264 HC XIII art 1.

265 Article 2, for example, provides that 'Belligerents are forbidden to move troops or convoys of either munitions of war or supplies across the territory of a neutral Power.'

266 HC XIII art 2. According to Article 10, however, the neutrality of a State 'is not affected by the mere passage through its territorial waters of war-ships or prizes belonging to belligerents.'

prize court in neutral territory, or from using neutral territory as a base of operations, respectively.[267] Article 18 of Hague Convention XIII provides that belligerent warships may not make use of neutral ports, roadsteads, or territorial waters to increase supplies of war material or their armament or for completing their crews.[268]

The approach of the Hague Conventions is significant: rather than broaching the issue solely from the perspective of the neutral State's duty of prevention, the inviolability of neutral States is dealt with from the perspective of duties towards neutrals and neutral rights. As de Bustamente notes:

> Instead of saying, for example, that the neutral must prevent the passage across its territory of the belligerent army, it is now held that the combatants must refrain from crossing neutral territory with their armies. This is not simply a different form of expression, but a radical change in the situation of both, and therefore in their international responsibility.[269]

This is not strictly accurate. The obligation is not the belligerent's alone; both the neutral and the belligerent are under reciprocal rights and duties in this area. Thus in Hague Convention V, while a belligerent is under a duty, under Articles 2 and 3, not to take certain action in neutral territory, the neutral State is under an obligation not to allow any of those belligerent actions to occur on its territory.[270]

The acknowledgement that neutrals had certain 'rights' stemming from their status was a deliberate development at the Second Hague Peace Conference. At the Conference France had submitted a text that proceeded from the perspective of the duties of a neutral State. In response to the draft, the Belgian delegate noted that it was important 'to call attention to the fact that neutrals not only have duties but that they also have rights.'[271] There was therefore a need to appreciate that the issue was not confined to the neutral's duty of prevention: 'the obligations of neutrals in this regard flow from an inhibition of general application which logically concerns belligerents primarily before affecting neutrals.'[272] Belgium therefore requested the inclusion of the statement that 'the territory of neutral States is

[267] HC XIII art 4; HC XIII art 5. However, the prohibition on the establishment of a prize court in neutral territory has 'long been the law of nations.' Hyde (n 27) 509.

[268] HC XIII art 18.

[269] A S de Bustamente 'The Hague Convention Concerning the Rights and Duties of Neutral Powers and Persons in Land Warfare' (1908) 2 AJIL 95, 97. See also S W D Rowson 'Modern Blockade: Some Legal Aspects' (1946) 23 BYBIL 346, 347: '[i]t is a comparatively modern notion that neutrals have rights against belligerents, who are under corresponding duties to neutrals.'

[270] HC V art 5.

[271] *Hague Conference Proceedings* vol III 174. The Belgian delegate continued: 'Being themselves strangers to the hostilities they have the primordial right to demand that they not be implicated in them directly or indirectly.'

[272] Ibid.

inviolable.'[273] A report on a draft of what would become Hague Convention XIII noted that:

> The starting-point of the regulations ought to be the sovereignty of the neutral State, which cannot be affected by the mere fact that a war exists in which it does not intend to participate. Its sovereignty should be respected by the belligerents, who cannot implicate it in the war or molest it with acts of hostility.[274]

The report went on to emphasize that the obligation contained in Article 1 of Hague Convention XIII was an obligation to respect another State's sovereignty, and therefore did not stem from the existence of war:

> The principle which it is proper to affirm at the outset is the obligation upon belligerents to respect the sovereign rights of neutral States. This obligation is not a consequence of the war any more than the right of the State to inviolability of its territory is a consequence of its neutrality. The obligation and the right are inherent in the very existence of States...[275]

As noted in Chapter 2, the neutral's inviolability was initially quite limited, as States could simply exchange a State's neutrality for belligerency through a declaration of war. Now, however, the inviolability of a neutral State is protected, not only under the law of neutrality, but also under the prohibition of the threat or use of force under Article 2(4) of the Charter.

b. The Inviolability of Neutral Territorial Waters

i. Passage through the neutral territorial sea

It has been noted that the passage of belligerent warships through neutral territorial waters is an anomaly that finds no parallel in land or aerial warfare.[276] During the drafting of Hague Convention XIII, the issue of belligerent passage through neutral territorial waters received considerable attention. At the time of the Second Hague Conference, there was disagreement as to the scope of innocent passage. The British delegation had sought to argue that innocent passage through territorial waters was a right exercisable at all times and could not be suspended in time of war. Other delegations were more receptive to the argument that passage could be suspended.

[273] Ibid. [274] *Hague Conference Proceedings* vol I 278, 290. [275] Ibid 290.
[276] Tucker *Neutrality at Sea* 232 n 80.

In the final formulation, the issue whether passage could be prohibited altogether was left unstated.[277] It was instead agreed at the Second Hague Conference that 'mere passage' of belligerent warships, naval auxiliaries and prizes through the neutral territorial sea could not be treated as a violation of the neutrality of the coastal State.[278] The result was Article 10 of Hague Convention XIII, which provides that:

> The neutrality of a Power is not affected by the mere passage through its territorial waters of war-ships or prizes belonging to belligerents.[279]

Questions arose as to the meaning of 'mere' passage. 'Mere' passage is used in the sense of 'innocent passage'; passage therefore must be sought purely for purposes of navigation and without prejudice to the security of the coastal State, and not for ulterior purposes, such as the evasion of capture.[280]

The phrase must be read in light of the other articles of the Convention.[281] In general terms, Article 1 provides that a belligerent must abstain from any act which would, if knowingly permitted by that belligerent, constitute a violation of neutrality.[282] A violation of the State's neutrality is defined in Article 2 as 'any act of hostility, including capture and the exercise of the right of search.'[283] But the concept of 'mere passage' must be read particularly in the context of Article 5, which prohibits belligerents from making use of neutral ports and waters as a base of operations, and Article 4, which prohibits a belligerent from setting up a prize court on a vessel in neutral waters.[284]

There is some doubt whether 'mere passage' is limited by a temporal requirement contained in Article 12 of Hague Convention XIII.[285] Article 12 provides that belligerent warships are not permitted to remain in the ports, roadsteads, or territorial waters of the neutral State for more than twenty-four hours.[286] The issue arose in the case of the *Altmark*, which took two days to pass through

[277] *Hague Conference Proceedings* vol III 701 (Annex 44 art 32), 720 (Annex 55); Higgins (n 26) 467–8.

[278] *Hague Conference Proceedings* vol I 297–8.

[279] HC XIII art 10.

[280] Tucker *Neutrality at Sea*; US *Law of Naval Warfare Manual* § 433 n 22.

[281] B MacChesney 'The Altmark Incident and Modern Warfare – "Innocent Passage" in Wartime and the Right of Belligerents to Use Force to Redress Neutrality Violations' (1957–1958) 52 *Northwestern ULR* 320, 332.

[282] HC XIII art 1.

[283] HC XIII art 2.

[284] HC XIII art 4; art 5. See US *Law of Naval Warfare Manual* § 433 n 22.

[285] For differing views see Castrén *Neutrality* 515–17; C H M Waldock 'The Release of the *Altmark's* Prisoners' (1947) 24 BYBIL 216, 227–35; D Schindler 'Commentary on the 1907 Hague Convention XIII Concerning the Rights and Duties of Neutral Powers in Naval War' in N Ronzitti (ed) *The Law of Naval Warfare: A Collection of Agreements and Documents with Commentaries* (Martinus Nijhoff, Dordrecht 1988) 193, 217.

[286] HC XIII art 12.

Norwegian territorial waters.[287] Norway claimed that the twenty-four hour rule was not applicable to passage through neutral waters, as opposed to stay in neutral ports.[288] The US *Law of Naval Warfare Manual* issued in 1955 adopted a compromise position, and stated that, if the twenty-four hour rule was not to be strictly observed with regard to mere passage, passage of more than twenty-four hours would nevertheless indicate that such passage was not being used for purposes of innocent navigation.[289]

The position remains unsettled. It has recently been suggested that the twenty-four hour rule does apply to passage through neutral territorial waters.[290] A number of military manuals reflect this position and state that innocent passage is limited to twenty-four hours.[291] The UK *Manual of the Law of Armed Conflict*, on the other hand, suggests that the twenty-four hour rule has lost its legal force even with regard to stay in neutral ports.[292] The UK *Manual* prefers the language of the law of the sea, and provides that a belligerent warship or auxiliary exercising rights of passage through neutral waters should do so 'continuously and expeditiously.'[293]

The UK position raises the issue of the relationship between 'mere passage' under the law of neutrality and 'innocent passage' under the peacetime law of the sea. The concept of 'innocent passage' is contained in the 1958 Convention on the Territorial Sea and the Contiguous Zone and the 1982 UN Convention on the Law of the Sea (LOSC).[294] Article 17 of the LOSC provides that 'ships of all States...enjoy the rights of innocent passage through the territorial sea.'[295] 'Passage' is defined within Article 18 to be passage that is 'continuous and expeditious.'[296] Article 19(1) of the LOSC notes that passage, to be characterized as innocent, must not be prejudicial to the 'peace, good order and security' of the coastal State. Article 19(2) then lists a series of acts that are prejudicial within the meaning of Article 19(1).[297]

There are reasons to doubt the application of the peacetime definition of innocent passage to the law of neutrality. First, there has 'never been any doubt' that the LOSC was dealing with the law of peace and not with the law of armed conflict at sea.[298] Moreover, it was noted on various occasions at the third UN

[287] For discussion see MacChesney (n 281); Waldock (n 285); E Borchard 'Was Norway Delinquent in the Case of the Altmark?'(1940) 34 AJIL 289.

[288] For the correspondence between the British and Norwegian governments, see Cmd 8012 (1950).

[289] US *Law of Naval Warfare Manual* § 433 n 23.

[290] Bothe (n 181) 593.

[291] Canada *LOAC Manual* § 810 (1); *San Remo Manual* § 21; *Helsinki Principles* 496 [2.2].

[292] UK *Manual of the Law of Armed Conflict* § 13.4.

[293] Ibid § 13.9D.

[294] Convention on the Territorial Sea and the Contiguous Zone (adopted 29 April 1958, entered into force 10 September 1964) 516 UNTS 205 art 14; LOSC art 17.

[295] LOSC art 17.

[296] Ibid art 18(2).

[297] Ibid art 19(2).

[298] E Rauch *The Protocol Additional to the Geneva Conventions for the Protection of Victims of International Armed Conflicts and the United Nations Convention on the Law of the Sea: Repercussions on the Law of Naval Warfare* (Duncker & Humblot, Berlin 1984) 19; A V Lowe 'The Commander's Handbook on the Law of Naval Operations and the Contemporary Law of the Sea' in H B Robertson

Conference on the Law of the Sea that the law of neutrality was unaffected by the LOSC. Thus Sweden stated that it:

> ...attached great importance to the question of the relation between the new Convention and the Conventions on the laws of war and of neutrality, which had been laid down in considerable detail in such long-standing and widely accepted international agreements as the Hague Conventions of 1907. It was [its] understanding that article 311, paragraph 2, provided for the continued application of these Conventions in time of war and that the rights and obligations resulting therefrom would not be affected by the new law of the sea.[299]

Secondly, it has been noted that grafting the peacetime law of the sea onto the law of armed conflict at sea is problematic in structural terms, because the trilateral relationship between opposing belligerents and a neutral State is different from the peacetime bilateral relationship between a flag State and a coastal State.[300]

There exist compelling reasons, however, to apply elements of the peacetime law of the sea in the context of armed conflict. First, the relationship between a belligerent and a neutral State is one of peace.[301] When an international armed conflict breaks out, the law of neutrality is applicable to non-participating States, but the peacetime relations between neutrals and belligerents are not wholly suspended.[302] As Rauch puts it, 'the law of neutrality is a branch of the law of peace, which has only been modified by the state of war between other subjects of international law. The law of neutrality itself is not a constituent part of the law of war.'[303]

Secondly, State practice indicates the acceptance of the innocent passage regime in time of armed conflict. During the conflict between Iran and Iraq, for example, Iran contended that it was entitled to prevent passage through its territorial sea on the basis that US actions were contrary to Article 19(2) of the LOSC.[304]

Jr (ed) *The Law of Naval Operations* (International Law Studies 64, US Naval War College, Newport 1991) 109, 131–2.

[299] UN Third United Nations Conference on the Law of the Sea OR vol XVI 53; UN Third United Nations Conference on the Law of the Sea OR vol XVII 54; UN Third United Conference on the Law of the Sea OR vol XIV 35. Another statement by Sweden may be found in (1994) 25 LOSB 36.

[300] MacChesney (n 281) 332. [301] *Helsinki Principles* [1.3]. [302] Ibid.

[303] Rauch (n 298) 37.

[304] UNSC 'Annex: Note Verbale dated 7 July 1988 from the Interests Section of the Islamic Republic of Iran in Washington addressed to the Embassy of Algeria in Washington' (15 March 1989) UN Doc S/20525. As to matters cited as being contrary to Article 19(2) of the LOSC, Iran states that 'In light of attacks on the Iranian ship, the *Ajr*, and on the Reshadat, Nasr and Salmon oil platforms, as well as the frequent warnings to the Islamic Republic of Iran's sea patrolling aircraft, the Government of the Islamic Republic of Iran not only considers the passage of the United States warships from its territorial sea as not being innocent, but it regards their presence in the Persian Gulf as a threat to its security.'

Thirdly, the duties of a neutral with regard its territory came into existence at a time when the territorial sea was comprised of a narrow band of water. Neutral waters now encompass the wider breadth of the territorial sea in line with the modern law of the sea.[305] As has been remarked, the extension of the three nautical mile territorial sea to twelve nautical miles removes over three million square miles of ocean from hostile action.[306]

It could, therefore, be suggested that the expansion of the territorial sea must be balanced by the adoption of the broader concept of innocent passage in the LOSC, rather than the narrower understanding of mere passage in the law of neutrality. Certain infringements of mere passage under the law of neutrality, for example, may not constitute 'non-innocent' passage under the law of the sea, because it is not prejudicial to the peace, good order or security of the coastal State.[307] For example, if the twenty-four hour rule is regarded as applicable to mere passage, a belligerent ship that takes longer than twenty-four hours to move through neutral waters would thereby violate the law of neutrality, but it would not violate of Article 19 of the LOSC.[308]

Article 10 of Hague Convention XIII is silent on whether passage may be prohibited altogether. At the Second Hague Conference, the issue was deliberately left to customary international law.[309] It would now appear to be established, however, that passage may be suspended by neutral States (except in international straits).[310] Military manuals suggest that passage through neutral territorial waters may be prohibited altogether.[311]

[305] See US *Naval Commander's Handbook* § 7.3.5. The *San Remo Manual* states (§ 14) that 'Neutral waters consist of the internal waters, territorial sea and, where applicable, the archipelagic waters, of neutral States.' H B Robertson Jr 'The "New" Law of the Sea and the Law of Armed Conflict at Sea' (Newport Paper 3, US Naval War College, Newport 1992) 16–17.

[306] L E Fielding 'Maritime Interception: Centrepiece of Economic Sanctions in the New World Order' (1992–1993) 53 *Louisiana LR* 1191.

[307] A Mayama 'The Influence of the Straits Transit Regime on the Law of Neutrality at Sea' (1995) 26 ODIL 1, 3.

[308] There remains some controversy whether the list of matters considered prejudicial in Article 19(2) is to be regarded as exhaustive or illustrative. It has been suggested, for example, that the list provides 'examples' of prejudicial passage: Shaw (n 130) 571; for a similar view that the list is illustrative see V Lowe 'The Impact of the Law of the Sea on Naval Warfare' (1987–1988) 14 SJILC 657, 668; D G Stephens 'The Impact of the 1982 Law of the Sea Convention on the Conduct of Peacetime Naval/Military Operations' (1998–1999) 29 *Cal Western ILJ* 283, 308. For the contrary view see J Astley III and M N Schmitt 'The Law of the Sea and Naval Operations' (1997) 42 AFLR 119, 131; 'Union of Soviet Socialist Republics-United States: Joint Statement with Attached Uniform Interpretation of Rules of International Law Governing Innocent Passage' (1989) 28 ILM 1444, 1446 [3].

[309] See *Hague Conference Proceedings* vol I 298, where it is noted that, while the predominant opinion expressed was that passage could be suspended, the question was not addressed in Article 10 but left 'under the empire of the general law of nations.' Turkey, Denmark, Sweden, Norway, and the US amended the original British draft to permit the closure of neutral territorial waters to passage: *Hague Conference Proceedings* vol III 723 (amendment of Norway).

[310] Oppenheim (7th edn) vol II 693.

[311] US *Law of Naval Warfare* § 433 note 22; *US Commander's Handbook* § 7.3.4; UK *Manual of the Law of Armed Conflict* § 13.9B; Canada *LOAC Manual* (2004) § 808; *San Remo Manual* § 19.

ii. Passage through international straits

Passage through international straits—waters in the territorial sea of one or more States but connecting two distinct portions of international waters—is not addressed by Hague Convention XIII. But the issue was considered at the Second Hague Conference, and opinion was divided. One group of States sought to ensure that a neutral State could not be permitted to close international straits to belligerent passage. Sweden considered that, while a neutral State had in fact the right to prohibit access to its territorial waters, straits occupied a special position, and suggested the inclusion of a provision that had been adopted by the *Institut de Droit International* in 1894: 'Straits which serve as a passage from one open sea to another open sea can never be closed.'[312] A similar view was taken by Denmark.[313]

In the *Case of the S S Wimbledon*, the Permanent Court of International Justice stated that:

> [W]hen an artificial waterway connecting two open seas has been permanently dedicated to the use of the whole world, such waterway is assimilated to neutral straits in the sense that even the passage of a belligerent man-of-war does not compromise the neutrality of the sovereign state under whose jurisdiction the waters in question lie.[314]

While this statement indicates that the neutrality of a coastal State is unaffected by the passage of belligerents, it does not address the question whether a neutral State is obliged to permit passage through international straits. There is some division between those writers who argue for the emergence of a customary right of belligerents to transit through neutral straits,[315] and those who suggest that such a right had not crystallized up to the period of the signature of the LOSC.[316] Practice, too, has been divided. On the one hand, the evidence is somewhat inconclusive with regard to whether a legal duty could be said to exist; on the other hand, examples of restrictions on belligerent passage have been rare. While it is not clear that the lack of restrictions can be said to indicate the existence of a duty,[317] practice certainly indicates that passage through neutral straits has been restricted only in exceptional cases.[318]

Governed solely by the law of neutrality, transit of neutral straits would be governed by the requirement of 'mere passage'; straits passage would therefore

[312] *Hague Conference Proceedings* vol I 297. [313] Ibid 297–8.

[314] *Case of the S S 'Wimbledon'* PCIJ Rep Series A No 1 15, 28.

[315] Tucker *Neutrality at Sea* 232–3 n 80; Castrén *Neutrality* 518; R R Baxter 'Passage of Ships Through International Waterways in Time of War' (1954) 31 BYBIL 187, 215; Mayama (n 307) 5.

[316] W H von Heinegg 'The Law of Naval Warfare and International Straits' in L C Green and M N Schmitt (eds) *The Law of Armed Conflict: Into the Next Millennium* (International Law Studies 71, US Naval War College, Newport 1998) 263, 268–9.

[317] Cf Baxter (n 315) 192. [318] Rauch (n 298) 44.

depend on it being 'innocent' as that phrase is understood.[319] The requirement of innocence would likely prohibit the passage of submerged submarines, and of overflight of neutral straits.[320] Moreover, it is likely that, under the law of neutrality, a neutral State would be entitled to impose certain security restrictions or conditions on the transit of international straits, as long as those restrictions were imposed impartially.[321]

The position with regard to passage through international straits was modified by the LOSC, which introduced the concept of transit passage.[322] The concept has been described as 'somewhere between freedom of navigation on the one hand and innocent passage on the other.'[323] It is much broader than the right of innocent passage.[324] It permits 'continuous and expeditious' transit of ships and may not be impeded.[325] Any laws and regulations relating to transit passage may not have the effect of denying, hampering, or impairing the right of transit passage.[326] Transit passage extends to aircraft.[327]

Ships exercising transit passage must proceed without delay, refrain from any threat or use of force, and refrain from any activities other than those incident to their normal modes of continuous and expeditious transit.[328] Transit may be conducted in 'normal mode.'[329] This term has commonly been interpreted as providing that submarines may exercise transit passage while submerged.[330]

Given the importance of international straits to navigation,[331] and given that the regime of transit passage offers considerable benefits to States engaged in naval operations, it is not surprising that States able to project naval force have sought to fold the transit passage regime into the framework of the law of armed conflict. It has been pointed out that the transit passage regime benefits from two key advantages over the mere passage regime of the law of neutrality. First, the neutral State has no ability to prevent passage because of non-innocence; as long as a belligerent is seeking transit passage for continuous and expeditious transit, it cannot be refused.[332] Secondly, according to the transit passage regime a neutral State is not permitted to impose restrictive measures, which it would arguably be allowed to do under the law of neutrality subject to the requirement of non-discrimination.[333] Hence a number of States have incorporated the transit passage regime into their military manuals.[334]

319 See, for example, MacChesney (n 281). 320 Mayama (n 307) 6–7.
321 For the suggestion that certain restrictions could be imposed see Baxter (n 315) 202.
322 LOSC art 37.
323 W M Reisman 'The Regime of Straits and National Security: an Appraisal of International Law Making' (1980) 74 AJIL 48, 68.
324 Lowe (n 298) 119. 325 LOSC art 38(1)–(2). 326 Ibid art 42(2).
327 Ibid art 38(1). 328 Ibid art 39(1). 329 Ibid art 38(2); art 39(1)(c).
330 See Rauch (n 298) 29–30.
331 L M Alexander 'International Straits' in H B Robertson Jr (ed) *The Law of Naval Operations* (International Law Studies 64, US Naval War College, Newport 1991) 91, 104–5.
332 Mayama (n 307) 9–10. 333 Ibid.
334 See UK *Manual of the Law of Armed Conflict* § 13.10–13.20; US *Naval Commander's Handbook* § 7.3.6; Germany *Humanitarian Law Manual* § 1126; Canada *LOAC Manual* § 812.

Article 39(1) of the LOSC provides that ships and aircraft involved in transit passage must refrain from the threat or use of force against the sovereignty, territorial integrity, or political independence of States bordering the strait.[335] Transiting States are also required to proceed without delay and to 'refrain from any activities other than those incident to their normal modes of continuous and expeditious transit unless rendered necessary by *force majeure* or distress.'[336] These requirements are contained in a number of military manuals.[337] They are additional to the requirements on transit imposed by the law of neutrality, including the duty not to use neutral straits as a sanctuary or as a base of operations.[338]

Under the LOSC, a State may not deny passage as a result of noncompliance with Article 39.[339] From the point of view of the law of neutrality, however, breach of the requirements of Article 39(1) will compromise the coastal State's neutrality under Articles 1 and 2 of Hague Convention XIII, and the neutral State is required to employ the means at its disposal to terminate the violation. If it does not use the means at its disposal to vindicate rights that have been violated, a neutral State is deemed to acquiesce in the violation of its rights.[340] In certain circumstances, therefore, if the violation of neutrality is not terminated, the opposing belligerent could take measures to respond to the threat posed by the violation.[341]

The application of the transit passage regime to the law of neutrality should be accepted for the same reasons as for the adoption of innocent passage. State practice is inconclusive with regard to the application of the transit passage regime to the law of neutrality.[342] The Iran-Iraq war provides some evidence of States having recourse to the concept of transit passage under the law of the sea. Much of the practice concerns the right of a belligerent, Iran, to prohibit or restrict transit passage by neutral ships.[343]

Iran first announced that it would, 'in view of its international obligations', keep the Strait of Hormuz open.[344] It subsequently attempted to close the Strait of Hormuz.[345] Iran insisted that the right of transit passage through a belligerent strait was not established in customary international law, and bound only State

[335] LOSC art 39(1)(b). [336] LOSC art 39(1)(a) and (c).

[337] UK *Manual of the Law of Armed Conflict* § 13.17; Canada *LOAC Manual* § 818; US *Naval Commander's Handbook* § 7.3.6; *San Remo Manual* § 30.

[338] UK *Manual of the Law of Armed Conflict* § 13.18; Canada *LOAC Manual* § 806; US *Naval Commander's Handbook* § 7.3.6; *San Remo Manual* § 30.

[339] Mayama (n 307) 17; Lowe (n 308) 671. [340] Tucker *Neutrality at Sea* 260–1.

[341] *San Remo Manual* § 22; UK *Manual of the Law of Armed Conflict* § 13.9E; Canada *LOAC Manual* § 811(2).

[342] Robertson Jr (n 305) 21–2.

[343] For the issues surrounding belligerent international straits see generally von Heinegg (n 316) 264–7; Baxter (n 315) 204.

[344] See (1981) 85 RGDIP 174. See also UNSC 'Letter dated 21 October 1980 from the Charge d'affaires of the Permanent Mission of Iran to the United Nations addressed to the Secretary-General' (22 October 1980) UN Doc S/14226.

[345] S Amin 'The Iran-Iraq War: Legal Implications' (1982) 6 MP 193, 209–10.

parties to the LOSC.[346] It therefore argued that it was entitled, on the basis of customary international law, to prevent passage through the Strait. This met with strong protest from neutral States, who suggested that the concept of transit passage was applicable even in belligerent international straits in time of international armed conflict. The Netherlands stated that:

> ...It is now quite generally recognised that a coastal State may extend its territorial sea to 12 sea miles, *provided* that the right of free passage through the resultant 'straits' (in the legal sense) continues in force.
>
> Like the right of free navigation on the high seas, the right of free passage is subject to certain restrictions when a coastal State is at war. Nevertheless, an absolute prohibition on the passage of ships flying neutral flags, without regard to the nature of their cargo and its hostile origin or destination, is certainly not in accordance with international law.[347]

The US and France issued similar protests.[348] Customary international law does not yet appear to support unrestricted passage through belligerent straits in time of war. It has been suggested that the *Corfu Channel Case's* affirmation of a right of States to send their warships through international straits during a technical state of war without authorization[349] provides 'some basis' for the conclusion that a belligerent is under an obligation to provide passage subject to reasonable measures of security and control.[350] However, the matter must remain subject to doubt.

Oman also claimed the Strait of Hormuz as its territorial sea.[351] At the third UN Conference on the Law of the Sea, Oman had rejected the concept of transit passage.[352] Oman subsequently contended that the application of the transit passage regime 'does not preclude a coastal State from taking such appropriate measures as are necessary to protect its interest of peace and security.'[353] Oman therefore rejected the application of the transit passage concept to the Strait of Hormuz.[354] Practice is therefore inconclusive with regard to the application of transit passage to neutral straits.

States have asserted the right to various defensive measures in neutral international straits. These measures, listed in military manuals, although varying

[346] UNSC 'Note Verbale dated 7 July 1988 from the Interests Section of the Islamic Republic of Iran in Washington addressed to the Embassy of Algeria in Washington' (15 March 1989) UN Doc S/20525. See also (1985) 5 LOSB 42.

[347] (1982) 13 NYIL 175, 259.

[348] For the reaction, of the US, see: (1985) 85 DSB 9; (1986) 86 DSB 71; (1987) 87 DSB 52; M N Leich 'Contemporary Practice of the United States Relating to International Law' (1984) 78 AJIL 885. For the reaction of France, see (1981) 27 AFDI 895; (1987) 33 AFDI 849.

[349] *The Corfu Channel Case* [1949] ICJ Rep 4, 28.

[350] Baxter (n 315) 204.

[351] Amin (n 345) 209.

[352] See S Mahmoudi 'Passage of Warships Through the Strait of Hormuz' (1991) 15 MP 338, 345.

[353] (1985) 5 LOSB 42.

[354] For strong criticism of Oman's position see Mahmoudi (n 352) 347.

slightly in detail, include the launching and recovery of aircraft, screen formation steaming, as well as acoustic and electronic surveillance.[355] It must be doubted whether some of these measures are compatible with innocent passage under the law of neutrality. In particular, there has been uncertainty regarding the compatibility of the launching and recovery of aircraft and the requirements of the LOSC, as the ability to launch and recover aircraft seems to be a very different proposition from the concept of overflight through international straits.[356]

c. Environmental Damage to Neutral States

In customary international law, 'due regard' must be given to the protection of the environment in any attack launched.[357] It could be argued that neutral States have an absolute immunity from environmental damage because of the neutral State's right to inviolability. As has been noted, however, the concept of the inviolability of the neutral State did not imply absolute immunity in the traditional law; the immunity of the neutral State was instead dependent on the neutral State discharging its neutral obligations. Hence under the traditional law the aggrieved belligerent could take action in neutral territory to redress the violation.

There was little discussion, until the Harvard Draft Convention on the Rights and Duties of Neutral States in Naval and Aerial War, of the possibility of belligerent damage to neutral States. Article 18 of the Draft Convention states that a 'belligerent shall not engage in hostile operations on, under or over the high seas so near to the territory of a neutral State as to endanger life or property therein.'[358] The commentary expresses the view that the article 'appears sound in principle although there is little express authority for it.'[359] In World War II, State practice regarding damage by belligerents to Swiss territory resulted in compensation.[360] While that practice indicates that belligerents will be liable for damage caused by belligerent acts, it appeared to confirm that neutral States do not, by virtue of their status alone, have a general immunity from environmental damage caused by international armed conflict.

Additional Protocol I contains a number of articles relating to environmental protection. Article 35(3) provides that:

355 UK *Manual of the Law of Armed Conflict* § 13.18; Canada *LOAC Manual* § 819; US *Naval Commander's Handbook* § 7.3.6; *San Remo Manual* § 30.

356 Lowe (n 298) 122; Mayama (n 307) 16.

357 J M Henckaerts and L Doswald Beck (eds) *Customary International Humanitarian Law* vol I (CUP, Cambridge 2005) 147.

358 Harvard Draft Convention on Neutrality (n 38) art 18.

359 Commentary on Harvard Draft Convention on Neutrality (n 51) 343.

360 On this point see Commission (EC) 'Protection of the Environment in Times of Armed Conflict: Report Established by a Study Group (Bothe, Cassese, Kalshoven, Kiss, Salmon and Simmonds)' (1984) 62–6.

> It is prohibited to employ methods or means of warfare which are intended, or may be expected, to cause widespread, long-term and severe damage to the natural environment.[361]

Article 55 appears in Part IV, on the protection of the civilian population, and provides that:

> 1. Care shall be taken in warfare to protect the natural environment against widespread, long-term and severe damage. This protection includes a prohibition of the use of methods or means of warfare which are intended or may be expected to cause such damage to the natural environment and thereby to prejudice the health or survival of the population.
> 2. Attacks against the natural environment by way of reprisals are prohibited.[362]

The literature is divided on the meaning of the 'natural environment' in these provisions and how they are to relate.[363] The most convincing view, however, is that Article 35(3) protects the natural environment in a general fashion while Article 55 protects the environment for the sake of the civilian population.[364]

There is nothing in either Article 35(3) or Article 55 that implies that they are limited to situations in which damage is caused to a State party. Hence the view has been put forward that Article 35(3) and Article 55 are to apply to neutral States as well.[365] This view presents certain difficulties, however. It is recognized that the threshold contemplated by Additional Protocol I is a high one: damage must be 'widespread, long-term and severe.' Since the relationship between belligerents and neutral States is governed by the law of peace, the peacetime customary law standard of damage may in fact be lower than that under Additional Protocol I. The *San Remo Manual* thus employs the peacetime standard, stating that methods and means of warfare should be employed with 'due regard for the natural environment taking into account the relevant rules of international law.'[366] Hence it must be concluded that neutral States enjoy no added protection from environmental damage arising out of armed conflict.

[361] AP I art 35(3). [362] AP I art 55. [363] See, for example, Dinstein (n 192) 202–3.

[364] See W H von Heinegg and M Donner 'New Developments in the Protection of the Natural Environment in Naval Armed Conflicts' (1994) 37 GYIL 281, 284–5.

[365] See the comments of R Lagoni in W H von Heinegg (ed) *Methods and Means of Combat in Naval Warfare: Report & Commentaries of the Round-Table of Experts on International Humanitarian Law Applicable to Armed Conflicts at Sea* (Bochumer Schriften 8, Universitätsverlag Brockmeyer, Bochum 1992) 115–16.

[366] *San Remo Manual* § 44.

9. Conclusion

The purpose of this chapter has been to consider the content of the rights and duties of neutral States, and to determine how those rights and duties have evolved since 1907. What the analysis has demonstrated is the continued recourse to elements of these rights and duties in contemporary State practice, but also the inadequacy of certain rules of neutrality in the present international landscape and the uncertainty as to whether these rules still apply.

The chapter first considered the contention that the law of neutrality had been reduced to its basic principles. Little evidence has been advanced for this claim, and positive international law demonstrates that many of the rights and duties of neutral States continue to be invoked. To the extent that the law of neutrality embodies a principle, it is the principle of impartiality. Although certain writers have contended that impartiality is a core duty of neutrality, impartiality in the law of neutrality is, in fact, a principle that guides the application of the duties of neutrality. In many ways, the principle of impartiality is the corollary of the principle of the equal application of the law of armed conflict between belligerents; the principle of impartiality in the law of neutrality similarly guides a neutral State's discharge of its obligations towards both belligerents. For example, the duty of impartiality guides the application of the duty of abstention, because if a neutral State tolerates the infringement of its neutral status by a belligerent, it fails to comply with the duty of abstention because that belligerent is provided with an advantage over its adversary.[367]

While the concept of impartiality has a strong claim to be regarded as a principle rather than a specific duty, therefore, the remainder of the chapter has been devoted to an analysis of the principal duties and rights of the neutral State. State practice in the twentieth and the twenty-first centuries indicates that the ambit of a number of these duties is unclear. For example, the duty of abstention, which may be said to occupy a fundamental place in the law of neutrality, has been constantly violated because its contours are quite unclear. The prohibition on the sale of military material, although referred to by States in numerous international armed conflicts, suffers from definitional uncertainties and a lack of clarity regarding the scope of the duty. Similarly, this is so with regard to the prohibition on economic assistance to a belligerent.

Many of the difficulties that surround the ambit of these neutral duties stems from the nineteenth century distinction between the State and the citizen that continues to be reflected in a number of rules and that has led to widespread violations of the rules of neutrality. The problem of volunteers is a case in point; the

[367] See the discussion in Commission (EC) 'Protection of the Environment in Times of Armed Conflict: Report Established by a Study Group (Bothe, Cassese, Kalshoven, Kiss, Salmon and Simmonds)' (1984) 51.

distinction between recruiting operations organized by a State and the departure of volunteers from neutral territory is of little assistance in clarifying, for example, the obligations of neutral States with regard to private military and security companies that may operate from their territory.

Other aspects of the content of the law of neutrality have not adapted to developments in international law with regard to the law on the use of force and the law of the sea. For example, while certain elements of the law of neutrality, such as the concept of a base of operations, have a certain currency in international law, other aspects of the neutral's duty of prevention, in particular the consequences of a neutral's failure to discharge its duty of prevention, are out of step with the law on the use of force. Nevertheless, based on its incorporation into various national military manuals, the rule is still considered to be valid by a number of prominent States.

Therefore, while the law of neutrality continues to be expressed in concrete rights and duties rather than principles, examination of a number of those rights and duties demonstrates that many of them are no longer adequate to the contemporary legal environment.

Chapter 4
Neutrality and the UN Charter

In his seminal article on Grotius and international society, Hedley Bull observed that '[t]he doctrine of collective security really literally amounts to an elimination of the right of neutrality; everybody has a duty to participate in the collective system.'[1] Following the devastation of World War II, it was envisaged that the law of war would take on a marginal cast, replaced by the UN Charter as the authoritative mechanism for the regulation of international security.[2] According to Fenwick—whose sentiments were shared by other writers—it was to be hoped that the Charter would usher in an 'advance from neutrality to collective responsibility' so that the law of war and neutrality could be written solely 'in the past tense.'[3]

According to the design of the Charter, aggression on the part of one State would be met with a community response by the Security Council.[4] This approach faltered as the original scheme of the Charter was frustrated by the political deadlock of the Cold War. As the prospects for collective security waned, the view emerged that there was some scope for the co-existence of the UN Charter and the law of neutrality.

But unlike the application of the law of armed conflict to UN forces, which has received extensive academic consideration, there has been little attempt to examine the relationship between the law of neutrality and the Charter in detail.[5] The purpose of this chapter is to move beyond summary analysis and to consider the ways in which the Charter, and the evolving practice of the Security Council, has affected the ability of States to exercise the rights and duties of neutrality.

[1] H Bull 'The Grotian Conception of International Society' in K Anderson and A Hurrell (eds) *Hedley Bull on International Society* (Macmillan, Basingstoke 2000) 95, 121.

[2] E C Stowell 'The Juridical Significance of World War II' (1944) 38 AJIL 106, 107; G Best *War and Law Since 1945* (Clarendon Press, Oxford 1994) 67.

[3] C G Fenwick '"The Old Order Changeth, Yielding Place to New"' (1953) 47 AJIL 84, 86–7.

[4] T M Franck *Recourse to Force: State Action Against Threats and Armed Attacks* (CUP, Cambridge 2002) 2.

[5] Important early work includes J F Lalive 'International Organisation and Neutrality' (1947) 24 BYBIL 73; T Komarnicki 'The Place of Neutrality in the Modern System of International Law' (1952-I) 80 RCADI 399; T Komarnicki 'The Problem of Neutrality under the United Nations Charter' (1953) 38 TGS 77; H J Taubenfeld 'International Actions and Neutrality' (1953) 47 AJIL 377. The most recent discussion of the topic appears in Swedish: O Bring *Neutralitetens uppgång och fall—eller den kollektiva säkerhetens historia* (Atlantis, Stockholm 2008).

1. UN Operations and the Law of Armed Conflict

a. Arguments for the Non-Application of the Law of Armed Conflict to UN Operations

Since the early years of the UN, various arguments were advanced as to why UN military operations were not bound by the law of armed conflict.[6] The most frequent arguments why UN military operations are not bound by the law of armed conflict have focused on two principal issues: (i) the equality of parties under the *jus in bello*; and (ii) the nature of UN enforcement action and its differences from traditional situations of international armed conflict.

i. Legal character of UN enforcement action

One argument deployed in support of the view that the United Nations need not comply with the law of armed conflict is that the law of armed conflict was formulated to apply between States, and that the situation cannot be extended by analogy to military action undertaken under the auspices of the UN. According to George Scelle, the law of armed conflict did not need to be updated in the era of the UN Charter because '[w]ar and the use of an international police force were two essentially different and even diametrically opposed ideas.'[7]

In 1952, the Committee on the Study of Legal Problems of the United Nations, set up by the American Society of International Law, agreed with Scelle that the use of force by the UN was of a different character to the use of force by a State.[8] The Committee concluded that UN forces were free to adhere to the law of armed conflict on a discretionary basis:

> In the present circumstances, then, the proper answer would seem to be, for the time being, that the United Nations should not feel bound by all the laws of war,

[6] S Wills 'Military Interventions on Behalf of Vulnerable Populations: the Legal Responsibilities of States and International Organisations Engaged in Peace Support Operations' (2004) 9 JCSL 387; J P Bialke 'United Nations Peace Operations: Applicable Norms and the Application of the Law of Armed Conflict' (2001) 50 AFLR 1; P C Szasz 'UN Forces and International Humanitarian Law' in M N Schmitt (ed) *International Law Across the Spectrum of Conflict: Essays in Honour of Professor L C Green on the Occasion of his Eightieth Birthday* (International Law Studies 75, US Naval War College, Newport 2000) 507; C Greenwood 'International Humanitarian Law and United Nations Military Operations' (1998) 1 YBIHL 3; D Shraga 'The United Nations as an Actor Bound by International Humanitarian Law' (1998) 5 IP 64; B D Tittemore 'Belligerents in Blue Helmets: Applying International Humanitarian Law to United Nations Peace Operations' (1997) 33 SJIL 61; C Greenwood 'Protection of Peacekeepers: The Legal Regime' (1996) 7 DJCIL 185; J Peck 'The UN and the Laws of War: How can the World's Peacekeepers be Held Accountable?' (1995) 21 SJILC 283; D Schindler 'United Nations Forces and International Humanitarian Law' in C Swinarski (ed) *Studies and Essays on International Humanitarian Law* (Martinus Nijhoff, The Hague 1984) 521.

[7] YBILC (1949) 51.

[8] Committee on Study of Legal Problems of the United Nations 'Should the Laws of War Apply to United Nations Enforcement Action?' (1952) 46 PAS 216, 220.

> but should select such of the laws of war as may seem to fit its purposes...adding such others as may be needed and rejecting those which seem incompatible with its purposes.[9]

Others acknowledged that, although the UN Charter does not mention 'war' or 'armed conflict' in its substantive articles, the law of armed conflict was nevertheless applicable to UN military operations: the regulation of conflict could not depend on the terminology used to describe a particular type of military operation.[10] The argument that UN enforcement action does not possess the character of war can no longer be regarded as decisive.[11]

ii. The aggressor state and the law of armed conflict

Perhaps the most dominant argument advanced in support of the view that the law of armed conflict did not apply to the UN concerned the legal status of the enemy. Since the prohibition of the threat or use of force in Article 2(4), a State that went to war illegally was in the position of an 'outlaw' and could not benefit from the law of armed conflict.[12] This argument was often framed in terms of the principle of *ex injuria jus non oritur*, according to which a State that has illegally initiated armed conflict cannot seek to obtain rights arising from the illegal situation.[13]

This view is defensible logically, but questionable on a number of grounds. First, the status of the maxim of *ex injuria jus non oritur* as a general principle of law is not established in international law.[14] Secondly, the application of the principle to armed conflict was considered unrealistic given the practical difficulties of implementing the Charter provisions on the use of force.[15] The discretionary concept of war therefore proved to be unworkable. Bowett noted as early as 1964 that 'it would appear to be as yet unaccepted that United Nations Forces, absent other legal considerations, are released from the control of the law of war because of the legal status of its opponent.'[16]

[9] Ibid.

[10] H J Taubenfeld 'International Armed Forces and the Rules of War' (1951) 45 AJIL 671, 673–4; F Seyersted *United Nations Forces in the Law of Peace and War* (A W Sijthoff, Leiden 1966) 197–203.

[11] Greenwood (n 6) 14.

[12] On the concept of 'outlaw' States generally see G Simpson *Great Powers and Outlaw States: Unequal Sovereigns in the International Legal Order* (CUP, Cambridge 2004).

[13] Q Wright 'The Outlawry of War and the Law of the War' (1953) 47 AJIL 365, 370–1.

[14] S Talmon 'The Constitutive Versus the Declaratory Theory of Recognition: *Tertium non Datur?*' (2005) 75 BYBIL 101, 128.

[15] See R D Sloane 'The Cost of Conflation: Preserving the Dualism of *Jus ad Bellum* and *Jus in Bello* in the Contemporary Law of War' (2009) 34 YJIL 47, 71.

[16] D W Bowett *United Nations Forces: A Legal Study of United Nations Practice* (Stevens & Sons, London 1964) 496.

b. Basis for the Application of the Law of Armed Conflict to UN Operations

The arguments advanced for the non-application of the law of armed conflict to UN operations are unconvincing, and practice now confirms that the law of armed conflict applies to UN military operations.[17]

In cases where Member States undertake enforcement action authorized by the UN Security Council but under national command and control, the situation is clear: those forces are bound by the law of armed conflict, as States parties to the relevant treaties have an obligation to ensure that their nationals are in compliance with the obligations contained in those treaties.

The situation is more difficult when the UN itself has command and control over enforcement action. The UN is not a party to the Hague Conventions of 1907 or the Geneva Conventions of 1949.[18] However, as the International Court of Justice stated in its Advisory Opinion on *Reparation for Injuries Suffered in the Service of the United Nations*, the UN 'is a subject of international law and capable of possessing international rights and duties.'[19] Hence the customary international law of armed conflict will apply to forces under UN command and control. The UN has itself repeatedly acknowledged that UN forces are to comply with the 'principles and spirit' of the law of armed conflict.[20] In 1999, the UN Secretary-General issued a bulletin which acknowledged that the fundamental 'rules and principles' of international humanitarian law are applicable to UN forces in situations of armed conflict.[21]

2. The UN Charter and the Law of Neutrality

While it is accepted that the law of armed conflict applies to UN forces engaged in UN peace operations, there are certain areas in which the inequality or imbalance between the UN and a State against which it is taking Chapter VII action has legal effect. This inequality extends to international responsibility for the consequences

[17] See, for example, UN Secretariat 'UN Secretary-General's Bulletin: Observance by United Nations Forces of International Humanitarian Law' (6 August 1999) UN Doc ST/SGB/1999/13; Institut de Droit International 'Conditions of Application of Humanitarian Rules of Armed Conflict to Hostilities in which United Nations Forces may be Engaged' (Session of Zagreb, 1971).

[18] Shraga (n 6) 67.

[19] *Reparation for Injuries Suffered in the Service of the United Nations* (Advisory Opinion) [1949] ICJ Rep 174, 179.

[20] UNGA 'Annex: Draft Model Agreement Between the United Nations and Member States Contributing Personnel and Equipment to the United Nations Peace-Keeping Operations' (23 May 1991) UN Doc A/46/185 [28]. The UN has also referred to the 'principles and spirit' of the law of armed conflict in Status of Forces Agreements (SOFAs) that it has concluded with host States. See Shraga (n 6) 68. For criticism see Greenwood (n 6) 22–3.

[21] 'UN Secretary-General's Bulletin' (n 17) [1.1].

of the unlawful use of force: following its 1990 invasion and occupation of Kuwait, Iraq was held liable for damage and loss arising from its unlawful use of force.[22] Another area in which the inequality between an aggressor and the UN is apparent is with regard to the law of occupation: there exist numerous instances in which the law of occupation, although in theory applicable to UN forces in a particular factual situation, has not been applied by UN forces.[23] It is arguably with regard to the law of neutrality, however, that there exists significant room for a differential application between the UN and an aggressor.[24]

The arguments advanced against the application of the law of armed conflict to the UN were similarly asserted with regard to the law of neutrality. It was generally perceived that the UN Charter had effected a profound modification of the rights and duties of neutral States, if it had not eliminated it entirely.[25] Arguments for the non-application of the law of neutrality to UN operations focus principally on the radical incommensurability between elements of the law of neutrality and the UN Charter itself.[26]

a. The Duty of Assistance to the UN

While the UN Charter does not contain any provision that prevents, in theory, compliance with the law of armed conflict, there are certain provisions of the Charter that appear to prevent a Member State adhering to the duties of neutrality by imposing certain obligations of co-operation.

The second limb of Article 2(5)—the duty not to assist a State against which the Security Council is taking enforcement action—would appear to be established in customary international law as a corollary of the prohibition of the use of force.[27] The first part of Article 2(5) of the Charter is potentially more radical; it provides that:

[22] See UNSC Res 687 (3 April 1991) UN Doc S/RES/687 [16].

[23] For treatment of the difficult question of when UN forces are bound by the law of occupation, see D Scheffer 'The Security Council and International Law on Military Occupations' in V Lowe et al (eds) *The United Nations Security Council and War: The Evolution of Thought and Practice since 1945* (OUP, Oxford 2008) 580; S Wills 'Occupation Law and Multi-National Operations: Problems and Perspectives' (2006) 77 BYBIL 256; A Roberts 'What is a Military Occupation?' (1984) 66 BYBIL 249, 289–91.

[24] H Lauterpacht 'The Limits of the Operation of the Laws of War' (1953) 30 BYBIL 206, 237.

[25] See, for example, UK *The Law of War on Land* [653](2). Cf US *Land Warfare Manual* [513].

[26] See, for example, C G Dehn 'The Effect of the United Nations Charter on the Development of International Law with Special Reference to the Status on Neutrality and the Hague and Geneva Conventions' in International Law Association Report of the Forty-First Conference (Cambridge 1946) (International Law Association, Cambridge 1946) 39, 42–3; 'The Present Position of "Neutral" States' (1947) 1 ILQ 212, 214.

[27] Seyersted (n 10) 286.

> All Members shall give the United Nations every assistance in any action it takes in accordance with the present Charter...[28]

The insertion of a positive duty to assist the UN marked an advance upon the Covenant of the League of Nations. An obligation to give the UN 'every assistance' in 'any action', when interpreted strictly, indicates an intention to prevent States from having reference to the law of neutrality at all. For example, if 'every assistance' is to include the provision of military forces for participation in armed conflict, as well as logistical assistance on a massive scale, Article 2(5) would appear to impose an obligation of partiality towards the UN in every circumstance; a State would be prevented not only from discharging its duties of neutrality, but may lose the status of a neutral State altogether.[29]

There is some evidence that this intention was behind the drafting of Article 2(5). Originally, Article 2(5) was drafted as two principles in the Dumbarton Oaks proposals.[30] The Norwegian delegate to the San Francisco Conference argued that the obligation of assistance contained in Article 2(5) required participation in collective action by the United Nations.[31] The French delegation suggested an addition to what would become Article 2(5): 'sans qu'un état puisse, pour s'y soustraire, invoquer un statut de neutralité.'[32] In referring to 'un statut de neutralité' the French delegation was referring to a status of permanent neutrality.[33] The amendment was eventually discarded because it was thought clear, from its terms, that permanent neutrality was incompatible with Article 2(5).[34]

The phrase 'any action', although on its face suggesting wide applicability, appears primarily to refer to enforcement action under Chapter VII.[35] Case law suggests a more restricted approach, however. The International Court of Justice has taken the view that the use of the phrase 'action' in Article 11(2) of the UN Charter refers to coercive or enforcement action pursuant to Chapter VII.[36] It is submitted that a similar meaning is to be given to the phrase 'any action' in Article 2(5), as a broader interpretation would blur the careful distinction between

[28] UN Charter art 2(5).

[29] H Meyrowitz *Le principe de l'égalité des belligérants devant le droit de la guerre* (Éditions A Pedone, Paris 1970) 343.

[30] L M Goodrich et al *Charter of the United Nations: Commentary and Documents* (3rd edn Columbia UP, New York 1969) 56.

[31] III UNCIO 355. [32] VI UNCIO 722. [33] Ibid.

[34] J A Frowein and N Krisch 'Article 2(5)' in B Simma et al (eds) *The Charter of the United Nations: A Commentary* (2nd edn OUP, Oxford 2002) 136, 137.

[35] In contrast, Article 25 of the Charter is not confined to decisions regarding enforcement action but applies to decisions of the Security Council taken in accordance with the Charter. See *Legal Consequences for States of the Continued Presence of South Africa in Namibia (South West Africa) Notwithstanding Security Council Resolution 276 (1970)* (Advisory Opinion) [1971] ICJ Rep 16, 52–3.

[36] *Certain Expenses of the United Nations (Article 17, paragraph 2 of the Charter)* (Advisory Opinion) ICJ Rep [1962] 151, 164–5. See also C F Amerasinghe 'The Charter *Travaux Préparatoires* and United Nations Powers to Use Armed Force' (1966) 4 CYIL 81, 92.

recommendations and binding obligations under Chapter VII and upset the structure of the Charter.[37]

It remains to be established what is meant by 'assistance.' Early interpretations of this phrase clearly contemplated military assistance. The *US Law of Naval Warfare Manual* issued in 1955 noted that, pursuant to Article 2(5), 'the members of the United Nations may be obliged to give assistance with their armed forces to the United Nations in its enforcement actions, the fulfilment of which obligation is incompatible with the status of neutrality.'[38] In 1955, it may still have been envisaged that the agreements under Article 43, placing national contingents at the disposal of the UN, would eventually come into existence. As is well known, however, no such agreements have been formulated, and there is no obligation to furnish military assistance to the UN in their absence.[39] Hence the conclusion must be that Article 2(5) could not impose upon Member States an obligation to provide military assistance.[40] Indeed, reference to the intentions of the drafters appears to indicate that States are under no obligation to give further assistance than is required from them on the basis of Articles 41 and 42.[41]

b. The UN and the Duty of Non-Assistance to an Aggressor

Pursuant to the second limb of Article 2(5), the UN Charter also imposes a duty of non-assistance on Member States, by requiring Member States to prohibit assistance to States against which the United Nations is taking preventive or enforcement action. Here the duty explicitly refers to action under Chapter VII.[42]

Like the first limb of Article 2(5), the obligation not to assist a State that is the object of Chapter VII action may override certain duties a State would otherwise have under the law of neutrality. For example, under Article 9 of Hague Convention XIII, a neutral State must not discriminate between belligerents in regard to admission into its ports, roadsteads, or territorial waters.[43] If admission into ports and territorial waters is regarded as 'assistance' however, then pursuant to Article 2(5) a neutral State would be required to discriminate between

[37] L M Goodrich and A P Simons *The United Nations and the Maintenance of International Peace and Security* (Greenwood Press, Westport 1955) 14; Frowein and Krisch (n 34) 138; Lalive (n 5) 78.

[38] US *Law of Naval Warfare Manual* 366.

[39] See, for example, H Blix *Sovereignty, Aggression and Neutrality* (Dag Hammarskjöld Foundation, Sweden 1970) 46.

[40] On this point see E de Wet *The Chapter VII Powers of the United Nations Security Council* (Hart, Oxford 2004) 261–2.

[41] Frowein and Krisch (n 34) 138.

[42] Ibid 137. Frowein and Krisch note that the concept of 'preventive' action contemplates action under Article 40 of the Charter.

[43] HC XIII art 9.

belligerents and to refuse admission to a State that is the object of preventive or enforcement action.[44]

c. The Duty to Implement Security Council Measures

Upon the Security Council making a determination under Article 39 and proceeding to measures under Articles 41 and 42, members of the Security Council are compelled to carry out those measures: Article 25 provides that UN members 'agree to accept and carry out the decisions of the Security Council in accordance with the present Charter.'[45] In contrast to a bilateral relationship between a violating and injured State, which creates only a right in the injured State to take action in response, there exists a direct relationship between Member States and the UN, and a duty to implement those measures if they are taken in accordance with Article 25.[46]

This necessarily means that the Charter will take priority over other international obligations. Article 103 provides that:

> In the event of a conflict between the obligations of the Members of the United Nations under the present Charter and their obligations under any other international agreement, their obligations under the present Charter shall prevail.[47]

Article 103 has been described as the 'basic law' for the international community.[48] It operates to ensure that obligations under the Charter are given priority over other international obligations when a situation of conflict between legal norms emerges.[49]

There exists some uncertainty, however, as to whether Article 103 prevails over both treaty and custom.[50] The drafting history indicates that this issue

[44] R R Baxter 'The Legal Consequences of the Unlawful Use of Force Under the Charter' (1968) 62 PAS 68, 73; Castrén *Neutrality* 435; cf Oppenheim (7th edn) vol II 649.

[45] UN Charter art 25.

[46] V Gowlland-Debbas 'Security Council Enforcement Action and Issues of State Responsibility' (1994) 43 ICLQ 55, 84; V Gowlland-Debbas 'The Functions of the United Nations Security Council in the International Legal System' in M Byers (ed) *The Role of Law in International Politics: Essays in International Relations and International Law* (OUP, Oxford 2000) 277, 293.

[47] UN Charter art 103.

[48] A Verdross 'General International Law and the United Nations Charter' (1954) 30 IA 342, 347.

[49] On this point see UNGA 'Fragmentation of International Law: Report of the Study Group of the International Law Commission' (13 April 2006) UN Doc A/CN.4/L.682 [333]-[334]. It has erroneously been claimed that Article 103 serves to invalidate the conflicting treaty: B Fassbender 'The United Nations Charter as Constitution of the International Community' (1998) 36 CJTL 529, 590.

[50] N D White and A Abass 'Countermeasures and Sanctions' in M D Evans (ed) *International Law* (2nd edn OUP, Oxford 2006) 509, 528.

was not specifically considered.[51] On its face, Article 103 speaks only of 'obligations under any other international agreement' and the strict position must be that Article 103 does not affect customary law obligations.[52] It has nevertheless been suggested that the object and purpose of the Charter demands its prevalence by analogy over customary obligations as well as treaties.[53] This now seems to be the dominant view, which is supported by the principle of *lex posterior derogat lex priori*.[54] In *R (Al-Jedda) v Secretary of State for Defence*, it was emphasized by Lord Bingham that the term 'obligations' in Article 103 should not be given a 'narrow, contract-based meaning.'[55] This view is also supported by the practice of the Security Council, which has been premised on the understanding that its resolutions prevail over conflicting customary obligations.[56] Thus if the law of neutrality and the obligations of the Charter may be said to conflict, the Charter obligations pursuant to Article 103 will prevail over the law of neutrality. To what extent two particular norms are in conflict is an issue that may be difficult to discern.[57] Pauwelyn has noted that a relationship of conflict exists between two norms of international law if one norm constitutes, has led to, or may lead to, a breach of the other.[58] Article 103 also has the effect of precluding wrongfulness in the law of responsibility.[59]

States have occasionally been drawn on the effects of the UN Charter on adherence to the Hague Conventions on neutrality. In 1955, in response to an enquiry by The Netherlands, the Soviet Union stated that the Charter took priority over the Hague Conventions:

[51] R Liivoja 'The Scope of the Supremacy Clause of the United Nations Charter' (2008) 57 ICLQ 583, 605.

[52] Y Dinstein 'The Interaction Between Customary International Law and Treaties' (2006) 322 RCADI 243, 418; A Orakhelashvili 'The Impact of Peremptory Norms on the Interpretation and Application of United Nations Security Council Resolutions' (2005) 16 EJIL 59, 69.

[53] R Bernhardt 'Article 103' in B Simma et al (eds) *The Charter of the United Nations: A Commentary* (2nd edn OUP, Oxford 2002) 1292, 1298–9.

[54] M Wood 'The UN Security Council and International Law: The Legal Framework of the Security Council' (Hersch Lauterpacht Memorial Lectures, University of Cambridge 2006) (7 November 2006) 19 <http://www.lcil.cam.ac.uk/Media/lectures/pdf/2006_hersch_lecture_1.pdf> accessed 20 December 2006.

[55] *R (Al-Jedda) v Secretary of State for Defence* [2008] 1 AC 332 [34] per Lord Bingham of Cornhill.

[56] 'Fragmentation of International Law' (n 49) [345].

[57] J Pauwelyn *Conflict of Norms in Public International Law: How WTO Law Relates to other Rules of International Law* (CUP, Cambridge 2003) 176; W Czapliński and G Danilenko 'Conflicts of Norms in International Law' (1990) 21 NYIL 3. On conflict in the context of the Security Council, see M Milanović 'Norm Conflict in International Law: Whither Human Rights?' (2009) 20 DJCIL 69; F Messineo 'The House of Lords in *Al-Jedda* and Public International Law: Attribution of Conduct to UN-Authorised Forces and the Power of the Security to Displace Human Rights' (2009) 56 NILR 35, 59–61.

[58] Bernhardt (n 53) 1296.

[59] Gowlland-Debbas 'Security Council Enforcement Action' (n 46) 88.

> The Government of the USSR recognises the Hague conventions and declarations of 1899 and 1907 ratified by Russia, of course only in so far as these conventions and declarations do not run counter to the Charter of the UNO...[60]

The Security Council rarely invokes the specific articles imposing obligations of implementation. One example when it did so was in relation to the impositions of sanctions on Iraq in 1990. Security Council Resolution 661 imposed a comprehensive embargo on Iraq.[61] Following lack of compliance with Resolution 661 by certain States which asserted their right to continue to trade with Iraq, Security Council Resolution 670 noted that the Council was '*determined also* to ensure respect for its decisions and the provisions of Articles 25 and 48 of the Charter of the United Nations,' and '*recall*[ed] the provisions of Article 103 of the Charter.'[62] Resolution 670 therefore emphasized that the obligations of the Charter prevailed over any obligations stemming from the law of neutrality.

Therefore conflicting obligations cannot be invoked in order to exempt a State from compliance with Security Council resolutions. Nor can other factors, such as economic necessity or *force majeure*, be relied upon as a basis for exemption.[63] This is so even though the economic impact of sanctions on third States may be severe. It is only the Security Council itself that has the power to exempt States from binding measures, under Article 48(1) of the Charter.[64] Pursuant to Article 50, a State may have recourse to the Security Council if confronted by special economic problems.[65]

The considerable scope of these obligations to implement the decisions of the Security Council, therefore, suggests a profound modification of the law of neutrality in circumstances when the Security Council takes action under Chapter VII. It is therefore necessary to examine in greater detail Chapter VII of the Charter and how it relates to the law of neutrality. In doing so it is necessary to distinguish between, on the one hand, the application of non-forcible measures by the UN Security Council and, on the other hand, UN military operations.

[60] *Pravda* (Moscow 9 March 1955) cited in G Ginsburgs 'The Soviet Union as a Neutral 1939-1941' (1958) 10 *Soviet Studies* 12, 33 n 14.

[61] UNSC Res 661 (6 August 1990) SCOR Resolutions and Decisions 19.

[62] UNSC Res 670 (25 September 1990) SCOR Resolutions and Decisions 24 preambular para 7 and preambular para 12.

[63] Gowlland-Debbas 'Security Council Enforcement Action' (n 46) 84.

[64] UN Charter art 48(1).

[65] On Article 50 see J Carver and J Hulsmann 'The Role of Article 50 of the UN Charter in the Search for International Peace and Security' (2000) 49 ICLQ 528. On the effect of sanctions on third States see UNGA 'Report of the Special Committee on the Charter of the United Nations and on the Strengthening of the Role of the Organisation: Implementation of the Provisions of the Charter of the United Nations related to Assistance to Third States affected by the Application of Sanctions under Chapter VII of the Charter' (22 August 1995) UN Doc A/50/361.

3. The Law of Neutrality and UN Non-Forcible Measures

Chapter VII of the UN Charter distinguishes between non-forcible measures decided by the UN Security Council under Articles 40 and 41, and forcible measures under Article 42.

a. Determination Under Article 39 of the UN Charter

Under Chapter VII of the Charter, the Security Council is directed to determine the existence of any threat to the peace, breach of the peace, or act of aggression under Article 39 and to decide on any enforcement measures.[66] There is deliberate room for flexibility in the interpretation of what constitutes a 'threat to the peace', a 'breach of the peace' or an 'act of aggression.'[67] These concepts are not defined anywhere in the Charter. Indeed, throughout the past two decades the scope of what is considered to constitute 'threats to international peace and security' has undoubtedly broadened.[68] Although the Council's discretion is broad, it is limited in certain respects.[69] In practice, the Council has most commonly found a 'threat' to international peace and security under Article 39.

Upon a finding under Article 39, the Security Council is empowered to proceed to enforcement action. Before it proceeds to measures under Article 41 and Article 42, however, the Council may, under Article 40, 'call upon the parties concerned to comply with such provisional measures as it deems necessary or desirable.'[70]

The language of Article 39 suggests that a determination of a threat to the peace, breach of the peace, or act of aggression must be made before the Security Council can decide on further action under Chapter VII. However, in practice the Security Council does not always make a determination under Article 39 before proceeding to enforcement action under Articles 41 or 42. Sometimes this is because the Council has passed multiple resolutions on the same topic, and so rather than reaffirming that a situation amounts to a threat to international peace and security it merely refers to a previous resolution.[71]

The Security Council has occasionally initiated action under Chapter VII without reference to Article 39 at all. Security Council Resolution 1160 imposed

[66] UN Charter art 39.

[67] On the flexibility of the Charter's provisions on peace and security see E C Luck 'A Council for All Seasons: The Creation of the Security Council and its Relevance Today' in V Lowe et al (eds) *The United Nations Security Council and War: The Evolution of Thought and Practice since 1945* (OUP, Oxford 2008) 61, 70–3.

[68] S Chesterman *Just War or Just Peace: Humanitarian Intervention and International Law* (OUP, Oxford 2001) chapter 4.

[69] Gowlland-Debbas 'Security Council Enforcement Action' (n 46) 93–4.

[70] UN Charter art 40.

[71] See Chesterman (n 68) 126.

sanctions against the Federal Republic of Yugoslavia, without explicitly noting the existence of a threat or breach of international peace and security, or an act of aggression. Instead, Resolution 1160 stated merely that it was acting under Chapter VII of the Charter.[72] Certain States registered objections. The Russian Federation stated that the resolution indicated that the situation in the region did not amount to a threat to international peace and security.[73] Egypt raised concerns about the constitutional basis of the resolution. It argued that the 'constitutional requirements of the Charter should in general be scrupulously followed and respected.'[74] The Federal Republic of Yugoslavia also argued that the resolution was constitutionally problematic.[75] The position of the UK appeared to be that the action under Chapter VII constituted an implicit determination of a threat to international peace and security. It noted in the Security Council that '... by acting under Chapter VII of the Charter, the Council considers that the situation in Kosovo constitutes a threat to international peace and security in the Balkans region.'[76] The US agreed that the situation implicitly constituted a threat to international peace and security.[77] The Security Council determined in a later resolution that the situation in Kosovo constituted a threat to international peace and security in the region.[78]

Nor do Security Council resolutions always—or even often—refer explicitly to Articles 41 or 42 in deciding upon measures to be taken. More commonly, Security Council resolutions refer 'globally' to Chapter VII and specify measures to be implemented without grounding them in specific articles of the Charter.[79]

It becomes necessary to determine what effect this procedure has on the law of neutrality. It has been contended that the obligations contained in Articles 2(5), 25, and 103 arise as soon as a determination is made under Article 39.[80] However, it is not clear that this is the case if the Security Council does not proceed further through Chapter VII. The Security Council may, in a particular instance, make a determination of a threat to international peace and security and then take no further action. At the outset of the hostilities between the United Kingdom and Argentina over the Falkland Islands, Security Council Resolution 502 determined—somewhat obliquely—that the situation constituted a breach of the peace.[81] It went on to demand an immediate cessation of hostilities, as well as the

[72] UNSC Res 1160 (31 March 1998) UN Doc S/RES/1160 preambular para 8.

[73] UNSC Verbatim Record (31 March 1998) UN Doc S/PV.3868 10 (Russian Federation). Despite stating that there existed no threat to international peace and security, the Russian Federation nevertheless voted in favour of Resolution 1160 imposing sanctions.

[74] Ibid 29 (Egypt).

[75] Ibid 16–17 (Federal Republic of Yugoslavia).

[76] Ibid 12 (United Kingdom).

[77] Ibid 13 (United States).

[78] UNSC Res 1199 (23 September 1998) UN Doc S/RES/1199.

[79] Gowlland-Debbas 'Security Council Enforcement Action' (n 46) 56.

[80] A Orakhelashvili 'The Power of the UN Security Council to Determine the Existence of a "Threat to the Peace"' (2006) 1 Irish YIL 61, 67.

[81] UNSC Res 502 (3 April 1982) SCOR Resolutions and Decisions 15.

withdrawal of all Argentine forces from the Islands.[82] Although it was not indicated explicitly, the Council appeared to be acting under Article 40. The Council did not proceed to take action under Articles 41 or 42.

Since Resolution 502 did not decide on enforcement action, the duty to assist the UN contained in the first limb of Article 2(5) did not explicitly apply. To the extent that the Security Council called for the withdrawal of Argentine forces, it could be argued that the second limb of Article 2(5) was applicable, as that limb has been interpreted as applying to preventive as well as enforcement action.[83] It may be suggested, therefore, that Resolution 502 modified the application of the law of neutrality, as States were prevented from giving 'assistance' to Argentina. The resolution prompted a number of States to depart from a position of neutrality and actively to assist the United Kingdom. The United States, for example, did not actively participate on the side of the United Kingdom, but nor did they comply with neutral duties. It provided significant levels of military aid to the UK, while suspending military aid and loan guarantees to Argentina.[84] Australia banned all imports from Argentina.[85] The European Community adopted sanctions against Argentina.[86]

Similarly, following Security Council 660, which explicitly invoked Article 40 after determining a breach of international peace and security in relation to Iraq's invasion of Kuwait, and proceeded both to condemn Iraq's invasion as well as demand its immediate withdrawal from Kuwait, States were prevented, under Article 2(5) of the Charter, from furnishing assistance to Iraq.[87]

As a matter of Charter law, a determination under Article 39 as well as identification of the State responsible for the breach or threat to the peace or act of aggression permits States to depart from the law of neutrality in favour of the United Nations.[88] At a minimum, however, identification of the State responsible for the determination under Article 39, as occurred in the Falkland Island crisis and the Kuwait crisis, will be necessary to modify the application of neutrality in favour of the United Nations. Absent a determination under Article 39 that identifies the responsible State, *or* further Security Council action under Articles 40 or 41, there exists no obligation on a State to modify the application of neutrality.

In practice, it is often difficult to separate a determination under Article 39 from the specific measures taken under Articles 41 or 42. The principal distinction of relevance for analysing the Charter's relationship with the law

[82] Ibid. [83] Frowein and Krisch (n 34) 137.

[84] See H S Levie *The Code of International Armed Conflict* vol II (Oceana Publications, London 1986) 793.

[85] (1987) 10 AYIL 571–7.

[86] See P J Kuyper 'Community Sanctions Against Argentina: Lawfulness under Community and International Law' in D O'Keeffe and H G Schermers (eds) *Essays in European Law and Integration* (Kluwer, Deventer 1982) 141.

[87] UNSC Res 660 (2 August 1990) SCOR Resolutions and Decisions 19 [1]-[2].

[88] For a similar formulation see *San Remo Manual* § 7–8.

of neutrality, therefore, will be the nature of the measures decided under Chapter VII.

b. The Law of Neutrality and Article 41 of the UN Charter

Article 41 of the Charter provides that:

> The Security Council may decide what measures not involving the use of armed force are to be employed to give effect to its decisions, and it may call upon the Members of the United Nations to apply such measures. These may include complete or partial interruption of economic relations and of rail, sea, air, postal, telegraphic, radio, and other means of communication, and the severance of diplomatic relations.[89]

It has been noted that the inclusive terms of Article 41 give the Security Council great flexibility in determining appropriate measures to be applied in response to a threat to international peace and security.[90]

Not all measures contemplated under Article 41 are necessarily inconsistent with the law of neutrality. For example, diplomatic relations could be severed between a neutral and a belligerent State without a violation of neutrality.[91] If economic sanctions are imposed by the Security Council on a target State that is a party to an international armed conflict, however, the obligations of the Charter are in conflict with the duties that flow from the status of neutrality. Therefore, upon a decision by the Security Council to impose sanctions under Article 41, the legal obligations contained in Article 2(5), Article 25, and Article 103 apply to the exclusion of the duties of the law of neutrality.

This does not mean that the status of neutrality is extinguished for those States that wish to have recourse to it; the imposition of sanctions does not entail participation in an armed conflict. However, it does mean that neutral States are required to deviate from their duties to the extent required by the decision of the Security Council. Hence neutrality continues to subsist but may not be applied equally between the belligerents; the neutral State is required to discriminate between the two.

However, for the law of neutrality to be engaged, and for it to be displaced under Article 41, there must exist an international armed conflict. Two principal scenarios may be envisaged. The first is when the Security Council imposes sanctions on a State engaged in an international armed conflict. The second is when

[89] UN Charter art 41.

[90] J M Farrall *United Nations Sanctions and the Rule of Law* (CUP, Cambridge 2007) 65.

[91] A Gioia 'Neutrality and Non-Belligerency' in H H G Post (ed) *International Economic Law and Armed Conflict* (Martinus Nijhoff, Dordrecht 1994) 51, 71.

an international armed conflict does not exist when sanctions are imposed and those sanctions continue after an international armed conflict breaks out involving the State that is the target of measures under Article 41.

An example of the first kind is provided by the Kuwait crisis in 1990–1991. Security Council Resolution 661 was decided under Chapter VII and addressed to 'all States.'[92] Resolution 661 called on States to prevent, *inter alia*, 'the sale or supply by their nationals or from their territories or using their flag vessels' weapons or military equipment.[93] Following this resolution there existed a direct conflict between the obligations of Member States under the Charter, on the one hand, and the duties of neutrality, on the other. The obligation to comply with Resolution 661 prevailed over the law of neutrality, by virtue of Articles 25 and 103 of the Charter. The target State could not seek to take countermeasures against neutral States for violating duties of neutrality.[94]

An example of the second type is provided by the international armed conflict between Afghanistan and coalition States in 2001. Security Council Resolution 1373, imposing various measures on States to prevent support for terrorism, apparently taken under Article 41, prevented States from applying the law of neutrality equally between the coalition and Afghanistan after the beginning of *Operation Enduring Freedom*.[95]

In practice, almost all the Security Council's decisions under Article 41 have been addressed to 'all States,' not only Member States.[96] Resolution 661, for example, was addressed to all States, 'including States non-members of the United Nations.'[97] The relationship between the Charter and non-members in the context of neutrality has been discussed elsewhere.[98] Now that almost every State is a member of the UN, the issue is of only minor academic interest.[99] Switzerland refused to comply with the Article 41 measures imposed on Southern Rhodesia in 1966.[100] However, Resolution 232 was addressed only to Member States, not 'all States.'[101] During the Kuwait crisis, Switzerland, a permanently neutral State

[92] UNSC Res 661 (n 61) [3]. The constitutional basis of the Charter was not mentioned; instead, the Council noted that it was acting under Chapter VII of the Charter.

[93] Ibid [3](c). [94] Gioia (n 91) 71; Lalive (n 5) 80.

[95] See also A Roberts 'Counterterrorism and the Laws of War: A Critique of the US Approach' (Address at The Brookings Institution, 11 March 2002) <http://www.brookings.edu/events/2002/0311terrorism.aspx> accessed 21 January 2007: 'The sanctions imposed by [the] UN Security Council even before September [2001] on the Taliban and Afghanistan themselves had ruled out pure neutrality on the traditional model.'

[96] Farrall (n 90) 67. [97] UNSC Res 661 (n 61) [5].

[98] D Thürer 'UN Enforcement Measures and Neutrality: The Case of Switzerland' (1992) 30 AdV 63, 69–72; Tucker *Neutrality at Sea* 176; Cf Verdross (n 48) 344–8.

[99] See Farrall (n 90) 66–8.

[100] UNSC Res 232 (16 December 1966) SCOR Resolutions and Decisions 7. See J F L Ross *Neutrality and International Sanctions: Sweden, Switzerland and Collective Security* (Praeger, New York 1989); B A Boczek 'Permanent Neutrality and Collective Security: The Case of Switzerland and the United Nations Sanctions Against Southern Rhodesia' (1969) 1CWRJIL 73.

[101] UNSC Res 232 (n 100) [2], [7].

and not a member of the UN at the time, agreed voluntarily to participate in the sanctions. In 1993, Switzerland noted that:

> By refusing to join in economic sanctions, Switzerland would end up providing moral and de facto support to the country that has broken the law, thwarting measures seeking to impose an economic blockade on that country, and deriving economic benefits from its position while every other country is burdened by participating in the boycott. Such non-participation would obviously be viewed by the international community as favouring the country against which the sanctions have been ordered, and would be very detrimental to Switzerland's image throughout the world.[102]

4. The Nature and Framework of UN Military Operations

The taxonomy of UN military operations is a complicated task. For purposes of examining how UN military operations interact with the law of neutrality, this taxonomy is of secondary importance to the question of when the UN itself becomes a party to an international armed conflict. As with determining when the law of armed conflict becomes applicable to UN military operations, the crucial question is not the authority under the Charter to engage in particular action, but the fact of participation by UN military operations in international armed conflict.[103]

It remains necessary, however, to consider the original design of Chapter VII with regard to military enforcement, before outlining how military enforcement has tended to operate in practice, through authorizations to individual States, groups of States, or regional organizations. This is not the only way in which a UN force may become a party to an international armed conflict. It is therefore necessary also to consider what is known variously as 'robust' or 'extended' peacekeeping operations.

a. The Original Concept of Military Sanctions under the UN Charter

To what extent the UN Charter establishes a system of collective security is a matter of contention.[104] What seems clear, however, is that there was no room for

[102] Switzerland Federal Department of Foreign Affairs 'White Paper on Neutrality: Annex to the Report on Swiss Foreign Policy for the Nineties' (29 November 1993) 19 <http://www.eda.admin.ch/etc/medialib/downloads/edazen/topics/intla/cintla.Par.0027.File.tmp/White_Paper_on_Neutrality.en.pdf> accessed 20 August 2007.

[103] Greenwood (n 6) 11.

[104] See A Roberts and D Zaum *Selective Security: War and the United Nations Security Council since 1945* (Adelphi Paper 395, Routledge, Abingdon 2008); B Urquhart 'Remarks' (1993) 87 PAS 284, 289.

States to remain neutral when the Security Council decided on the use of force.[105] Under the original plan of Chapter VII, Article 43 was of seminal importance. Article 43(1) states that:

> All Members of the United Nations, in order to contribute to the maintenance of international peace and security, undertake to make available to the Security Council, on its call and in accordance with a special agreement or agreements, armed forces, assistance, and facilities, including rights of passage, necessary for the purpose of maintaining international peace and security.[106]

The special agreements were to be negotiated 'as soon as possible' upon the initiative of the Security Council.[107] Under Article 45, in order to enable the United Nations to take urgent military measures, 'Members shall hold immediately available national air-force contingents for combined international enforcement action.'[108]

Under the original scheme of Chapter VII Member States would not have been able to have recourse to the status of neutrality. As Judge Ammoun noted in the ICJ's advisory opinion on the *Legal Consequences for States of the Continued Presence of South Africa in Namibia (South West Africa)*:

> If the provisions of the Charter concerning collective security could have been implemented according to the letter and in the spirit of the San Francisco Conference, there would have been no place for neutrality, at least among States Members of the United Nations.[109]

This continues to be the analysis followed by military manuals, which state that the status of neutrality is lost if military action is ever taken pursuant to Article 43 and Article 42 as originally contemplated.[110]

As is well known, the agreements that were to be concluded under Article 43 have never materialized, despite hopes that the end of the Cold War could have led to the signing of such agreements.[111] Article 43 itself has been described as a 'dead letter.'[112] In the absence of Article 43 agreements, there is no obligation on Member States to participate in UN military operations.[113]

105 Meyrowitz (n 29) 346. 106 UN Charter art 43(1). 107 UN Charter art 43(3).
108 UN Charter art 45.
109 Separate Opinion of Vice-President Ammoun *Legal Consequences for States of the Continued Presence of South Africa in Namibia* (n 35) 92.
110 See for example US *Operational Law Handbook* XIV (B)(2).
111 See UNGA Report of the Secretary-General 'An Agenda for Peace: Preventive Diplomacy, Peacemaking and Peace-Keeping' (17 June 1992) UN Doc A/47/277 [43].
112 *Al-Jedda* (n 55) [29] per Lord Bingham of Cornhill. 113 Gioia (n 91) 73.

b. Authorizations to use military force

Although Chapter VII could not be implemented in the way originally envisaged, the system was sufficiently adaptable to permit the Security Council to take forcible measures in ways not originally contemplated. In its advisory opinion on *Certain Expenses of the United Nations* the ICJ indicated this flexibility:

> [A]n argument which insists that all measures taken for the maintenance of international peace and security must be financed through agreements concluded under Article 43, would seem to exclude the possibility that the Security Council might act under some other Article of the Charter. The Court cannot accept so limited a view of the powers of the Security Council under the Charter. It cannot be said that the Charter has left the Security Council impotent in the face of an emergency situation when agreements under Article 43 have not been concluded.[114]

Subsequent practice confirms that the absence of agreements under Article 43 is not a barrier to enforcement action taken under Article 42.[115] As Frowein has pointed out, action under Article 42 was frequently interpreted as limited to direct action with forces made available to the Security Council under Article 43, but this is not the only possible interpretation of Article 42.[116] According to Article 42 actions may include demonstrations, blockades, and other operations by air, sea, or land forces 'of members' of the United Nations. There is no reference to Article 43.[117] However, one aspect of the relationship between Articles 42 and 43 is that the Security Council cannot oblige Member States to place armed forces at its disposal without agreements according to Article 43.[118]

The Security Council may not, therefore, compel participation by Member States, which has important consequences for the application of the law of neutrality.

In response to the failure of Chapter VII to function as envisaged, the Security Council has adapted by authorizing military enforcement measures passed under

[114] *Certain Expenses of the United Nations* (n 36) 167.

[115] F Berman 'The Authorisation Model: Resolution 678 and Its Effects' in D Malone (ed) *The UN Security Council: From the Cold War to the 21st Century* (Boulder, Lynne Rienner 2004) 153; D Sarooshi *The United Nations and the Development of Collective Security: The Delegation by the UN Security Council of its Chapter VII Powers* (Clarendon Press, Oxford 1999) 144; O Schachter *International Law in Theory and Practice* (Martinus Nijhoff, Dordrecht 1991) 395–6; J W Halderman 'Legal Basis for United Nations Armed Forces' (1962) 56 AJIL 971.

[116] J A Frowein 'Legal Consequences for International Law Enforcement in Case of Security Council Inaction' in J Delbrück (ed) *The Future of International Law Enforcement: New Scenarios—New Law?* (Duncker & Humblot, Berlin 1993) 111, 112.

[117] Ibid.

[118] R Higgins *Problems and Process: International Law and How We Use It* (OUP, Oxford 1994) 265–6; J A Frowein and N Krisch 'Article 43' in B Simma et al (eds) *The Charter of the United Nations: A Commentary* vol I (2nd edn OUP, Oxford 2002) 760, 763.

Chapter VII. The classic form of such resolutions is Security Council Resolution 678, which 'authorise[d] Member States co-operating with the Government of Kuwait...to use all necessary means to uphold and implement resolution 660 (1990) and all subsequent relevant resolutions and to restore international peace and security in the area.'[119] Since this formula was first used against Iraq, the practice of authorizations has been widely used by the Security Council. This practice has been criticized for its putative concessions to unilateralism and national interest, and for providing States with broad, open-ended mandates subject to little oversight.[120] Others have suggested that the delegation of enforcement to certain States tempers the more Panglossian elements of the Charter, and acknowledges that not every State will seek to be involved in every UN action.[121]

As Sarooshi has argued, although the Security Council has, since 1990, used the language of 'authorizing' certain measures, it may be more accurate to refer to the grant of power as a 'delegation': whereas an authorization denotes the conferral of limited authority to undertake a particular, circumscribed function, a delegation indicates a broader and more open-ended grant of power.[122] In conformity with the Security Council's own terminology, however, the term 'authorization' will be used here.

Of course, 'authorizations' under the Charter encompass a wide spectrum of activity and do not always sanction the use of military force. When military force is contemplated, the Security Council typically has recourse to euphemisms such as 'all necessary means'[123] or 'all necessary measures'[124]

The basis for such authorizations to use force has been disputed. During the debate on Security Council Resolution 678, for example, Yemen protested that the resolution did not identify any specific article in Chapter VII.[125] Cuba protested that the resolution was 'in total disregard of the procedures established by the Charter.'[126] A number of writers also disputed the legality of the resolution and argued that the use of force was based in collective self-defence under Article 51.[127] However, there now exists little doubt that Resolution 678 authorized enforcement action under Chapter VII. Coalition troops pointed to Resolution 678 as their authority for undertaking the action; and the Resolution itself, in

[119] UNSC Res 678 (29 November 1990) SCOR Resolutions and Decisions 27.

[120] On this see Chesterman (n 68) 179–95.

[121] See A Roberts 'The United Nations and International Security' (1993) 35 *Survival* 3, 16–19.

[122] Sarooshi (n 115) 13. Cf Berman (n 115).

[123] For example, UNSC Res 678 (n 119) [2]; UNSC Res 940 (31 July 1994) UN Doc S/RES/940 [4]; UNSC Res 1528 (27 February 2004) UN Doc S/RES/1528 [8], [16].

[124] For example, UNSC Res 1264 (15 September 1999) UN Doc S/RES/1264 [3]; UNSC Res 1484 (30 May 2003) UN Doc S/RES/1484 [4]; UNSC Res 1529 (29 February 2004) UN Doc S/RES/1529 [6].

[125] UNSC Verbatim Record (29 November 1990) UN Doc S/PV.2963 33 (Yemen).

[126] Ibid 58 (Cuba).

[127] See, for example, E V Rostow 'Until What? Enforcement Action or Collective Self-Defence?' (1991) 85 AJIL 506.

referring to the restoration of international peace and security, would sit uncomfortably in a Resolution based upon the right of self-defence.[128]

The lack of UN oversight and limits imposed on the States authorized under Resolution 678 has caused disquiet; but the power of the Security Council to engage in such authorization of force is widely recognized. There is some dispute over where in the UN Charter such a power is to be found. One suggestion is that such competence stems from the UN's inherent power to authorize the use of force as well as a flexible approach to the UN Charter.[129] The most persuasive argument, however, locates the Security Council's ability to authorize enforcement action in principles of international institutional law, as well as based in the subsequent practice of UN organs.[130]

The ability of the Security Council to authorize the use of force under Chapter VII is now broadly accepted. In the 'Supplement to An Agenda for Peace', UN Secretary-General Boutros Boutros-Ghali acknowledged that neither the Security Council nor the Secretary-General had the capacity to 'deploy, direct, command and control' enforcement actions.[131] The 'Brahimi Report' on United Nations Peace Operations of 2000 went further, noting that 'The panel recognises that the UN does not wage war. Where enforcement action is required it has consistently been entrusted to coalitions of willing States, with the authorisation of the Security Council, acting under Chapter VII of the Charter.'[132]

c. 'Extended' Peacekeeping

During the Cold War, peacekeeping emerged out of the failure of the Security Council's Chapter VII enforcement powers. The concept of peacekeeping was a legal innovation, and the constitutional basis for it in the Charter remains a point of academic contention, if largely without practical significance.[133]

Although governed by consent with the host State, the nature of peacekeeping has always been accompanied by the risk that a peacekeeping force could become involved in hostilities. This was evident as early as the 1960s, when the

[128] Higgins (n 118) 262; Sarooshi (n 115) 177; C Greenwood 'New World Order or Old? The Invasion of Kuwait and the Rule of Law' (1992) 55 MLR 153, 169; C Warbrick 'The Invasion of Kuwait by Iraq' (1991) 40 ICLQ 965.

[129] H Freudenschuß 'Between Unilateralism and Collective Security: Authorisations of the Use of Force by the UN Security Council' (1994) 5 EJIL 492, 526.

[130] Sarooshi (n 115) 142–66.

[131] UNGA 'Supplement to An Agenda for Peace: Position Paper of the Secretary-General on the Occasion of the Fiftieth Anniversary of the United Nations' (25 January 1995) UN Doc A/50/60-S/1995/1 [77].

[132] UNGA 'Report of the Panel on United Nations Peace Operations' (21 August 2000) UN Doc A/55/305-S/2000/809 [55].

[133] A Orakhelashvili 'The Legal Basis of the United Nations Peace-Keeping Operations' (2002–2003) 43 VJIL 485.

peacekeeping mission in the Congo, ONUC, became increasingly embroiled in the aftermath of independence.[134] Security Council Resolution 161 authorized ONUC to take 'all appropriate measures to prevent the occurrence of civil war in the Congo...including the use of force, if necessary, in the last resort.'[135] The nature of peacekeeping took on an increasingly robust cast during the 1990s, and the controversies that arose over the extension of ONUC's mandate were to be raised anew with regard to peacekeeping operations in Somalia and Yugoslavia during the 1990s.[136]

The difference between peacekeeping and peace enforcement is emphasized in peacekeeping doctrine. The difference is commonly explained as a difference between minimal uses of force at a tactical level in self-defence (for peacekeeping), and the use of force at a strategic and international level, authorized under Charter VII of the Charter (in peace enforcement).[137]

Reality does not always adhere to these distinctions. Numerous peacekeeping operations since 1990 appear to operate in a 'grey zone' that renders indistinct the concepts of impartiality and partiality.[138] Thus the UN's peacekeeping operation in Yugoslavia, UNPROFOR, was set up as a traditional peacekeeping force to manage the cease-fire, even though the cease-fire was at the time tenuous and unstable.[139] UNPROFOR's mandate, however, gradually expanded, and from February 1993, the Security Council began to refer to Chapter VII operations in its resolutions on UNPROFOR.[140] The practice of the Security Council throughout the 1990s of enlarging the mandate of what initially began as peacekeeping operations means that a clear line between peacekeeping and enforcement cannot always be drawn.

It should also be emphasized that the law of armed conflict does not track the structure of the Charter. The law of armed conflict is not applicable solely in circumstances where the Security Council has authorized the use of force under Chapter VII. It is entirely conceivable that a peacekeeping force established with the consent of the host State could become involved in armed conflict through the use of force in self-defence.

[134] See M Berdal 'The Security Council and Peacekeeping' in V Lowe et al (eds) *The United Nations Security Council and War: The Evolution of Thought and Practice since 1945* (OUP, Oxford 2008) 175, 182–4.

[135] UNSC Res 161 (21 February 1961) UN Doc S/4741 [1].

[136] C Gray *International Law and the Use of Force* (3rd edn OUP, Oxford 2008) 263.

[137] See, for example, UNDPKO *United Nations Peacekeeping Operations: Principles and Guidelines* (2008) <http://pbpu.unlb.org/pbps/Library/Capstone_Doctrine_ENG.pdf> access 21 January 2009 [2.2].

[138] J Boulden 'Mandates Matter: An Exploration of Impartiality in United Nations Operations' (2005) 11 GG 147, 151.

[139] R Higgins 'The New United Nations and the Former Yugoslavia' (1993) 69 IA 465.

[140] For comprehensive treatment see M Weller 'Peace-Keeping and Peace Enforcement in the Republic of Bosnia and Herzegovina' (1996) 56 ZaöRV 70.

It has been suggested, for example, that clashes between UNPROFOR and Bosnian Serb forces became increasingly intense throughout 1993 and 1994, and that an international armed conflict in the sense of common Article 2 of the Geneva Conventions existed by the summer of 1994.[141] In theory, the UN acknowledges that its forces will observe the 'principles and spirit' of international humanitarian law in enforcement action and in peacekeeping when force used in self-defence rises to the level of armed conflict.[142] However, the application of the law of armed conflict to UN peace operations has frequently been denied.[143]

Practice demonstrates that a high threshold must be reached before UN forces will be regarded as involved in an international armed conflict. The 1994 Convention on the Safety of United Nations and Associated Personnel provides that personnel on UN operations may not be the object of attack, but excludes from protection those forces engaged in enforcement action under Chapter VII.[144] If attacks against peacekeepers, even against those engaged in using force in self-defence, are prohibited under the Convention, it would seem that a high threshold must be crossed before the law of armed conflict is viewed as applicable.[145] There has been an extreme reluctance, by both States and the UN itself, to acknowledge that UN forces involved in extended or robust peacekeeping are to be regarded as parties to an armed conflict.[146] Given this reality, it would appear unlikely that participation in peacekeeping will raise substantive issues concerning the law of neutrality. In practical terms, it is most probable that issues of neutrality will arise in military enforcement action.

5. UN Military Operations and the Law of Neutrality

a. Military Participation in UN Enforcement Actions

The application of the law of neutrality to enforcement action authorized under Chapter VII on a significant scale and directed against a State, like the actions against Korea in 1950 and Iraq in 1990, raises a number of issues.

[141] Greenwood (n 6) 23–4. [142] See 'Secretary-General's Bulletin' (n 17) [1.1].

[143] Greenwood (n 6) 24. NATO appears to follow a similar approach. See NATO *Peace Support Operations* (AJP - 3.4.1, 2001) [4B6]: 'The PSF [Peace Support Force] will not generally be a party to the conflict, yet certain LOAC [Law of Armed Conflict] principles may be applied.'

[144] UN Convention on the Safety of United Nations and Associated Personnel (adopted 9 December 1994, entered into force 15 January 1999) 2051 UNTS 363 art 7(1). For the Convention's application see art 2(2).

[145] Greenwood (n 6) 24–5; Wills (n 6) 402–3.

[146] For example, an Italian Commission of Enquiry on the activities of UNOSOM in Somalia did not express a view as to whether UN forces were engaged in an armed conflict or a police operation. See N Lupi 'Report of the Enquiry Commission on the Behaviour of Italian Peace-keeping Troops in Somalia' (1998) 1 YIHL 375. In the *Brocklebank* case, the Canadian Court Martial Appeal Court found no evidence of an armed conflict in Somalia during peacekeeping operations. *The Queen v Brocklebank* [1996] 134 DLR (4th) 377. See also K Boustany 'Brocklebank: a Questionable Decision of the Court Martial Appeal Court of Canada' (1998) 1 YIHL 371.

Attempts have been made to deny the application of neutrality to such enforcement action. These arguments rely primarily on the contention that such enforcement action is not equivalent to interstate 'war' and therefore does not trigger the law of neutrality.[147] It is true that the Security Council action in Korea generated considerable debate as to whether that conflict could be considered to be 'war.'[148] Certain States explicitly denied the existence of a state of war.[149] The Kuwait crisis in 1990 again led to denials by some States that a state of war existed.[150] In some cases, however, denial of the characterization of the conflict as a 'war' appeared to be for domestic consumption, and was not a considered statement on the matter for purposes of international law.[151] The relevant question was whether an international armed conflict existed between the UN-authorized force and the target State: the label attached to the UN-authorized forces was irrelevant.[152] As Bowett noted, the analogy between UN action and police action is unrealistic from the point of view of the application of the law of armed conflict:

> This competence possessed by a United Nations Force to engage, to the extent determined by its mandate, in international armed conflict may be considered equivalent to 'belligerency'...Thus 'enforcement action' as conceived in Chapter VII necessarily comprehends the assumption of belligerent status by the Forces of the United Nations charged with the responsibility of restoring or maintaining international peace.[153]

There is no reason of principle why a different approach should be taken with regard to the law of neutrality.

In these types of enforcement action, it seems clear that the status of neutrality is not extinguished for States that wish to have recourse to it.[154] In the absence of Article 43 agreements, there is no obligation to take part in military action authorized by the Security Council. As Oscar Schachter has noted, there is an important distinction between obligations and authorizations in the UN system.[155] In ordinary speech, to 'authorize' means 'to permit or allow or licence, not to require or oblige.'[156] In contrast to decisions issued under the Charter—for

147 This suggestion is made by S Chesterman 'Neutrality and its Discontents' (Swiss Security Policy Hearings 2009) <http://www.sipol09.ethz.ch/Transkriptionen/Ausland/Prof.-Simon-Chesterman> accessed 12 December 2009.

148 L C Green 'The Nature of the "War" in Korea' (1951) 4 ILQ 462.

149 See (1983) 54 BYBIL 534.

150 (1991) 66 BYBIL 704.

151 Italy referred to the conflict as an 'international policing operation', but the denial of the existence of war or armed conflict was for constitutional reasons. *Keesing's* (1991) 37941. See also the statement of Italian Prime Minister Andreotti in (1988–1992) 8 IYIL 264.

152 See generally H Meyrowitz 'La guerre du Golfe et le droit des conflits armés' (1992) 96 RGDIP 551, 555–7.

153 Bowett (n 16) 499–500.

154 M Voelckel 'Faut-il encore déclarer la guerre?' (1991) 37 AFDI 7, 22.

155 Schachter (n 115) 395.

156 *Al-Jedda* (n 55) [31] per Lord Bingham of Cornhill.

example, measures taken under Article 41 – authorizations do not compel States to adopt a certain course of action but merely give them the power to do so.[157] In this respect, the practice of the Security Council in authorizing States to use force bears some similarities to the era of the League of Nations, and the League Council's recommendatory functions.[158]

i. Enforcement action in Korea (1950)

The early practice of the Security Council concerning the UN action in Korea confirms this.[159] Upon the invasion by North Korea of South Korea on 24 June 1950, the Security Council first determined that North Korea's actions constituted a 'breach of the peace,' and 'called upon' all Members to 'render every assistance to the United Nations in the execution of this resolution and to refrain from giving assistance to the North Korean authorities.'[160] Security Council Resolution 83 of 27 June 1950 noted that North Korea had refused to cease hostilities and withdraw to the thirty-eighth parallel. It recommended that the UN Members 'furnish such assistance to the Republic of Korea as may be necessary to repel the armed attack and to restore international peace and security.'[161] The reference to 'armed attack' seems to frame the response in terms of collective self-defence. But this changed on 7 July 1950, when the Security Council passed Resolution 84. This Resolution recommended that 'all Members providing military forces and other assistance pursuant to the aforesaid Security Council resolutions' make that assistance available to a 'unified commander under the United States' and authorized the unified command to use the UN flag 'in the course of operations against North Korean forces.'[162]

The nature of the UN action in Korea remains a subject of some dispute.[163] While some have claimed that the action should be seen as collective self-defence,[164] it is better classified as enforcement action.[165] The root of much of the confusion is Security Council Resolution 83, which is drafted in capacious terms and seemingly refers both to the Council's enforcement powers and to self-defence. Security Council Resolution 84, however, makes it clear that the basis of the action is the Security Council's enforcement power. As Bowett notes of Resolution 84, 'the recommendation operated as an authorisation to Members to take action which, without such authorisation, might have been illegal.'[166]

[157] Berman (n 115) 157. [158] Chesterman (n 68) 169.
[159] For background to the hostilities in Korea, see N J Padelford 'The United Nations and Korea: A Political Résumé' (1951) 5 IO 685.
[160] UNSC Res 82 (25 June 1950) UN Doc S/1501.
[161] UNSC Res 83 (27 June 1950) UN Doc S/1511.
[162] UNSC Res 84 (7 July 1950) UN Doc S/1588. [163] Gray (n 136) 258–9.
[164] J A Frowein and N Krisch 'Article 39' in B Simma et al (ed) *The Charter of the United Nations: A Commentary* (2nd edn OUP, Oxford 2002) 717, 728.
[165] Sarooshi (n 115) 169–70; Seyersted (n 10) 33. [166] Bowett (n 16) 32.

Because the authorization granted a power to States to act, there was no obligation to dispatch troops or take other military measures. While many States did in fact send military forces, others, such as Sweden, took advantage of the recommendatory character of the resolution and did not participate militarily.[167] States that wished to do so were permitted to adhere to the status of neutrality. A number of States did, in fact, explicitly claim neutrality during the hostilities, notably China and the Soviet Union.

China's right to claim neutrality was widely accepted; while States protested against various violations by China of its neutral duties, they did not protest against its neutral status. For example, a number of States protested that Chinese soldiers were being recruited into the North Korean military forces. China responded that such individuals were 'volunteers' and therefore not a violation of its duties as a neutral.[168]

The Soviet Union also adhered to a position of neutrality during the conflict. In the Security Council, the Soviet Union stated that the Hague Conventions were 'in full force to-day, and the armed forces of the United States are obliged to observe them.'[169] The Soviet Union addressed numerous claims concerning violation of neutral duties to the United States.[170] The US refused to entertain Soviet claims for reparations for violations of neutrality, not because it saw the law of neutrality as inapplicable, but because it argued that the action had been taken by United Nations forces and so the claims should have been directed to the UN.[171]

ii. Enforcement action in Iraq (1990)

Whereas the action in Korea was couched in the more traditional language of recommendation, the Security Council's practice in response to Iraq's aggression against Kuwait demonstrated a striking transformation in the use of authorizations.[172]

Resolution 665 provided the first authorization to Member States to use force, and called on Member States 'co-operating with the Government of Kuwait' to use:

> such measures commensurate to the specific circumstances as may be necessary under the authority of the Security Council to halt all inward and outward maritime shipping, in order to inspect and verify their cargoes and destinations and to ensure strict implementation of the provisions related to such shipping laid down in resolution 661 (1990).[173]

[167] E Karsh 'International Co-operation and Neutrality' (1988) 25 JPR 57, 61.

[168] Taubenfeld (n 5) 392–3. See also R Higgins *United Nations Peacekeeping 1946–1967: Documents and Commentary* vol II (OUP, Oxford 1970) 180.

[169] UNSC Verbatim Record (7 September 1950) SCOR Resolutions and Decisions 9.

[170] Seyersted (n 10) 110–11. [171] Ibid 187. [172] Berman (n 115) 167.

[173] UNSC Res 665 (25 August 1990) SCOR Resolutions and Decisions 21 [1].

The phrasing of the Security Council's authorization is significant: Resolution 665 'was addressing the United States and all other nations which had *chosen* to respond to Kuwait's request. There was no *requirement* for any state to send ships or other assistance.'[174]

The crucial resolution enshrining the 'authorisation model' to use military force was, however, Security Council Resolution 678. Resolution 678, passed under Chapter VII of the Charter, authorized 'Member States co-operating with the Government of Kuwait' to 'use all necessary means' to restore international peace and security in the area.[175] As with the UN action in Korea, considerable debate has turned on whether this resolution actually authorized enforcement action or recognized the right of collective self-defence. As noted above, there is now little doubt that the resolution authorized enforcement action.

At the beginning of the conflict the question of whether the law of armed conflict applied was never seriously debated and seems to have been assumed from the outset.[176] Security Council Resolution 670 acknowledged, for example, the applicability of the Fourth Geneva Convention.[177]

Practice indicates that the law of neutrality was also seen as applicable and acknowledged by the parties to the conflict. The phrasing of the resolution limits the authorization to those States 'co-operating with the Government of Kuwait.' Participation in the use of force was therefore discretionary. The resolution is an implicit acknowledgement that there remains scope for neutrality in UN-authorized measures.[178] A number of States explicitly indicated their neutrality during the hostilities. Most notably, Iran and Jordan both emphasized their neutrality during the conflict.[179] India also adopted a position of neutrality.[180] The ability to claim the status of neutrality was a position recognized by other States.[181]

[174] J G Dalton 'The Influence of Law on Seapower in Desert Shield/Desert Storm' (1993) 41 Naval LR 27, 44 (emphasis in original).

[175] UNSC Res 678 (29 November 1990) SCOR Resolutions and Decisions 27.

[176] A Roberts 'The Laws of War in the 1990-91 Gulf Conflict' (1993/1994) 18 IS 124, 142.

[177] UNSC Res 670 (25 September 1990) SCOR Resolutions and Decisions 24 [13].

[178] A Roberts 'From San Francisco to Sarajevo: The UN and the Use of Force' (1995) 37 *Survival* 7, 12; A Hurrell 'Collective Security and International Order Revisited' (1992) 11 *Int Relations* 37, 47; S P Subedi 'Neutrality in a Changing World: European Neutral States and the European Community' (1993) 42 ICLQ 238, 253.

[179] *Keesing's* (1990) 37696; *Keesing's* (1991) 37942.

[180] 'War in the Gulf; India Says It Will Withdraw US Planes' Refueling Right' *New York Times* (New York, 18 February 1991); 'War in the Gulf; Refueling of Jets in India to Stop' *New York Times* (New York, 20 February 1991).

[181] 'United States: Department of Defence Report to Congress on the Conduct of the Persian Gulf War – Appendix on The Role of the Law of War' (1992) 31 ILM 612, 637.

b. Non-Military Support for UN Enforcement Action

The voluntary character of participation in military measures authorized by the Security Council seems clearly established. A more complicated question concerns the obligations to assist States acting pursuant to an authorization. If authorizations are not obligations under the Charter, and since Article 25 *prima facie* does not apply, it is not clear whether States that wish to claim the status of neutrals are obliged to discriminate in their adherence to neutral duties.

A textual interpretation of the Charter suggests that a neutral State would not be required to modify its duties of neutrality during enforcement action authorized by the Security Council because Article 103 prevails over general international law only when the Security Council imposes 'obligations.' Since an authorization does not compel Member States to take action, but simply confers on them a discretionary power to do so, there is no relevant 'obligation' under the Charter to which Article 103 grants priority.[182] The concept of an 'obligation' under the Charter has, according to this view, a clear meaning that cannot be extended to encompass authorizations.

As a matter of principle, this view is compelling. The Charter should not lightly be presumed to have prevailed over general international law. As Bernhardt explains, Article 103:

> represents a partial suspension of the basic international law maxim *pacta sunt servanda*. Such a suspension is only acceptable in the case of a conflict between obligations, the superior or stronger of which should prevail. If a certain measure or form of behaviour is merely recommended without being legally obligatory, existing treaty obligations must be respected and the recommendation cannot be followed.[183]

Against this view, a functional approach suggests that to interpret Article 103 in a narrow way would fatally impair the efficacy of the Charter. It would, in effect, negate the innovations of the Security Council to function in the area of international peace and security absent agreements under Article 43. Given that authorizations attempt to delegate the powers of the UN itself, States that are acting pursuant to such delegations are acting on behalf of the United Nations itself.[184] Accordingly, authorizations should be seen as more than mere recommendations to act because of their 'legal nature and density.'[185]

[182] Frowein and Krisch (n 164) 729. [183] Bernhardt (n 53) 1296.

[184] R Kolb 'Does Article 103 of the Charter of the United Nations Apply only to Decisions or also to Authorisations Adopted by the Security Council?' (2004) 64 ZaöRV 21, 32.

[185] Ibid.

This view provides a compelling argument in terms of the States acting in conformity with the authorizations, but it is not clear that it is equally persuasive with regard to States that have chosen not to act upon an authorization. Nevertheless, this approach to the interpretation of Article 103 has been favoured in recent case law. In *R (Al-Jedda) v Secretary of State for Defence*, Lord Bingham noted that a purposive approach to Article 103 as applicable to authorizations 'reflect[s] the practice of the UN and member states as it has developed over the past 60 years.'[186] The meaning of the phrase 'obligations' in Article 103 should not, he argued, be given a 'narrow, contract-based meaning.'[187] As Lord Bingham made clear, however, this view was directed to those States that were acting in accordance with the authorization:

> As is well known, a large majority of States chose not to contribute to the multinational force, but *those which did* (including the UK) became bound by articles 2 and 25 to carry out the decisions of the Security Council in accordance with the Charter so as to achieve its lawful objectives.[188]

The effect of authorizations on States that were not contributing to the multinational force was not canvassed.

It seems to be established that Member States that are not directly participating in the measures authorized have a *power* to discriminate in favour of the UN-authorized force. It has been suggested that a determination under Article 39 that identifies the responsible State would permit a State to depart from the law of neutrality. Equally, an authorization to Member States to use all 'necessary means' permits a State to depart from the law of neutrality. Thus a number of States during the Kuwait crisis adopted measures in favour of the coalition action without participating directly in hostilities. Spain provided logistical, humanitarian and political support for Allied forces in the Gulf while eschewing direct military involvement.[189] The Torrejón air base was used by a substantial number of US forces en route to the Gulf.[190] Portugal provided similar logistical support but did not send troops.[191] Turkey authorized the US Air Force to station 96 warplanes at a base in Incirlik. These aircraft later joined the air offensive against Iraq.[192]

In departing from the law of neutrality, the State would not incur international responsibility: an authorization under Chapter VII would act as a circumstance precluding wrongfulness. In this regard, the International Law Commission has noted that 'sanctions applied in conformity with the provisions of the Charter would certainly not be wrongful in the legal system of the United Nations, even though they might conflict with other treaty obligations incumbent upon the

[186] *Al-Jedda* (n 55) [33] per Lord Bingham of Cornhill. [187] Ibid [34].
[188] Ibid (emphasis added). [189] *Keesing's* (1991) 37942. [190] Ibid. [191] Ibid.
[192] Ibid 37936.

State applying them.'[193] The ILC proceeded to note that '[t]his view would, moreover, seem to be valid not only in cases where the duly adopted decision of the Organisation authorising the application of a sanction is mandatory for the Member States but also where the taking of such measures is merely recommended.'[194]

Whether there is an obligation for Member States not actively participating to act in accordance with an authorization is more difficult to evaluate and will depend on whether the Security Council intended to displace general international law. The Security Council's power to override general international law is not, however, without controversy. This question has arisen most recently with regard to the law of occupation.[195] Much will turn on the precise terms of the relevant Security Council resolution, and the particular character of the rule that the Security Council is attempting to modify or displace.[196] Sir Michael Wood has noted that:

> The extent to which SCRs [Security Council Resolutions] should be interpreted taking into account applicable rules of international law, whether general international law or particular treaties, depends on the analysis of the intentions of the Security Council (as evidenced by the text of the resolution and the surrounding circumstances). If it appears that the Council was intending to lay down a rule irrespective of the prior obligations of States, in general or in particular, then that intention would prevail; if, conversely, it appears that the Council was intending to base itself on existing legal rules or an existing legal situation, then its decisions ought certainly to be interpreted taking those rules into account.[197]

In the Kuwait crisis, it was clear States that wished to remain neutral were required to discriminate in their application of neutral duties pursuant to Resolution 661, which had imposed an economic embargo on Iraq. Thus the declarations of neutrality issued by Jordan and Iran were subordinate to their obligation to comply with Resolution 661. The US outlined its position in a Department of Defence Report:

> It was the US position during the Persian Gulf crisis that, regardless of assertions of neutrality, all nations were obligated to avoid hindrance of Coalition

[193] (1979) II(ii) YBILC 119. [194] Ibid.

[195] UNSC Res 1483 (22 May 2003) UN Doc S/RES/1483. See Scheffer (n 23) 580; A Roberts 'Transformative Military Occupation: Applying the Laws of War and Human Rights' (2006) 100 AJIL 580.

[196] On this see A Orakhelashvili 'The Post-War Settlement in Iraq: the UN Security Council Resolution 1483 (2003) and General International Law' (2003) 8 JCSL 307.

[197] M Wood 'The Interpretation of Security Council Resolutions' (1998) 2 MPYBUNL 73, 92.

> operations undertaken pursuant to, or in conjunction with, UNSC decisions, and to provide whatever assistance possible.[198]

Resolution 665 'call[ed] upon' Member States co-operating with Kuwait that were deploying maritime forces to the Gulf to 'use such measures commensurate to the specific circumstances as may be necessary under the authority of the Security Council' to halt all inward and outward maritime shipping to verify cargo.[199] This has correctly been interpreted as an authorization to States, issued after some uncertainty concerning the ability of States to interdict shipping to verify compliance with Resolution 661.[200]

Paragraph 3 'request[ed] all States to provide, in accordance with the Charter of the United Nations, such assistance as may be required' to the States co-operating with Kuwait.[201] This suggests that there is no obligation on non-belligerent or neutral States to provide assistance; the request is purely recommendatory. Paragraph 3 of Resolution 678 was in similar terms; it requested all States to provide 'appropriate support' for the actions of the States engaging in hostilities with Iraq.[202] As the International Court of Justice has emphasized, the language of a resolution must be analysed carefully for its binding effect.[203] A recommendation by a UN organ cannot be converted into an obligation without further agreement by the States concerned.[204] There is no indication, from the terms of these resolutions, that it is mandatory to provide support to States acting in accordance with UN authorizations.

However, a persuasive case can be made that Article 2(5) should apply to UN-authorized action and would modify the rights and duties of neutrality in favour of UN forces. Textually, there is no reference to Article 2(5) as applying only when 'obligations' are involved or when 'decisions' have been taken; rather, the principle of Article 2(5) applies both in 'any action' and in 'preventive or enforcement action': terms which, admittedly, have been interpreted as referring to the same sort of action: enforcement action under Chapter VII.[205]

The first limb of Article 2(5)—the duty of positive assistance—does, however, seem to have a textual restriction: the obligations contained within it apply to action the Security Council takes 'in accordance with the present Charter.' While it was not contemplated by the founders of the UN that the Security Council could authorize States to take a certain course of action, this interpretation of the Charter is now confirmed by subsequent practice and there is no serious objection that they are unlawful or inconsistent with the Charter.

198 'United States: Department of Defence Report to Congress' (n 181) 638.

199 UNSC Res 665 (n 173) [1].

200 This point is addressed in greater detail in Chapter 5.

201 UNSC Res 665 (n 173) [3].

202 UNSC Res 678 (n 119) [3].

203 *Legal Consequences for States of the Continued Presence of South Africa in Namibia* (Advisory Opinion) (n 35) 41.

204 Schachter (n 115) 395.

205 Frowein and Krisch (n 34) 138; Lalive (n 5) 78.

State practice confirms the view that Article 2(5) is applicable to authorizations. Italian Prime Minister, Giulio Andreotti, stated on 16 January 1991 that:

> The Second paragraph of decision 678 gives countries which, like Italy, cooperate in the Arab peninsula, the power to adopt all the necessary measures for supporting and implementing the pertinent decisions of the Security Council, starting with decision 660. These measures include, as outlined in Article 2 of the Charter, the obligation of members to give the United Nations – and I quote – 'every assistance in any action which it undertakes in accordance with the provisions of this Charter.'[206]

Members, by and large, were willing to offer support. Jordan announced that, despite its stance of neutrality, it would comply with UN Resolutions.[207] It is suggested that, on the basis of Article 2(5) and Article 49 of the Charter, there is a duty on States to modify the rights and duties of neutrality in favour of UN-authorized action.

c. Modalities of Support for UN Enforcement Action

State practice indicates various forms of support for UN-authorized action, from logistical assistance to the provision of military bases and the stationing of troops. The duty to co-operate under the first limb of Article 2(5) is, as the US Department of Defence Report suggested, essentially subjective and according to capacity.[208] At minimum, however, States must avoid hindering UN-authorized forces.[209] For States that wish to remain neutral, this will entail adjustment of neutral rights and duties in a number of areas.

i. Internment

According to Article 11 of Hague Convention V, a neutral State that receives on its territory troops belonging to belligerent armies is required to intern them.[210] During the hostilities that followed Security Council Resolution 678, reports arose of Iraqi aircraft landing in Iran. On 29 January 1991, the coalition claimed that nearly 100 aircraft were in Iran. Iran stated that it would hold the aircraft until the end of hostilities.[211]

Iran stated that it would apply this rule equally to both belligerents; it was noted that all aircraft would be 'confiscated' and their pilots kept in custody, and it was emphasized that 'this policy would be applied to all parties which violate

[206] (1988–1992) 8 IYIL 264. [207] Dalton (n 174) 54.
[208] 'United States: Department of Defence Report' (n 181) 638. [209] Ibid.
[210] HC V art 11. [211] *Keesing's* (1991) 37936.

Iranian air, land or sea spaces.'[212] The US disagreed with this view. It advised Iran 'that, in light of UNSC Resolution 678, Iran would be obligated to return downed Coalition aircraft and aircrew, rather than intern them.'[213] It was the US position during the Gulf conflict, that 'entry into Iranian (or Jordanian) airspace to rescue downed aviators would be consistent with its international obligations as a belligerent, particularly in light of Resolution 678.'[214] This view demonstrated, the US report argued, the 'modified nature of neutrality in these circumstances.'[215]

ii. Transit rights over neutral airspace

On land, the territory of neutral States is regarded as inviolable.[216] Early UN practice indicated no change in this rule. Neutral States had the absolute right to prohibit UN use of neutral territory. In the UN action in Korea, for example, China protested on numerous occasions at UN incursions into its airspace.[217] The US 'admitted the possibility that its planes had inadvertently violated neutral territory and expressed its regret and its willingness to assume responsibility.'[218] The US issued instructions to soldiers under UN command not to intrude onto Chinese territory despite its view that China was assisting North Korean forces.[219]

The action in the Gulf in 1990 seems to suggest a development of State practice towards the view that, if States are acting pursuant to a UN authorization, 'the world community would expect the "neutral" to preclude the aggressor from operating in or entering its territory, but to allow UN-authorised forces to operate there.'[220] Ireland assented to the provision of landing and transit rights to US aircraft during the hostilities.[221] During August and September 1990, more than 1,500 military aircraft flew over Irish airspace.[222]

Austria also permitted the use of its airspace. Austria 'decided that overflights by US military transport aircraft would not be inconsistent with its neutral obligations.'[223] Austria permitted in February 1991 103 US tanks to cross Austrian territory by rail from Germany to Italy.[224] Switzerland did not permit transit of its airspace by combat aircraft or aircraft carrying troops and ammunition.[225] It

[212] Ibid 37942. 'Rafsanjani News Conference Iran's Neutrality; Iraqi planes; Relations with USA' SWB (London, 5 February 1991).

[213] 'United States: Department of Defence Report' (n 181) 639. [214] Ibid. [215] Ibid.

[216] HC V art 1. [217] Higgins (n 168) 226–9. [218] Seyersted (n 10) 111–12.

[219] See the telegram dated 13 November 1950 contained in J G Verplaetse, 'The *ius in bello* and Military Operations in Korea 1950-1953' (1963) ZaöRV 679, 709–10.

[220] J Astley III and M N Schmitt 'The Law of the Sea and Naval Operations' (1997) 42 AFLR 119, 147.

[221] L Heffeman and A Whelan 'Ireland, the United Nations and the Gulf Conflict: Legal Aspects' (1991) 3 ISIA 115, 127.

[222] *Keesing's* (1991) 37942. [223] 'United States: Department of Defence Report' (n 181) 640.

[224] *Keesing's* (1991) 37989.

[225] (1992) 2 SZIER 596; Swiss Federal Ministry of Foreign Affairs 'White Paper on Neutrality' (n 102) 18. Cf 'United States: Department of Defence Report' (n 181) 640.

indicated that it was prepared to re-examine Swiss practice in the area.[226] However, since the Kuwait crisis, Switzerland has concluded that support for coercive military measures decided or authorized under the UN Charter is compatible with neutrality. Since 1993, Switzerland has allowed foreign troops to use Swiss territory for overflight as long as the operation is backed by a Security Council mandate or authorization.[227]

iii. Use of the territorial sea and neutral ports

Hague Convention XIII provides that belligerent rights may not be asserted in neutral territory.[228] Article 9, however, provides that a neutral State must impose any restrictions on access to its ports or territorial waters on the basis of impartiality.[229] Numerous other provisions of Hague Convention XIII proceed on the basis that access to neutral ports and territorial waters is to be granted on the basis of impartiality.[230]

When a determination under Article 39 is made that identifies the responsible State, or enforcement action is authorized, the neutral State must accordingly adjust its application of these rules. Since refuelling and resupply in neutral ports may constitute 'assistance' under Article 2(5), the neutral State is under an obligation to prevent the State which is the object of the enforcement action from using its ports or territorial waters. This is the minimum that is required under the second limb of Article 2(5). Failure to comply with it would constitute 'aid or assistance' under Article 41(2) of the ILC's Articles on State Responsibility.[231]

Whether a neutral State is under an obligation to permit access to its ports by a UN-authorized force is a more difficult question. Quincy Wright argued in 1953 that the UN could 'authorise measures to assure isolation of the aggressor and to prevent third-state assistance to the aggressor even though those measures go beyond the normal powers of a belligerent to interfere with commerce at sea.'[232] Those measures would now include interception of vessels in neutral territorial waters.[233]

[226] (1992) 2 SZIER 596.

[227] Switzerland Federal Department of Foreign Affairs 'Swiss Neutrality in Practice Current Aspects: Report of the Interdepartmental Working Group of 30 August 2000' (30 August 2000) <http://www.eda.admin.ch/eda/en/home/topics/intla/cintla/ref_neutr.html> accessed 21 December 2006 4–5.

[228] HC XIII art 1. [229] Ibid art 9. [230] Ibid art 10–25.

[231] ILC 'Report of the International Law Commission on the Work of its 53rd Session' (23 April – 10 August 2001) UN Doc A/56/10 art 41(2).

[232] Q Wright 'The Outlawry of War and the Law of War' (1953) 47 AJIL 365, 375. Wright notes, however, that this discretion is 'not unlimited.'

[233] It should be noted parenthetically that the characterization of the conflict as either UN enforcement action or collective self-defence may have real consequences for the scope of measures exercisable in maritime interdiction operations: if the action is viewed as collective self-defence interdiction measures could not go beyond those available under the law of neutrality, whereas if the action is viewed as a Chapter VII enforcement action, the law of naval warfare may be adapted to encompass broader rights. On this point see Wright (n 232) 375; C Greenwood 'Self-Defence and the Conduct of

UN Resolution 665, authorizing maritime interdiction in the Gulf, built on Resolution 661, which imposed an economic embargo on Iraq. Following the passage of Resolution 665, Coalition States conducted maritime interception operations in the Persian Gulf, the Gulf of Oman, and the Red Sea, and managed to divert almost all goods headed into or out of Iraq.[234]

The powers granted under Resolution 665 were (probably deliberately) imprecisely phrased: the degree of force that could be used to verify cargoes, and in what circumstances, was left up to the co-operating States themselves.[235] The measures contemplated by Resolution 665 are analogous to blockade action.[236] The difference, however, is that under the terms of the Resolution interception measures could be extended to the territorial seas of neutral and non-belligerent States.[237] While there was apparently support for the view that neutral States would have to allow the UN-authorized force to use their territorial seas, this did not come to pass.[238] The territorial seas and international straits of certain States were used by the coalition force for interception purposes, but only with the permission of the littoral State.[239]

However, it is increasingly accepted that the territorial seas of neutral and non-belligerent States must be made available for UN-authorized maritime operations.[240] Subsequent Security Council resolutions authorizing maritime interdiction measures have presumed a wide spectrum of permissible action. At the outbreak of hostilities in the Federal Republic of Yugoslavia (FRY), for example, the Security Council imposed an embargo on all deliveries of weapons and military equipment.[241] This embargo was maintained after Yugoslavia's

International Armed Conflict' in Y Dinstein (ed) *International Law in a Time of Perplexity: Essays in Honour of Shabtai Rosenne* (Martinus Nijhoff, Dordrecht 1989) 273, 285.

[234] On the visit and search of Iraqi and neutral vessels see *Keesing's* (1990) 37695. For data on the number of vessels searched, see W H von Heinegg 'The Current State of International Prize Law' in H H G Post (ed) *International Economic Law and Armed Conflict* (Martinus Nijhoff, Dordrecht 1994) 5, 6–7.

[235] Dalton (n 174) 45.

[236] G P Politakis 'UN-Mandated Naval Operations and the Notion of Pacific Blockade: Comments on Some Recent Developments' (1994) 6 AJICL 173, 191; Y Dinstein *War, Aggression and Self-Defence* (4th edn CUP, Cambridge 2005) 295.

[237] L Fielding 'Maritime Interception: Centrepiece of Economic Sanctions in the New World Order' (1992–1993) 53 *Lousiana LR* 1191, 1224–5; R McLaughlin 'United Nations Mandated Naval Interdiction Operations in the Territorial Sea?' (2002) 51 ICLQ 249.

[238] Dalton (n 174) 53. Iran protested at certain actions of US warships. See UNSC 'Letter Dated 23 October 1990 From the Permanent Representative of the Islamic Republic of Iran to the United Nations Addressed to the Secretary-General' (24 October 1990) UN Doc S/21902; UNSC 'Letter Dated 23 October 1990 From the Permanent Representative of the Islamic Republic of Iran to the United Nations Addressed to the Secretary-General' (24 October 1990) UN Doc S/21903. On one occasion, Iran protested that US warships were present in Iranian territorial waters. See UNSC 'Letter Dated 23 October 1990 From the Permanent Representative of the Islamic Republic of Iran to the United Nations Addressed to the Secretary-General' (24 October 1990) UN Doc S/21904.

[239] Fielding (n 237) 1223.

[240] McLaughlin (n 237) 273–4.

[241] UNSC Res 713 (25 September 1991) UN Doc S/RES/713 [6].

dissolution and thus applied to all the successor States of the FRY.[242] In Security Council Resolution 787 the Security Council authorized Member States to enforce the embargo. Paragraph 11 called upon all States to take 'all necessary steps' to ensure that none of their exports were diverted to the Former Republic of Yugoslavia.[243] Acting under Chapter VII, as well as Chapter VIII of the Charter, paragraph 12 calls on all States:

> ...acting nationally or through regional agencies or arrangements, to use such measures commensurate with the specific circumstances as may be necessary under the authority of the Security Council to halt all inward or outward maritime shipping in order to inspect and verify their cargoes and destinations and to ensure strict implementation of the provisions of resolutions 713 (1991) and 757 (1992).[244]

These measures included, according to Security Council Resolution 820, the prohibition of maritime traffic from entering the territorial sea of the FRY, except where authorized or when in *force majeure*.[245] This demonstrates the considerable discretion of the Security Council to authorize measures going beyond the traditional law. This would extend to taking action in the territorial sea of a neutral State.[246]

6. Conclusion

According to the original design of the UN Charter, States would not have been able to have recourse to the law of neutrality. As Fenwick forcefully argued:

> What is said of the old laws of war is equally if not more true of the old law of neutrality, which has passed away with the new law of collective responsibility. Even in the case of recognised States which have not been admitted into the United Nations, it is not to be believed that they will be able to claim, if they should be so unwise as to attempt to do so, the former rights of neutrals and perhaps block the action of the United Nations against the aggressor...[247]

Subsequent practice has demonstrated that there exists greater room under the Charter for neutrality than perceived by those writing at the time of its creation.

[242] UNSC Res 727 (8 January 1992) UN Doc S/RES/727 [6]; see also UNSC 'Further Report of the Secretary-General Pursuant to Security Council Resolution 721' (5 January 1992) UN Doc S/23363 [33].

[243] UNSC Res 787 (16 November 1992) UN Doc S/RES/787 [11].

[244] Ibid [12].

[245] UNSC Res 820 (17 April 1993) UN Doc S/RES/820 [28].

[246] McLaughlin (n 237) 274.

[247] Fenwick (n 3) 86–7.

In part, the acceptance of a position of neutrality under the Charter was a matter of political expediency and a concession to *realpolitik* during the Cold War. As a group of Swedish military experts concluded, in an analysis conducted before Sweden joined the UN:

> ...the member States will not be obliged to participate in enforcement measures...[and] are free in such a war to observe neutrality in the traditional sense. This does not mean that a smaller State does not run any risk to be drawn into a great power war. But if this happens, it will not be as a consequence of its membership in the United Nations.[248]

This chapter has sought to trace in some detail the way in which the Security Council may override the law of neutrality. The procedure of Chapter VII suggests that States are *released* from their obligations of neutrality upon the Security Council identifying the State responsible for a threat or breach of the peace, or an act of aggression, under Article 39 of the Charter, or proceeding further through the suite of options of Chapter VII. The imposition of sanctions under Article 41 during a situation in which neutrality is applicable, or becomes applicable, *obligates* States to adhere to the obligations of the Charter rather than the law of neutrality.

With regard to the use of military force authorized by the Security Council, somewhat paradoxically, the increasing flexibility of the Security Council's decision-making practices has led to a greater tolerance for positions of abstention from UN Security Council action. The failure to conclude agreements under Article 43 of the Charter has obviously played a significant part in this; the inability of the Security Council to compel Member States to contribute military forces has led to the *de facto* acceptance of non-participation on the part of many States and an increasing reliance on coalitions to undertake military tasks.

Just because the Security Council cannot compel military participation in UN-authorized action does not mean, however, that neutral duties are completely unaffected by Security Council military enforcement action. The practice of States and case law suggests that the Security Council does not need explicitly to displace the law of neutrality; instead, the increasing acceptance that Article 103 and Article 2(5) are applicable to Security Council authorizations appears to indicate that UN obligations will prevail over the duties of neutrality, and the developing State practice reviewed demonstrates certain *de minimus* forms of discrimination in favour of UN military operations.

[248] *Kommentar till Förenta Nationernas stadga* (Stockholm 1945) cited in Blix (n 39) 47.

Chapter 5
The Exercise of Belligerent Rights Against Neutrals

Under the traditional law of neutrality at sea, belligerents are able to take certain measures in relation to the control of neutral shipping and aircraft. The ability of belligerents to undertake measures to interfere with neutral shipping has, in the traditional law, given rise to the possibility of direct confrontation between traditional belligerent 'rights' or powers, on the one hand, and the right of neutrals to enjoy peacetime freedoms of commerce, on the other.[1]

The traditional law provides that neutral shipping is required to submit to these belligerent measures of control. These measures of control are, principally, the right to undertake visit, search, and seizure to prevent contraband from reaching an enemy port; the right to set up a blockade in order to prevent ingress or egress to and from enemy territory; and the ability to set up certain 'maritime exclusion zones' for the conduct of naval warfare. While these measures developed to govern the interaction of neutrals and belligerents at sea, there is an increasing recognition that these measures are equally applicable to aerial warfare. Pursuant to the traditional law, neutrals are required to acquiesce in these belligerent measures, as long as such action is in conformity with the law of naval warfare and is not undertaken in the territorial waters or airspace of a neutral State.

The view that neutral shipping must automatically submit to these belligerent powers of control is increasingly challenged by theoretical and practical developments, both of which suggest that the *jus ad bellum* has had increasing effect on the interaction between belligerent and neutral States. It is the purpose of the present chapter to evaluate the extent to which the neutral's duty of acquiescence to belligerent measures has been affected by the impact of the law on the use of force.

[1] As a number of writers have pointed out, the use of the term 'belligerent rights' is inaccurate. The law of armed conflict does not itself grant 'rights' to belligerents but instead, as Adam Roberts points out, 'suffers them to take certain actions.' See A Roberts 'The Equal Application of the Law of War: a Principle under Pressure' (2008) 90 IRRC 931, 935. For similar views see F Bugnion 'Guerre juste, guerre d'aggression et droit international humanitaire' (2002) 84 IRRC 523, 532 n 17; A Orakhelashvili 'Overlap and Convergence: The Interaction Between *Jus ad Bellum* and *Jus in Bello*' (2007) 12 JCSL 157, 165; C Greenwood 'The Relationship between *Ius ad Bellum* and *Ius in Bello*' (1983) 9 RIS 221, 227–8. Because of its popular usage and for the purpose of convenience, the term 'belligerent rights' will continue to be used throughout this chapter.

1. The UN Charter and Belligerent Rights

a. The Uncertain Status of Belligerent Rights

Under traditional international law, the presence of a state of war permitted belligerents as of right, but according to certain limits, to take measures against neutral shipping. The ability to exercise these belligerent rights under the law of armed conflict now that the concept of war is prohibited is open to doubt.

There has long been general uncertainty regarding the extent of the UN Charter's effect on the exercise of belligerent rights, and particularly regarding belligerent interference with neutrals. This uncertainty first became apparent following the cessation of hostilities between Israel and the Arab States in 1948. Following the signature of an armistice agreement, Egypt closed the Suez Canal and continued to intercept Israeli and third party merchant vessels.[2] In 1950, it published a contraband list.[3] Throughout, Egypt claimed that a state of war continued to exist between Israel and Egypt, despite the armistice agreement, and that it was therefore permitted to exercise belligerent controls.[4] Israel protested against Egypt's actions.

The Security Council Resolution of 1 September 1951 characterized Egypt's action as unjustifiable under the circumstances but did not discuss whether traditional belligerent rights remained on foot alongside the Charter: it noted that 'neither party can reasonably assert that it is actively a belligerent, or requires to exercise the right to visit, search and seizure for any legitimate purpose of self-defence.'[5] The Resolution has been marshalled in support of the view that the UN Charter does not support the exercise of traditional belligerent rights.[6]

Examined more closely, however, the Resolution is ambiguous; and its disjunctive form presumably has some intention or meaning. It could therefore be argued that the Resolution contemplates two distinct scenarios governed by different legal frameworks: when a State is 'actively a belligerent'—i.e. when a State will possess all the powers of a belligerent in wartime—and when a State is in a

[2] For a thorough review of the issues see generally S Dinitz 'The Legal Aspects of the Egyptian Blockade of the Suez Canal' (1956–1957) 45 Geo LJ 169; T D Brown Jr 'World War Prize Law Applied in a Limited War Situation: Egyptian Restrictions on Neutral Shipping with Israel' (1965–1966) 50 Minn LR 849; L Gross 'Passage Through the Suez Canal of Israeli-Bound Cargo and Israeli Ships' (1957) 51 AJIL 530.

[3] Dinitz (n 2) 171. Egypt also established a prize court. On this see generally J Trappe 'On the Jurisdiction of the Egyptian Prize Court, 1948-1960' (1959–60) 15–16 REDI 60.

[4] See 'Conclusions du gouvernement égyptien au sujet des plaintes des gouvernements étrangers quant à la visite des navires neutres et la saisie des objets de contrabande dans les ports egyptiens' (1951) 7 REDI 235, 238.

[5] UNSC Res 95 (1 September 1951) UN Doc S/2322. For background, see 'The Security Council and the Suez Canal' (1952) 1 ICLQ 85.

[6] R Higgins 'Legal Limits to the Use of Force by Sovereign States: United Nations Practice' (1961) 37 BYBIL 269, 311; E Lauterpacht 'The Legal Irrelevance of the "State of War"' (1968) 62 PAS 58.

state of peace, in which circumstance the law of self-defence will prevail. The Resolution appears to leave open the effect of the UN Charter on the exercise of belligerent rights against neutrals.

It is not clear, however, whether the legal situation is governed by such a binary classification, and that questions of self-defence are irrelevant to an assessment of the interaction between neutrals and belligerents. According to the traditional law, a determination that war or armed conflict exists automatically brings into operation, vis-à-vis parties to an armed conflict, belligerent rights of visit, search, seizure, and blockade. Pursuant to this approach both belligerents are entitled to take these measures against neutrals. There are reasons of principle and practice to question this approach in light of the Charter provisions on the use of force.

b. The Peaceful Relationship Between Belligerents and Neutrals

The relationship between neutrals and belligerents is inherently one of peace.[7] The law of peace is not replaced *in toto* by the presence of armed conflict, and is only modified to a certain extent required by the law of maritime neutrality.[8] If the fact is fully acknowledged that the relationship between belligerents and neutrals is one of peace, it would appear to follow that any interference by belligerents with neutral shipping or aviation must be judged not only under the law of neutrality, but also under the *jus ad bellum*.

This suggests a difference in relationship between the *jus ad bellum* and the law of neutrality, on the one hand, and between the *jus ad bellum* and the *jus in bello*, on the other. Much debate has surrounded the precise relationship between the *jus ad bellum* and the *jus in bello*. In particular, views differ on the precise impact of the *jus ad bellum* on the *jus in bello*, and how the two regimes overlap. A prominent view suggests that, once an 'armed conflict' comes into existence, analysis under the *jus ad bellum* yields to the *jus in bello*, as the former is generally thought not to apply to individual acts of violence within the course of the armed conflict itself.

The situation is different under the law of neutrality. There is no situation of armed conflict between a neutral and a belligerent State; the relationship, as stated above, is one of peace. This means, however, that the *jus ad bellum* will necessarily and logically have an impact on the evaluation of belligerent interference with neutrals. In other words, now that war is unlawful in international law, analysis of the reach of belligerent measures against neutrals cannot be confined only to the law of neutrality: whether such measures are justified must also be evaluated under the law on the use of force. This means that the *jus ad bellum* is relevant not

[7] *Helsinki Principles* 499 ([1.3]).

[8] Ibid.

only to the initial use of force, but to each interaction between belligerents and neutrals. Because of the peaceful relationship between belligerents and neutrals, each act of interference by belligerents against neutrals is subject to a two-tiered test; for such an act to be lawful, it must be justified under both the *jus ad bellum* and the law of neutrality.[9]

This approach is also supported by logic. It would be contrary to the thrust of the UN Charter and the direction of international law to contend that a State may exercise an arsenal of belligerent powers against commercial neutral shipping and aircraft simply because it had engaged in an act of aggression resulting in a situation of armed conflict. The right of belligerents to interfere with neutrals is no longer analysed solely under the law of neutrality. Instead, that interference must be judged under the law on the use of force as well.

c. Belligerent Rights and the Law of the Sea

In protesting against belligerent interference with neutral shipping, States frequently make reference to the right to freedom of navigation. In the Iran-Iraq war, for instance, in protesting against indiscriminate attacks on neutral shipping, States frequently invoked the right to freedom of navigation and the law of the sea.[10] Security Council Resolutions also reaffirmed the right to freedom of navigation as a principle to be respected alongside the law of neutrality.[11]

The fact that States and the Security Council frequently refer to the right of freedom of navigation alongside the law of neutrality and the law of naval warfare reaffirms the view that the relationship between parties to an armed conflict and non-participants is one of peace. As Wolfrum writes, '[e]ven in times of war, the freedom of navigation cannot be regarded as suspended between States that are not parties to the conflict.'[12] The law of the sea and the law of naval warfare no

[9] M Bothe 'Neutrality in Naval Warfare: What is Left of Traditional International Law?' in A J M Delissen and G J Tanja (eds) *Humanitarian Law of Armed Conflict: Challenges Ahead—Essays in Honour of Frits Kalshoven* (Martinus Nijhoff, Dordrecht 1991) 387, 392–3.

[10] See UNSC Verbatim Record (25 May 1984) UN Doc S/PV.2541 [17] (Kuwait); [35] (Qatar) [74]-[75] (Senegal); UNSC Verbatim Record (25 May 1984) UN Doc S/PV.2542 [5] (Jordan); [30] (Ecuador); [38]-[42] (Sudan); [57] (Panama); UNSC Verbatim Record (29 May 1984) UN Doc S/PV.2543 [7], [16] (Bahrain); [47]-[49] (Somalia); [64]-[66] (Germany); [73] (United Arab Emirates); [83] (Oman); UNSC Verbatim Record (30 May 1984) UN Doc S/PV.2545 [11] (Djibouti); [25] (United States); [49] (Turkey); [62] (Tunisia); [76] (Egypt); UNSC Verbatim Record (1 June 1984) UN Doc S/PV.2546 [17] (Liberia); [23] (China); [29] (the Netherlands)' [51] (Pakistan); [69] (Soviet Union); [75]-[78] (United Kingdom); [91]-[92] (India); [100] (Malta).

[11] UNSC Res 540 (31 October 1983) SCOR Resolutions and Decisions 6 [3]; UNSC Res 552 (1 June 1984) SCOR Resolutions and Decisions 15 [2].

[12] R Wolfrum 'Military Activities on the High Seas: What are the Impacts of the UN Convention on the Law of the Sea?' in L C Green and M N Schmitt (eds) *The Law of Armed Conflict: Into the Next Millennium* (International Law Studies 71, US Naval War College, Newport 1998) 501, 506.

longer exist in separate spheres.[13] The modern law of the sea must, therefore, be taken into account in any discussion of the interaction between belligerents and neutrals.

The link between the 1982 UN Convention on the Law of the Sea (LOSC) and the law of naval warfare is not straightforward and has generated a considerable amount of literature. It is clear that the LOSC has not replaced the rights and duties of neutrality. Article 87 of the LOSC states that freedom of the high seas is to be exercised 'under the conditions laid down by this Convention and by other rules of international law.'[14] In certain areas, however—for example, in relation to innocent passage through the territorial sea and navigation through international straits—the law of neutrality must be reconciled with the provisions of the LOSC.[15]

Generally, however, military matters do not feature prominently in the LOSC.[16] Indeed, the LOSC makes no mention of the traditional law of naval warfare, which has led to erroneous speculation that this body of law has been superseded. Article 88 provides that the high seas will be reserved for peaceful purposes.[17] Some ambiguity has attached to this phrase, with uncertainty surrounding whether the phrase is intended to prohibit all military activities completely or only breaches of the threat or use of force contrary to Article 2(4) of the UN Charter.[18] The meaning of the phrase 'peaceful purposes' in The Antarctic Treaty, for example, carries the former meaning: all military measures are prohibited.[19]

[13] As the US *Naval Commander's Handbook* states, 'in the last half century, the concepts of "peace" and "war" have become blurred to the extent that it is not always possible to draw neat distinctions between the two.' US *Naval Commander's Handbook* § 4.1.

[14] LOSC art 87(1). For discussion of the meaning of 'other rules' as inclusive of the law of armed conflict see G K Walker *The Tanker War 1980–1988: Law and Policy* (International Law Studies 74, US Naval War College, Newport 2000) 487–9.

[15] For consideration of these issues see W H von Heinegg 'The United Nations Convention on the Law of the Sea and Maritime Security Operations' (2005) 48 GYIL 151; J Astley III and M N Schmitt 'The Law of the Sea and Naval Operations' (1997) 42 AFLR 119; A Mayama 'The Influence of the Straits Transit Regime on the Law of Neutrality at Sea' (1995) 26 ODIL 1; V Lowe 'The Impact of the Law of the Sea on Naval Warfare' (1987–1988) 14 SJILC 657; A V Lowe 'The Laws of War at Sea and the 1958 and 1982 Conventions' (1988) 12 MP 286; D G Stephens 'The Impact of the 1982 Law of the Sea Convention on the Conduct of Peacetime Naval/Military Operations' (1998–1999) 29 *Cal Western ILJ* 283; H B Robertson Jr 'Theatre of Operations in Naval Warfare: Different Maritime Areas' in W H von Heinegg (ed) *Regions of Operations of Naval Warfare: Reports and Commentaries of the Round-Table of Experts on International Humanitarian Law Applicable to Armed Conflicts at Sea* (Bochumer Schriften Band 25, Universitätsverlag Brockmeyer, Bochum 1995) 1; H B Robertson Jr *The "New" Law of the Sea and the Law of Armed Conflict at Sea* (Newport Paper No 3, US Naval War College, Newport 1992); B H Oxman 'The Regime of Warships Under the United Nations Convention on the Law of the Sea' (1984) 24 VJIL 809.

[16] D Stephens 'The Legal Efficacy of Freedom of Navigation Assertions' in R B Jacques (ed) *Issues in International Law and Military Operations* (International Law Studies 80, US Naval War College, Newport 2000) 235, 237.

[17] LOSC art 88.

[18] B A Boczek 'Peaceful Purposes of the United Nations Convention on the Law of the Sea' (1989) 20 ODIL 359.

[19] The Antarctic Treaty (adopted 1 December 1959, entered into force 23 June 1961) 402 UNTS 71 art 1.

Article 88 should not, however, be read in isolation but in context and in light of the LOSC's object and purpose.[20] In particular, Article 88 must be read together with Article 301, which states that in exercising rights or performing their obligations under the LOSC, States must 'refrain from any threat or use of force against the territorial integrity or political independence of any State, or in any other manner inconsistent with the principles of international law embodied in the Charter of the United Nations.'[21] The effect of Article 88 and Article 301, it has been noted, is to tie the use of force at sea to the UN Charter's restrictions on the use of force.[22]

This lends further support to the view that the exercise of belligerent rights against neutrals has been restricted considerably by the law on the use of force contained in the Charter and by the central importance of the peacetime right to freedom of navigation in the LOSC. Any restriction on the freedom of navigation of neutral shipping should therefore be regarded as an exceptional measure that must be justified under the Charter provisions on the use of force.

d. Belligerent Rights and the Prohibition on the Threat or Use of Force

It may be objected that certain belligerent action permissible under the law of neutrality, such as the exercise of the power of visit and search over merchant vessels, does not constitute a violation of the use of force under the UN Charter.[23] This is because of the recognized distinction between warships and merchant ships. While the extension of the right of self-defence to cover warships is generally acknowledged, and warships are manifestations of sovereign territory, the case of merchant shipping is different. Merchant ships 'are mere private chattels, lumps of floating steel often situated many miles from the flag State and having little connection, even of an economic nature, with that State, and it is more difficult to explain why they should come within the doctrine of self-defence.'[24] The visit and search of a merchant ship, for example, does not involve the use of force

[20] Vienna Convention on the Law of Treaties (adopted 23 May 1969, entered into force 27 January 1980) 1155 UNTS 331 art 31(1).

[21] LOSC art 301.

[22] S Kaye 'Freedom of Navigation in a Post 9/11 World: Security and Creeping Jurisdiction' in D Freestone, R Barnes and D M Ong (eds) *The Law of the Sea: Progress and Prospects* (OUP, Oxford 2006) 347, 353; A V Lowe 'The Commander's Handbook on the Law of Naval Operations and the Contemporary Law of the Sea' in H B Robertson Jr (ed) *The Law of Naval Operations* (International Law Studies 64, US Naval War College, Newport 1991) 109, 131.

[23] Cf O Bring 'Comments' in I F Dekker and H H G Post (eds) *The Gulf War of 1980–1988* (Martinus Nijhoff, Dordrecht 1992) 243, 243.

[24] A V Lowe 'Self-Defence at Sea' in W E Butler (ed) *The Non-Use of Force in International Law* (Martinus Nijhoff, Dordrecht 1989) 185, 188–9.

against the flag State giving rise to a violation of Article 2(4) of the Charter.[25] The General Assembly's Declaration of Aggression includes as an example of aggression an attack on the 'marine merchant fleet'; it would appear, then, that an attack on an individual merchant ship is not to be considered an act of aggression.[26]

This view may be challenged. It is increasingly accepted that Article 51 may extend to cover the use of force to protect merchant shipping when those vessels are attacked.[27] During the Iran-Iraq War, the rules of engagement of both the United Kingdom and the United States permitted the use of force to protect merchant shipping from attacks.[28] The Netherlands has stated that:

> Deliberate attacks and, at the same time, because of the means employed, indiscriminate attacks against merchant shipping in whatever part of the Gulf fall clearly outside the scope of the permissible use of armed force.[29]

The International Court of Justice in *Oil Platforms* considered whether a State could exercise self-defence in response to attacks on its merchant shipping.[30] In its written pleadings, Iran took the view that individual merchant ships are not considered to be manifestations of the flag State protected by Article 2(4) of the Charter.[31] By contrast, the United States stated in its pleadings that attacks on merchant shipping could amount to an armed attack and trigger a response under Article 51 of the Charter.[32]

The International Court of Justice did not in fact deal directly with the question whether a strike against a single merchant ship could trigger the right of self-defence by the State to which it was flagged.[33] The Court instead focused on the requirement, stated by the Court in *Military and Paramilitary Activities in and*

[25] Bothe (n 9) 393. [26] Ibid.

[27] C Greenwood 'Comments' in I F Dekker and H H G Post (eds) *The Gulf War of 1980–1988* (Martinus Nijhoff, Dordrecht 1992) 212, 213–14.

[28] For the UK position see C Gray 'The British Position with Regard to the Gulf Conflict' (1988) 37 ICLQ 420, 425–6. For the US rules of engagement see 'United States: Secretary of Defence Report (Weinberger Report) to the Congress on Security Arrangements in the Persian Gulf' (1987) 26 ILM 1433, 1454.

[29] UNSC Verbatim Record (1 June 1984) UN Doc S/PV.2546 [31].

[30] *Oil Platforms (Islamic Republic of Iran v United States of America)* [2003] ICJ Rep 161.

[31] *Oil Platforms (Islamic Republic of Iran v United States of America)* (2003) ICJ Pleadings: *Reply and Defence to Counter-claim submitted by the Islamic Republic of Iran* (10 March 1999) <http://www.icj-cij.org/docket/index.php?p1=3&p2=3&k=0a&case=90&code=op&p3=1> accessed 21 August 2007 [7.13].

[32] *Oil Platforms (Islamic Republic of Iran v United States of America)* (2003) ICJ Pleadings: *Rejoinder submitted by the United States of America* (23 March 2001) <http://www.icj-cij.org/docket/index.php?p1=3&p2=3&k=0a&case=90&code=op&p3=1> accessed 21 August 2007 [5.19]-[5.22].

[33] Kammerhofer finds an 'implication' in paragraphs 50–61 of the Judgment that the sinking of civilian vessels may constitute an armed attack in the sense employed by Article 51 of the UN Charter. See J Kammerhofer 'Oil's Well that Ends Well? Critical Reflections on the Merits Judgement in the *Oil Platforms* Case'(2004) 17 LJIL 695, 706–7. This appears to be based on the view that the Court did not explicitly rule out the possibility that an attack on a civilian vessel may constitute an armed attack.

against Nicaragua, to distinguish 'the most grave forms of the use of force (those constituting an armed attack) from other less grave forms.'[34]

This approach to self-defence has been subjected to strong criticism. It has been pointed out that the Court in *Military and Paramilitary Activities in and against Nicaragua* dealt with a specific factual scenario: whether the acts of irregular forces could ever amount to an armed attack.[35] Hence it has been suggested that the requirement that acts reach a certain level of gravity is not applicable to attacks by conventional forces, and that the test was therefore wrongly applied in *Oil Platforms*.[36] If it is accepted that an attack by conventional forces need not meet the requirement of gravity, it has been suggested that an attack on a merchant vessel may indeed amount to an armed attack:

> Other than with its reference to a 'frontier incident' (presumably an isolated instance in which border forces may be acting without authority), the Court was not suggesting that a particular level of gravity is required before a direct attack, involving the use of deadly force by a State's regular armed forces, will qualify as an armed attack. There is certainly nothing in the Court's discussion in *Nicaragua* implying that missile and mine attacks on naval and commercial vessels are anything less than an armed attack.[37]

In his separate opinion in *Oil Platforms*, Judge Simma disagreed with the Court's distinction between different levels of gravity of the use of force. Instead, he suggested, the use of force not amounting to an armed attack, 'for instance against individual ships', could justify in response 'proportionate defensive measures' on the part of the victim, also not amounting to an armed attack.[38]

Despite these proposals, it must be concluded that *Oil Platforms* does not address conclusively the question whether interference with a merchant ship may be classified as a breach of Article 2(4) of the Charter. The most persuasive view is that, while visit and search of neutral shipping or aircraft does not constitute a breach of the prohibition of the use of force, it does necessarily rely on the threat of force to compel compliance.[39] The wrongfulness of such action will be

[34] *Oil Platforms* (n 30) [51] (citing *Military and Paramilitary Activities in and against Nicaragua (Nicaragua v United States of America)* [1986] ICJ Rep 14 at [191]).

[35] See *Military and Paramilitary Activities in and against Nicaragua* (n 34) [195].

[36] See D Raab '"Armed Attack" After the *Oil Platforms* Case' (2004) 17 LJIL 719, 724–245.

[37] W Taft IV 'Self-Defence and the *Oil Platforms* Decision' (2004) 29 YJIL 295. For a similar view that the gravity requirement is not required for an armed attack to arise, see 'The Chatham House Principles of International Law on the Use of Force in Self-Defence' (2006) 55 ICLQ 963, 966, 969–71.

[38] *Oil Platforms* (n 30) (Separate Opinion of Judge Simma) [12].

[39] C Greenwood 'The Effects of the United Nations Charter on the Law of Naval Warfare' in W H von Heinegg (ed) *Visit, Search, Diversion and Capture: the Effect of the United Nations Charter on the Law of Naval Warfare* (Bochumer Shriften Band 24, Universitätsverlag Brockmayer, Bochum 1995) 133, 163.

precluded if it can be shown that the belligerent was acting in accordance with the law of self-defence.[40]

2. The Law of Self-Defence and Neutrals

a. Self-Defence against Neutrals

Self-defence under Article 51 of the UN Charter is an exception to the prohibition on the threat or use of force contained in Article 2(4) of the Charter.[41] Self-defence is therefore a response to the violation of territorial integrity (or political independence) of a State.[42] At first glance, the ability to take measures in self-defence against third States is difficult to comprehend. The right of self-defence is, after all, available only in response to an armed attack and therefore seems inadequate as a legal basis for interference with third States.[43] The position of a neutral State, after all, is in no way impaired by the fact that another State has committed aggression.[44] In this regard it has been remarked that the concept of necessity is a better foundation on which to ground interference by belligerents with neutrals.[45] The State of necessity, in contrast to that of self-defence, is characterized by the fact that a State, faced with the violation of its essential interests, infringes the rights of an innocent State.[46]

Nevertheless, international law grants latitude to States engaged in self-defence to affect incidentally the rights of third States. In its commentary to Article 21 of the Articles on State Responsibility, it is noted that:

> The essential effect of article 21 is to preclude the wrongfulness of conduct of a State acting in self-defence vis-à-vis an attacking State. But there may be effects vis-à-vis third States in certain circumstances... The law of neutrality distinguishes between conduct as against a belligerent and conduct as against a neutral. But neutral States are not unaffected by the existence of a state of war.

[40] ILC 'Report of the International Law Commission on the Work of its 53rd Session' (23 April–10 August 2001) UN Doc A/56/10 art 21.

[41] Y Dinstein *War, Aggression and Self-Defence* (4th edn CUP, Cambridge 2005) 177.

[42] See generally C Gray *International Law and the Use of Force* (3rd edn OUP, Oxford 2008) chapter 4.

[43] 'Commentary' (Remarks of T Halkiopoulos) (1987–1988) 14 SJILC 581, 583.

[44] Bothe (n 9) 394–5.

[45] See D W Bowett *Self-Defence in International Law* (Manchester UP, Manchester 1958) 173; G Schwarzenberger 'Report on Some Aspects of the Principle of Self-Defence in the Charter of the United Nations and the Topics Covered by the Dubrovnik Resolution' in International Law Association Report of the Forty-Eighth Conference (New York, 1958) (International Law Association, New York 1958) 550, 569–75; A Gioia 'Neutrality and Non-Belligerency' in H H G Post (ed) *International Economic Law and Armed Conflict* (Martinus Nijhoff, Dordrecht 1994) 51, 102 n 199.

[46] A Verdross 'Règles générales du droit international de la paix' (1929) 30 RCADI 279, 488–9.

> Article 21 leaves open all issues of the effect of action in self-defence vis-à-vis third States.[47]

This passage is not entirely straightforward and its language is somewhat oblique. But the thrust of it is that it allows that the right of self-defence may in certain circumstances extend to measures against neutral States. This view is supported by other statements made during the International Law Commission's (ILC's) work on the topic of State responsibility. In his Second Report on State Responsibility, Special Rapporteur James Crawford noted that: 'A State exercising an inherent right of self-defence of a State has certain belligerent rights, even as against neutrals.'[48] This strongly suggests that belligerents are permitted by the law of self-defence to take measures affecting third States.[49]

Indeed, it seems that this approach is not a modification of the law of neutrality in light of the UN Charter but the elaboration of a principle of considerable historical pedigree. There is evidence in prize law that self-defence was considered the basis for interference with neutral ships. In the *Le Louis* case, Lord Stowell stated that:

> I can find no authority that gives the right of interruption to the navigation of States in amity upon the high seas, excepting that which the rights of war give to both belligerents against neutrals. This right, incommodious as its exercise may occasionally be to those who are subjected to it, has been fully established in the legal practice of nations, having for its foundation the necessities of self-defence, in preventing the enemy from being supplied with the instruments of war, and from having his means of annoyance augmented by the advantages of maritime commerce…
>
> If it be asked why the right of search does not exist in time of peace as well as in war, the answer is prompt; that it has not the same foundation on which alone it is tolerated in war – the necessities of self-defence.[50]

[47] ILC 'Report of the International Law Commission on the Work of its 53rd Session' (23 April–10 August 2001) UN Doc A/56/10 art 21.

[48] 'Second Report on State Responsibility by Mr James Crawford, Special Rapporteur: Addendum' (30 April 1999) UN Doc A/CN.4/498/Add.2 [300]. This is a broader view of self-defence than that taken in the Commentary to Article 34 in the 1996 Draft Articles. See ILC 'Report of the International Law Commission on the Work of its 32nd Session' (5th May–25th July 1980) UN Doc A/35/10 at 61.

[49] See also J-M Thouvenin 'Circumstances Precluding Wrongfulness in the ILC Articles on State Responsibility: Self-Defence' in J Crawford, A Pellet and S Olleson (eds) *The Law of International Responsibility* (OUP, Oxford 2010) 455, 464–5.

[50] *The Le Louis Case* (1817) 2 Dodson 210, 243–5. For further discussion see B Cheng *General Principles of Law as applied by International Courts and Tribunals* (Grotius Publications, Cambridge 1987) 77–83.

There appears, therefore, to be historical support for the view that self-defence is the foundation of belligerent action against neutrals.[51] If the foundation for action against neutrals is to be found in the law of self-defence, however, the principles of necessity and proportionality must be satisfied.

b. The Principles of Necessity and Proportionality

It is an established principle that self-defence must satisfy the requirements of necessity and proportionality to be lawful.[52] Necessity and proportionality are not mentioned explicitly in Article 51 but are part of customary international law.[53] These principles apply to self-defence in customary international law as well as self-defence taken under Article 51 of the Charter.[54] According to a minority view, the principle of proportionality does not apply in circumstances when the use of force in self-defence leads to the outbreak of war.[55] This view, however, does not reflect State practice and the better approach is that the principles of necessity and proportionality apply regardless of how an armed conflict is characterized by the belligerents. Nevertheless, the scale and the intensity of an armed conflict are undoubtedly important factors in determining what will be necessary and proportionate action.[56]

There exists some uncertainty about the meaning of necessity and proportionality. Necessity requires that force may be used only if absolutely essential for the purpose of repelling or intercepting an armed attack: it denotes that no alternative form of redress, other than the use of force, is available.[57] As well as being necessary, a response in self-defence must also be proportionate. There is disagreement as to how precisely proportionality is to be measured.[58] It has been contended, for example, that proportionality means proportionality between the

[51] See also S Neff 'Prerogatives of Violence: In Search of the Conceptual Foundations of Belligerents' Rights' (1997) 38 GYIL 41, 46.

[52] *Military and Paramilitary Activities in and against Nicaragua* (n 34) [194]; *Legality of the Threat or Use of Nuclear Weapons* (Advisory Opinion) [1996] ICJ Rep 226 [141]; *Oil Platforms* (n 30) [51]; *Case Concerning Armed Activities on the Territory of the Congo (Democratic Republic of the Congo v Uganda)* 2005 <http://www.icj-cij.org/docket/index.php?p1=3&p2=3&k=51&case=116&code=co&p3=4> accessed 20 December 2007 [147].

[53] These principles derive from the *Caroline* incident. See 'Correspondence between Great Britain and the United States, respecting the Arrest and Imprisonment of Mr. McLeod, for the Destruction of the Steamboat Caroline (March, April 1841)' (1840–41) 29 BFSP 1126. See also R Y Jennings 'The Caroline and Mcleod Cases' (1938) 32 AJIL 82.

[54] *Legality of the Threat or Use of Nuclear Weapons* (n 52) [41].

[55] ILC 'Addendum to the Eighth Report on State Responsibility by Mr Roberto Ago' (1980) II(i) YBILC [121] (Ago); Dinstein (n 41) 240.

[56] Greenwood (n 39) 150; R Sloane 'The Cost of Conflation: Preserving the Dualism of *Jus ad Bellum* and *Jus in Bello* in the Contemporary Law of War' (2009) 34 YJIL 47, 68.

[57] Dinstein (n 41) 209–10.

[58] T M Franck 'On Proportionality of Countermeasures in International Law' (2008) 102 AJIL 715, 716.

damage inflicted and the response taken in self-defence.[59] The better view, however, is that any action in self-defence must be proportionate to the objective of countering, repelling or intercepting the armed attack.[60] There is, therefore, a clear link between the principles of necessity and proportionality.[61]

c. The Relationship Between Self-Defence and Neutrality

The view that the basis for belligerent interference with neutral shipping is now found in the law of self-defence and not derived from a state of war was expressed by the United Kingdom, during the Iran-Iraq war.[62] From mid-1985, Iran increasingly stopped and searched neutral merchant shipping for contraband.[63] In response to the exercise of visit and search by Iran of a British merchant ship, the *Barber Perseus*, the United Kingdom stated that:

> The United Kingdom upholds the general principle of the freedom of navigation on the high seas. However, under Article 51 of the United Nations Charter a state such as Iran, actively engaged in an armed conflict, is entitled in exercise of its inherent right of self-defence, to stop and search a foreign merchant ship on the high seas if there is reasonable ground for suspecting that the ship is taking arms to the other side for use in the conflict. This is an exceptional right: if the suspicions prove to be unfounded and if the ship has not committed acts calculated to give rise to suspicion, then the ship's owners have a good claim for compensation for loss caused by the delay.[64]

The United Kingdom claimed, therefore, that the law of self-defence provided the basis for interference with merchant shipping.[65]

The response to the *Barber Perseus* incident marked a development in the UK legal position. Initially the UK framed its position in the traditional terms of 'war'

[59] See, for example, E P J Myjer and N D White 'The Twin Towers Attack: an Unlimited Right to Self-Defence?' (2002) 7 JCSL 5, 8.

[60] C H M Waldock 'The Regulation of the Use of Force by Individual States in International Law' (1952) 81 RCADI 451, 464; Ago (n 55) [121]. See also E Cannizzaro 'Contextualising Proportionality: *Jus ad Bellum* and *Jus in Bello* in the Lebanese War' (2006) 88 IRRC 779, 783–4.

[61] K Trapp 'Back to Basics: Necessity, Proportionality, and the Right of Self-Defence against Non-State Terrorist Actors' (2007) 56 ICLQ 141, 146. The ICJ in *Oil Platforms* noted that the target of force in self-defence was also a relevant consideration in determining whether self-defence is lawful. See *Oil Platforms* (n 30) [74]. This has been interpreted as adding a separate requirement in order for self-defence to be lawful: J A Green 'The Oil Platforms Case: An Error in Judgment?' (2004) 9 JCSL 357, 380, 384. The better view is that the target selected in self-defence will be a factor in calculating whether the principle of proportionality is satisfied.

[62] On the British position on the Iran-Iraq war generally see Gray (n 28); C Gray 'The British Position with Regard to the Gulf Conflict (Iran-Iraq): Part 2' (1991) 40 ICLQ 464.

[63] *Keesing's* (1986) 34514.

[64] (1986) 57 BYBIL 583.

[65] Ibid 635; see also (1988) 59 BYBIL 581.

and 'neutrality,'[66] and referred to the UK's 'neutrality obligations.'[67] However, as the hostilities progressed and attacks on neutral shipping increased, the UK's terminology changed. In 1984, the UK referred to its 'neutrality in the conflict,' but it was careful to note that its neutrality was a 'policy,' rather than an obligation, underscoring its optional nature.[68] It subsequently dropped the language of neutrality altogether, referring instead to its 'impartiality' in the 'conflict'.[69] Similarly, the UK avoided any reference to the doctrine of neutral 'convoy', and stated that its warships 'accompanied' British flag vessels.[70]

The shift in terminology demonstrates the UK's concern that Article 51 of the Charter, and not the law of naval warfare, constitutes the basis for interference with neutral shipping.[71] But there remains some uncertainty as to how the UK's emphasis on the law of self-defence relates to the law of naval warfare and neutrality. On one view, the UK's approach suggests that the law of self-defence comprehensively and exclusively governs the ability of belligerents to intercept merchant shipping. According to another view, the law of naval warfare and neutrality continues to exist, but the law of self-defence now constitutes an additional level of legal restraint.

Questioned in the House of Commons as to whether it was the intention of the UK government to abolish the right of visit and search, the Minister of State responded as follows:

> Yes; I take my hon. Friend's point. None the less, we are anxious that the Iranians should act extremely cautiously. Our position is based on the general principle of freedom of navigation and the United Nations charter.[72]

It seems clear that the UK did not intend to suggest that the law on the use of force had completely superseded the law of naval warfare. Instead, the UK emphasis on the law of self-defence sought to add another level of legal restraint,

[66] See statements contained in (1982) 53 BYBIL 559 ('neutral in the war'); (1983) 54 BYBIL 549 ('neutral in this war').

[67] See (1981) 52 BYBIL 520.

[68] (1984) 55 BYBIL 597.

[69] (1985) 56 BYBIL 534; (1987) 58 BYBIL 638–9; 'Second Report from the Foreign Affairs Committee, Current UK Policy Towards the Iran/Iraq Conflict, June 1988' in A De Guttrey and N Ronzitti (eds) *The Iran-Iraq War (1980–1988) and the Law of Naval Warfare* (Grotius Publications, Cambridge 1993) 291, 315–316, 329; 'Answers by the Prime Minister, 11 July 1988' in ibid 357–8; 'Statement by the Permanent Representative of the UK to the UN before the UN Security Council, 1 June 1984' in ibid 380.

[70] D R Humphrey 'Belligerent Interdiction of Neutral Shipping in International Armed Conflict' (1997) 2 JCSL 23, 34.

[71] A V Lowe 'United Kingdom: Commentary' in A De Guttry and N Ronzitti (eds) *The Iran-Iraq War (1980–1988) and the Law of Naval Warfare* (Grotius Publications, Cambridge 1993) 241, 244. The General Council of British Shipping reproduced the text of Article 51 of the UN Charter to be passed on to masters of British merchant ships entering the Gulf. See C Greenwood 'Remarks' (1988) 82 PAS 146, 159.

[72] (1986) 57 BYBIL 584.

grounded in the principles of necessity and proportionality, to the conduct of hostilities at sea. This is clear from the UK *Manual on the Law of Armed Conflict,* which states, in its chapter on maritime warfare:

> In considering the rules set out in this chapter, it is necessary to bear in mind at all times one point of central importance, namely that the conduct of armed conflict at sea is subject to the limitations imposed by the UN Charter on all use of force. One particularly important aspect of those limitations is that even when resort to force is justified, it should not exceed what is necessary and proportionate to the achievement of the goal for which force may be used.[73]

The UK *Manual* makes it clear that the law of maritime warfare has not been superseded by the limitations of the UN Charter, but that the Charter imposes another level of legal scrutiny: the conduct of armed conflict must not transgress the principles of necessity and proportionality.[74]

In the context of the Iran-Iraq war, it was therefore not enough for Iran to justify its visit and search of neutral merchant shipping under the law of neutrality.[75] According to the UK's approach, Iran would also have been required to show that the visit and search of neutral shipping was necessary and proportionate under the law of self-defence. If action against neutral shipping is neither necessary nor proportionate in self-defence, a belligerent would not be justified in taking action against neutral shipping, even if such action were conducted in accordance with the law of neutrality. In other words, a belligerent is no longer automatically entitled, by the fact of armed conflict or war, to take sweeping measures against neutral commerce; its entitlement to take those measures is limited by the restraints of the UN Charter.

It should be emphasized, however, that there exists no positive obligation *durante bello* on neutrals to resist the exercise of visit and search undertaken by a belligerent that has resorted to armed conflict illegally. In those armed conflicts in which there is no determination of illegality under the *jus ad bellum*, neutral shipping may tolerate interference by both sides. Even though a neutral ship may tolerate the aggressor's exercise of visit and search, that tolerance does not stem from an attitude of legal conviction.[76]

[73] UK *Manual of the Law of Armed Conflict* § 13.3.

[74] See ibid § 12.2; § 12.44; § 12.81; § 12.98; § 13.46; § 13.91; § 13.106.

[75] See UNSC 'Letter Dated 19 July 1985 from the Permanent Representative of the Islamic Republic of Iran to the United Nations Addressed to the Secretary-General' (22 July 1985) UN Doc S/17348.

[76] Orakhelashvili (n 1) 193.

d. Criticisms of the Link Between the *Jus ad Bellum* and Neutrality

This position has been subjected to various objections. First, it has been suggested that the imposition of constraints derived from the law of self-defence to the conduct of hostilities undermines the principle that the rules of armed conflict should apply equally to both sides of the armed conflict, regardless of which side is acting lawfully under the *jus ad bellum*.[77]

This view takes as its starting point the view that the constraints of the *jus ad bellum* recede once an armed conflict exists and the *jus in bello* comes into play.[78] However, there exists a growing body of practice and scholarly opinion that the *jus ad bellum* no longer recedes once an armed conflict is being waged, but continues to apply throughout the conduct of hostilities. Instead, the principles of necessity and proportionality in the *jus ad bellum* remain relevant throughout the course of the armed conflict.[79] Thus in a case of self-defence, it is not enough for a State to invoke self-defence and then to suggest that its subsequent acts comply with the law of armed conflict. It must also demonstrate that its conduct throughout the armed conflict is proportionate under the *jus ad bellum*.[80] The destruction of a military objective, for example, will need to satisfy not only the requirements of the law of armed conflict in relation to targeting, but must also be proportionate to the ends of self-defence.[81] While the concept of proportionality in the law of armed conflict is concerned with collateral damage to civilians and civilian objects, the concept of *jus ad bellum* proportionality takes into account a broader, architectural set of questions, including interference with third States.[82]

One prominent example of this approach is the UK's conduct during the armed conflict with Argentina over the Falkland Islands. During the conflict, the United Kingdom stated that its military operations were conducted 'within the framework of the Charter' and that its operations had been reported to the Security

[77] W H von Heinegg 'The Current State of International Prize Law' in H H G Post (ed) *International Economic Law and Armed Conflict* (Martinus Nijhoff, Dordrecht 1994) 5, 22; W H von Heinegg '"Benevolent" Third States in International Armed Conflicts: The Myth of the Irrelevance of the Law of Neutrality' in M N Schmitt and J Peijic (eds) *International Law and Armed Conflict: Exploring the Faultlines* (Martinus Nijhoff, Leiden 2007) 543, 562–3.

[78] See *Legal Consequences of the Construction of a Wall in the Occupied Palestinian Territory* (Advisory Opinion) 2004 ICJ Pleadings CR2004/1 <http://www.icj-cij.org/docket/index.php?p1=3&p2=4&k=5a&case=131&code=mwp&p3=2> accessed 21 August 2006, 44 (Abi-Saab): 'Once an armed conflict is brought into being, the *jus in bello* (or international humanitarian law) comes into play, as the *lex specialis* governing the ensuing situation regardless of the *jus ad bellum*.'

[79] See J G Gardam 'Proportionality and Force in International Law' (1993) 87 AJIL 391, 404; Sloane (n 56) 68–9; R Lagoni 'Remarks' (1988) 82 PAS 161, 162–3.

[80] Greenwood (n 1) 223.

[81] Gardam (n 79) 404. Such an approach also seems to find confirmation in *Oil Platforms*, where the ICJ stated that: 'The United States must also show that its actions were necessary and proportional to the armed attack made on it, and that the platforms were a legitimate military target open to attack in the exercise of self-defence.' (*Oil Platforms* (n 30) [51]).

[82] J G Gardam 'A Role for Proportionality in the War on Terror' (2005) 74 NJIL 3, 5.

Council.[83] Its use of military force, it stated on a number of occasions, was governed by necessity and proportionality of self-defence.[84] The UK Attorney General advised the British war cabinet that an attack on the Argentine mainland would go beyond a proportionate response.[85] Almost every aspect of the UK campaign was justified in detail according to whether an action was a necessary and proportionate response to the armed attack.[86] When the British navy targeted the *General Belgrano*—an Argentine cruiser that was a legitimate military objective under the *jus in bello*—the debate on the legality of its sinking was conducted almost entirely according to whether it was justified under the *jus ad bellum*.[87]

This approach does not threaten the equality of belligerents under the *jus in bello*. After all, a State acting in self-defence cannot excuse an act that is contrary to the law of armed conflict.[88] Conversely, compliance with the law of armed conflict will not excuse a violation of the *jus ad bellum*.[89] The objection that such an approach would undermine the equality of belligerents is even less persuasive with regard to the relationship between the *jus ad bellum* and the law of neutrality. Even those who deny the application of the *jus ad bellum* throughout the conduct of hostilities between belligerents accept that the law of neutrality is the area of the *jus in bello* that has been most deeply modified by the UN Charter.[90] Indeed, even if one rejects the view that the requirements of necessity and proportionality under the *jus ad bellum* apply throughout the course of an armed conflict vis-à-vis the belligerents themselves, it seems difficult to maintain that the principles of necessity and proportionality do not apply throughout the course of an armed conflict to the interactions between belligerents and neutrals, which is based in the law of peace.[91]

Secondly, this approach has been criticized for its vagueness and potential for abuse.[92] It has been suggested that to tie the exercise of belligerent rights to the application of the principles of necessity and proportionality would open a wide margin of discretion.[93] Von Heinegg argues that the application of this approach would imply that belligerents have greater latitude to interfere with merchant shipping as an armed conflict escalates, and so would have an incentive to ratchet

[83] See (1983) 54 BYBIL 545; (1984) 55 BYBIL 591–2; (1985) 56 BYBIL 526.

[84] See W J Fenrick 'Legal Aspects of the Falklands Naval Conflict' (1985) 24 RDPM 243, 245.

[85] Ibid 249. [86] Greenwood (n 39) 149. [87] Greenwood (n 80) 223–4.

[88] Greenwood (n 39) 164. [89] Ibid. [90] Ibid 160.

[91] C Greenwood 'Self-Defence and the Conduct of International Armed Conflict' in Y Dinstein (ed) *International Law at a Time of Complexity: Essays in Honour of Shabtai Rosenne* (Martinus Nijhoff, Dordrecht 1989) 273, 283; J Gardam *Necessity, Proportionality and the Use of Force by States* (CUP, Cambridge 2004) 176.

[92] W H von Heinegg 'The Current State of the Law of Naval Warfare: A Fresh Look at the *San Remo Manual*' in A M Helm (ed) *The Law of War in the 21st Century: Weaponry and the Use of Force* (International Law Studies 82, US Naval War College, Newport 2006) 269, 285. See also 'Commentary' (Remarks of H B Robertson) (1987–1988) 14 SJILC 581, 586.

[93] von Heinegg (n 77) 24.

up hostilities to take advantage of these rights. He suggests that a crucial element of restraint would be lost.[94]

However, application of the traditional law alone brings with it its own uncertainties: most notably, whether belligerent rights may be exercised in an armed conflict that is not classified as a war.[95] If the traditional law applies upon the outbreak of armed conflict and is unrestricted by the *jus ad bellum*, a belligerent would be permitted to take extensive measures against neutrals remote from the theatre of armed conflict. If the full battery of belligerent rights against neutrals is available only when an armed conflict is classified as a war, however, there arise considerable difficulties in determining how to define war in international law. It is suggested that the application of the *jus ad bellum* as a further constraint on belligerent action against neutrals provides greater certainty and is more consistent with contemporary international law.

3. The Law of Contraband

The view that belligerent interference with neutral commerce must meet a double test to be lawful—justified under both the *jus ad bellum* as well as the law of neutrality—is not only theoretically coherent but is reflected in various instances of State practice. On numerous occasions, justification of belligerent interference with neutral shipping has been conducted by reference to the law of self-defence.

a. The Exercise of Visit and Search and Self-Defence

i. Iraq: maritime interdiction in the Persian Gulf (1990)

An embargo was imposed on Iraq pursuant to Security Council Resolution 661, which was passed four days after Iraq invaded Kuwait in 1990.[96] Resolution 661 was, however, silent on whether measures could be taken against shipping attempting to breach the embargo. The matter was resolved by the passage of Resolution 665, which has been described as 'the fundamental conceptual precedent for modern UN naval interdiction operations.'[97] In the short period between the passage of Resolutions 661 and 665, however, the question arose whether certain States acting in self-defence of Kuwait were permitted to exercise visit and search against merchant shipping to enforce compliance with Resolution 661.[98]

[94] Ibid. [95] See generally Humphrey (n 70).

[96] UNSC Res 661 (6 August 1990) SCOR Resolutions and Decisions 19 [3].

[97] R McLaughlin 'United Nations Mandated Naval Interdiction Operations in the Territorial Sea' (2002) 51 ICLQ 249, 261. UNSC Res 665 (25 August 1990) SCOR Resolutions and Decisions 21.

[98] The view that naval operations during the Kuwait crisis were based in the law of self-defence has been criticized in V Gowlland-Debbas 'Security Council Enforcement Action and Issues of State

Resolution 661 imposed obligations on all States to comply with the embargo on Iraq during a situation of international armed conflict, so no State (except non-members of the UN at the time, such as Switzerland) was strictly in the position of a neutral State.[99] Nevertheless, the events that transpired between Resolution 661 and 665 concerned the relationship between those States that claimed to be acting in collective self-defence of Kuwait, and those that did not.[100]

Resolution 661 was passed on 6 August 1990. On 12 August 1990, Kuwait made a formal request for assistance to the United States and to the United Kingdom, asking those States to take military and other steps necessary to ensure that economic measures were complied with.[101] The US took the view that the request from Kuwait furnished a sufficient legal basis for the interdiction of shipping to enforce the Security Council Resolution.[102] Similarly, the British Foreign and Commonwealth Minister of State stated that Article 51 provided the legal authority to take measures to 'reinforce the economic weapon that was put in place under the Security Council Resolution.'[103] On 12 August, the US Secretary of State announced an interdiction policy that included the use of force against ships attempting to breach the embargo.[104] US Special Warning Notice No 80 of 17 August 1990 stated that:

> (1) In response to requests from the legitimate government of Kuwait and in exercising the inherent right of collective self-defence recognised under Article 51 of the UN Charter, United States forces will, in co-operation with regional and allied forces, conduct a maritime operation to intercept the import and export of commodities and products to and from Iraq and Kuwait that are prohibited by Security Council Resolution 661.
>
> [...]

Responsibility' (1994) 43 ICLQ 55, 88–9. Cf S Lyons 'Naval Operations in the Gulf' in P Rowe (ed) *The Gulf War in International and English Law* (Routledge, London 1993) 155, 157–8.

[99] For the view that the law of armed conflict was in operation between Iraq and Kuwait, see C Greenwood 'New World Order or Old? The Invasion of Kuwait and the Rule of Law' (1992) 55 MLR 153, 171.

[100] See J G Dalton 'The Influence of Law on Seapower in Desert Shield/Desert Storm' (1993) 41 Naval LR 27, 33–4.

[101] UNSC 'Letter Dated 12 August 1990 from the Permanent Representative of Kuwait to the United Nations Addressed to the President of the Security Council' (13 August 1990) UN Doc S/21498.

[102] UNSC 'Letter Dated 16 August 1990 from the Charge d'affaires A I of the United States Mission to the United Nations Addressed to the Security Council, 16 August 1990' (16 August 1990) UN Doc S/21537; 'United States Department of Defense, Press Release Concerning Naval Interdiction, 16 August 1990' in E Lauterpacht et al (eds) *The Kuwait Crisis: Basic Documents* (Cambridge International Documents Series I, Grotius, Cambridge 1991) 247.

[103] 'Transcript of a Press Conference Given by the British Foreign and Commonwealth Minister of State, Mr William Waldegrave, 13 August 1990' in *The Kuwait Crisis* (n 102) 245–6.

[104] Dalton (n 100) 34.

(6) Failure of a ship to proceed as directed will result in the use of the minimum level of force necessary to ensure compliance.[105]

According to the US and British position, they were entitled, pursuant to the right of collective self-defence, to take visit and search measures against third States in order to enforce Resolution 661. On the same day, the first interdictions in Operation Desert Shield took place, when Iraqi tankers were visited and searched in the Red Sea and the Persian Gulf.[106]

There was, however, considerable opposition to the US and UK stance. Other States on the Security Council—France, the Soviet Union, Canada, and Malaysia—refused to participate unless the interdiction operations were brought under the authority of Article 42 of the Charter.[107] Sudan and Jordan protested against the interdiction regime, and Sudan asked for clarification from the Security Council whether a blockade could be established under Resolution 661.[108] Even amongst those States prepared to act on the basis of self-defence, it was thought that the passage of a further Resolution explicitly authorizing such interdiction was politically preferable.[109]

Resolution 665, passed on 25 August 1990, brought the interdiction operations under the authority of the Security Council.[110] Resolution 665 raised a host of legal issues, notably in relation to the sequencing of measures under Articles 41 and 42 of the Charter.[111] This was not the only source of uncertainty. What also remained opaque in Resolutions 661 and 665 was the interrelationship between the Charter and the traditional law. States that questioned the US and UK use of collective self-defence to enforce Resolution 661 did not raise concerns about the resort to measures against third States. Instead, they objected to the recourse to collective self-defence, on the basis that the Security Council, following the passage of Resolution 661, remained seized of the matter and had exclusive competence to order further measures.[112]

If this issue is put to one side, the question arises whether visit and search by the US and UK was permissible. It seems clear that States acting on the basis of collective self-defence were in principle permitted to take measures to enforce

[105] 'Special Warning No. 80 issued by the United States Department of the Navy, 17 August 1990' in *The Kuwait Crisis* (n 102) 248.

[106] McLaughlin (n 97) 259.

[107] Dalton (n 100) 34–5.

[108] See UNSC 'Letter Dated 20 August 1990 From the Permanent Representative of Jordan to the United Nations Addressed to the Secretary-General' (20 August 1990) UN Doc S/21571; UNSC 'Note Verbale Dated 19 August 1990 From the Charge D'Affaires A I of the Permanent Mission of the Sudan to the United Nations Addressed to the President of the Security Council' (21 August 1990) UN Doc S/21574.

[109] Dalton (n 100) 37–8.

[110] UNSC Res 665 (n 97) [1].

[111] McLaughlin (n 97) 255–7.

[112] For different views on this issue, see T M Franck and F Patel 'UN Police Action in Lieu of War: "The Old Order Changeth"' (1991) 85 AJIL 63; E V Rostow 'Until What? Enforcement Actions of Collective Self-Defence?' (1991) 85 AJIL 506.

Resolution 661, and that it was the fact that they claimed to be acting in self-defence, and not merely because they were in an armed conflict and could therefore exercise belligerent rights against neutrals, that proved decisive.

Whether the measures could exceed the measures available to belligerents against neutrals is a more uncertain question. It has been noted that, during the conflict, State practice indicated that 'the legality of a State's resort to force has a subtle impact on the perception by that State of the means that can legitimately be used to achieve its goal.'[113] It is certainly clear that the States involved saw the maritime *jus in bello* applicable to the conflict: the US, for example, set up two prize courts, one in the southern district of New York and one in the northern district of California, in order to adjudicate cases arising out of Operation Desert Storm.[114]

Although it has been asserted that a State acting in self-defence may take action against neutrals that exceeds the limits of the traditional law,[115] it is suggested that the better view is that the traditional law serves as the threshold beyond which a State acting in self-defence may not cross.[116] After all, the traditional law regulating the relationship between belligerents and neutrals was formulated at a time when war was legal; it is unlikely in the extreme that the principles of necessity and proportionality would permit the rights of non-participants to be interfered with to a greater extent in an era in which the threat or use of force is prohibited.[117]

Given the reality that, although not technically neutral, a number of States wished to remain non-participants and not actively to assist Kuwait, the UK and the US would not have been permitted to exercise against merchant shipping any measures that went beyond measures that would have been available under the law of neutrality. Indeed, given that every interference by the US and the UK with 'neutral' shipping would have to be justified as necessary and proportionate for Kuwait's self-defence, it is likely that those States would be prevented from exercising the plenitude of the traditional law.

ii. Kosovo: interdiction of oil tankers by NATO forces (1999)

The background to the crisis in Kosovo is well known.[118] During the course of the armed conflict between NATO States and the Federal Republic of Yugoslavia (FRY), it became clear that air strikes on air refineries by NATO were not having the desired impact on the flow of oil into the FRY. Indeed, the FRY continued to receive petroleum imports from a number of States, principally Russia.

113 Gardam (n 79) 393.
114 Astley III and Schmitt (n 15) 143 n 98.
115 For this view see S Neff *The Rights and Duties of Neutrals* (Manchester UP, Manchester 2000) 212–13.
116 Greenwood (n 91) 285.
117 See D P O'Connell *The Influence of Law on Seapower* (Manchester UP, Manchester 1975) 160.
118 For a discussion of the background, see S Chesterman *Just War or Just Peace: Humanitarian Intervention and International Law* (OUP, Oxford 2001) 206–10.

Russia continued to supply oil to the Montenegrin port of Bar, and refused to support a European-led embargo.[119] This continued supply of oil to the FRY led NATO to contemplate the exercise of visit and search of merchant shipping.[120] NATO spokesman Jamie Shea emphasized that the aim of such a visit and search regime had the aim of curtailing petroleum imports to the FRY so as 'to have a decisive impact on military operations in Yugoslavia.'[121] In a debate in the House of Lords, the Parliamentary Under-Secretary of State at the Foreign and Commonwealth Office stated that:

> ...the law in this area is of course complex. There is customary law, treaties and international conventions. I assure the noble Lord that all these areas will be considered not only by NATO but also by legal advisors here. We have to make any embargo as effective as we can. NATO is working out military options. We shall take into account any rules of engagement as well as international law.[122]

Since there existed an international armed conflict at the relevant time between the States of NATO and the FRY, the law of neutrality was applicable, and offered one possible basis for the interception of merchant ships carrying contraband.[123] However, States exhibited a reluctance to rely solely on the belligerent rights of visit and search based on the existence of armed conflict.[124] At one point in the discussions amongst NATO States, a blockade of the Montenegrin port of Bar was contemplated, as a possible extension of existing military operations.[125] However,

[119] S Castle 'War in the Balkans: Embargo – NATO Sidesteps Oil Stand-off With Russia' *The Independent* (London 1 May 1999) <http://www.independent.co.uk/news/war-in-the-balkans-embargo—nato-sidesteps-oil-standoff-with-russia-1090613.html?cmp=ilc-n> accessed 9 December 2009.

[120] 'Russia to Ignore NATO Embargo' *BBC News* (London, 25 April 1999) < http://news.bbc.co.uk/1/hi/world/europe/327498.stm> accessed 9 December 2009; 'Turning Off Serbia's Oil Supply' *BBC News* (London 29 April 1999) < http://news.bbc.co.uk/1/hi/world/europe/330589.stm> accessed 9 December 2009.

[121] 'Press Conference by Dr Jamie Shea and Brigadier General Guiseppe Marani' (29 April 1999) <http://www.nato.int/koSovo/press/p990429a.htm> accessed 10 December 2009.

[122] Hansard HL vol 600 col 436 (29 April 1999).

[123] C Greenwood 'The Applicability of International Humanitarian Law and the Law of Neutrality to the Kosovo Campaign' in A E Wall (ed) *Legal and Ethical Lessons of NATO's Kosovo Campaign* (International Law Studies 78, US Naval War College, Newport 2003) 35, 39.

[124] G Walker 'Application of the Law of Armed Conflict During Operation Allied Force: Maritime Interdiction and Prisoner of War Issues' in A E Wall (ed) *Legal and Ethical Lessons of NATO's Kosovo Campaign* (International Law Studies 78, US Naval War College, Newport 2003) 85, 94; N Butler 'From Collective Defence to Peace Enforcement' in A Schnabel and R Thakur (eds) *Kosovo and the Challenge of Humanitarian Intervention* (United Nations University Press, Tokyo 2000) 273, 279; N Ronzitti 'Commentary' in A Wall (ed) *Legal and Ethical Lessons of NATO's Kosovo Campaign* (International Law Studies 78, US Naval War College, Newport 2003) 113, 118.

[125] UK Parliament 'Kosovo: Operation "Allied Force"' (HC Library Research Papers 99/48, 1999) 60 <http://www.parliament.uk/documents/commons/lib/research/rp99/rp99-048.pdf> accessed 10 December 2009.

a number of States, including France, Italy, and Denmark, stated that recourse to a blockade was not a possible course of action.[126]

It was suggested by these States that a further Security Council Resolution would be necessary in order to interfere with neutral shipping. The US was more amenable to the use of the law of neutrality as a legal basis for interceptions, but evidently did not view the assertion of traditional belligerent rights as adequate to undertake such interceptions, and sought to argue that Security Council Resolution 1160 provided legal authority for action.[127] Security Council Resolution 1160, passed under Chapter VII, had imposed sanctions on the Federal Republic of Yugoslavia, deciding:

> that all States shall, for the purposes of fostering peace and stability in Kosovo, prevent the sale or supply to the Federal Republic of Yugoslavia, including Kosovo, by their nationals or from their territories or using their flag vessels and aircraft, of arms and related matériel of all types, such as weapons and ammunition, military vehicles and equipment and spare parts for the aforementioned, and shall prevent arming and training for terrorist activities there.[128]

Resolution 1160 could not, however, be used as a legal basis for the proposed interception measures. First, Resolution 1160 made no mention of an embargo on petroleum or petroleum products. Secondly, even if Resolution 1160 had embargoed petroleum products, there was no authorization granted to individual States to enforce it. Thirdly, unlike the situation under Resolution 661, in which there was a basis for the interdiction measures in the *jus ad bellum*, namely collective self-defence, the intervention in Kosovo was highly contentious, and finds no foothold in the positive law.[129]

Ultimately, the legal basis of the visit and search of neutrals during the conflict was not resolved amongst NATO allies. Instead, a voluntary visit and search regime was established to search the vessels of flag States participating in the

[126] See B Møller 'The Nordic Countries: Whither the West's Conscience?' in A Schnabel and R Thakur (eds) *Kosovo and the Challenge of Humanitarian Intervention* (United Nations University Press, Tokyo 2000) 151, 156. Denmark participated in the NATO action and contributed military forces. See H Klingenberg 'Elements of Nordic Practice 1999: Denmark' (2000) 69 NJIL 333, 333–6.

[127] See F L Kirgis 'NATO Interdiction of Oil Tankers' *ASIL Insights* (April 1999) <http://www.asil.org/insigh33.cfm> accessed 10 December 2009.

[128] UN SC Res 1160 (31 March 1998) UN Doc S/RES/1160 at [8]. Interestingly, Resolution 1160 did not explicitly characterize the situation as a threat to international peace and security. The sanctions in Resolution 1160 were reaffirmed in UNSC Res 1199 (23 September 1998) UN Doc S/RES/1199 at [7].

[129] On the legality of the NATO intervention, see Chesterman (n 118) 206–17; D Kritsiotis 'The Kosovo Crisis and NATO's Application of Armed Force against the Federal Republic of Yugoslavia' (2000) 49 ICLQ 330; I Brownlie and C J Apperley 'Kosovo Crisis Inquiry: Memorandum on the International Law Aspects' (2000) 49 ICLQ 878; C Chinkin 'The Legality of NATO's Action in the Former Republic of Yugoslavia (FRY) under International Law' (2000) 49 ICLQ 910; V Lowe 'International Legal Issues Arising in the Kosovo Crisis' (2000) 49 ICLQ 934.

petroleum embargo.[130] The reluctance to rely on the framework offered by the law of neutrality, and to assert belligerent rights against third-State shipping on the basis of the existence of an armed conflict alone, is suggestive of the trend towards the 'double test' requirement sketched above; ultimately, in the absence of clear legality under the *jus ad bellum*, recourse to the traditional law of naval warfare to neutral shipping appears doubtful.[131]

Nevertheless, a caveat to this analysis should be registered. It must be kept in mind that the pronouncements of States on the legal situation surrounding the proposed interception measures are difficult to discern. The NATO States were eager to avoid a direct confrontation with Russia, which opposed the embargo and whose ships would have been subject to interdiction measures. The fact that the destination of shipping was in Bar, in Montenegro—which sought to distance itself from the regime in Belgrade and remain politically neutral—also may have added to NATO reluctance to enforce the embargo.[132] Nevertheless, it remains the case that no State sought to rely on the law of neutrality and the exercise of belligerent rights springing from a situation of armed conflict as a legal basis for interdiction measures. A clear link was sought between the operation of the law of neutrality and the *jus ad bellum*.

iii. Afghanistan: Operation Enduring Freedom (2001–present)

Operation Enduring Freedom, established in the wake of the terrorist attacks launched by Al Qaeda against the United States on 11 September 2001, originally involved 27 States participating in collective self-defence measures.[133] One component of *Operation Enduring Freedom* is maritime interdiction operations. Those interdiction operations are of two types. One involves the interdiction of shipping suspected of carrying Al Qaeda members fleeing the theatre of combat in Afghanistan. The other involves the interdiction of contraband destined for Al Qaeda.[134]

Operation Enduring Freedom has raised difficult questions about the scope of self-defence against terrorist attack.[135] Although originally based in the law of self-defence, there exist significant doubts whether the requirements of necessity and proportionality could possibly be satisfied. As Christine Gray writes, '[t]he

[130] See I H Daalder and M E O'Hanlon *Winning Ugly: NATO's War to Save Kosovo* (Brookings, Washington DC 2000) 146.
[131] For a similar view see Brownlie and Apperley (n 129) 901.
[132] Greenwood (n 123) 56.
[133] United States Department of State Fact Sheet 'Operation Enduring Freedom' (31 January 2006) <http://2001-2009.state.gov/r/pa/prs/ps/2006/60083.htm> accessed 10 March 2010.
[134] M A Becker 'The Shifting Public Order of the Oceans: Freedom of Navigation and the Interdiction of Ships at Sea' (2005) 46 HILJ 131, 151–2.
[135] For discussion see Gray (n 42) 208–16.

longer *Operation Enduring Freedom* continues, the further it is detached from its initial basis in self-defence.'[136]

This ambiguity extends to the maritime component of *Operation Enduring Freedom*. The maritime component was first mentioned in Security Council Resolution 1776, which made reference to the maritime component of *Operation Enduring Freedom* but did not specify its legal basis.[137] The lack of clarity was criticized by Russia in the Security Council debate on the resolution.[138]

To add further ambiguity to this already complicated picture, the visit and search of merchant shipping requires the existence of an international armed conflict and, controversially, the US characterizes *Operation Enduring Freedom* as part of a broader 'war on terror' that brings with it many of the characteristics of an international armed conflict.[139] This assertion has attracted strong criticism as a legally untenable response to terrorism.[140] Whether there exists an international armed conflict between the US and al Qaeda is a question that cannot be comprehensively addressed here. Serious doubts must exist, however, as to whether interdiction measures against merchant shipping could be taken on the basis of an armed conflict 'of unpredictable duration and undefined territorial boundaries.'[141]

What will be addressed here is the justification for interdiction measures linked specifically to the theatre of hostilities in Afghanistan.[142] An international armed conflict has undoubtedly existed between Afghanistan and the US-led coalition. The international armed conflict began on 7 October 2001.[143] In November 2002, the International Committee of the Red Cross (ICRC) communicated to various governments that, in its opinion, the international armed conflict had been transformed into a non-international armed conflict on 19 July 2002, after the establishment of an Afghan transitional government.[144] Others have claimed that the conflict became non-international in character even earlier.[145] Whether an

[136] Ibid 206. [137] UNSC Res 1776 (19 September 2007) UN Doc S/RES/1776.

[138] UNSC Verbatim Record (19 September 2007) UN Doc S/PV.5744.

[139] For a discussion of the overlap between operations in Afghanistan and the wider 'war on terror' in *Operation Enduring Freedom* see G S Corn 'Making the Case for Conflict Bifurcation in Afghanistan: Transnational Armed Conflict, al Qaida and the Limits of the Associated Militia Concept' in M N Schmitt (ed) *The War in Afghanistan: A Legal Analysis* (International Law Studies 85, US Naval War College, Newport 2009) 181.

[140] See, for example, G Rona 'Official Statement on Behalf of the ICRC' (16 March 2004) <http://www.icrc.org/Web/eng/siteeng0.nsf/html/5XCMNJ> accessed 20 May 2008.

[141] N Melzer *Targeted Killing in International Law* (OUP, Oxford 2008) 266.

[142] In the Security Council, Russia sought to limit the maritime component of *Operation Enduring Freedom* to combating terrorism in Afghanistan and argued it 'should not be used for other purposes.' See UNSC Verbatim Record (19 September 2007) UN Doc S/PV.5744.

[143] A Roberts 'Afghanistan and International Security' in M N Schmitt (ed) *The War in Afghanistan: A Legal Analysis* (International Law Studies 85, US Naval War College, Newport 2009) 3, 8–9.

[144] The memorandum has not been made public. See A Roberts 'The Laws of War in the War on Terror' in F L Borch and P S Wilson (eds) *International Law and the War on Terror* (International Law Studies 79, US Naval War College, Newport 2003) 175, 194.

[145] See Y Arai-Takahashi 'Disentangling Legal Quagmires: The Legal Characterisation of the Armed Conflicts in Afghanistan Since 6/7 October 2001 and the Question of Prisoner of War Status' (2002) 5 YBIHL 61, 97.

international armed conflict continues to exist between the US and Afghanistan is a much more difficult question.

Because of the uncertainties that plague the application of the law of armed conflict to all aspects of *Operation Enduring Freedom*, most States engaged in the maritime component of *Operation Enduring Freedom* have sought to rely on the authority of Article 51 of the Charter as the basis for maritime interception operations.[146] The exercise of traditional belligerent rights to the maritime component of *Operation Enduring Freedom* has been described by a UK Judge Advocate with the UK Royal Navy as an 'implausible' approach.[147] According to this view:

> ...operations under Article 51 may not avail themselves of the full range of rights usually available to belligerents in an international armed conflict. The effect of this would be to say, for example, that although maritime units may use force such as is necessary and proportional, they may be required to do so within the peacetime rules and conventions which apply at sea, a case in point being the United Kingdom's fairly conservative view of the doctrine of flag State consent.[148]

The reliance of these States on the law of self-defence—and, in practice, on the consent of the flag State to conduct stop and search—further demonstrates the reluctance of States to rely solely on the law of contraband.

iv. Israel's interception of merchant shipping (2001–2002)

Israel claims to have been engaged in an armed conflict with Hamas and other armed Palestinian groups since 2000.[149] Israeli case law has supported this categorization of the situation.[150] While Israel has been somewhat reluctant to define the type of armed conflict it has been engaged in, the Israeli Supreme Court has held that the law of international armed conflict is applicable.[151]

[146] K O'Rourke 'Panel III Commentary – Maritime and Coalition Operations' in F L Borch and P S Wilson (eds) *International Law and the War on Terror* (International Law Studies 79, US Naval War College, Newport 2003) 297, 298 (the USA); P Cronin 'Panel III Commentary – Maritime and Coalition Operations' in ibid 301 (Australia); J-G Perron 'Panel III Commentary – Maritime and Coalition Operations' in ibid 309 (Canada).

[147] N Brown 'Panel III Commentary – Maritime and Coalition Operations' in F L Borch and P S Wilson (eds) *International Law and the War on Terror* (International Law Studies 79, US Naval War College, Newport 2003) 303, 305.

[148] Ibid 305–6. See also P J Kwast 'Maritime Interdiction of Weapons of Mass Destruction in an International Legal Perspective' (2007) 38 NYIL 163, 238 n 429 for the position of the Netherlands.

[149] Israeli Ministry of Foreign Affairs 'The Operation in Gaza (27 December 2008–18 January 2009): Factual and Legal Aspects' (July 2009) [30] <http://www.mfa.gov.il/NR/rdonlyres/E89E699D-A435-491B-B2D0-017675DAFEF7/0/GazaOperationwLinks.pdf> accessed 12 November 2009.

[150] *Public Committee against Torture in Israel v Israel* (2007) 46 ILM 375 [16] and cases cited therein.

[151] Ibid [25].

On the basis of this categorization, therefore, the law of maritime warfare would be applicable to Israeli maritime operations, and the law of neutrality provides a basis for the visit and search of neutral merchant shipping for contraband. In two incidents in which Israel engaged in the interception of neutral shipping, however, Israel sought to justify its conduct under the law of self-defence.

On 6 May 2001, the Israeli Navy intercepted a merchant ship containing weapons en route from Lebanon to the Gaza Strip.[152] Then, on 4 January 2002, the Israeli Navy intercepted the *Karine A*, a merchant ship sailing under the flag of Tonga,[153] which contained weapons bound for the Palestinian Authority.[154] In reporting this action to the UN, Israel did not refer to the law of neutrality or naval warfare, but contended that the seizure of the ship constituted a 'vital act of self-defence.'[155]

The practice reviewed suggests that belligerents no longer rely solely on the fact of armed conflict or war to assert the right of visit and search of neutral shipping. The evidence suggests instead the development of a rule that belligerents during an armed conflict must conduct their operations not only in accordance with the law of neutrality, but also by reference to the principles of necessity and proportionality under the *jus ad bellum*.

b. The Content of the Doctrine of Contraband

i. Erosion of the distinction between absolute and conditional contraband

The State practice reviewed above suggests that greater interference with neutrals may be justified as an armed conflict increases in scale. There may be room to doubt, however, whether belligerents could ever exercise, as against neutrals, the full battery of belligerent rights permissible in pre-Charter international law, when war was unregulated. In other words, one of the effects of the principles of necessity and proportionality, as well as the pressure imposed by the principle of freedom of navigation in the law of the sea, is that the doctrine of contraband may have been narrowed.

The first half of the twentieth century saw the reverse trend. Belligerents increasingly broke down the distinction between absolute and conditional contraband in order to exercise more intrusive measures of control against

[152] UNGA 'Letter dated 9 May 2001 from the Permanent Representative of Israel to the United Nations addressed to the Secretary-General' (9 May 2001) UN Doc A/56/69-S/2001/459.

[153] 'Weapons Ship Mystery Deepens' *BBC News* (London 10 January 2002) <http://news.bbc.co.uk/1/hi/world/middle_east/1753233.stm> accessed 20 July 2009.

[154] See Israel Ministry of Foreign Affairs 'Seizing of the Palestinian Weapons Ship *Karine A*' (4 Jan 2002) <http://www.mfa.gov.il/MFA/Government/Communiques/2002/Seizing%20of%20the%20Palestinian%20weapons%20ship%20Karine%20A%20-> accessed 20 July 2009.

[155] UNGA 'Letter dated 4 January 2002 from the Permanent Representative of Israel to the United Nations addressed to the Secretary-General' (4 January 2002) UN Doc A/56/766-S/2002/25.

neutrals. Already in World War I, the distinction between absolute and conditional contraband was blurred.[156] World War II marked a further shift in the practice of contraband control towards increasingly expansive belligerent rights.[157]

The erosion of the distinction between absolute and conditional contraband has continued since 1945. In the two conflicts between India and Pakistan, in 1965 and 1971, no material distinction was made between absolute and conditional contraband.[158] The desuetude of the distinction between absolute and conditional contraband seems to be confirmed by the unified view of contraband followed in a number of military manuals and by various writers.[159]

The content of the law of contraband and its enforcement in modern times received its most extensive examination during the Iran-Iraq war. The British position raised the possibility of a more restricted view of contraband. British statements indicated that the doctrine of contraband extended only to arms and war material; that is, to what was previously known as 'absolute contraband.'[160] During the Falklands crisis, the British position appeared to be even more restrictive, as the UK expressed the view that the law of self-defence did not extend to visit and search of a French vessel carrying arms to Argentina.[161]

During the conflict, Iran made no distinction between absolute and conditional contraband: among the items seized by Iranian patrols included explosives, automobile spare parts, electrical appliances, and water-cooling devices.[162] In one incident in 1985, the Kuwaiti cargo ship *Al-Muharrag* was diverted to the Port of Bandar Abbas by Iranian forces. Upon visit and search, it was determined that out of 10,500 tons of cargo aboard, 4,500 tons were 'logistical goods' bound for Iraq. In seizing these goods as contraband, Iran made reference to Hague Convention XIII on neutrality in naval war.[163]

Kuwait protested against the seizure of these goods, and argued that the action by Iran amounted to a violation of the right to freedom of navigation. It also argued that the action was a violation of Security Council Resolution 552.[164] Kuwait issued further protests against the seizure of the Kuwaiti ships *Ibin*

[156] See, for example, *The Hakan* [1918] AC 148, 151.

[157] See G G Fitzmaurice 'Some Aspects of Modern Contraband Control and the Law of Prize' (1945) 22 BYBIL 73.

[158] W H von Heinegg 'Visit, Search, Diversion and Capture in Naval Warfare: Part II, Developments Since 1945' (1992) 30 CYIL 89, 94–9.

[159] *San Remo Manual* § 148; US *Naval Commander's Handbook* § 7.4.1; UK *Manual of the Law of Armed Conflict* § 13.5(h); Canada *LOAC Manual* GL-4; *Helsinki Principles* [5.2.3]. See also L C Green *The Contemporary Law of Armed Conflict* (3rd edn, Manchester UP, Manchester 2008) 192.

[160] (1986) 57 BYBIL 583–4.

[161] See (1982) 53 BYBIL 469.

[162] B A Boczek 'Law of Warfare at Sea and Neutrality: Lessons from the Gulf War' (1989) 20 ODIL 239, 261.

[163] UNSC 'Letter dated 19 July 1985 from the Permanent Representative of the Islamic Republic of Iran to the United Nations Addressed to the Secretary-General' (22 July 1985) UN Doc S/17348.

[164] UNSC 'Letter dated 10 July 1985 from the Permanent Representative of Kuwait to the United Nations Addressed to the Secretary-General' (11 July 1985) UN Doc S/17335.

Shaheed on 7 July 1984; the *Al-Wattyah* on 4 September 1985; the *Al-Massilah* on 6 September 1985; an Italian vessel, the *Merzario Britania* on 6 September 1985; and the Chinese vessel *Jing Jiang* on 12 September 1985.[165] Kuwait contended that since all of these merchant ships were sailing in international waters, Iran had no right to intercept them.[166] Kuwait therefore appeared to contend that there was no basis for belligerent interference with neutral shipping, and that the situation was governed entirely by the law of peace. Kuwait went further than the UK in its restrictive approach: on its view, the doctrine of contraband was apparently not applicable in any sense to the armed conflict then taking place between Iran and Iraq.

In response, Iran stated that, while it was respectful of the freedom of navigation of ships in the Gulf, it was its established legal right under the law of neutrality to inspect ships suspected of carrying 'military hardware' or 'arms' to Iraq.[167] On this evidence, Iran's view of the reach of contraband goods is remarkably similar to that of the United Kingdom, although Iran viewed fuel as contraband as well.[168]

The argument has been advanced that a public proclamation of trade policy during armed conflict may in certain circumstances increase the burden on belligerents to demonstrate a 'reasonable basis' for exercising visit and search. The UK's official and publicly declared policy throughout the Iran-Iraq war was not to sell arms or 'lethal equipment' to either belligerent.[169] The US also made public statements, following an increase in the targeting of neutral shipping, to the effect that its merchant shipping was not carrying oil exported from Iraq.[170] Von Heinegg suggests that these types of statements may indicate a trend towards the establishment of a new customary rule, to the effect that a belligerent must satisfy a more stringent test to undertake visit and search when a State has announced a prohibition on the sale of weapons.[171] No such customary rule could be said to have come into existence at the present time, however.

ii. The influence of Additional Protocol I

The State practice from the Iran-Iraq war suggests that belligerents may be restricted to the capture of material that constitutes absolute contraband only. It is necessary to consider whether what may constitute contraband is further

[165] UNSC 'Annex to the Letter dated 20 September 1985 from the Permanent Representative of Kuwait to the United Nations Addressed to the Secretary-General' (20 September 1985) UN Doc S/17482.

[166] Ibid.

[167] UNSC 'Letter dated 25 September 1985 from the Permanent Representative of the Islamic Republic of Iran to the United Nations Addressed to the Secretary-General' (25 September 1985) UN Doc S/17496.

[168] Ibid.

[169] (1986) 57 BYBIL 644; 58 BYBIL 638.

[170] (1987) 87 DSB 60–1; (1987) 87 DSB 42; (1988) 88 DSB 44.

[171] von Heinegg (n 158) 122.

restricted by Articles 54(2) and 54(3) of Additional Protocol I. Article 54(2) provides that it is prohibited to:

> attack, destroy, remove or render useless objects indispensible to the survival of the civilian population, such as foodstuffs, agricultural areas for the production of foodstuffs, crops, livestock, drinking water installations and supplies and irrigation works, for the specific purpose of denying them for their sustenance value to the civilian population or the adverse Party, whatever the motive, whether in order to starve out civilians, to cause them to move away, or for any other motive.[172]

The application of Additional Protocol I to naval warfare is a topic that has been extensively debated. There is general agreement that the general rules of Article 35–41, on methods and means of warfare, are applicable to naval warfare.[173] The uncertainty surrounds the application of Section I of Part IV of Additional Protocol I, which deals with the protection of the civilian population, to naval warfare. Article 49(3) provides that:

> The provisions of this Section apply to any land, air or sea warfare which may affect the civilian population, individual civilians or civilian objects on land. They further apply to all attacks from the sea or from the air against objectives on land but do not otherwise affect the rules of international law applicable in armed conflict at sea or in the air.[174]

Article 49(3) is an obscure provision and has been subjected to different interpretations. Attention to the language used in Article 49(3) indicates that its effect on naval warfare goes beyond attacks by naval forces on land warfare.[175] Indeed, the two sentences appear to concern different issues. Article 49 is concerned primarily with 'attacks', defined as 'acts of violence against the adversary, whether in offence or in defence.'[176] Article 49(3) contains two sentences. The first does not explicitly concern attacks; it instead covers 'any land, air or sea warfare which may affect the civilian population, individual civilians or civilian objects on land.' The second sentence provides that the provisions of Section I 'further apply to all attacks' emanating from the sea or the air against objectives on land. The use of 'sea warfare' is broader than 'attacks' and indicates that the scope of Article 49(3),

[172] AP I art 54(2).

[173] W H von Heinegg 'The Law of Armed Conflict at Sea' in D Fleck (ed) *The Handbook of International Humanitarian Law* (2nd edn OUP, Oxford 2008) 475, 491.

[174] AP I art 49(3).

[175] E Rauch *The Protocol Additional to the Geneva Conventions for the Protection of Victims of International Armed Conflicts and the United Nations Convention on the Law of the Sea: Repercussions on the Law of Naval Warfare* (Duncker & Humblot, Berlin 1984) 58.

[176] AP I art 49(1).

taken as a whole, is wider than its second sentence indicates.[177] The use of 'further' in the second sentence of Article 49(3) rather than 'therefore' or a similar expression indicates that the second sentence of Article 49(3) is not meant to explain the first but may instead be concerned with a different issue.[178]

A review of the *travaux préparatoires* indicates that the Working Group expressed a reluctance to attempt a review and revision of the law of armed conflict at sea but ultimately left matters unresolved.[179] In those circumstances, the plain meaning of the text read in light of its object and purpose must prevail.[180] In opposition to this view it has been suggested that the distinctions between military objectives and civilian objects, and between combatants and the civilian population, cannot be transposed to the very different field of naval warfare.[181] Since much of the law of naval warfare, including the law of blockade and contraband, affects neutral shipping and is not directed solely at military objectives, the acceptance of the application of Additional Protocol I to naval warfare would impermissibly transform the traditional law.[182]

The debate has lost a degree of practical significance now that certain rules of Section I of Part IV are considered customary international law. The view closest in line with the text and the object and purpose of Additional Protocol I, it is suggested, is that Section I is not limited to naval bombardment but is applicable to all maritime warfare affecting the civilian population, individual civilians or civilian objects on land. Hence, the provisions of Section I of Part IV will apply, in theory, to the doctrine of contraband.[183] However, it must be kept in mind that Additional Protocol I is confined to the relationship between the parties to an international armed conflict, so the effects of it on aspects of the law of neutrality can be extended only by analogy.[184]

[177] See N Ronzitti 'Le droit humanitaire applicable aux conflits armés en mer' (1994) RCADI 9, 39; W J Fenrick 'Intervention' (1987) 26 RDPM 137, 138.

[178] Rauch (n 175) 66.

[179] Ibid 61–6. For a summary of some of the concerns, see also Y Sandoz et al (eds) *Commentary on the Additional Protocols of 8 June 1977 to the Geneva Conventions of 12 August 1949* (Martinus Nijhoff, Geneva 1987) 605–6; W A Solf 'Intervention' (1987) 26 RDPM 149.

[180] Rauch (n 175) 66. While the Vienna Convention came into force in 1980, three years after the passage of Additional Protocol I, the general rule of treaty interpretation was established at the time as a rule of customary international law.

[181] H Meyrowitz 'Le Protocole Additionnel I aux Conventions de Genève de 1949 et le droit de la guerre maritime' (1985) 89 RGDIP 243, 254–6; for this view, see also H B Robertson Jr 'The Principle of the Military Objective in the Law of Armed Conflict' (1997–1998) 8 USAFAJLS 35, 40.

[182] Meyrowitz (n 181) 255. For Rauch's reply to Meyrowitz, see E Rauch 'Le droit contemporain de la guerre maritime: quelques problèmes créés par le Protocole additionnel I de 1977' (1985) 89 RGDIP 958.

[183] See also G J F van Hegelsom 'Methods and Means of Combat in Naval Warfare' in W H von Heinegg (ed) *Methods and Means of Combat in Naval Warfare: Report & Commentaries of the Round-Table of Experts on International Humanitarian Law Applicable to Armed Conflicts at Sea* (Bochumer Schriften Band 8, Universitätsverlag Brockmeyer, Bochum 1992) 1, 9–10.

[184] von Heinegg (n 158) 132–3.

The question arises whether Article 54(2) has had an effect on what may be treated by belligerents as contraband, particularly dual-use items susceptible to use in war as well as peace. On first glance, Article 54(2) would appear to modify what may properly be treated as contraband, as it would be prohibited for a belligerent to 'remove' objects 'indispensible to t he survival of the civilian population.' On this reading, a belligerent may not treat as contraband such goods as irrigation works or water installations, even if they are used in the enemy's military effort.[185]

Such an interpretation is qualified by the requirement that such removal must be 'for the specific purpose of denying' those goods 'for their sustenance value to the civilian population or the adverse Party.' A strict reading of this provision would suggest that removal of such goods for a different purpose—i.e. to prevent contraband from reaching an enemy—would not contravene Article 54(2). Article 54(2) is qualified by Article 54(3), which confirms the former's limited effect on the law of contraband. According to this provision, Article 54(2) will not apply to goods that are either used for sustenance solely for the members of the armed forces or are in direct support of military action, provided that action against these objects does not leave the civilian population with such inadequate food or water as to cause its starvation or force its movement.[186]

The effect of such provisions is to leave the law of contraband largely unaffected. Contraband control must not be directed to the removal of goods indispensible to the survival of the civilian population if such removal is either for the purpose of denying sustenance value to the civilian population, or may be expected to leave the civilian population with such inadequate supplies of food and water as to cause starvation or movement.

iii. The doctrine of continuous voyage and contraband

Circumstances may arise when contraband is transported indirectly to an enemy destination. This may occur, for instance, when contraband is shipped to a port adjacent to belligerent territory and subsequently transported over a land border.

The doctrine of continuous voyage emerged to respond to this scenario.

According to it, when goods are manifested to a neutral port that serves as a transit point to the enemy, the transportation is deemed to be one continuous carriage to the enemy State, and the goods are therefore liable to seizure.[187]

The contours of the doctrine may be traced to the Napoleonic wars.[188] It was developed through the jurisprudence of the US Supreme Court, which applied

[185] It should be noted, moreover, that the list of items in Article 54(2) of AP I is illustrative rather than exhaustive.

[186] AP I art 54(3).

[187] Tucker *Neutrality at Sea* 270.

[188] See *The Maria* (1805) 5 Ch Rob 365.

the doctrine throughout the American Civil War.[189] In *The Kim*, decided during World War I, it was stated that:

> ...the doctrine of continuous voyage or transportation, both in relation to carriage by sea and to carriage over land, had become part of the law of nations at the commencement of the present war, in accordance with the principles of recognised legal decisions, and with the views of a great body of modern jurists, and also with the practice of nations in recent maritime warfare.[190]

In relying on the doctrine, the practice has been for a belligerent to adduce evidence sufficient to create a 'reasonable suspicion' of ultimate enemy destination. The burden then falls on the neutral claimant to demonstrate innocent destination.[191]

Again, the Iran-Iraq war serves as the most recent and detailed State practice in this area, principally because neutral shipping was not able to reach Iraq. During the conflict, Kuwait and Saudi Arabia were widely suspected of serving as transit points for contraband ultimately destined for Iraq.[192] Iran responded to this situation by conducting attacks against Kuwaiti and Saudi Arabian shipping, in those States' territorial waters, and against neutral shipping destined for Kuwaiti and Saudi Arabian ports. The question arose whether Iran was permitted to visit and search neutral shipping destined for Kuwait or Saudi Arabia.

At first glance it could be argued that Security Council Resolution 552 forbade recourse to the continuous voyage doctrine. Resolution 552 '[r]eaffirms the right of free navigation in international waters...for shipping en route to and from all ports and installations of the littoral States that are not parties to the hostilities.'[193] It could be argued that the Security Council is here emphasizing the priority of the principle of freedom of navigation over the doctrine of continuous voyage. Resolution 552 was concerned primarily with direct attacks on neutral shipping, not with the doctrine of contraband. Security Council meetings confirm that the focus was on belligerent attacks on merchant shipping.[194] A number of States protested against attacks in Kuwaiti and Saudi Arabian waters and against attacks on

[189] The US Supreme Court upheld the doctrine in *The Prize Cases* (1862) 66 US (1 Black) 635; *The Peterhoff* (1866) 68 US (1 Wall) 28; *The Springbok* (1866) 68 US (1 Wall) 1; *The Bermuda* (1868) 68 US (1 Wall) 514.

[190] *The Kim* [1915] P 215, 275.

[191] Tucker *Neutrality at Sea* 272–4.

[192] The Jordanian port of Aqaba was also suspected of serving as a transit port for Iraq. See (1983) 54 BYBIL 467.

[193] UNSC Res 552 (1 June 1984) SCOR Resolutions and Decisions 15 [2].

[194] See, for example, the comments of Jordan in UNSC Verbatim Record (25 May 1984) UN Doc S/PV.2542 [10]-[11].

ships *en route* to Kuwait and Saudi Arabia but did not state that those ships could not be visited and searched for contraband.[195]

The Netherlands put forward a view that could be interpreted as suggesting the restriction of the doctrine of continuous voyage:

> As to the legal aspects of the attacks on shipping in the Gulf, let me observe that under international law belligerents may take measures to restrict shipping to and from ports of the other belligerents. Such measures do, of necessity, affect the rights of third States under whose flags such shipping is conducted. Imperfect as it may be in this field, international law nevertheless contains certain restrictions as to the implementation of such measures.[196]

The Representative of the Netherlands went on to note that 'we strongly hope that the Council's call not to interfere with shipping *en route* to and from States that are not party to the hostilities will be scrupulously respected.'[197] It has been contended that the statement by the Netherlands concerns the language of continuous voyage.[198] While the language of 'interfere with' rather than 'attack' could be considered to be significant, it is notable that other States focused almost exclusively on attacks against neutral shipping and not the belligerent right of visit and search.[199]

The British view, which articulated a restrictive view of contraband, contains nothing to indicate that visit and search pursuant to the doctrine of continuous voyage was no longer lawful. Indeed, the British statement after the *Barber Perseus* incident says nothing about goods being transported 'directly' to the enemy; if the United Kingdom wished to indicate that indirect shipment was immune from visit and search it could clearly have done so. The British view that visit and search may be conducted if there are 'reasonable grounds for suspicion' that the merchant is transporting contraband to the enemy is, in fact, very close to the test under the traditional law.

The US also permitted searches of its shipping on the basis of the continuous voyage doctrine. In January 1986, armed Iranian sailors intercepted the US

[195] See ibid (Sudan) [38]. See also UNSC Verbatim Record (29 May 1984) UN Doc S/PV.2543 [7]-[8] (Bahrain), [76] (United Arab Emirates); UNSC Verbatim Record (1 June 1984) UN Doc S/PV.2546 [23] (China).

[196] UNSC Verbatim Record (1 June 1984) UN Doc S/PV.2546 [31].

[197] Ibid [37].

[198] A Gioia and N Ronzitti 'The Law of Neutrality: Third States' Commercial Rights and Duties' in I F Dekker and H H G Post (eds) *The Gulf War of 1980–1988* (Martinus Nijhoff, Dordrecht 1992) 221, 232. Gioia and Ronzitti accept, however, the continuing validity of the continuous voyage doctrine.

[199] See, however, the remarks of Kuwait: UNSC Verbatim Record (25 May 1984) UN Doc S/PV.2541 [22].

freighter *President Taylor* in international waters. Although bound for Fujaira, a port in Oman, the US permitted the ship to be boarded and searched.[200]

The 1990–1991 Gulf War provides further evidence that the doctrine of continuous voyage remains a component of the law. In the period after the passage of Resolution 661 until the passage of Resolution 665, ships heading for ports other than Kuwait or Iraq were stopped and boarded if there was reason to suspect that they were carrying cargo destined for Iraq or Kuwait.[201]

4. The Law of Blockade

a. Blockade and the UN Charter

Considerable controversy surrounds the present application of the law of blockade. Because it is mentioned as one of the measures that may be taken by the Security Council under Article 42 of the Charter, there has arisen an apprehension that blockade is impermissible as a means of maritime warfare, even when mounted in self-defence.

Following the decision of various coalition States to take interdiction measures to enforce Security Council Resolution 661, passed in response to Iraq's invasion of Kuwait in 1990, several States issued protests against what they argued was a blockade and therefore unlawful except when established in accordance with Article 42.[202] The UN Secretary-General, Javier Pérez de Cuéllar, seemed to agree, declaring that it was not correct to describe the coalition operation as a blockade, as such an action could be undertaken only in accordance with Article 42.[203] However, the preferable characterization of the US and UK interdiction operations prior to the passage of Resolution 665 is that these States were involved in visit and search for contraband and were not engaged in the imposition of a blockade.

Contrary to the UN Secretary-General's assertion, there is no reason why the mention of a blockade as one of the measures that may be taken under Article 42 cannot also be taken by States acting in self-defence.[204] Indeed, as early as 1950,

[200] See D L Peace 'Major Maritime Events in the Persian Gulf Between 1984 and 1991: A Juridical Analysis' (1990–1991) 31 VJIL 545, 549.

[201] Ibid 560–1; Astley III and Schmitt (n 15) 143 n 98.

[202] UNSC 'Letter Dated 15 August 1990 from the Permanent Representative of the Libyan Arab Jamahiriya to the United Nations Addressed to the Secretary-General' (16 August 1990) UN Doc S/21529.

[203] 'UN Press Release: Clarification of the Reported Statement by the UN Secretary-General Concerning the Imposition of a Naval Blockade, 16 August 1990' in *The Kuwait Crisis* (n 102) 247.

[204] For the view that a blockade against neutral warships is illegal unless mandated under Article 42, see Bothe (n 9) 394–5.

a blockade was initiated by States acting in defence of the Republic of Korea.[205] The blockade was taken after Security Council Resolution 83 had recommended that Members of the United Nations 'furnish such assistance to the Republic of Korea as may be necessary to repel the armed attack and to restore international peace and security in the area.'[206] The blockade was not taken under Article 42 of the Charter but was instead mounted as an act of collective self-defence.[207]

Although the UN General Assembly referred to blockade as an example of an act of aggression in its definition of aggression formulated in 1974, this should not be read as precluding the imposition of blockade in self-defence.[208] Since the imposition of a blockade in self-defence must be necessary and proportionate, however, it is likely that its use has been restricted considerably in international law.

b. The Effect of Additional Protocol I on the Law of Blockade

It is clear that Articles 54 and 70 of Additional Protocol I will apply to the initiation of a blockade, further restricting belligerent action. Article 54(1) provides that starvation of civilians as a method of warfare is prohibited. Hence, recourse to the types of blockades instituted in both World Wars, such as the 'hunger blockade' of Germany in World War I, is now prohibited.

It has been argued that such a prohibition is too sweeping, in light of the fact that the delegates to the Diplomatic Conference did not intend to modify the law of blockade.[209] This view is contrary to rules of treaty interpretation and is contradicted by the meaning of Article 49(3). While the Australian delegation at the Diplomatic Conference argued that Article 54 does not affect the rules of naval blockade,[210] this may not be used to displace the text of Additional Protocol I. A blockade is clearly an act of sea warfare 'which may affect the civilian population, individual civilians or civilian warfare on land' in Article 49(3).

[205] On the blockade generally see M W Cagle and F A Manson *The Sea War in Korea* (United States Naval Institute, Annapolis 1957) chapter 9.

[206] UNSC Res 83 (27 June 1950) UN Doc S/1511.

[207] W H von Heinegg 'Naval Blockade' in M N Schmitt and A R Thomas (eds) *International Law Across the Spectrum of Conflict: Essays in Honour of Professor L C Green on the Occasion of his Eightieth Birthday* (International Law Studies 75, US Naval War College, Newport 2000) 203, 211. US Admiral Sherman noted that, while all warships not under United Nations command, including Russian, would be permitted to enter North Korean ports, all merchant shipping would be barred. See Cagle and Manson (n 205) 281.

[208] UNGA Res 3314 (14 December 1974) UN Doc A/RES/3314 (XXIX) para 3(c).

[209] For this view see Y Dinstein *The Conduct of Hostilities under the Law of International Armed Conflict* (2nd edn CUP, Cambridge 2010) 225.

[210] *Official Records of the Diplomatic Conference on the Reaffirmation and Development of International Humanitarian Law Applicable in Armed Conflicts, Geneva 1974–1977: Volume VI* (Federal Political Department, Bern 1978) 220 (CDDH/SR.42).

A naval blockade to prevent the import of foodstuffs in order to hasten the end of an armed conflict by means of starvation is prohibited.[211] The rule of Article 54(1) has hardened into a rule of customary international law.[212] This principle has been incorporated into the *San Remo Manual*, which states that the establishment of a blockade is prohibited if: (i) it has the sole purpose of starving the civilian population or denying it other objects essential for its survival; or (ii) the damage to the civilian population is, or may be expected to be, excessive in relation to the concrete and direct military advantage anticipated from the blockade.[213]

Regarding humanitarian assistance, it is first necessary to recall Article 23 of the Fourth Geneva Convention, which provides that:

> Each High Contracting Party shall allow the free passage of all consignments of medical and hospital stores and objects necessary for religious worship intended only for civilians of another High Contracting Party, even if the latter is its adversary. It shall likewise permit the free passage of all consignments of essential foodstuffs, clothing and tonics intended for children under fifteen, expectant mothers and maternity cases.[214]

It is clear that Article 23(1) contemplated a situation of blockade.[215] The provision was, nevertheless, extremely limited; the obligation is owed only to a circumscribed group of the population.

Article 70(1) of Additional Protocol I expands the scope of humanitarian assistance to the entire civilian population. If the establishment of a blockade leads to inadequate provision of food, medical supplies, clothing, means of shelter, and other supplies essential to the survival of the civilian population, relief actions which are humanitarian and impartial and conducted without any adverse distinction shall be undertaken subject to the agreement of the parties concerned.[216] Some uncertainty surrounds the meaning of 'parties concerned', and particularly whether a blockading party has the discretion to reject relief offers because of considerations of military necessity.[217]

On the terms of Article 70(1), it has been suggested that one cannot yet speak of a genuine obligation to enable free passage of humanitarian assistance.[218]

[211] See M Bothe 'Commentary on the 1977 Additional Protocol I' in N Ronzitti (ed) *The Law of Naval Warfare: A Collection of Agreements and Documents with Commentaries* (Martinus Nijhoff, Dordrecht 1988) 760, 764; Green (n 159) 205.

[212] J-M Henckaerts and L Doswald-Beck (eds) *Customary International Humanitarian Law* vol I (CUP, Cambridge 2005) 186.

[213] *San Remo Manual* § 102.

[214] GC IV art 23.

[215] J S Pictet (ed) *Commentary IV: Geneva Convention Relative to the Protection of Civilian Persons in Time of War* (ICRC, Geneva 1958) 178–9.

[216] AP I art 70(1); *San Remo Manual* § 103.

[217] Rauch (n 175) 91.

[218] Dinstein (n 209) 227.

While it has been argued that a blockading power has an 'unrestricted discretion' to agree or not to agree to the passage of relief consignments,[219] this perhaps goes too far: customary international law now appears to support the view that consent must not be refused on arbitrary grounds.[220]

Both the *San Remo Manual* and the UK *Manual of the Law of Armed Conflict*, which follows it, provides that the blockading party has an obligation to provide for free passage of foodstuffs and essential supplies, subject to:

(a) the right to prescribe the technical arrangements, including search, under which such passage is permitted; and
(b) the condition that the distribution of such supplies shall be made under the local supervision of a Protecting Power or a humanitarian organization which offers guarantees of impartiality, such as the International Committee of the Red Cross.[221]

The parties to the conflict themselves must allow and facilitate rapid and unimpeded passage of all relief consignments, equipment, and personnel, even if the assistance is destined for the civilian population of the adverse party.[222]

c. The Establishment of Blockades in Contemporary International Law

State practice with regard to blockade has been relatively sparse.[223] Blockades that raise questions concerning neutral rights are even rarer in recent international law. As with visit and search, an examination of State practice appears to confirm the influence of the principles of necessity and proportionality in the *jus ad bellum* upon the law of maritime warfare. The existence of an armed conflict no longer automatically entitles a belligerent to set up a blockade affecting neutral shipping. For a blockade against neutral shipping to be valid, it must meet not only the requirements of the traditional law but also be necessary and proportionate under the law of self-defence.[224]

Early State practice after the example of the blockade of North Korea suggests a distinct reluctance by States to have recourse to a full blockade, affecting neutral as well as belligerent shipping, absent clear justification in self-defence.

i. India's blockade of East Pakistan (1971)

The armed conflict between India and Pakistan in 1971 was not lengthy but it was of considerable intensity and scale. On 3 December 1971, Pakistan bombed

[219] Rauch (n 175) 92. [220] Henckaerts and Doswald-Beck (n 212) 197.
[221] *San Remo Manual* § 103. See *Helsinki Principles* [5.3]
[222] AP I art 70(2); GC IV art 23. US *Naval Commander's Handbook* § 7.7.3.
[223] T D Jones 'The International Law of Maritime Blockade – A Measure of Naval Economic Interdiction' (1983) 26 How LJ 759.
[224] For a similar view see Gioia and Ronzitti (n 198) 233.

Indian airfields and shelled various Indian positions along the India-West Pakistan border.[225] On the same day, Pakistan published a list of contraband, in which it acknowledged that a 'state of war exists between Pakistan on the one hand and India on the other.'[226] Neutral States indicated that belligerents were entitled to take measures of economic warfare.[227]

India announced a blockade of East Pakistan on 4 December 1971.[228] Questions arose about whether the blockade had been mounted in conformity with the law of naval warfare.[229] Its short duration has also been criticized; the blockade has been described as 'so short lived and so aberrant in its purposes and enforcement, as to offer no clear deducible result.'[230]

ii. US mining of North Vietnamese ports (1972)

During the conflict between North and South Vietnam, caution was exercised by the US not to initiate blockade measures. This caution appeared to be based in the view, as the director of the International Law Division of the US Navy explained, that a blockade could be asserted only during a state of war, which did not exist between the US and North Vietnam.[231] Instead of the exercise of belligerent rights incident to a state of war, maritime measures were exercised on the basis of collective self-defence of South Vietnam.[232] *Operation Sea Dragon*, which began in 1966 and which involved the visit and search of North Vietnamese shipping in the territorial sea of North Vietnam, was predicated on the principle of self-defence.[233]

The issue of a blockade against North Vietnam arose in 1972. Following a significant military assault by North Vietnamese forces in South Vietnam, on 8 May 1972 President Nixon ordered the mining of North Vietnamese ports, including Haiphong Harbour.[234] There was some uncertainty whether this action amounted

[225] G Warner 'Review Article: Nixon, Kissinger and the Breakup of Pakistan, 1971' (2005) 81 IA 1097, 1111.

[226] 'Contemporary Practice of the United States Relating to International Law' (1972) 66 AJIL 378, 386; A K Pavithran 'The Indo-Pakistan War of 1971' (1972) 3 East JIL 247.

[227] The US noted that '[t]he two countries have declared a state of war between them and, under this declaration, they have the right of blockade.' *Foreign Relations of the United States 1969–1976: Vol XI South Asia Crisis 1971* (United States Government Printing Office, Washington DC 2005) 698. A US warning was transmitted to US merchant vessels acknowledged that neutral shipping could be visited and searched on the high seas or in the ports of either belligerent. For the text see 'Contemporary Practice of the United States Relating to International Law' (1972) 66 AJIL 378, 386.

[228] von Heinegg (n 158) 96. [229] O'Connell (n 117) 130. [230] Humphrey (n 70) 27.

[231] G E Carlisle 'The Interrelationship of International Law and United States Naval Operations in Southeast Asia' (1967–1968) 22 JAGJ 8, 11–12.

[232] Ibid 12.

[233] Humphrey (n 70) 31; see also D P O'Connell 'International Law and Contemporary Naval Operations' (1970) 44 BYBIL 19, 35.

[234] (1972) 66 DSB 747, 749.

to a blockade.[235] The US itself denied that its action amounted to a blockade. While acknowledging that a blockade would have been a lawful response to the North Vietnamese activities, the US Department of State legal advisor stated that this was not, in fact, what the mining of Haiphong Harbour amounted to:

> ...the United States and the Republic of Vietnam have resorted instead to lesser measures of collective self-defence in order to achieve maritime interdiction. To have declared a blockade could have implied, under traditional international law, a whole range of actions which would have extended the area of hostilities and risked grave dangers of widening the conflict.[236]

It was therefore argued that the action taken did not amount to a blockade in the traditional sense because of its restricted scope and effects; it did not involve action on the high seas and it was stated that the action was not intended to interfere with the rights of neutral States.[237] In reporting the US actions to the Security Council, it was stressed that the action was taken as a measure of self-defence and therefore restricted in extent and purpose.[238]

iii. Iran's blockade of the Shatt al-Arab (1980)

The law of blockade did not play a significant role in the Iran-Iraq war. At the beginning of the conflict, Iran closed the Shatt al-Arab river.[239] As with many other instances of blockade after 1945, there is some doubt whether this action met the traditional criteria for the blockade to be legally valid.[240] It has been calculated that the blockade affected 71 neutral vessels.[241] The blockade of Iraqi ports led ships to use Kuwait as a destination for cargo ultimately destined for Iraq.[242]

Whether Iran was entitled to set up a blockade was disputed. It has been remarked that a number of States accepted the blockade in view of the lack of

[235] For a discussion of different views expressed at the time, see F B Swayze 'Traditional Principles of Blockade in Modern Practice: United States Mining of Internal and Territorial Waters of North Vietnam' (1977) 29 JAGJ 143, 160. See also US *Naval Commander's Handbook* § 7.7.5.

[236] 'Contemporary Practice of the United States Relating to International Law' (1972) 66 AJIL 836, 836–8.

[237] Ibid 838. On the protection of neutrals during the action, see B A Clark 'Recent Evolutionary Trends Concerning Naval Interdiction of Seaborne Commerce as a Viable Sanctioning Device' (1972–1973) 27 JAGJ 160.

[238] See UNSC 'Letter Dated 8 May 1972 from the Permanent Representative of the United States to the United Nations Addressed to the President of the Security Council' (9 May 1972) UN Doc S/10631.

[239] Boczek (n 162) 243.

[240] Gioia and Ronzitti (n 198) 234.

[241] von Heinegg (n 207) 212; Boczek (n 162) 257.

[242] J A Roach 'Missiles on Target: Targeting and Defence Zones in the Tanker War' (1990/1991) 31 VJIL 593, 603.

protests.[243] The UK, however, protested against the blockade as an act that was neither necessary nor proportionate for self-defence.[244]

iv. Israel's aerial and maritime blockade of Lebanon (2006)

On 12 July 2006, eight Israeli soldiers were abducted and two killed by Hezbollah forces. This event triggered an Israeli military response and a quick escalation into open hostilities between Hezbollah forces and Israel.[245] On the same day, Israel announced that Hezbollah's attack was an 'act of war' to which it was responding in self-defence.[246]

One component of Israel's military response was the imposition of an aerial and naval blockade. On 13 July 2006, Israel entered Lebanese territorial waters to impose a comprehensive blockade of Lebanese ports and harbours.[247] The next day, Israel imposed an aerial blockade.[248] The justification given by Israel was that it had entered Lebanese territorial waters in order to prevent terrorists and weapons and other material from reaching Israel.[249]

The blockades did not give rise to confrontation between Israel and neutral shipping. Concerns were raised, however, as to whether the blockades could be considered to be necessary and proportionate under the law of self-defence. Lebanese government authorities argued that the imposition of the Israeli blockades was a disproportionate response.[250] Concerns about the proportionality of the blockades were frequently folded into larger questions about the proportionality of Israel's armed response.[251]

243 von Heinegg (n 207) 212. 244 (1988) 59 BYBIL 581.

245 For a summary of the conflict see UNSC 'Report of the Secretary-General on the Implementation of Security Council Resolution 1701 (2006)' (28 June 2007) UN Doc S/2007/392 [2].

246 See for example UNGA 'Identical Letters Dated 12 June 2006 from the Permanent Representative of Israel to the United Nations addressed to the Secretary-General and the President of the Security Council' (12 June 2006) UN Doc A/60/937; 'Statement by Foreign Ministry Deputy DG Gideon Meir' (13 July 2006) <http://www.mfa.gov.il/MFA/About+the+Ministry/MFA+Spokesman/2006/Statement%20by%20Foreign%20Ministry%20Deputy%20DG%20Gideon%20Meir%2013-Jul-2006> accessed 28 June 2009.

247 See UNGA 'Report of the Commission of Inquiry on Lebanon Pursuant to Human Rights Council Resolution S-2/1' (23 November 2006) UN Doc A/HRC/3/2 [268].

248 Ibid.

249 See H M Fattah and S Erlanger 'Israel Blockades Lebanon; Wide Strikes by Hezbollah' *New York Times* (New York 14 July 2006) <http://www.nytimes.com/2006/07/14/world/middleeast/14mideast.html> (accessed 12 November 2006); 'Israel Imposes Lebanon Blockade' *BBC News* (London 13 July 2006) < http://news.bbc.co.uk/1/hi/5175160.stm> accessed 10 June 2008.

250 See 'Israel Imposes Lebanon Blockade' *BBC News* (London 13 July 2006) < http://news.bbc.co.uk/1/hi/5175160.stm> accessed 10 June 2008.

251 For discussion of proportionality during the Israel-Lebanon war, see A Zimmermann 'The Second Lebanon War: *Jus ad Bellum, Jus in Bello* and the Issue of Proportionality' (2007) 11 MPYBUNL 99; Cannizzaro (n 60); M N Schmitt '"Change Direction" 2006: Israeli Operations in Lebanon and the International Law of Self-Defence' in M D Carsten (ed) *International Law and Military Operations* (International Law Studies 84, US Naval War College, Newport 2008) 265.

v. Israel's blockade of Gaza (2009–2010)

Since 2009, Israel has maintained a blockade of the Gaza Strip on the basis that Israel is engaged in an armed conflict with Hamas, which is the elected government in Gaza.[252] It first announced the blockade of Gaza during *Operation Cast Lead*, the armed conflict between Israel and Hamas in the Gaza strip from 27 December 2008 until 18 January 2009. The blockade was announced on 3 January 2009, at a distance of 20 miles from the coast.[253] At the time, the blockade was established, according to Israel, for a 'clear military necessity'—to prevent the military strengthening of Hamas by stopping the smuggling of weapons and the entry of terrorists into the Gaza Strip.[254]

Israel has sought to maintain the blockade beyond the duration of *Operation Cast Lead*, which came to an end with a unilateral Israeli ceasefire on 18 January 2009.[255] There have been a number of incidents of merchant ships attempting to breach the blockade. On 5 February 2009, the merchant vessel *Tali*, which was flying the flag of Togo, attempted to enter the Gaza Strip. While at sea, the vessel was contacted and informed that it would not be able to enter Gaza due to the existence of the blockade. It was intercepted and boarded by the Israeli Navy.[256] On 31 May 2010, Israel intercepted a six-ship flotilla carrying humanitarian aid that was attempting to breach the blockade.[257] Clashes between activists and Israeli special forces aboard the largest ship in the flotilla, the *Mavi Marmara*, resulted in the deaths of nine civilians.[258]

Israel argues that it was entitled to take action against the *Mavi Marmara* because it was attempting to breach the blockade. This raises questions whether the blockade was legally established under international law.[259] While the

[252] See 'MFA Legal Expert Sarah Weiss Maudi on the Legal Aspects of Gaza Aid' (26 May 2010) http://www.mfa.gov.il/MFA/HumanitarianAid/Palestinians/Legal_aspects_Gaza_aid:26-May-2010.htm> accessed 2 June 2010.

[253] Israeli Defence Force Military Advocate General 'Interception of the Gaza Flotilla – Legal Aspects' <http://www.mag.idf.il/592-4071-en/patzar.aspx> (accessed 20 June 2010).

[254] Ibid.

[255] 'Israel Holds its Fire: Statement by PM Ehud Olmert' (17 January 2009) <http://www.mfa.gov.il/MFA/Government/Speeches+by+Israeli+leaders/2009/Statement_PM_Ehud_Olmert_17-Jan-2009.htm> accessed 20 January 2009; 'Israel Declares Ceasefire in Gaza' *BBC News* (London 18 January 2009) <http://news.bbc.co.uk/1/hi/world/middle_east/7835794.stm> accessed 18 January 2009.

[256] Israel Defence Force 'Israel Navy Intercepts Cargo Boat, 5 Feb 2009' (5 February 2009) <http://idfspokesperson.com/2009/02/06/israel-navy-intercepts-cargo-boat-5-feb-2009-1344-ist> accessed 21 June 2009; Israel Ministry of Foreign Affairs 'Cargo Boat Attempting Illegal Entry to Gaza Intercepted' (5 February 2009) <http://www.mfa.gov.il/MFA/Government/Communiques/2009/Cargo_boat_illegal_entry_Gaza_waters_intercepted_5-Feb-2009.htm?WBCMODE=PresentationUnpYair+Tsaban> accessed 21 June 2009.

[257] 'Deaths as Israeli Forces Storm Gaza Aid Ship' *BBC News* (London 31 May 2010) <http://www.bbc.co.uk/news/10195838> accessed 1 June 2010.

[258] T Buck, D Dombey and D Strauss 'Israel Condemned After Flotilla Attack' *Financial Times* (London 31 May 2010) <http://www.ft.com/cms/s/0/b09c57f6-6c80-11df-91c8-00144feab49a.html?ftcamp=rss> accessed 2 June 2010.

[259] C Lynch 'Israel's Flotilla Raid Revives Questions of International Law' *Washington Post* (Washington DC 1 June 2010) <http://www.washingtonpost.com/wp-dyn/content/article/2010/06/01/

blockade appeared to meet the traditional criteria under the law of maritime warfare, there exists considerable doubt whether Israel was entitled to maintain a blockade.

Since 18 January 2009, Israel maintains its blockade of Gaza as 'a legitimate and recognised measure under international law that may be implemented as part of an armed conflict at sea.'[260] Israel has stated that it is engaged in an armed conflict, without specifying whether this conflict is international or non-international in character.[261] Israel appears to view the situation with Hamas as a *sui generis* situation, neither strictly international nor non-international but combining elements of both.[262] It has indicated that it considers this armed conflict to have been in progress for a considerable duration.[263]

The concept of blockade is unknown to non-international armed conflict, except if there has been recognition of belligerency.[264] For the blockade to be valid under the law of armed conflict, then, it must be shown that an international armed conflict existed at the relevant time.

One possibility is that Israel, as an Occupying Power of Gaza, is engaged in an international armed conflict. Common Article 2 of Geneva Convention IV sets out that the Convention applies to 'all cases of partial or total occupation of the territory of a High Contracting Party, even if the said occupation meets with no armed resistance.'[265] This means that belligerent occupation may constitute the sole manifestation of the existence of armed conflict between two States.[266] Israel denies that it is an Occupying Power following its withdrawal of certain measures of control from Gaza in 2005. However, scholarly opinion suggests that this was at

AR2010060102934.html?hpid=topnews> accessed 2 June 2010; A Hirsch 'Was the Gaza Flotilla Raid Legal?' *Guardian* (London 1 June 2010) <http://www.guardian.co.uk/law/afua-hirsch-law-blog/2010/jun/01/gaza-freedom-flotilla-international-law> accessed 2 June 2010.

[260] Israel Ministry of Foreign Affairs 'The Gaza Flotilla and the Maritime Blockade of Gaza – Legal Background' (31 May 2010) <http://www.mfa.gov.il/MFA/Government/Law/Legal+Issues+and+Rulings/Gaza_flotilla_maritime_blockade_Gaza-Legal_background_31-May-2010.htm> (accessed 1 June 2010) [2].

[261] See Israel Defence Forces Military Strategic Information Section 'Operation "Sea Breeze" – Legal Aspects' (n.d.) (copy on file with author). A similar view is apparent in some Israeli case law. See *Jaber Al-Bassiouni Ahmed et al v Prime Minister and Minister of Defence* (30 January 2008) HCJ 9132/07 [12] per President Beinisch.

[262] Israeli Ministry of Foreign Affairs 'The Operation in Gaza (27 December 2008–18 January 2009): Factual and Legal Aspects' (29 July 2009) <http://www.mfa.gov.il/MFA/Terrorism-+Obstacle+to+Peace/Hamas+war+against+Israel/Operation_in_Gaza-Factual_and_Legal_Aspects.htm> accessed 29 November 2009 [30].

[263] Israel's report on *Operation Cast Lead* suggests that Israel has been in an armed conflict with Hamas and other Palestinian groups since October 2000. See ibid [36].

[264] For the *sui generis* situation in Algeria, which involved the visit and search of shipping during a situation of non-international armed conflict, see Humphrey (n 70) 30; von Heinegg (n 158) 101; P Norton 'Between the Ideology and the Reality: The Shadow of the Law of Neutrality' (1976) 17 HILJ 249, 272–5.

[265] GC IV art 2.

[266] Y Dinstein *The International Law of Belligerent Occupation* (CUP, Cambridge 2009) 32.

best only a partial withdrawal and that the law of occupation continues to govern Israel's conduct.[267]

Even if it is accepted that an international armed conflict exists between Gaza and Israel because Israel is deemed an Occupying Power, it is not clear that the blockade would be validly initiated under the law of armed conflict, because there is scope for doubt whether a blockade initiated by an occupier of its own occupied territory is legally permissible.[268]

Another ground on which an international armed conflict may exist is to suggest that a declaration of blockade itself creates a situation of international armed conflict between the blockading and the blockaded power, much in the manner that the existence of occupation creates an international armed conflict. There is considerable evidence in traditional international law that a declaration of blockade creates a state of war: in non-international armed conflict recourse to a blockade by the metropolitan State constituted recognition of belligerency and an indication that the conflict should be treated as an inter-State war.[269] There are, it is suggested, strong reasons of principle to resist this view. There is no practice since the nineteenth century to the effect that a declaration of blockade automatically brings about a situation of armed conflict—as distinct from the initiation of a blockade during an existing armed conflict.

Even if this argument is accepted, however, and the view is taken that the declaration of blockade during *Operation Cast Lead* created an international armed conflict,[270] this would provide no reason to permit the enforcement of a blockade after the cessation of hostilities. As noted, Israel's unilateral ceasefire was announced on 18 January 2009. While the enforcement of a blockade during a ceasefire was permissible in traditional international law, because a ceasefire did not terminate the state of war, it is highly doubtful whether this view can be maintained in the era of the UN Charter.[271] It is useful at this point to recall the statement of the Security Council following Egypt's claims to visit and search the ships of Israel and third States following the armistice of 1949.[272] In that

[267] Ibid 276–80. See also UNHRC 'Human Rights in Palestine and other Occupied Arab Territories: Report of the United Nations Fact-Finding Mission on the Gaza Conflict' (25 September 2009) UN Doc A/HRC/12/48 [276]-[279].

[268] 'Harvard Draft Convention on Rights and Duties of Neutral States in Naval and Aerial War' (1939) AJILS 167, 692.

[269] W L Walker 'Recognition of Belligerency and Grant of Belligerent Rights' (1937) 23 TGS 177, 187.

[270] See, for example, Human Rights Watch *White Flag Deaths: Killings of Palestinian Civilians During Operation Cast Lead* (August 2009) 51 <http://www.hrw.org/en/reports/2009/08/13/white-flag-deaths> accessed 2 September 2009.

[271] For the modern view that ceasefires and armistices effectively terminate an armed conflict, see C Gray 'After the Ceasefire: Iraq, the Security Council and the Use of Force' (1994) 65 BYBIL 135, 142; R Higgins 'The June War: The United Nations and Legal Background' (1968) 3 JCH 253, 268; J Stone *Legal Controls of International Conflict* (Maitland Publications, Sydney 1959) 644.

[272] UNSC Res 95 (1 September 1951) UN Doc S/2322.

instance, the Security Council rejected Egypt's contention that it was actively a belligerent or exercising visit and search for purposes of self-defence.[273]

d. Enforcement of Blockade

Enforcement of a blockade involves the stop and seizure of a vessel attempting to breach the blockade.[274] It is established that a vessel can be seized for mere breach of a blockade; it does not need to be carrying contraband.[275]

Views differ as to when a vessel attempting to breach a blockade may be stopped and seized. European States adhered to the view that a vessel could be seized for breaching a blockade only in the immediate area of operations of the blockading force.[276] The Declaration of London largely followed the European approach, providing that the seizure of neutral vessels for violation of blockade could be carried out 'only within the radius of action of the warships assigned to maintain an effective blockade.'[277] The Declaration also made it clear that the doctrine of continuous voyage did not apply to blockades: a vessel on its way to a non-blockaded port could not be captured for breach of blockade.[278]

In contrast, the view favoured by the UK and US was that a belligerent was entitled to seize a 'blockade runner' at any stage of its voyage; the belligerent did not have to wait until the vessel had passed the blockade line, or entered the vicinity of maritime operations.[279] This view held that the doctrine of continuous voyage was also applicable to blockades. Hence a vessel en route to a neutral port could be seized for breach of blockade if the neutral port served as a transit route to an area under blockade.[280]

The US *Naval Commander's Handbook* continues to adhere to this approach to breach of blockade:

> Attempted breach of blockade occurs from the time a vessel or aircraft leaves a port or airfield with the intention of evading the blockade, and for vessels exiting the blockaded area, continues until the voyage is completed [...] It is immaterial that the vessel or aircraft is at the time of the interception bound for neutral territory, if its ultimate destination is the blockaded area. There is a presumption of attempted breach of blockade where vessels or aircraft are bound for a neutral port or airfield serving as a point of transit to the blockaded area.[281]

[273] Ibid. [274] Bothe (n 9) 398. [275] Ibid. [276] Tucker *Neutrality at Sea* 293–4.
[277] Declaration Concerning the Laws of Naval War (signed 26 February 1909) 208 CTS 338 art 17.
[278] Ibid art 19. [279] Tucker *Neutrality at Sea* 293. [280] Castrén *Neutrality* 306.
[281] US *Naval Commander's Handbook* § 7.7.4.

It is doubtful whether the statement of the US *Naval Commander's Handbook* reflects contemporary international law. This is not only because the doctrine of continuous voyage is controversial as applied to blockade and does not appear to reflect customary international law. More importantly, granting a right to belligerents to seize a blockade runner anywhere on the high seas cannot be reconciled with the principles of necessity and proportionality under the law of self-defence, or with the principle of freedom of navigation enjoyed by non-participants during time of armed conflict.[282] The US broad interpretation of the enforcement of blockades has not been followed by the UK or Germany, and no similar statement is contained in the *San Remo Manual.*

Given the paucity of State practice on blockades since 1945, it is not surprising that there is only minimal State practice with regard to breach of blockade. However, the issue did arise during Israel's interception of shipping attempting to breach its blockade in May and June 2010. Legal advice concerning the interception of the *Mavi Marmara* relied on the US *Naval Commander's Handbook's* broad statement concerning where and when a vessel attempting to breach a blockade may be captured.[283]

In July 2010, Israel prepared to intercept a Libyan merchant ship preparing to breach the blockade.[284] On 13 July 2010, the Israeli Foreign Ministry, in an apparent retreat from the view contained in the *US Naval Manual*, advised the Israeli Defence Force to wait until the Libyan vessel reached the territorial waters of the Gaza Strip before intercepting it.[285] The ship's documentation stated that it was heading for an Egyptian port and not for Gaza.[286] This indicates some reluctance to enforce the doctrine of continuous voyage with regard to blockade.

The Israeli Foreign Ministry indicated that similar advice had been provided regarding the enforcement of the blockade against the Turkish flotilla:

> We recommend that any enforcement be carried out only if the blockade is actually breached or at least at maximum proximity to the closure zone, so as to create a clearly justified basis for the action. As will be recalled, we recommended [in the Turkish flotilla] that action be taken as close as possible to the blockade

[282] von Heinegg (n 207) 216.

[283] See 'Operation "Sea Breeze": Legal Aspects' (n 261). The advice notes that 'Israel had the authority to capture the vessels, from the moment they left the territorial waters of neutral States.' See also 'The Gaza Flotilla and the Maritime Blockade of Gaza – Legal Background' (n 260) [8] (citing the US *Naval Commander's Handbook*).

[284] A Pfeffer and A Harel 'IDF Preparing for Forceful Interception of Libya-sponsored Aid Ship Bound for Gaza' *Haaretz* (Tel Aviv 13 July 2010) <http://www.haaretz.com/print-edition/news/idf-preparing-for-forceful-interception-of-libya-sponsored-aid-ship-bound-for-gaza-1.301557> accessed 14 July 2010.

[285] B Ravid 'Foreign Ministry Advises IDF: Don't Stop Gadhafi Ship Until it Approaches Gaza Waters' *Haaretz* (Tel Aviv 13 July 2010) < http://www.haaretz.com/print-edition/news/foreign-ministry-advises-idf-don-t-stop-gadhafi-ship-until-it-approaches-gaza-waters-1.301561> accessed 14 July 2010.

[286] Ibid.

zone. It was explained that this was operationally impossible, however certainly in this case, when there is only one ship, this is possible.[287]

It is difficult to deduce a rule of customary international law in light of the recent practice of one State. However, it is suggested that the influence of the Charter suggests that enforcement of blockade should occur only in the region of naval action; any greater degree of interference outside the area of blockade would infringe the principle of freedom of navigation.

5. The Law of Exclusion Zones

Maritime exclusion zones share certain similarities to blockades, but they have given rise to more controversy, owing to some uncertainty as to what precisely they entail. The first modern recourse to an exclusion zone was during the Russo-Japanese war.[288] War zones were next resorted to in World War I and II, but no attempt was made to define the concept with any precision.[289]

It has been remarked that there is neither uniform usage of the term 'maritime exclusion zone' nor 'a general consensus as to the details of the concept.'[290] The term covers a wide spectrum of activity. At one end of the spectrum, the establishment of an exclusion zone may serve simply to indicate the theatre of hostilities so that neutral shipping can steer clear of it. At the other extreme, a maritime exclusion zone may be used to disclaim all responsibility for targeting neutral shipping, effectively rendering an exclusion zone a 'free-fire zone.'[291] The latter is clearly illegal.

Since 1945, exclusion zones have rarely been invoked, but have been resorted to in large-scale conflicts involving naval power.[292] Unlike the law of blockade, which has a considerable historical pedigree, it has been suggested that exclusion zones are *lex ferenda*.[293] The concept is included in the military manuals of various States, however, so it is likely that they are now a recognized feature of maritime warfare.[294] The principal area of contention is the relationship between exclusion zones and the law of neutrality, because the establishment of an exclusion zone may constitute a significant restriction on the principle of freedom of navigation.[295] Hence any imposition of an exclusion zone must be strictly limited

287 Ibid. 288 Wolfrum (n 12) 505.

289 For a discussion of the history of exclusion zones see R Leckow 'The Iran-Iraq Conflict in the Gulf: The Law of War Zones' (1988) 37 ICLQ 629, 631–3. See also W J Fenrick 'The Exclusion Zone Device in the Law of Naval Warfare' (1986) 24 CYIL 91; G P Politakis 'Waging War at Sea: the Legality of War Zones' (1991) 38 NILR 125.

290 von Heinegg (n 173) 540. 291 Ibid 544. 292 Leckow (n 289) 633.

293 Ibid 644; Fenrick (n 289) 124–5.

294 UK *Manual of the Law of Armed Conflict* § 13.77–13.80; US *Naval Commander's Handbook* § 7.9; Canada *LOAC Manual* § 852–5.

295 Wolfrum (n 12) 506.

in scale, duration, and effects on neutral shipping, and must be able to meet the requirements of necessity and proportionality under the law of self-defence.[296]

a. Exclusion Zones in the Iran-Iraq War (1982–1983)

The Iran-Iraq war saw the most extensive and sustained use of exclusion zones since 1945. Exclusion zones were proclaimed by both Iran and Iraq during the conflict.[297] However, it is difficult to assess the use of exclusion zones in the Iran-Iraq war because, as Fenrick pointed out while the conflict was in progress, 'neither belligerent appears to be paying particular heed to legal issues in determining their courses of action.'[298]

Iran proclaimed an exclusion zone that ran the length of the Gulf, close to the Iranian coast.[299] It could be argued that in its confinement to an area close to its territorial sea, Iran's exclusion zone was a necessary and proportionate act of self-defence under Article 51.[300] Its targeting methods, however, rendered the zone illegal. Iran targeted neutral shipping entering the zone, which exceeded the boundaries of proportionality.[301]

Similarly, Iraq attacked neutral shipping entering its exclusion zone, which was based around an Iranian oil facility on Kharg Island in the Gulf.[302] On 15 August 1982, Iraqi President Saddam Hussein declared that 'foreign shipping companies have only themselves to blame if their ships approach [Kharg Island].'[303] On 25 November 1983, Iraq declared that all shipping in the north of the Gulf could be the object of attacks.[304] While Iraq attempted to justify its conduct on the basis that its exclusion zone was consistent with self-defence,[305] its frequent and indiscriminate targeting of neutral shipping was widely condemned.[306]

Exclusion Zones in the Falklands War (1982)

Exclusion zones were also utilized in the armed conflict between the UK and Argentina over the Falkland Islands. Both belligerents resorted to a series of exclusion zones.[307]

[296] Gioia and Ronzitti (n 198) 234.

[297] See generally Leckow (n 289); M Jenkins 'Air Attacks on Neutral Shipping in the Persian Gulf: The Legality of the Iraqi Exclusion Zone and Iranian Reprisals' (1985) 8 BCICLR 517.

[298] Fenrick (n 289) 121.

[299] M Bothe 'Neutrality at Sea' in I F Dekker and H H G Post (eds) *The Gulf War of 1980–1988* (Martinus Nijhoff, Dordrecht 1992) 205, 210.

[300] Gioia and Ronzitti (n 198) 235; Lagoni (n 79) 163.

[301] Leckow (n 289) 637.

[302] *Keesing's* (1982) 31850.

[303] Ibid.

[304] *Keesing's* (1984) 32689.

[305] *Keesing's* (1982) 31850.

[306] Fenrick (n 289) 117.

[307] For a classification of these zones see Fenrick (n 84) 249–50; Fenrick (n 289) 109.

On 7 April 1982, the United Kingdom declared a Maritime Exclusion Zone (MEZ) two hundred miles from the centre of the Falkland Islands.[308] Within this zone, any Argentine warships and naval auxiliaries would be treated as hostile. The MEZ did not, however, affect neutral shipping. On 28 April 1982, the UK announced that the MEZ would be converted into a Total Exclusion Zone (TEZ). The TEZ applied not only to Argentine naval forces but to any other ship, whether naval or merchant vessel, acting in support of the Argentine occupation of the Islands, as well as to aircraft. The announcement of the TEZ stated that:

> The exclusion zone will also apply to any aircraft, whether military or civil, which is operating in support of the illegal occupation. Any ship and any aircraft, whether military or civil, which is found within this zone without authority from the Ministry of Defence in London will be regarded as operating in support of the illegal occupation and will therefore be regarded as hostile and will be liable to be attacked by British Forces.[309]

The expansion of the MEZ into a TEZ was justified as necessary and proportionate under the law of self-defence.[310] However, as the announcement makes clear, the UK reserved the right to attack neutral aircraft and shipping simply because of their presence within the zone. It is difficult to see how this approach—deeming all neutral shipping and aviation within a certain zone to be liable to attack—could be justified under either the law of naval warfare or under the law of self-defence.[311] The UK *Manual of the Law of Armed Conflict* provides that '[p]articular care must be taken before initiating hostile action against neutral vessels' and that any such attack is subject both to the UN Charter and to satisfaction of the definition of military objective.[312] The TEZ was criticized by the Soviet Union as an impermissible restriction on the freedom of the seas.[313]

Nevertheless, no neutral shipping or aircraft was in fact targeted within the TEZ, and it seems probable that the UK would not have attacked on sight neutral vessels that were in the zone, but would have first considered whether they were engaging in a form of unneutral service rendering them a lawful target.[314] The most charitable view of the British position is that 'its naval units were not forced to really enforce the TEZ vis-à-vis neutral vessels and aircraft or, what is more

308 Fenrick (n 84) 250.

309 UNSC 'Letter dated 28 April 1982 from the Permanent Representative of the United Kingdom of Great Britain and Northern Ireland to the United Nations addressed to the President of the Security Council' (28 April 1982) UN Doc S/15006.

310 Ibid.

311 For this concern see US *Naval Commander's Handbook* § 7.9.

312 See UK *Manual of the Law of Armed Conflict* § 13.46–13.48. For neutral civil aircraft, see § 12.43–12.44.

313 Fenrick (n 289) 111.

314 D G Stephens 'Law of Naval Warfare and Zones' in R Jaques (ed) *Maritime Operational Zones* (US Naval War College, Newport 2006) 4-1, 4-12.

likely, the proclamation of the TEZ was nothing but a most effective ruse of war because it obviously induced the Argentine forces to avoid the area.'[315]

The geographical placement of the zones also lends weight to the view that they were necessary and proportionate under the law of self-defence. The TEZ was limited to an area where commercial traffic was minimal.[316] By contrast, as the *San Remo Manual* points out, '[z]ones located in isolated areas far from normal shipping routes, such as those used in the Falklands, are less likely to raise objections than zones on major shipping routes such as those in the Persian Arabian Gulf.'[317]

In response to the British zones, Argentina established a series of its own exclusion zones.[318] It first established a 200 nautical mile zone around the Islands. It then imposed a 200 nautical mile zone around the Argentine coast. It eventually declared the entire South Atlantic to be a 'war zone', rendering every British vessel, whether merchant or military, liable to attack.[319] This geographical expansion cannot be considered a necessary and proportionate measure and also infringes the rules of targeting.[320]

Exclusion Zones in *Operation Iraqi Freedom* (2003–2004)

On 20 March 2003, the US announced a warning, asserting belligerent rights in the course of the maritime phase of *Operation Iraqi Freedom*.[321] This Notice to Mariners advised that '[a]ll maritime vessels or activities that are determined to be threats to coalition naval forces will be subject to defensive measures, including boarding, seizure, disabling or destruction, without regard to registry or location.'[322] It went on to note that:

> Vessels operating in the Middle East, Eastern Mediterranean Sea, Red Sea, Gulf of Oman, Arabian Sea and Arabian Gulf are subject to query, being stopped, boarded and searched by US/Coalition warships operating in support of operations against Iraq. Vessels found to be carrying contraband bound for Iraq or carrying and/or laying naval mines are subject to detention, seizure and destruction.[323]

[315] W H von Heinegg 'Current Legal Issues in Maritime Operations: Maritime Interception Operations in the Global War on Terrorism, Exclusion Zones, Hospital Ships and Maritime Neutrality' in R B Jaques (ed) *Issues in International Law and Military Operations* (International Law Studies 80, US Naval War College, Newport 2006) 207, 217. For a similarly favourable view see Leckow (n 289) 634.

[316] Fenrick (n 84) 256. [317] *San Remo Manual* § 106.2. [318] Fenrick (n 289) 111–12.

[319] Ibid 113. [320] Ibid. [321] US *Naval Commander's Handbook* § 7.9.

[322] Maritime Liaison Office (MARLO) Bahrain 'MARLO Advisory Bulletin 06-03' (20 March 2003) (contained as Appendix B to US *Naval Commander's Handbook*).

[323] Ibid.

As the US *Naval Commander's Handbook* points out, this announcement did not amount to the establishment of a maritime exclusion zone but served to indicate the exercise of belligerent rights in a specific area.[324]

In 2004, after attacks on Iraqi oil terminals, the US issued a new notice to mariners stating that 'warning zones' had been established around the Iraqi terminals.[325] 'Exclusion zones' were established with regard to two terminals, which entailed the temporary suspension of innocent passage through Iraqi territorial waters.[326]

No protests were reported following the implementation of the zones, and there were no instances of confrontation between belligerent and neutral shipping within the zone.[327] There was therefore no attempt by a neutral State to exercise its right of innocent passage in a belligerent territorial sea, in contrast to the attempt by the US, during the Iran-Iraq war, to exercise its navigational rights in Iran's territorial sea.[328] Indeed, the paucity of State practice with regard to the relationship between belligerents and neutrals in maritime exclusion zones is notable. It is apparent, however, that the establishment of maritime exclusion zones is not *per se* questioned by neutrals but indicates that any such establishment will have to respect the principle of freedom of navigation and conform to the principles of necessity and proportionality in self-defence.

6. Conclusion

Now that the threat or use of force is prohibited in international law, legal principle would suggest that belligerents are limited in their ability to take belligerent measures against neutrals that were previously dependent on a state of war for their operation—such as the right of visit and search, the right to establish a blockade, and the right to set up exclusion zones. Because the relationship between belligerents and neutrals is a peaceful one, interference by belligerents with neutral shipping and aircraft will have to satisfy a double test in order to be lawful: such interference must meet the requirements of necessity and proportionality under the *jus ad bellum*, and also meet the requirements of the law of neutrality and naval warfare.

[324] US *Naval Commander's Handbook* § 7.9. See Stephens (n 314) 4–15 for discussion of exclusion zones in the eastern Mediterranean.

[325] HYDROPAC 795/04 (030850Z MAY 2004) (contained as Appendix C to US *Naval Commander's Handbook*).

[326] Ibid. [327] Stephens (n 314) 4–18.

[328] For the Iranian argument, contending that US passage would not be 'innocent' under Article 19 of the LOSC, see UNSC 'Letter dated 15 March 1989 from the Charge D'Affaires A I of the Permanent Mission of the Islamic Republic of Iran to the United Nations Addressed to the Secretary-General' (15 March 1989) UN Doc S/20525.

State practice suggests, therefore, that after the first half of the twentieth century, which saw the expansion of belligerent rights against neutrals to an alarming degree, the situation has, in many respects, been reversed by the influence of the Charter and the peacetime freedoms of the sea on the law of naval warfare. The requirement that belligerent interference with neutrals is lawful only if such action is necessary and proportionate means that recourse to the full range of belligerent rights against neutrals, as found in the law of contraband and blockade, will be impermissible in most armed conflicts. Instead, the scope of permissible belligerent action against neutrals has probably been narrowed considerably, demonstrating the overlap between the law of the UN Charter and the law of neutrality.

Conclusion

The traditional law of neutrality is a body of law that sits uncomfortably with certain elements of what is a central pillar of contemporary international law, the law on the use of force. For that reason, it tends to occupy a marginal existence in much contemporary armed conflict, and a number of writers have sought to dismiss its existence in contemporary international law.

This book has sought to provide an examination of the way in which the law of neutrality continues to exist and operate, albeit often obscurely, in recent international armed conflict. In doing so, it begins from a framework that distinguishes between the status of neutrality in international law, on the one hand, and the rights and duties that flow from that status, on the other hand. It has proceeded in four main steps. First, questions surrounding the applicability of the status of neutrality, which raise a number of theoretical and practical difficulties, have been examined. Secondly, the contemporary content of neutrality has been examined. Thirdly, the monograph has moved to an examination of when the content of neutrality may be modified or displaced, in the context of Security Council enforcement action under Chapter VII of the UN Charter. Fourth, the impact of the *jus ad bellum* on the interaction between belligerents and neutrals has been investigated.

Chapter 1 has sought to address arguments that neutral status is now an optional position for States. Developments in the law on the use of force have led to suggestions by a number of writers that neutrality is no longer an obligatory body of law that comes into existence upon hostilities reaching a certain threshold, as the traditional law provided; instead, they suggest, neutrality is now an optional legal status that may be invoked in certain circumstances, largely dependent on the State's volition. In almost all instances, non-participating States are free to occupy any position along a spectrum ranging from strict neutrality, on the one hand, to a position of non-belligerency, on the other. Proponents of this thesis claim for this concept of optional neutrality considerable explanatory power, and seek to demonstrate that the phenomenon of non-belligerency can account for the widespread deviation from the duties of neutrality in contemporary international armed conflicts.

This argument is difficult to sustain. While it has certain attractions, it is not reflected in customary international law, which continues to support the view that neutrality becomes obligatory for States that are not parties to an international armed conflict. The law of neutrality is *prima facie* applicable to non-participating States rather than an optional position that States are free to discard at will.

Acceptance of the argument of Chapter 1 does not overlook the effects on the law of neutrality of the comprehensive transformation of the law on the use of force in the twentieth century. As is developed in subsequent chapters, the law on the use of force has had a considerable impact on the way in which the status of neutrality may be modified, exchanged, or terminated; and it has also had a considerable effect on States' exercise of belligerent rights against neutrals. However, an examination of State practice does not suggest the development of a new legal rule to the effect that neutrality is an entirely optional position.

Chapter 2 has been devoted to an examination of when precisely the status of neutrality is triggered, and when it comes to an end. Here the prevailing view is that the law of neutrality comes into existence upon war being declared or otherwise evident. This view, however, suffers from certain difficulties and no longer accurately reflects the behaviour of States. What is suggested is that the *status* of neutrality is applicable upon an armed conflict coming into existence, but that this status may not automatically entail all the duties under the traditional law of neutrality.

Instead, it is suggested, the duties of neutrality may expand as an international armed conflict expands. Just as a belligerent's ability to take measures against neutral shipping will expand as an international armed conflict increases in intensity and scope (a development which is examined in Chapter 5), so too will a neutral's duties increase as an international armed conflict intensifies and broadens. This approach, it is suggested, is the best means of reconciling principle with the conduct of States. The way in which neutral status is terminated is then examined. The question of when a neutral State becomes a participant in an international armed conflict is one that has not received a large amount of attention. It has been tentatively suggested that the current state of the law indicates that the threshold here is quite high. In the area of the termination of neutrality, the law on the use of force has had a fundamental effect and has modified the traditional law. The law of neutrality did not itself regulate a belligerent's ability to terminate a State's neutrality by a declaration of war or invasion of its territory.[1] The ability of a neutral State to preserve its neutrality depended primarily on its strength relative to the belligerents and its ability to repel violations of its neutrality. Under the UN Charter, this position has now changed; a belligerent violates not only the law of neutrality, but also the UN Charter, in using force against a neutral State.

Chapter 3 has turned from the status of neutrality to the question of the content of neutrality. It has sought to examine in some detail the rights and duties that continue to attach to neutral status. Rather than an approach that suggests

[1] Oppenheim (3rd edn) vol II 406.

that neutrality consists of a series of principles rather than concrete rules, the analysis of Chapter 3 suggests that States continue to invoke the substantive rights and duties of neutrality, but in a not entirely satisfactory way. Many of the duties of neutrality are hindered by fundamental uncertainties and do not reflect developments in the law on the use of force or the modern law of the sea. Moreover, the distinction between neutral States and neutral citizens, which is a central tenet of Hague Conventions V and XIII, creates considerable obstacles in the path towards development of effective duties for neutral States.

Chapter 4 then considers the way in which neutrality has been affected by the practice of the UN Security Council in the area of international peace and security. While it was originally thought that the UN Charter had abolished comprehensively the ability of States to remain neutral, the failure of the UN Charter provisions on collective security to work as intended have led to a greater role for neutrality than envisaged by the founders of the UN Charter. The practice of authorizations to UN Member States to use military force has meant that States that choose not to participate in such UN-authorized action do not lose their status of neutrality. UN Security Council decisions taken under Chapter VII do, however, permit Member States to deviate from their duties of neutrality, and the view appears to be developing that States that choose not to participate in UN-authorized military action are nevertheless subject to certain obligations to assist that UN-authorized military action and to adjust the duties of neutrality accordingly.

Chapter 5 turns to an examination of the doctrines of economic warfare which parties to an international armed conflict have traditionally utilized to interfere with neutral shipping. While in the traditional law of neutrality, belligerents were entitled to utilize the doctrines of contraband, blockade, and war zones upon the existence of a state of war, the practice of the twentieth and twenty-first centuries suggest that, in their interactions with neutrals, belligerents are now subject to more onerous restraints. State practice demonstrates that, in these areas, belligerents are now required to justify the exercise of these traditional belligerent rights not only in accordance with the law of neutrality, but also in accordance with the *jus ad bellum*.

What is apparent from this study is that while parts of the law of neutrality are no longer relevant to the contemporary international legal order, others have demonstrated a surprising durability despite being considerably reshaped. Since the law of neutrality remains the most developed body of rules regulating the interactions of parties and non-parties in international armed conflict, it is likely that its rights and duties will continue to be invoked for some time. After all, the purpose that animates the law of neutrality—the prevention of the spread and escalation of armed conflict—remains an important one. Nevertheless, much of the law of neutrality languishes in a state of disrepair. There exists, for instance, a need for many of the duties of neutrality to be rethought for the twenty-first century, and to be developed with regard to other areas of international law.

ANNEX

The Historical Development of Neutrality

Neutrality is difficult to define. Throughout history, it has been understood in radically different ways. In 1895, Thomas Lawrence wrote of neutrality as an institution of continuous, sometimes discontinuous, movement across time. Neutrality contained 'rules that have been observed for ages, and rules that have been developed in our own time.' Some had gained adherence over long usage, while others were 'shifting and uncertain.' Neutrality contained principles 'that are still warmly supported and fiercely decried.'[1]

Any adequate understanding of neutrality as a legal concept must attempt to examine it historically. Indeed, it has been said that the 'law of neutrality is based less upon logic than upon history.'[2] One might add that it has been based less on doctrine than upon power. The belligerent seeks to exercise maximum control over neutral commerce in the prosecution of economic warfare; the neutral seeks to preserve its ability to trade in war as in peace, unfettered by belligerent interference. It is this conflict between the objectives of belligerents and neutrals that has, throughout the centuries, defined the scope of neutral duty and configured the boundaries of freedom of commerce during wartime.

The purpose of this annex is to examine the emergence and development of the concept of neutrality as a field of relations between belligerent and neutral States. While it is not possible here to outline a possible methodological framework, the annex presents a number of methodological issues that require brief description. Practitioners of intellectual history, at least those associated with the methodology of the so-called Cambridge School, emphasize the primacy of context. This approach privileges an 'ideal of containment'—that the horizon of meaning is fixed by context—over an 'ideal of movement' that traces the operation of a concept beyond its immediate contextual confinement.[3] Indeed, the Cambridge School's most prominent representative, Quentin Skinner, has argued that it is a mistake 'to write histories of ideas tracing its morphology of a given concept over time.'[4] This approach counsels disaggregation over generalization and cautions against any attempt to assimilate distinct concepts into sweeping narratives of

[1] T J Lawrence The Principles of International Law (2nd edn Macmillan, London 1895) 473.

[2] L Preuss, 'The Concepts of Neutrality and Nonbelligerency' (1941) 218 *Annals* 97, 100.

[3] See generally P E Gordon, 'Contextualism and Criticism in the History of Ideas' in D M McMahon and S Moyn (eds) *Rethinking Modern Intellectual History* (OUP, 2014) 32; M Jay, 'Historical Explanation and the Event: Reflections on the Limits of Contextualisation' (2011) 42 NLH 557.

[4] Q Skinner, 'Meaning and Understanding in the History of Ideas' (1969) 8 HT 3, 48.

change.[5] A focus on containment to the exclusion of movement, however, appears ill suited to the history of legal concepts inasmuch as such history seeks to trace the development of concepts across time.[6]

One of the benefits of a contextual approach is its opposition to treating historical phenomena as a developing sequence of elaboration and earlier concepts as anticipations of present concerns, or in viewing historical investigation as an exercise in lexicography.[7] The tradition of conceptual history (*Begriffsgeschichte*) shares with contextual approaches a methodological hostility towards the examination of historical concepts through a contemporary lens.[8] It is, however, able more fully to accommodate the study of conceptual change. Conceptual history insists on the importance of alternating a contextual approach with an approach that examines change in the meaning of concepts across time.[9] Both these approaches—synchronic analysis of concepts in particular situations, and diachronic analyses tracing changes over time in the meaning of concepts—are brought together in the process of historical enquiry.[10]

The practice of conceptual history has its own methodological pitfalls, which cannot be examined in any detail here.[11] Nevertheless, the emphasis on both diachronic alongside synchronic accounts of concepts will be important methodological tools in the examination of neutrality in international legal history. The objective of this annex is not to search for disparate usages throughout history or to unearth a definitive origin or pedigree. Instead, it seeks to offer an account of how historical change gave rise to the development of neutrality as a legal relationship: a legal status that gives rise to legal relationships between neutrals and belligerents.

[5] D Armitage, *Foundations of Modern International Thought* (CUP 2013) 30.

[6] A Orford, 'On International Legal Method' (2013) 1 LRIL 166, 172; A Orford, 'The Past as Law or History? The Relevance of Imperialism for Modern International Law' in M Toufayan, E Tourme-Jouannet and H Ruiz Fabri (eds) *Droit international et nouvelles approches sur le tiers-monde: entre répétition et renouveau* (Société de legislation compare 2013) 97. See also M Koskenniemi, 'Histories of International Law: Significance and Problems for a Critical View' (2013) 27 TICLJ 215.

[7] For this criticism see R Tuck, *Natural Rights Theories* (CUP 1979) 1. As Samuel Moyn points out, the practice of anticipation is evident in much historical human rights scholarship. S Moyn, *The Last Utopia: Human Rights in History* (Belknap Press 2010) 6. For this problem in international law, see M Koskenniemi, 'Vitoria and Us: Thoughts on Critical Histories of International Law' (2014) 22 *Rechtsgeschichte* 119.

[8] M Bevir, '*Begriffsgeschichte*' (2000) 39 HT 273, 277. Conceptual history is most prominently associated with the work of Reinhart Koselleck. See for example the essays collected in R Koselleck *The Practice of Conceptual History: Timing History, Spacing Concepts* (Stanford UP 2002). A detailed account is M Richter, *The History of Political and Social Concepts: A Critical Introduction* (OUP 1995). A useful examination is J-W Müller, 'On Conceptual History' in D M McMahon and S Moyn (eds) *Rethinking Modern European Intellectual History* (OUP 2014) 74.

[9] Borrowing from linguistic theory, conceptual history terms these modes 'synchronic' and 'diachronic' analysis. For an explanation and comparison with the Cambridge School approach see M Richter, 'Conceptual History (*Begriffsgeschichte*) and Political Theory' (1986) 14 PT 604, 620–3.

[10] H E Bödeker, 'Concept – Meaning – Discourse. *Begriffsgeschichte* Reconsidered' in I Hampsher-Monk, K Tilmans and F van Vree (eds) *History of Concepts: Comparative Perspectives* (Amsterdam UP 1998) 51.

[11] For some of these criticisms see, for example, Bevir (n 8).

Some principal claims emerge from this examination. First, the power or the right of belligerents to take prize measures emerged historically prior to the concept of neutrality as a distinct legal status held by third States during war. Secondly, this power of belligerents to take action during wartime against commerce destined for or aiding the enemy increasingly came up against neutral assertions of a 'natural' right of commerce for their citizens. This, however, gave rise to the paradoxical state of affairs, according to which a neutral State decried belligerent interference with the shipping of its nationals yet refused to assume responsibility for those actions. This tension led to a fundamental tension at the heart of neutral obligation between the duties of abstention and impartiality. It was this tension that afflicted the nineteenth century practice of neutrality and attempts to codify the law of neutrality and naval warfare in the early twentieth century.

1. The Emergence of Prize Law

In his magisterial volumes on the history of international law, Verzijl remarks that '[w]riters on the subject...are hesitant about the first emergence of the term and the concept of neutrality.'[12] There is little agreement amongst historians and lawyers as to the concept's pedigree. One view places the birth of neutrality as early as the twelfth century.[13] Other claims for neutrality's historical pedigree place its birth in the fourteenth or fifteenth century.[14]

Some of this divergence is based on uncertainty about the precise object of description. While the technical term 'neutrality' may be traced back no further than the fifteenth century, recognition of non-participation as a fact can be traced to earlier sources.[15] The concept of non-participation clearly appears in

[12] J H W Verzijl, *International Law in Historical Perspective* IX-B (Sijthoff & Noordhoff 1979) 15.

[13] Grewe traces the beginnings of the practice of neutrality to the twelfth century to the feudal relations between vassals and princes. See W Grewe, *The Epochs of International Law* (M Byers (ed and tr)) (Walter de Grutyer 2000) 68. Wolff Heintschel von Heinegg has argued that 'neutrality' was first acknowledged in 1164, during war between Pisa and Genoa. W H von Heinegg, 'Visit, Search, Diversion and Capture: Conditions of Applicability' in W H von Heinegg (ed) *Visit, Search, Diversion and Capture: the Effect of the United Nations Charter on the Law of Naval Warfare* (Bochumer Schriften zur Friedenssicherung und zum Humanitären Völkerrecht Band 24, Universitätsverlag Brockmeyer 1995) 1, 2.

[14] See P C Jessup and F Deák, *Neutrality: Its History, Economics and Law. Volume I: The Origins* (Columbia UP 1935) 4; T E Holland, *Lectures on International Law* (T A Walker and W L Walker (eds)) (Sweet & Maxwell 1933) 407.

[15] J Westlake, *International Law* II (CUP 1907) 161: 'The fact of neutrality is as old as war, but the technical term from the root is not traced by Nys further back than to treaties and edicts drawn up in French at the close of the fifteenth century..., before which time we have *stille sitzen*, to sit still—*unpartyschung*, impartiality—*guerrae abstinentia*, abstintence from the war—and, especially with regard to naval war, to be *in treuga*, in truce, *in pace*, or simply a friend, *amicus*.'

Thucydides' account of the Peloponnesian War, for example.[16] Similar degrees of non-participation are referred to in ancient India.[17]

Any form of non-participation grounded in a principle recognizing the equality of belligerents, however, was unknown to the Middle Ages.[18] Just war doctrine viewed war as a matter of enforcing the collective good.[19] Principles governing recourse to force took precedence over those governing the conduct of hostilities.[20] Since there was no position 'outside' natural law, there was little theoretical basis for a position that did not take sides in a just conflict. That basis became possible only after the breakdown of the unity of the Christian Church and the gradual emergence of divergent doctrinal positions on war.[21]

Belligerents came into contact with non-participants through attempts to capture property at sea in order to prevent it from reaching enemy ports. The small size of professional navies meant that these captures at sea were in practice undertaken by privateers sailing under letters of marque or reprisal—essentially licences from a foreign power to private ships to carry out captures in response to previous injury.[22] The position of 'admiral' was created to command the issuance and revocation of letters of marque or reprisal.[23]

[16] Thuycidides, *The War of the Peloponnesians and the Athenians* (J Mynott (ed)) (CUP 2013) I, 33–7. For discussion see G Hawthorn, *Thucydides on Politics* (CUP 2014) 31–2. More generally, R A Bauslaugh, *The Concept of Neutrality in Classical Greece* (University of California Press 1991); S Shepperd, 'The Laws of War in the Pre-Dawn Light: Institutions and Obligations in Thucydides' *Peloponnesian War*' (2004–2005) 43 CJTL 905, 922–4. For an example of an ancient non-participant State preventing its citizens from enrolling in a belligerent army see N Toogood, '"Athens Aids Eritrea": A State's Jurisdiction Over Its Citizens' Actions' (1997) 47 CQ 295.

[17] See K K R Sastry, 'A Note on Udasina: Neutrality in Ancient India' (1954) IYIA 131; S V Viswanatha, *International Law in Ancient India* (Longmans, Green & Co 1925) 32–5; 185–6.

[18] M H Keen, *The Laws of War in the Late Middle Ages* (Routledge & Kegan Paul 1965) 208.

[19] Grewe (n 13) 107.

[20] J T Johnson, *Just War Tradition and the Restraint of War: a Moral and Historical Inquiry* (Princeton UP 1981) 47–48, 123.

[21] J T Johnson, *Ideology, Reason and the Limitation of War: Religious and Secular Concepts 1200–1740* (Princeton UP 1975) 8–9. Vitoria argued that a war could, in effect, be fought justly by both sides due to 'invincible ignorance' on the part of one belligerent. See F de Vitoria, 'On the American Indians' in *Political Writings* (A Pagden and J Lawrance (eds)) (CUP 1991) 282–3. Gentili, similarly, argued that both belligerents may go to war in the belief that their cause is just. A Gentili, *De Jure Belli Libri Tres* (J C Rolfe (tr)) Clarendon Press 1933) 31–2.

[22] It would seem that the earliest mention of letters of marque was in 1293. R G Marsden (ed) *Documents Relating to Law and Custom of the Sea* I (Navy Records Society, London 1915) 19. On the development of letters of marque see R de Mas Latrie, *Du droit de marque, ou droit de représailles au Moyen Âge* (A Franck, Paris 1883). Letters of reprisal were issued permitting the bearer to seize property of a foreign power's subjects in reprisal for injury suffered by the bearer at the hands of that foreign power. For letters of reprisal dating from 1295 see Marsden, *Documents* I 38. See G Clark, 'The English Practice with Regard to Reprisals by Private Persons' (1933) 27 AJIL 694. For the Elizabethan practice see K R Andrews, *Elizabethan Privateering: English Privateering during the Spanish War, 1585–1603* (CUP 1964); J E Thomson, *Mercenaries, Pirates and Sovereigns: State-Building and Extraterritorial Violence in Early Modern Europe* (Princeton UP 1994) 82–3; M Kempe, '"Even in the Remotest Corners of the World": Globalised Piracy and International Law, 1500-1900' (2010) 5 JGH 353.

[23] The word 'admiral' seems to have entered common usage in records soon after an agreement with Flanders in 1297. Marsden, *Documents* I 46. But an order of the King to William de Leyburne (the first admiral) dates from 1296. This order commands the admiral to apply the rule that friends' goods found in a friendly ship were to be restored to the friends and enemy goods found in the same ship were to be delivered to the captors: Marsden, *Documents* I 42.

Rules concerning capture at sea were developed primarily in treaties but were also contained in sets of regulations or practices issued to seafaring communities. The most well known is the Consolate of the Seas (*Consolato del Mare*), which is believed to be a collection of traders' practices for merchants in Barcelona.[24] The *Consolato* set out various rules for the confiscation of ships and cargo. The most straightforward provides that enemy goods found in enemy ships render the ship and the goods good prize. If enemy property was found on the ship of the friend, the ship could be seized but only the enemy goods were good prize and the ship itself had to be released. Freight was to be paid to the ship for the amount it would have earned at the delivery port. Friends' goods on enemy ships were not subject to confiscation.[25]

Rules to this effect were agreed in treaties. In 1353, a treaty of alliance between the King of England, King Edward III, and the King of Portugal made detailed provision for the regulation of captures at sea. The treaty provided that, if either treaty party were at war with a third enemy power, property belonging to either treaty party would be returned, or full restitution would be made, if the property were found in an enemy's ship—so long as there was no evidence that that power was allied with the enemy.[26]

Dispute over the requirements of this 1353 treaty gave rise to one of the first exercises of the admiral's jurisdiction over matters of prize. French sailors captured a Portuguese ship carrying Portuguese goods. The goods, then in possession of the French, were then recaptured by an Englishman and brought to England. Portugal claimed restoration of these goods under the terms of the treaty. The admiral disagreed and condemned the goods as 'prize' belonging to the English captors. A letter from Edward III to the King of Portugal affirmed the decision of the admiral, on the basis that the goods seized had been spoiled by the original French captors and were of French ownership at the time of seizure by the English.[27]

A distinct admiralty court was created in England to adjudicate these and other disputes applying maritime law, but was only seldom invoked until later centuries.[28] Relevant practice and rules were collated in the *Black Book of the Admiralty*.[29] The admiralty court heard disputes in three principal areas: civil or

[24] S S Jados (ed) *Consulate of the Sea and Related Documents* (University of Alabama Press 1975) ch 276. It is believed the document dates to the late fourteenth century, although this is disputed. The author is unknown.

[25] S Neff, *The Rights and Duties of Neutrals* (Manchester UP 2000) 11 terms this the 'character-of-the-cargo' rule on capture.

[26] An English translation and extract is contained in Marsden, *Documents* I 78–80.

[27] Marsden, *Documents* I 81.

[28] R G Marsden, 'Early Prize Jurisdiction and Prize Law in England (Part I)' (1909) 24 EHR 675, 681.

[29] T Twiss (ed) *Monumenta Juridica: The Black Book of the Admiralty* (6 vols, Longman & Co 1871–6).

'instance' jurisdiction, which encompassed a wide array of commercial cases; cases concerned with crimes committed at sea; as well as the law of prize. Sitting in prize jurisdiction, the court distinguished acts of piracy from lawful capture ('good prize'), as well as ensuring that the admiral received a share of the goods taken by privateers. The requirement that all captures to be good prize must be brought before the High Court of Admiralty for adjudication was established in the late sixteenth century.[30]

One of the most important practical questions was the status of enemy goods found aboard the ships of friends, and the status of property owned by friends found aboard enemy ships. During the war with Spain that began in 1585, England adopted the following rules. Property owned by a subject of Spain could be seized, whether found in friendly or enemy ships.[31] If Spanish property was found in a friendly ship, the property could be claimed in prize but freight was payable to the master of the ship.[32] Carriage of Spanish property in friendly ships did not result in the condemnation of the ship as good prize; the ship, and the property belonging to friendly subjects, was to be restored to the legal owners.[33] Friendly-owned property found aboard enemy ships was not good prize and was to be returned to its owner. This practice was consistent with the rules set down in the *Consolato del Mare,* but it is doubtful whether that document was of direct influence.[34]

Another doctrine, less favourable to friendly commerce, viewed the ownership of the ship, rather than the ownership of the goods, as determinative for purposes of capture. This was the practice of the Spanish admiralty in relation to matters of prize during its war with England. Spanish authorities condemned as prize all goods, regardless of ownership, captured in an enemy ship.[35] This doctrine was

[30] Mandatory adjudication of captures by the 'high courte of the Admiralty' was established by an Order in Council dated 20 July 1589: Marsden, *Documents* I 252. It seems there was a practice of foreign powers giving their consent to the condemnation of a foreign prize by the High Court of Admiralty. Marsden, *Documents* I 282. The first example of condemnation of a ship as lawful prize appears to be the case of the Spanish vessel *St Anthony,* also in 1589: Marsden, *Documents* I 254.

[31] Marsden, *Documents* I 306.

[32] See for example the 1598 case of the *Roebuck,* concerning the confiscation of Spanish salt, Marsden, *Documents* I 291.

[33] For an example of the restoration of a German ship, the *St Michael,* and the German-owned goods aboard it, see Marsden, *Documents* I 302.

[34] Marsden, 'Early Prize Jurisdiction' (n 28) 694. There is considerable controversy over the status of the *Consolato* as a collection of basic rules operating as ancient custom, which particular treaties affirmed or modified. For an approach that adopts this position see Wheaton (8th edn, n 158) §445; A P Higgins, 'The Growth of International Law, Maritime Rights and Colonial Titles 1648-1763' in J H Rose et al (eds) *The Cambridge History of the British Empire* I (CUP 1929) 538, 550. C J Kulsrud, *Maritime Neutrality to 1780* (Little, Brown and Company 1936) 15–16; 130. On this view the rules of the *consolato* function somewhat similarly to relationship between the international minimum standard and modern bilateral investment treaties. The more persuasive view is that the *Consolato* constituted no such customary or baseline rule and that the position outside treaty law was highly unsettled; see R Pares, *Colonial Blockade and Neutral Rights* (Clarendon Press 1938) 154 n1.

[35] See the 1587 statement by one Francisco Tassis, resident in London, concerning the practice of the Spanish admiralty in taking as prize all goods, regardless of ownership, in enemy ships: Marsden,

also adopted in a Marine Ordinance promulgated by the French King François I in 1543, during the war with Emperor Charles V.[36] But this Ordinance went further than the Spanish practice by providing that carriage of enemy goods in the ships of friends rendered the cargo and the ship good prize.[37] It may be that this expansive decree was in response to the practice of English merchants falsely claiming ownership of goods that were in fact owned by subjects of the Emperor or the French King; it was in response to this practice of 'cloaking' or 'colouring' that King Henry VIII had proclaimed his 'newtrality' in 1536.[38] Debate over the general applicability of these contending positions would continue almost ceaselessly until the middle of the nineteenth century. Whether there existed any general rule of international law absent a prevailing treaty provision is a matter of considerable uncertainty.

A special class of goods was that useful to the war effort, which could be captured without payment of freight. These were contraband, or prohibited, goods. As early as 1293, there exists practice that war materials destined for an enemy port could be seized when the ships containing such goods were found within English ports.[39] In 1589, Queen Elizabeth I proclaimed that all ships engaged in the trade of food, war materials, and shipping stores voluntarily to Spain would be condemned as prize without payment of freight; a subsequent proclamation allowed Dutch vessels to trade with Spain but under stringent prohibitions with regard to certain items.[40] The High Court of Admiralty later granted its seal to the proclamation.[41]

Treaties of alliance were common modes for the listings of contraband. In the Treaty of Southampton between England and the United Provinces of 17 September 1625, a treaty of alliance against Spain, in addition to a general

Documents I 249, 250: '...all goodes laden in an unfree bottom, (as they nowe terme Englishe shippe by reason of the trowbles), to what nation soever they appertayne, are by that lawe and order merely confiscate and good prize.'

[36] *Recueil général des anciennes lois françaises* 12 (Belin Leprieur 1821) 854.

[37] The rule was restated in the Marine Ordinance of 15 March 1584, during the war with Spain: *Recueil général des anciennes lois françaises* 14 (Belin Leprieur 1821) 556, 579. England later came to adopt the rule in its 1665 war against the Dutch. France protested against this practice on the basis that the rule was no longer followed by French courts. See R G Marsden (ed) *Documents Relating to Law and Custom of the Sea* II (Navy Records Society, London 1915) 62, 63. See the response to the French protest by the Prize Commissioners (ibid 64), stating that the rule condemning all goods found on an enemy's ship was the 'ancient law' of England and other nations. For a survey of the changes in French practice see E Schnakenbourg, 'From "Hostile Infection" to "Free Ships, Free Goods": Changes in French neutral trade legislation (1689–1778)' in K Stapelbroek (ed) *Trade and War: The Neutrality of Commerce in the Inter-State System* (Helsinki Collegium for Advanced Studies 2011) 95.

[38] The proclamation appears in Marsden, *Documents* I, 149–50.

[39] Marsden, *Documents* I, 21–31.

[40] For the background to the proclamation and for reactions of other powers, see E P Cheyney, 'International Law under Queen Elizabeth' (1905) 20 EHR 659. For the order issued to Dutch traders see Marsden, *Documents* I, 262.

[41] Marsden, *Documents* I, 317. The seal of the High Court of Admiralty was granted in 1601.

prohibition on all trade between either of the contracting parties and Spain, 'munitions de bouche et de guerre', war materials and victuals, silver, leather, iron, and shipping materials destined for Spain were declared contraband. Ships carrying such contraband, as well as the prohibited cargo, were to be declared good prize and condemned.[42] A subsequent proclamation of 31 December 1625 by the English King Charles I stated that the prohibition of contraband items was justified by the law of nations.[43] A similar point was made in a proclamation of contraband in 1627, which stated that 'his Majestie doth put in practice no innovation, since the same course hath beene held, and the same penalties have beene heretofore inflicted by other States and princes upon the like occasions.'[44] However, it must be borne in mind that these treaties were expressions of immediate needs rather than of general principle.[45] Exemptions from blanket proclamations or treaty rules could be granted.[46]

Early practice indicates that certain actions, distinct from the carriage of certain goods, were considered so closely allied to a belligerent as to give rise to a right of capture. In 1604, a Dutch ship captured a Venetian ship that was trading south of the tropics under licence from Spain.[47] Because it was 'universally known' that Spain claimed to treat as hostile all ships trading south of the tropics, the Venetian acceptance of a licence from Spain was tantamount to alliance, and the ship good prize in Holland, then at war with Spain.[48] This recognition of activity rendering a 'friendly' ship an auxiliary or ally of a belligerent prefigures both the later controversy concerning the carriage of colonial commerce and the nineteenth century doctrine of 'unneutral service.'[49]

2. The Appearance of Neutrality in Doctrine

Hugo Grotius entitles a chapter of *De Jure Belli ac Pacis,* written in 1625, 'On those who are of neither side in war'. [50] As a number of writers have pointed out,

[42] Traité de Ligue Offensive et Défensive entre Charles I Roi de la Grande Bretagne, et les Provinces-Unies des Pays-Bas (signed 17 September 1625) 5(2) Dumont 478, art 20. The treaty is notable for its emphasis on the concept of enemy destination; those vessels suspected of taking their course towards Spain were obliged to stop and to be visited (art 22).

[43] Rymer XVIII 259.

[44] Marsden, *Documents* I, 433, 435. The proclamation stated that both the ship and the goods were good prize if found in possession of the prohibited contraband.

[45] P C Jessup and F Deák, 'The Early Development of the Law of Neutral Rights' (1931) 46 PSQ 481, 488.

[46] See, for example, Marsden, *Documents* I, 460, for favourable rules afforded to merchants from Hamburg.

[47] On the concept of 'lines of amity' see A P Higgins, 'International Law and the Outer World, 1450-1648' in J H Rose et al (eds) *The Cambridge History of the British Empire* I (CUP 1929) 183, 187–8; C Schmitt, *The* Nomos *of the Earth in the* Jus Publicum Europaeum (G L Ulmen (tr)) (Telos Press 2003) 92–9.

[48] Marsden, *Documents* I, 345. [49] Ibid.

[50] H Grotius, *De Jure Belli ac Pacis Libri Tres* (F W Kelsey (tr)) (OUP 1925) book III ch XVII.

what Grotius describes is very far from a 'theory' of neutrality.[51] If a just belligerent could be identified, then it was incumbent upon non-belligerent States not to do anything to hinder that just belligerent, nor to do anything that will assist the unjust belligerent.[52] If doubt existed, however, as to which party had just cause, Grotius counselled impartiality as the wisest course for the non-belligerent: '[i]n a doubtful matter, however, those at peace should show themselves impartial to either side in permitting transit, in furnishing supplies to troops, and in not assisting those under siege.'[53] Indeed, Grotius notes that '[i]t will even be of advantage to make a treaty with either party that is waging war, in order that it may be permissible to abstain from war while retaining the goodwill of either, and to render to each the common duties of humanity.'[54]

Grotius, then, identified two distinct limbs to the position of *medii* or non-belligerent powers. A duty of abstention existed that prevented, in a situation of identifiable just war, assistance to the wrongful belligerent. A position of impartiality was the right course of conduct in a situation in which just cause could not be identified. But these distinct duties were not treated with a great deal of precision. Thus Grotius identifies as one aspect of impartiality the obligation not to assist those under siege; yet this obligation would appear conceptually closer to a duty of abstention than of impartiality.[55]

Grotius also devotes attention to the rights of belligerents. From those who are 'at peace', nothing should be taken from them by belligerents 'except in case of extreme necessity.'[56] Grotius then elaborates different classes of goods. Some things, such as weapons, are useful only in war. Other items were never of use in war. In between these two categories were items potentially for use in war as well as for peace, such as money, ships, provisions, and naval equipment.[57] Items for war were always capable of seizure, since 'he who supplies an enemy with things necessary for warfare is on the side of the enemy.'[58] Items incapable of use in war were not to be subject to interference. Whether items in the third category could be seized was determined on the basis of necessity. If a belligerent is unable to protect itself without seizing the goods, it may do so but with the duty to make restitution.[59] This distinction between prohibited contraband goods and 'free goods' was mirrored in treaty practice of the period. For example, the Treaty of the

[51] Oppenheim (1st edn) II 303; W E Hall, *Hall's International Law* (A P Higgins (ed)) (8th edn OUP 1924) 693; Grewe (n 13) 216–17.

[52] Grotius (n 50) 786. [53] Ibid.

[54] Ibid 787. In support of this approach Grotius quotes Livy: 'Let them desire peace with either side, as befits impartial friends; let them not intervene in the war.' (ibid). He ends the chapter by quoting Archidamus, King of Sparta: 'It is a good thing to remain quiet.'

[55] Ibid 786. [56] Ibid 783. [57] Ibid 602. [58] Ibid.

[59] Ibid. Grotius notes that if the enforcement of the belligerent's right was hindered by the supply of goods, and the supplier had known that this would result from the supply of the goods (Grotius gives the example of a belligerent holding a port under blockade) then the supplier would be liable to the belligerent for injury inflicted.

Pyrenees, signed between France and Spain in 1659, defined contraband as 'all sorts of Fire-Arms, and all things belonging to them.'[60] 'Free goods', on the other hand, were defined as 'anything belonging to the nourishment and sustenation of Life.'[61] The practice of stating contraband items in treaty form became common practice by the middle of the seventeenth century.[62]

Grotius wrote from within a framework that was beholden in many respects to just war doctrine.[63] A number of jurists after Grotius seized on his distinction between the law of nature and the law of nations (*jus gentium*) and insisted on the primacy of positive law.[64] Richard Zouche, the Regius Professor of Civil War at Oxford, distinguished further between the law of nations and the *jus inter Gentes*, the law between nations.[65] The *jus inter Gentes* required a clear distinction between States at peace and States at war, and the relationship between the two.[66] Unsurprisingly given his maritime law practice (he would later become a judge of the High Court of Admiralty), Zouche's study is notable for its detailed attention to questions of maritime capture. Noting the practice of the period that enemy goods rendered all goods on board liable to seizure, Zouche follows Grotius in stating that this approach is not required by the law of nations and that enemy ships merely raise a presumption that the cargo on board is also of enemy character.[67] In relation to the status of friendly ships carrying enemy goods, Zouche opposes the French approach of the Marine Ordinance with the view that it is 'more equitable' to 'release the ships of a friendly power after removing their cargoes, unless they carry contraband'.[68] In relation to contraband, Zouche cites approvingly Grotius's distinction between free goods, warlike items ('persons who supply such things to enemies are regarded as taking their side'), and conditional goods that may be seized in particular circumstances, namely 'if their carriage may hinder a surrender which is expected.'[69]

Although Zouche adhered to many of Grotius's views, there was little doctrinal consistency amongst writers. An adherent of Zouche's voluntarist approach,

[60] Treaty of the Pyrenees (signed 7 November 1659) 5 CTS 325, art 12. [61] Ibid, art 13.

[62] P Jessup and F Deák, 'The Early Development of the Law of Contraband of War II' (1933) 48 PSQ 62, 75.

[63] The classic study of Grotius and just war is P Haggenmacher, *Grotius et la doctrine de la guerre juste* (Presses Universitaires de France 1983).

[64] Thomas Hobbes and Samuel Pufendorf were the two most prominent writers who sought to conflate the two. On this point see Armitage (n 5) ch 4.

[65] R Zouche, *An Exposition of Fecial Law and Procedure, or of the Law between Nations, and Questions concerning the Same* (J L Brierly (tr)) (Carnegie Institution of Washington 1911) 1.

[66] For Zouche, States at peace had relationships of alliance or friendship with belligerents. See ibid 4–7. He makes it clear that friends and allies are not synonymous with those who 'espouse the same side in war' (ibid 120).

[67] Ibid 122.

[68] Ibid 122. Zouche cites approvingly the *Consolato del Mare*, pursuant to which one who seizes enemy goods in a friendly ship is bound to pay freight for the part of the voyage performed.

[69] Ibid 123. Zouche also devoted attention to the question of when during a voyage a ship carrying contraband could be captured (ibid 124–5).

Johann Textor's work is striking in his explicit reference in his *Synopsis Juris Gentium* of 1680 to 'the law of neutrality'.[70] Neutrality for Textor is a 'right' of equal friendship, a relationship founded on treaty alone: 'strictly speaking and in the usage of the Law of Nations, those only are neutrals who derive their middle position from consent or agreement.'[71] The primary duty of neutrality is an obligation to abstain from 'hostile acts' against either belligerent.[72] Textor devotes much of his chapter on neutrality to the permissibility of neutral trade. Part of the 'right' of equal friendship on the part of the neutral, founded on agreement, is the right to engage in commerce with either party: '[i]t would be absurd for parties to be put by agreement in a condition of friendship one with the other, and yet for commerce between them to be forbidden, so that, simply for the sake of bringing a little more advantage to the other party, they are unable to contract one with the other.'[73] There was no difficulty in admitting the permissibility of trade in non-warlike material. But Textor extended his general principle to the supply of weapons as well, on the basis that the neutral does not itself use the arms against the belligerent, and provided that both sides are treated alike by the neutral.[74] This right to trade then came up against a belligerent's interest in intercepting these items en route to an enemy port.[75]

Textor's ambitious *laissez-faire* approach marks a striking attempt to carve out a right to engage in commerce on the part of the neutral merchant and its government. The doctrine had little immediate effect on the practice of maritime warfare, which saw increasingly invasive measures applied to the trade of non-belligerent shipping.[76] Yet it prefigured in important respects the more celebrated doctrines of neutrality elaborated in the eighteenth century.

3. Neutrality and Jealousy of Trade

The law of nations in the eighteenth century began to correspond to an autonomous set of norms capable of imposing structure on an international order underpinned by State sovereignty.[77] It was in the eighteenth century that

[70] J W Textor, *Synopsis Juris Gentium* II (J P Bate (tr)) (Carnegie Institution 1916) chapter 26. For an (uncharitable) assessment of Textor's theory of neutrality see Ludwig von Bar's introduction, who describes Textor's approach to neutrality as 'retrograde and artificial' in comparison with the approach of Grotius (22a).

[71] Ibid 273. [72] Ibid 278. [73] Ibid 279.

[74] Ibid 280. Nor did Textor suggest there was any distinction whether the trade is conducted 'on public or private account.'

[75] Ibid 280–1.

[76] During the war with Louis XIV's France, England and the Netherlands agreed to seize as good prize all ships sailing for France, which effectively amounted to a ban on neutral commerce with an enemy belligerent. See the documents of 1689 in Marsden, *Documents* II, 130–2.

[77] E Jouannet, *The Liberal-Welfarist Law of Nations: A History of International Law* (CUP 2012) 13. For the role of sovereignty relating to the conduct of warfare see J Q Whitman, *The Verdict of Battle: The Law of Victory and the Making of Modern War* (Harvard UP 2012) 19.

neutrality became theorized as a particular status with definite content, both in particular conflicts and in the writings of Cornelius van Bynkershoek, Emer de Vattel and Martin Hübner.[78]

Bynkershoek, in particular, is widely seen as the first jurist to develop neutrality into a distinct sphere of the law of nations.[79] First, unlike many earlier writers, Bynkershoek distinguished between 'allies' and 'neutrals'. 'Allies' were those States bound to belligerents by treaties of mutual assistance or alliance. 'Neutrals' (*non hostii*) were those 'who belong to neither belligerent party and owe no services to either party by treaty obligations.'[80] This was an understanding markedly different from Textor's understanding of neutrality as a purely conventional relationship. Second, for Bynkershoek a position of neutrality gave rise to particular rights and duties. Neutrals, he argues:

> must in every way guard against interfering in the war, and against showing favouritism toward or prejudice against either belligerent. This is the meaning of the phrase in Livy: 'let them not intervene in the war,' that is, let them not show preference to either belligerent so far as concerns the war, and this is the only proper course for neutrals.[81]

This is an understanding of neutrality that emphasizes the requirements of impartiality and abstention on the part of the neutral. Moreover, Bynkershoek divorced the application of neutrality from the morality of war. The requirements of neutrality instead meant that the 'question of justice and injustice' did 'not concern the neutral, and it is not his duty to sit in judgement between his friends who may be fighting each other, and to grant or deny anything to either belligerent through considerations of the relative degree of justice.'[82]

Both Vattel and Hübner were responding, in very different ways, to the rise of the concept of 'jealousy of trade,' the conjunction of politics and economics that transformed international relations into a theatre of 'perpetual commercial war.'[83] The Seven Years' War, fought between 1754 and 1763, demonstrated the role of commerce in fuelling warfare.[84] Maritime space became a theatre of market competition but also a space of increasing juridification.[85] Vattel and Hübner

[78] Grewe (n 13) 371 argues that these three writers built the foundations of modern neutrality law.

[79] Hall (8th edn, n 51) 698; G G Butler and S Macoby, *The Development of International Law* (Longmans, Green and Co 1928) 232; Grewe (n 13) 373. For wider treatment see K Akashi, *Cornelius van Bynkershoek: His Role in the History of International Law* (Kluwer 1998).

[80] C van Bynkershoek, *Quaestionum Juris Publici Libri Duo* (T Frank (tr)) Clarendon Press 1930) 60.

[81] Ibid 61. [82] Ibid 61.

[83] I Hont, *Jealousy of Trade: International Competition and the Nation-State in Historical Perspective* (Belknap Press 2005) 6.

[84] Ibid 34; Kulsrud (n 34) 64–70 David Hume's essay 'Of the Jealousy of Trade' was published during the conflict. D Hume, *Political Essays* (K Haakonssen (ed)) (CUP 1994) 150.

[85] See M Foucault, *Security, Territory, Population: Lectures at the Collège de France 1977–1978* ((M Senellart (ed) and G Burchell (tr)) Palgrave Macmillan 2007) 337; M Foucault, *The Birth of Biopolitics:*

approached the role of commerce in war, and the role of international law in governing this relationship, from strikingly different perspectives.[86]

Like Pufendorf before him, Vattel considered that the law of nations was the law of nature applied to States. The law of nature demanded mutual aid; it was a duty to do 'everything in our power for the preservation and happiness of others, as far as such conduct is reconcilable with our duties towards ourselves.'[87] The most important way in which States could foster the international society required by natural law was through trade, provided that such trade did not conflict with a State's primary duty of self-preservation and was compatible with the balance of power.[88]

The concept of neutrality served to preserve the law of nature's emphasis on mutual aid through commerce during warfare. Vattel emphasized that it was the right of every nation to remain 'neuter' upon the outbreak of war: 'if either of the belligerent powers attempted to force them to a junction with him, he would do them an injury, inasmuch as he would be guilty of an infringement on their independency in a very essential point.'[89] Neutrals are those who 'remain common friends to both parties, without favouring the arms of the one to the prejudice of the other.'[90]

Vattel elevated impartiality to the apex of neutral duties.[91] Yet what was subsumed under a general concept of impartiality was in fact two subsidiary obligations, depending on whether or not the activity in question was associated directly with hostilities. First, Vattel argued that impartiality required a State to 'give no assistance where there is no obligation to give it' and to refuse 'voluntarily to furnish troops, arms, ammunition, or any thing of direct use in war.'[92] Thus in a sphere 'directly' concerned with war, Vattel counsels abstention for the neutral, on the basis that 'it would be absurd that a State should at one and the same time assist two nations at war with each other; and besides it would be impossible to do it with equality.'[93] The second obligation was imposed in relation to 'whatever does not relate to war'. In this sphere, a neutral nation must not refuse to one of

Lectures at the Collège de France 1978–1979 ((M Senellart (ed) and G Burchell (tr)) Palgrave Macmillan 2008) 56.

[86] For a comparison of these authors see K Stapelbroek, 'Universal Society, Commerce and the Rights of Neutral Trade: Martin Hübner, Emer de Vattel and Ferdinando Galiani' in P Korkman and V Mäkinen (eds) *Universalism in International Law and Political Philosophy* (Helsinki Collegium for Advanced Studies 2008) 63.

[87] E de Vattel, *Le droit des gens, ou principes de la loi naturelle appliqués à la conduite et aux affaires des nations et des souverains* (London, 1758) book II §2; The translation as E de Vattel *The Law of Nations, Or, Principles of the Law of Nature, Applied to the Conduct and Affairs of Nations and Sovereigns, with Three Early Essays on the Origin and Nature of Natural Law and on Luxury* (B Kapossy and R Whatmore (eds)) (Liberty Fund 2008) will be used in what follows.

[88] See I Nakhimovsky, 'Vattel's Theory of the International Order: Commerce and the Balance of Power in the Law of Nations' (2007) 33 HEI 157.

[89] Vattel (n 87) book III §106. [90] Ibid, book III §103. [91] Ibid, book III §104.

[92] Ibid. [93] Ibid.

the belligerent parties what it grants to the other, and in carrying out its existing commerce the neutral causes no injury to a belligerent.[94]

However, while neutrals were free to continue trade to belligerents, belligerents were entitled to seize those goods on the basis of necessity. Neutrals 'suffer accidentally' from this predicament: 'I do not oppose their right: I only assert my own; and if our rights clash with and reciprocally injure each other, that circumstance is the effect of inevitable necessity.'[95] This licensed broad powers of belligerent visit and search of neutral vessels. Yet Vattel emphasized limits to belligerent rights in the distinction between contraband and free goods, a distinction 'on which Europe seems to be generally agreed.'[96]

Vattel notably drew a sharp distinction between the activities of a neutral State and its citizens. While it was 'the general custom of Europe' for a neutral State, upon receiving a declaration of war, to order its subjects to refrain from trade in contraband, Vattel noted that a belligerent 'does not impute to the neutral sovereigns these practices of their subjects.'[97] Since the belligerent could not prevent the conveyance of contraband, the belligerent had the right to conduct visit and search.[98]

Vattel's approach appeared to be one that saw commercial rivalry as part of the natural order; the clashing interests of belligerents and neutrals assisted the preservation of the balance of power. The approach of Vattel's contemporary, the Danish writer Martin Hübner, adopted a different approach to neutral trade.[99] His 1759 treatise, *De la saisie des bâtimens neutres,* was the first work devoted exclusively to the law of neutrality.[100] According to Hübner, the doctrine of contraband was a doctrine resulting from the reality of jealousy of commerce.[101] The principle of necessity did not prevail in every circumstance to afford belligerent rights of interference; instead, the only rights that could be enjoyed by the belligerent were those conferred by the law of neutrality. There was no possible conflict between belligerent and neutral rights.[102] Yet the war then in progress while Hübner was writing would lead to the emergence of two doctrines circumscribing neutral trading rights. The first was the Rule of the War of 1756. The second was the Doctrine of Continuous Voyage.

Commerce between imperial centres and their colonies became a new instrument to augment sovereign power and to increase the balance of trade.[103] Colonial trade was generally closed to the exclusive use of the metropolitan power to which the colony belonged.[104] In 1756, however, owing to British blockades of French

[94] Ibid, book III §110. [95] Ibid, book III §111. [96] Ibid. [97] Ibid, book III §113.

[98] Ibid, book III §114.

[99] Hübner's reflections on neutral trade were first set out in the second volume of his essay on the history of natural law. See M Hübner, *Essai sur l'histoire du droit naturel* II (n.p. 1758) 116–32.

[100] M Hübner, *De la saisie des bâtimens neutres, ou Du Droit qu'ont les Nations Belligérantes d'arrêter les Navires des Peuples Amis (n.p. 1759).*

[101] Hübner, *Essai* (n 99) 120–4. [102] Hübner, *De la saisie* II (n 100) 93–4.

[103] Kulsrud (n 34) 67. [104] *The Immanuel* (1799) 2 C Rob 186; 165 ER 284.

colonial ports, France invited Dutch merchants to carry out French West Indian trade on its behalf and issued special licences to Dutch traders in order to do so. Under the Anglo-Dutch Treaty of 1674, the principle of 'free ships, free goods' was recognized; a neutral ship was immune from belligerent interference.[105] This was in contrast to the general principle that the British law officers had stated was dictated by the law of nations, that enemy goods on board the ship of a friend were subject to seizure.[106] Under the 1674 treaty, Dutch merchants could transport enemy (French) goods without risk of capture of the goods by the British. British privateers responded by seizing Dutch ships serving French colonial ports.[107]

A number of contemporaneous British pamphlets and treatises denounced the Dutch practice of carrying French trade, even though the practice was consistent with the treaty of 1674.[108] There was a critical distinction between carrying on trade with a belligerent and carrying out trade on a belligerent's behalf, which corresponded to the concept of old and new trade.[109] The Rule of the War of 1756 provided that neutrals could not enter into trade in wartime in a domain that was denied to them in peacetime.[110] The carriage of goods between a country and its colonial ports was restricted to its own national ships. If a neutral in time of war was allowed to trade with an enemy's colony which had been closed to that neutral in peacetime, by that act the neutral merchant was considered by the British as an enemy ship liable to capture.[111] Although the context was different, the principle distinguishing between trading with an enemy and trading on behalf of an enemy was not new, as demonstrated by the example of the Venetian merchants trading south of the 'line' in 1604.[112]

105 Treaty of Navigation and Commerce (England-Netherlands), 10 December 1674, 13 CTS 255, art VIII.

106 See the report of the Law Officers as to the action of Frederick II in withholding payment of interest on the Silesian loan, in response to the Prussian 'Exposition des motifs fondés sur le droit des gens': Marsden, *Documents* II, 348, 350–5.

107 For background see generally Pares (n 34) 180–204.

108 Thus James Marriott, in his famous letter to Dutch merchants in England, wrote that '[e]very Subject of Holland, that acts as a real Dutchman, will most certainly be treated as such, but the Dutchman who puts upon himself as borrowed character, has little Reason to complain, if he is treated like what he appears to be, the Deserter of his own Country, and the Enemy of its Ally.' J Marriott, *A Letter to the Dutch Merchants in England* (M Cooper 1759) 6. See also J Marriott, *The Case of the Dutch Ships Considered* (4th edn, T Harrison 1778). Other contemporaneous accounts critical of the Dutch practice include C Jenkinson (Lord Liverpool), *Discourse on the Conduct of the Government of Great Britain, in respect to Neutral Nations, during the Present War* (Helton Bradley 1759); R Lee, *A Treatise of Captures in War* (Sandby 1759).

109 Pares (n 34) 186.

110 See the discussion in Grewe (n 13) 407. The background to the doctrine is also discussed in H J Bourguignon, *Sir William Scott, Lord Stowell: Judge of the High Court of Admiralty, 1798–1828* (CUP 1987) 225–8.

111 See also V Enthoven, 'Neutrality: Atlantic Shipping in and after the Anglo-Dutch Wars' in P J Stern and C Wennerlind (eds) *Mercantilism Reimagined: Political Economy in Early Modern Britain and Its Empire* (OUP 2014) 328, 342; T Helfman, 'Commerce on Trial: Neutral Rights and Private Warfare in the Seven Years' War' in K Stapelbroek (ed) *Trade and War: The Neutrality of Commerce in the Inter-State System* (Helsinki Collegium for Advanced Studies 2011) 14.

112 See Marsden, *Documents* I, 345 (n 22).

The Doctrine of Continuous Voyage was formulated to deal with a related problem: the carriage of enemy colonial goods to neutral ports prior to an ultimate onward journey to enemy 'home' ports.[113] Dutch traders attempted to circumvent the application of the Rule of the War of 1756 by trading with its own West Indian colonies, St Eustatius and Curaçao, even though the cargo loaded there had come from one of the French islands, involving French colonial trade.[114] The solution of the British prize courts was to treat the shipment of the cargo as one continuous journey, beginning at the French port.[115] This doctrine could not have come into being without the Rule of 1756, pursuant to which the first part of the voyage, the carriage of colonial trade, was prohibited to the neutral.[116] The doctrine took shape later on. At the beginning of its war with France in 1793, a British Order in Council stated that all vessels trading between France and French colonies should be brought before prize courts for adjudication on the basis of the Rule of the War of 1756. As well as protesting that the Rule of the War of 1756 was not international law,[117] American merchants devised ways to continue to trade with colonial ports, eliciting strong protest.[118] The doctrine of continuous voyage was developed in response to this.[119]

Pursuant to the doctrine, prize courts would look to the ultimate destination of goods rather than the port at which they were immediately offloaded.[120] A sea voyage involving several intermediate stops would be considered as one voyage. But there were difficulties in determining when a voyage could be considered continuous. When cargo was merely transferred from one vessel to another at the first port before continuing its journey, there was no difficulty in determining that the journey was continuous.[121] For example, in the case of the *Polly*, decided in 1800, the ship had been carrying sugar, fish, and cocoa from America to Spain. The sugar and cocoa had been imported into America from Havana, which was a Spanish colony. The captors had argued that, had the journey been from Havana to Spain, the presence of cocoa and sugar made the journey a violation of the Rule of the War of 1756 as an entry into colonial trade.[122] What was key was the intention of the shipper; in order to do so, all surrounding circumstances, including

[113] O H Mootham, 'The Doctrine of Continuous Voyage, 1756-1815' (1927) 8 BYBIL 63. For possible earlier manifestations of the doctrine see D J Llewelyn Davies, 'Enemy Property and Ultimate Destination During the Anglo-Dutch Wars 1664-7 and 1672-4' (1934) 15 BYBIL 21; D J Llewelyn Davies, 'The Development of Prize Law under Sir Leoline Jenkins' (1936) 21 TGS 149, 158.

[114] Bourguignon (n 110) 229. [115] Ibid. [116] Pares (n 34) 222–3.

[117] For American criticism of the Rule of the War of 1756, see an anonymous pamphlet published by James Madison, which was issued in 1805: *Examination of the British Doctrine, which subjects to Capture a Neutral Trade, not open in Time of Peace* (np, nd).

[118] The American practice was criticised by James Stephen in *War in Disguise; or, the Frauds of the Neutral Flags* (Whittingham 1805).

[119] H W Briggs, *The Doctrine of Continuous Voyage* (John Hopkins Press 1926) 13–14.

[120] Pares (n 34) 204–25.

[121] *Thomyris (Russel)* (1808) Edw 17, 19; 165 ER 1017, 1018. The most detailed opinion on continuous voyage is *The William* (1806) 5 C Rob 385; 165 ER 817.

[122] *Polly (Laskey)* (1800) 2 C Rob 361, 369; 165 ER 344, 347.

the landing of goods and the payment of import duties, were important to determine the continuity of the voyage.[123] The doctrine of continuous voyage soon began to be applied more expansively and was applied by British prize courts not only to the Rule of the War of 1756 and the transportation of enemy goods, but also to the French coasting trade and to blockade and contraband.[124]

The effect of these doctrines was to increase the power of belligerents to control trade, and to link neutrality increasingly with the concept of impartiality associated with Bynkershoek and Vattel.[125] The core of this was the right of belligerents to exercise visitation and search of neutral ships.[126] Relatedly, the obligation of neutrals to submit to visitation and search was a manifestation of a more fundamental obligation on the part of impartiality.[127] It was the 'grand fundamental duty of neutrality' 'not to relieve one belligerent from the infliction of his adversaries' force' and 'not to relieve the distresses of one belligerent, to the prejudice of another.'[128] Neutrality as a fundamental stance of non-participation and impartiality appears to have taken definite shape by the end of the Seven Years' War.[129]

The concept of impartial neutrality became most prominently associated with the United States. Upon the outbreak of the War of the First Coalition between France and other European powers in 1793, the United States issued a proclamation which stated that 'the duty and interest of the United States require, that they should with sincerity and good faith adopt and pursue a conduct friendly and impartial toward the belligerent powers.'[130] This proclamation, with its emphasis on impartiality as the core of neutral obligation, has been referred to frequently as one of the precursors to the modern form of neutrality.[131] The proliferation of treaties of alliance meant, however, that instances of 'pure' neutral impartiality were rare.[132] A State could maintain its neutrality while furnishing troops to a belligerent pursuant to pre-existing treaties.[133]

[123] Briggs (n 119) 22.

[124] Pares (n 34) 217–21; Mootham (n 113) 65–6. On the coasting trade see *The Ebenezer (Christensen)* 6 C Rob 250; 165 ER 920. On blockade and contraband see Briggs (n 119) ch 3.

[125] For this argument see T Helfman, 'Neutrality, the Law of Nations, and the Natural Law Tradition: A Study of the Seven Years' War' (2005) 30 YJIL 549; T Helfman, 'Commerce on Trial: Neutral Rights and Private Warfare in the Seven Years' War' in K Stapelbroek (ed) *Trade and War: The Neutrality of Commerce in the Inter-State System* (Helsinki Collegium for Advanced Studies 2011) 14, 40.

[126] The classic statement granting a right of belligerents to exercise visit and search even against a merchant ship travelling is that of Sir William Scott in *Maria (Paulsen)* (1799) 1 C Rob 340, 360; 165 ER 199, 206.

[127] Bourguignon's study of Sir William Scott notes the important influence of Bynkershoek and Vattel on his jurisprudence. See Bourguignon (n 110) 260.

[128] *Rendsborg (Nyberg)* (1802) 4 C Rob 121, 126; 165 ER 557, 559. Italics omitted.

[129] A similar chronology is accepted by Higgins (n 34) 553.

[130] J D Richardson (ed) *A Compilation of the Messages and Papers of the Presidents 1789–1897* I (Government Printing Office 1896) 156.

[131] Hall (8th edn, n 51) 707.

[132] Thus at the time of the 1793 proclamation of neutrality by the United States, there existed a treaty of alliance between the United States and France: Treaty of Alliance (signed 6 February 1778) 46 CTS 447. On this point see C S Hyneman, 'Neutrality during the European Wars of 1792-1815' (1930) 24 AJIL 279.

[133] For examples see Hall (8th edn) 700–2. Hall notes that it was in 1788 that the right of a State to furnish troops under treaty came under question as contrary to neutrality.

The concept of distinct prohibitions on the neutral State was in the course of development. The levying of troops in neutral territory was widely viewed to be permissible and was sanctioned by Vattel. '[W]hen it is the custom of a nation, for the purpose of employing and training her subjects, to permit levies of troops in favour of a particular power', he notes, the opposing belligerent may object only when threatened with invasion or when the levying is conducted for the prosecution of 'an odious and evidently unjust cause.'[134] In similar fashion passage through neutral territory was seen as compatible with the status.[135] It had been longstanding practice that belligerent actions were not to occur in neutral territory.[136] By the turn of the eighteenth century, prize law distinguished between 'remote' uses of neutral territory by belligerents (such as procuring provisions) and 'proximate' acts of war; the latter included the act of a belligerent warship in launching hostile expeditions from neutral territory.[137] Similarly, the US practice stated that neutral waters could not be used as a staging ground from which to launch hostile operations.[138] The US protested strongly against the attempt by France in 1792 to grant commissions to American citizens to raid English commerce.[139]

The increasingly assertive practices of belligerents at sea, both during the Seven Years' War and subsequently, provoked neutral response. The practice of neutral convoy—placing merchant shipping under the escort of military frigates—was developed in response to the increasingly broad exercise of visitation and search propounded by the British prize court. The commander's word as to the innocence of the cargo, these neutrals asserted, was sufficient for belligerents to waive visitation and search.[140] Those critical of British belligerent practices, such as the French diplomat, the Comte d'Hauterive, contended that neutral commerce should be free from belligerent disturbance.[141] His views gave succour to those agitating in favour of a coalition of neutral powers in defence of neutral convoy

[134] Vattel (n 87) book III §110. [135] Ibid, book III §119.

[136] The illegality of the practice was recognized in 1562. See Marsden, *Documents* I, 172. The capture of prizes in the territorial waters of friends was viewed as illegal in 1564 (ibid 179).

[137] *Twee Gebroeders (No 1) (Alberts)* (1800) 3 C Rob 162, 164; 165 ER 422, 423.

[138] 'The Secretary of State to the Governors of the several States, 16 April 1795' *American State Papers: Documents, Legislative and Executive, of the Congress of the United States: Foreign Relations* I (Gales and Seaton, Washington 1833) 608.

[139] Moore, *Digest* VII §1295. [140] Bourguignon (n 110) 180–1.

[141] C Hauterive, *State of the French Republic at the End of the Year VIII* (L Goldsmith (tr)) (J S Gordon 1801). In a famous response, Friedrich von Gentz defended British practice as a contribution to the balance of power. F von Gentz, *On the State of Europe before and after the French Revolution: being an Answer to the Work entitled De l'état de la France à la fin de l'an VIII* (John Herries (tr)) (5th edn Hatchard 1804). On the figure of Gentz generally, see G Mann, *Secretary of Europe: the Life of Friedrich Gentz, Enemy of Napoleon* (W H Woglom (tr)) (Yale University Press 1946). Thomas Brooke Clarke offered a defence of Britain in response to Hauterive: T B Clarke, *An Historical and Political View of the Disorganisation of Europe* (T Cadell and W Davies 1803). For the debate see M Forsyth, 'The Old European States-system: Gentz versus Hauterive' (1980) 23 HJ 521; I Nakhimovsky, *The Closed Commercial State* (Princeton UP 2011) ch 2.

and committed to resistance to British belligerent powers.[142] Russia, joined by Denmark, Sweden, and Prussia, notably sought to defend Denmark's right to neutral convoy, which Britain had denied, as well as the principle of 'free ships, free goods'.[143] This was, however, a short-lived assertion of neutral power. In April 1801, the British navy defeated the Danish fleet. Shortly after Paul I of Russia's assassination, Britain entered into the Convention of St Petersburg with Russia, which reasserted the position that enemy property could be seized on neutral ships.[144]

4. Neutrality in the Nineteenth Century

a. Neutrality as a Status

According to Thomas Holland, by the end of the eighteenth century, the topic of neutrality had become 'the most important of all those dealt with by the Law of Nations.'[145] Neutrality came to be viewed as a factual position with a particular legal status. This was closely connected to the particular status of the concept of war in international law in the nineteenth century. Fundamental to the nineteenth century, international legal order became the clear separation between states of peace and war. The existence of war brought into operation a different legal order that created separate statuses. According to Sir Travers Twiss, '[a]ll, who take part

[142] This was not the first instance of so-called 'armed neutrality'; as early as 1613, the Netherlands, Lübeck and Sweden combined to resist Danish belligerent practices: Treaty of Alliance for the Protection of Navigation and Commerce (Netherlands-Lübeck), 5(2) Dumont V(ii) 231; Treaty of Alliance (Netherlands-Sweden), 5 April 1614, 5(2) Dumont V(ii) 245. See Kulsrud (n 34) 296–322. A later armed neutrality emerged during the American Revolution in 1780 against Britain. The armed neutrality sought to ensure that navigation between neutral ports was respected; that contraband was limited to munitions of war; that the principle of 'free ships free goods' was followed; and that blockades were applicable only if effectively enforced. J B Scott, *The Armed Neutralities of 1780 and 1800: A Collection of Official Documents Preceded by the Views of Representative Publicists* (OUP 1918); On this see I de Madariaga, *Britain, Russia and the Armed Neutrality of 1780: Sir James Harris's Mission to St Petersburg during the American Revolution* (Hollis & Carter 1962).

[143] O Feldbaek, 'The Anglo-Danish Convoy Conflict of 1800' (1977) SJH 161. A key work in defence of neutral convoy was that of J F W Schlegel, *Upon the Visitation of Neutral Vessels under Convoy; or, an Impartial Examination of a Judgment pronounced by the English Court of Admiralty the 11th June, 1799, in the Case of the Swedish Convoy* (de Juge (tr))(Debrett 1801). The case to which Schlegel referred was the *Maria (Paulsen)* decided by Sir William Scott (discussed at n 122). Responses to Schlegel's treatise were immediately forthcoming by British lawyers. See most prominently R Ward, *A Treatise of the Relative Rights and Duties of Belligerent and Neutral Powers in Maritime Affairs: in which the Principles of Armed Neutralities and the Opinions of Hubner and Schlegel are Fully Discussed* (Diplomatic Review Office 1875 (first published 1801)); A Croke, *Remarks on Mr Schlegel's Work upon the Visitation of Neutral Vessels under Convoy* (Wilks and Taylor 1801). The treaty establishing the armed neutrality is the Convention between Russia and Sweden for the Re-establishment of an Armed Neutrality (signed 4(16) December 1800) 55 CTS 411.

[144] Convention of St Petersburg (Great Britain-Russia)(signed 17 June 1801) 56 CTS 105.

[145] Holland (n 14) 399.

in the war, are Belligerents; all, who stand aloof from the contention of the Belligerents, are neutral.'[146] As the Law Officers of the Crown noted:

> neutrality, both according to the law of nations and the municipal law of this country, means the neutrality of one State, as between two or more States who are at war between themselves; and has no bearing upon a state of peace, however probable a future war may be, or however much, or however reasonably, war may be apprehended.[147]

The status of neutrality therefore existed alongside a formal state of war and did not apply to other applications of force such as reprisals, pacific blockades, and intervention. Whether a state of war in fact existed was often a matter of belligerent intention, of 'animus belligerendi'.[148] Certain situations could, however, demonstrate factually the existence of a state of war, most notably the establishment of a blockade, which if enforced against third States was necessarily a situation of war rather than of reprisal.[149] However, non-participants did not have a legal right to adopt the *status* of neutrality in the way that belligerents could invoke the state of war. Neutral status was granted only to non-participant States if the belligerents chose to treat them as such, through the process of recognition.

The subjective nature of the state of war doctrine meant that the process of recognition of neutrality by belligerents was of paramount importance.[150] Recognition of neutrality by belligerents in the nineteenth century was constitutive in character.[151] Recognition of neutrality by belligerents transformed the *de facto* neutral position of factual non-participants into *de jure* neutrals bound by the law of neutrality and its rights and duties. As with recognition of Statehood in nineteenth century international law, recognition of neutrality functioned as a 'juristic baptism' that brought into existence the rights and duties of neutrality.[152] Such recognition was however, in most instances artificial or at least implicit, typically brought about through belligerent acquiescence in the assertion of neutral rights.[153] The importance of recognition meant that a formal declaration of neutrality was symbolic but not required by international law.[154]

[146] T Twiss, *The Law of Nations Considered as Independent Political Communities: On the Rights and Duties of Nations in Time of War* (2nd edn Clarendon Press 1875) 436.

[147] McNair *International Law Opinions* III 152. The opinion was in response to a request by Ecuador to Great Britain to prohibit the construction of ships by Peru in British ports, and to refuse a loan to the Peruvian government, during a period of prospective hostilities that did not amount to formal war.

[148] I Brownlie, *International Law and the Use of Force by States* (Clarendon Press 1963) 27.

[149] 76 BFSP 426–7.

[150] J Lorimer, *Institutes of the Law of Nations* II (William Blackwood and Sons 1884) 130; Oppenheim (1st edn) II 316.

[151] In non-international armed conflicts that demonstrated the characteristics of an international war, the situation was reversed: the recognition of insurgents as belligerents created the legal relationship of neutrality between third States and the dueling belligerent parties.

[152] J Crawford, *The Creation of States in International Law* (2nd edn OUP 2006) 16.

[153] Oppenheim (1st edn) II 406.

[154] Hackworth, *Digest* VII 352.

According to one school of thought, there was no duty to recognize a non-participant State's neutrality. A belligerent that refused to recognize another State's neutrality did not violate international law because the status of neutrality was dependent on belligerent acknowledgement and was not an independent right.[155] Acceptance of neutrality by a belligerent could be conditional and accompanied by the imposition of certain conditions on the neutral State.[156] According to this approach, once established through belligerent recognition, the status of neutrality could be 'exchanged' for belligerency during the hostilities. An extinction of neutral status could occur in two ways. First, the neutral could become a belligerent simply by abandoning its neutral position and voluntarily entering the war on the side of one of the belligerents, usually by formally joining hostilities through direct military action. Secondly, the neutral State could become a belligerent through a declaration of war issued against it. Hence neutrality was defined not as a right but as an 'attitude' perfected through recognition.[157]

An opposing school of thought emphasized that neutrality was a legal right that adhered to a State choosing that status independent of recognition. This approach emphasized the right to claim neutrality as an attribute of State sovereignty.[158] Perhaps the foremost expositor of this view was the Swedish jurist Richard Kleen, who contended that the right of an independent State to stay neutral during a war was 'un droit incontestable et inaliénable.'[159] In practice, the question of recognition was secondary to whether a state of war existed. If a situation of war was acknowledged to exist, those States that were factually non-participants in the hostilities became *de jure* neutrals unless their conduct was radically at odds with holding that status. If their conduct did depart from neutrality, the question was whether that departure was a mere violation of neutrality that could be corrected, or an act or series of acts amounting to full belligerency on one side of the conflict.

b. The Development of Belligerent Rights against Neutrals

In the nineteenth century, the rules governing belligerent interference with neutral commerce developed with much greater precision than previously known. First, privateering was abolished. Secondly, the question of the seizure of enemy and

155 Oppenheim (1st edn) II 406.

156 During the Russo-Japanese War of 1904–1905, belligerent recognition of China's neutrality was made dependent on China's fulfillment of certain stipulations imposed by the belligerents. A S Hershey, 'Some Questions of International Law Arising from the Russo-Japanese War II: The Hay Note and Chinese Neutrality' (1904) 16 TGB 375.

157 Oppenheim (1st edn) II 301; 316.

158 See, for example, *Wheaton's International Law* (Dana (ed)) (8th edn Little, Brown, Boston 1866) §414.

159 R Kleen, *Lois et usages de la neutralité d'après le droit international conventionnel et coutumier des états civilisés* I (A Chevalier-Marescq 1898) 75.

neutral non-contraband property was finally settled. Thirdly, the doctrine of contraband became increasingly categorized by prize courts yet the subject of profound contestation. Fourthly, similarly contested was the concept of blockade, which became an increasingly deployed method of warfare. Finally, the separate category of 'unneutral' service developed to encompass cases analogous to, but more serious than, carriage of contraband, such as the conveyance of troops and dispatches.

Impetus for a number of these developments derives from the 1856 Declaration of Paris, which has been described as 'the most important international instrument regulating the rights of belligerents and neutrals at sea which received something like universal acceptance.'[160] The Declaration of Paris contains four articles:

1. Privateering is, and remains, abolished;
2. The neutral flag covers enemy's goods, with the exception of contraband of war;
3. Neutral goods, with the exception of contraband of war, are not liable to capture under enemy's flag;
4. Blockades, in order to be binding, must be effective, that is to say, maintained by a force sufficient really to prevent access to the coast of the enemy.[161]

i. Privateering

Since the thirteenth century, rulers had granted letters of marque to privateers, licensing them to engage in acts of warfare at sea in place of, or alongside, naval forces.[162] But by the time of the Declaration of Paris, the use of privateers had declined with the ascendance of professional navies. The United States was opposed to the abolition of privateering announced in the Declaration and did not become a party to it for that reason, even though the evidence suggests that Britain granted to neutrals the privileges of the 'free ships, free goods' rule in exchange for the abolition of privateering.[163]

ii. Private property at sea

The Declaration affirmed the rule that had been the subject of so much historical contention, namely that 'free ships make free goods'. Prior to the Declaration there was considerable divergence in practice as to the status of enemy goods on neutral ships and neutral goods on enemy ships. Treaties overlaid whatever

[160] H W Malkin, 'The Inner History of the Declaration of Paris' (1927) 8 BYBIL 1, 2.

[161] Paris Declaration Respecting Maritime Law (signed 16 April 1856, entered into force 16 April 1856) 115 CTS 1.

[162] Kulsrud (n 34) 36–8.

[163] J M Lemnitzer, '"That Moral League of Nations Against the United States": The Origins of the 1856 Declaration of Paris' (2013) 35 IHR 1068.

customary practice could be said to exist. There was general evidence, however, that enemy goods could be seized whether carried on enemy or neutral ships absent a treaty relationship. A treaty could frequently guarantee the rule of 'free ships, free goods.'[164] But there is little evidence of general acceptance of the 'free ships, free goods' principle before the middle of the nineteenth century.[165] The long-maintained British position was that the goods of an enemy on board a friend's ship could be taken.[166]

During the Crimean War, the neutral powers naturally sought to assert the rule in favour of immunity of property on neutral ships.[167] Britain and France found themselves in the rare position of being allied belligerents and needed to standardize their practice of maritime warfare.[168] They agreed to waive the right of seizing enemy property on board a neutral vessel.[169] This was a temporary concession rather than recognition of a changed customary rule. The Declaration of Paris confirmed in its second rule that '[t]he neutral flag covers an enemy's goods, with the exception of contraband of war.'[170]

The Declaration was criticized as a craven concession of British naval power.[171] Yet it was not necessarily a concession on the state of customary international law. In the American Civil War, British Admiralty instructions stated that the 'free ships, free goods' rule was conventional in nature.[172] As noted, the United States did not accede to the Declaration; examination of its practice, therefore, provides some indication of the Declaration's customary status. American writers took the view that the rule was 'a concession made by the belligerent to the neutral, and it gave to the neutral flag a capacity not given to it by public law.'[173] The US treaty practice following the Declaration of Paris indicates the rule's conventional nature. Pursuant to a number of treaties entered into by the US, the contracting parties agree to the acceptance of the 'free ships, free goods' principle, as well as

[164] *The Nereide* (1815) 9 Cranch 388. [165] Moore, *Digest* VII 440.

[166] This view is expressed comprehensively in the 'Report of the Law Officers as to the Action of Frederick II in withholding Payment of Interest on the Silesian Loan' in Marsden, *Documents* II, 348–74. Sir William Scott expresses the view that 'free ships, free goods' is an 'inadmissible rule' in *Maria (Paulsen)* (1799) 1 C Rob 340, 360; 165 ER 199, 206.

[167] C H Stockton, 'The Declaration of Paris' (1920) 14 AJIL 356, 358.

[168] Malkin (n 160) 13; C I Hamilton, 'Anglo-French Seapower and the Declaration of Paris' (1982) 4 IHR 166, 172.

[169] 46 BFSP 36.

[170] Paris Declaration Respecting Maritime Law (signed 16 April 1856, entered into force 16 April 1856) 115 CTS 1 art 2.

[171] T G Bowles, *Maritime Warfare* (2nd edn W Ridgway 1878) 22. Bowles went on to note (82) that the Declaration 'is false in fact, false in its statement of doctrine, of principle, and of maritime law, and, as far as Great Britain is concerned, was signed without any known authority.' For the more sympathetic continental view, see L B Hautefeuille, *Des droits et devoirs des nations neutres en temps de guerre maritime* II (3rd edn Guillaumin 1868) 281.

[172] 'Papers Relating to Belligerent and Neutral Rights, 1861-1865' (1928) 34 AHR 77, 82. The nature of the concession was acknowledged by US President Pierce; see Moore, *Digest* VII 449–50.

[173] *Kent's Commentary on International Law* (J T Abdy (ed)) (2nd edn Deighton Bell & Co, Cambridge 1878) 320.

the principle that neutral non-contraband property found on an enemy ship is immune from capture, and to apply them 'to the commerce and navigation of all such powers and states as shall consent to adopt them as permanent and immutable.'[174] Similar treaty concessions had, in fact, been concluded in similar form prior to 1856, and these treaties do not express the view that the rule is in conformity with general international law.[175] Indeed, these treaties are in the nature of bargains, often conceding the 'free ships, free goods' principle in exchange for permitting capture of neutral goods on enemy ships.[176] Upon the outbreak of war in Spain, however, the US government stated that it would apply the rule that the neutral flag covered enemy goods (except for contraband) and that neutral non-contraband goods were exempt from seizure when carried under an enemy flag, and it appeared to do so from recognition that such rules were recognized international law.[177]

iii. Contraband

The Declaration of Paris stated that contraband was an exception to the 'free ships, free goods rule', but did not provide any detail as to what was covered by the term. This may have been in part because, as Thomas Holland expressed it, '[w]hether any given article should be treated as contraband is, in the first instance, entirely a question for the belligerent Government and its Prize Court.'[178] Certain issues had been resolved and constituted consistent rules. All forms of contraband required enemy destination; the goods in question had to be shipped to an enemy port. Goods going to a neutral port, 'cannot come under the description of contraband, all goods going there being equally lawful.'[179] The

[174] Rights of Neutrals at Sea (United States—Peru) (signed 22 July 1856, entered into force 31 October 1857) 10 Bevans 1019, art 1; Treaty of Amity, Commerce and Navigation; Extradition (United States—Haiti) (signed 3 November 1864, entered into force 22 May 1865) 8 Bevans 614, art 19; Treaty of Amity, Commerce, and Navigation; Extradition (United States—Dominican Republic) (signed 8 February 1867, entered into force 5 October 1867) 7 Bevans 162, art 15.

[175] Rights of Neutrals at Sea (United States—Russia) (signed 22 July 1854, entered into force 31 October 1854) 11 Bevans 1214, art 1; Rights of Neutrals at Sea (United States—Two Sicilies) (signed 13 January 1855, entered into force 14 July 1855) 11 Bevans 1191, art 1.

[176] Treaty of Peace, Amity, Navigation and Commerce (United States—Colombia) (signed 3 October 1824, entered into force 27 May 1825) 6 Bevans 855, art 12; Treaty of Peace, Amity, Commerce, and Navigation (United States—Central American Republic) (signed 5 December 1825, entered into force 2 August 1826) 6 Bevans 503, art 14; Treaty of Peace, Friendship, Navigation, and Commerce (signed 20 January 1836, entered into force 31 May 1836) 12 Bevans 1038, art 15; Treaty of Peace, Friendship, Navigation, and Commerce (United States—Ecuador) (signed 13 June 1839, entered into force 9 April 1842) 7 Bevans 296, art 15; Treaty of Amity, Navigation, and Commerce (United States—El Salvador) (signed 2 January 1850, entered into force 2 June 1852) 7 Bevans 462, art 15.

[177] Moore, *Digest* VII 452–3. The conflict prompted the United States to revive its position that all private property at sea except for contraband should be immune from capture. C Savage, *Policy of the United States toward Maritime Commerce in War* (US Government Printing Office 1934) 103. For earlier US proposals towards the immunity of private property at sea, see ibid, 46–53; 98–100.

[178] T E Holland, *Letters to "The Times" upon War and Neutrality 1881–1920* (3rd edn Longman's, Green, and Co 1921) 130.

[179] *Imina (Vroom)* (1800) 3 C Rob 167; 165 ER 424.

consequences of the presence of contraband were also tolerably clear; unlike earlier prize practice, which applied the doctrine of infection to condemn the ship as well as the cargo, the modern practice was that only the cargo was subject to condemnation.[180] The appropriate penalty for the owner of the ship was the simple loss of freight and expenses.[181]

The nineteenth century debates turned on the viability of the distinction originally made by Grotius between three different categories of goods: absolute contraband (goods useful for war); conditional contraband (dual-use items, capable of deployment for warlike or peaceful purposes); and free goods. There was no disagreement that weapons and munitions of war constituted contraband 'by the Common Law and usage of Nations.'[182] Nor was there disagreement that there were certain goods that were 'free goods' incapable of being put to hostile purposes.[183] Contraband was, of course, frequently defined in treaties in order to avoid disagreement in particular instances.[184] Yet there was fundamental controversy as to whether the doctrine should acknowledge the concept of conditional contraband at all.

The British view was that conditional contraband did exist and the task of the prize court was to determine whether particular goods were in fact contraband and whether they could be seized. First, destination was evidence of use. Shipment to a military port was evidence that the items were indeed being used for warlike purposes and could be seized as contraband. Shipment to a commercial port was evidence *prima facie* that the goods were intended for peaceful use and did not constitute contraband.[185] Secondly, goods in their native state were to be treated more leniently than manufactured goods, since that would indicate non-military use.[186] Thirdly, if the shipped cargo was the direct product of the neutral trader's country of nationality, a presumption would arise that the goods were not

[180] *Neutralitet (Burning)* (1801) 3 C Rob 295, 296; 165 ER 469, 470. In this case Sir William Scott noted two exceptions, which would subject the ship to condemnation. First, where the owner of the contraband cargo is the owner of the ship, and secondly, where the ship is sailing under false papers or a false destination. See also *Franklin (Segerbrath)* (1801) 3 C Rob 217, 224; 165 ER 441, 444. A third exception was if the ship resisted visit and search. The US approach was that contraband articles contaminate the non-contraband parts of a cargo if belonging to the same owner. *The Peterhoff* (1866) 72 US (5 Wall) 28.

[181] *Ringende Jacob (Kreplien)* (1798) 1 C Rob 89, 90; 165 ER 107, 107.

[182] Article 6 of Admiral Milne's Additional Instructions of June 20, 1861, in 'Papers Relating to Belligerent and Neutral Rights, 1861-1865' (1928) 34 AHR 77, 83.

[183] Lawrence gives the example of pianos and children's toys as inherently peaceful goods. T J Lawrence, *War and Neutrality in the Far East* (Macmillan and Co 1904) 142.

[184] For example, Treaty of Amity, Commerce and Navigation; Extradition (United States—Haiti) (signed 3 November 1864, entered into force 22 May 1865) 8 Bevans 614, art 20. For a list containing a list of contraband as well as free goods, see Treaty of Amity and Commerce (United States—France) (signed 6 February 1778, entered into force 17 July 1778) 7 Bevans 763, art 26.

[185] *Jonge Margaretha (Klausen)* (1799) 1 C Rob 188; 165 ER 143. See also *The Peterhoff* (1866) 72 US (5 Wall) 28, 58.

[186] *Jonge Margaretha (Klausen)* (1799) 1 C Rob 188; 165 ER 143; *Evert (Everts)* (1803) 4 C Rob 354; 165 ER 638.

contraband.[187] If these exceptions applied, the doctrine of pre-emption rather than seizure would be applied; the cargo would be restored to the owner as long as security was given to sell the cargo in England.[188]

Conditional contraband as a category could be open to abuse. The difficulty, for the belligerent at least, was in finding a 'general test of essentiality' of the nature of the items in question or in securing proof that the delivery of particular articles would be essential to the war effort.[189] The uncertainties of this test led many continental lawyers to assert that the category of conditional contraband did not exist.[190] They sought to limit the category of contraband to what would be considered 'absolute' contraband: munitions, naval stores, and shipbuilding materials. In 1896, the *Institut de droit International* passed a resolution stating that conditional contraband was abolished.[191] There was also fundamental uncertainty as to what constituted contraband. At the West African Conference of 1884–1885 the issue of coal became a source of contention. Russia and France took the view that coal could not be regarded as contraband, while Britain and the US argued it was contraband when destined for naval or military use, but not when destined for commerce.[192] Yet the category of conditional contraband remained controversial and continued to be employed in naval warfare, for example by Japan in its war with Russia.[193]

The contradiction between preserving the freedom of commerce for neutral individuals and the increasingly stringent obligations on neutral States resulted in belligerent powers regarding the definition of contraband as a continual source of contention throughout the nineteenth century. During the Spanish-American War of 1898, a number of States, as part of their declared positions of neutrality, prohibited their citizens from trading in war material with belligerents.[194] This was a symptom of increasing uncertainty as to the activities that it was incumbent on the neutral State to prevent (such as the fitting out of warships in its ports) and activities it was not required to prevent, such as the trade in contraband carried out by its subjects. Indeed, the neutral in the latter case had a duty not to interfere: 'it is bound to leave those of its subjects who engage in them to be dealt with by the belligerent against whom they are

[187] *Kent's Commentary* (n 173) 337 notes that pitch and tar would be contraband unless the produce of the country whence they are exported, in which case they are subject to pre-emption.

[188] For an early example of the doctrine, see *Vryheid* (1778) Hay & M 188; 165 ER 44.

[189] Hall (8th edn, n 51) 781.

[190] T Ortolan, *Règles internationales et diplomatie de la mer* II (4th edn Plon 1864) 178–80; for a summary of the continental position see Wheaton (8th edn) §501 n 226; R Kleen, 'La droit de la contrebande de guerre' (1893) 25 RDILC 18.

[191] See J B Scott (ed) *Resolutions on the Institute of International Law Dealing with the Law of Nations* (OUP 1916) 129, section 4.

[192] Lawrence (n 183) 157–8.

[193] Lawrence (n 183) 148–9.

[194] E J Benton, *International Law and Diplomacy of the Spanish-American War* (Johns Hopkins UP 1908) 185, 195–6.

directed.'[195] The carriage of contraband was for the belligerent to police through the exercise of visit and search.[196] The neutral State's position in regard to contraband was, according to Lawrence, one of 'passive non-interference.'[197] Yet there was a distinction between an article of contraband and the fitting out of a neutral ship, and 'when the acts of those under its control amount to more than mere trading, and become something akin to active participation in the war, then it must step in and prevent its territory from being made the starting-point of expeditions or the base of operations.'[198] This appeared to be an attempt to reconcile the increasing obligations incumbent on neutral States with the right of commerce of neutral citizens. Whether this was a convincing distinction, or whether the development of international law required the prevention of contraband, was keenly debated.[199]

iv. Blockade

In earlier centuries, the law of blockade was viewed as analogous in a maritime context to siege warfare on land. Its objective is not merely to prevent the importation of goods to a blockaded port, but also to prevent the export of goods.[200] The nineteenth century saw a considerable amount of blockade practice, such that it could be remarked in 1878 that 'among the rights of belligerents, there is none more clear and incontrovertible, or more just and necessary in the application, than that which gives rise to the law of blockade.'[201]

The Declaration of Paris emphasized that blockades, in order to be binding, had to be effective. Disagreement surrounded the meaning of this criterion. The continental approach required greater stringency from belligerents. A blockade was considered effective only if ships were in the immediate vicinity of the blockading port and there was a manifest danger for the ship to enter.[202] This was based on an approach advanced by French authors that blockade is an act of territorial maritime jurisdiction by the belligerent.[203] Any act of interruption, howsoever caused, raised the blockade; to be re-established it would need to be declared and notified anew.[204]

The British understanding of effectiveness was looser, but had become more rigorous in its rejection of so-called 'paper blockades', declared but unaccompanied

[195] Bowles (n 171) 42. Bowles drew a distinction between direct and indirect participation with distinct legal responsibility. The neutral State was responsible for preventing acts of direct participation; the belligerent was responsible for stopping acts of indirect participation.

[196] McNair, *International Law Opinions* III 136–7. [197] Lawrence (n 183) 181.

[198] Ibid. Lawrence applied this view to argue that Britain was required to prevent departure of two Japanese battleships constructed in Britain.

[199] See J Westlake, 'Is it Desirable to Prohibit the Export of Contraband of War?' in L Oppenheim (ed) *The Collected Papers of John Westlake on Public International Law* (CUP 1914) 362.

[200] *Kent's Commentary* (n 173) 343.

[201] Ibid 340. [202] Hall (8th edn, n 51) 856. [203] Hautefeuille (n 171) II 178.

[204] C Phillipson (ed) *Smith's International Law* (5th edn Dent 1918) 373.

by warships capable of preventing entry to the port in question.[205] A blockade continued to be viewed as effective even if a ship entered the blockaded port owing to the temporary absence of a blockading vessel or the temporary disruption of the blockading force due to weather.[206] On the British view, the distance of the blockading force from the port was immaterial; all that was necessary was the presence of a force sufficient to capture vessels attempting ingress.[207] The occasional absence of a blockading force, due to stress of weather, for example, was held not to constitute an interruption of a blockade; but if the blockade is raised by the forces of an enemy or a diversion of forces, the blockade ceases to exist. If it is to be re-established, it must be declared and notified again.[208]

Although expressed in oblique terms, the Declaration of Paris's requirement of effective blockades was seen as leaning towards the continental approach to effectiveness.[209] It was the continental approach to the effectiveness of blockades that had been advanced by the neutrals in the armed neutralities of 1780 and 1800. This view also finds support in nineteenth century treaty practice; Wheaton argued that the authority of 'modern treaties', particularly the Convention of St Petersburg signed upon the conclusion of the Armed Neutrality of 1800, indicated that effectiveness required 'the actual presence of a maritime force, stationed at the entrance of the port, sufficiently near to prevent communication.'[210] The United States during its war with Spain in 1898 stated that, to be effective and binding, a blockade 'must be maintained by a force sufficient to render ingress to or egress from the port dangerous.'[211]

The Anglo-American and continental approaches also diverged with regard to notification of blockade and breach of blockade. The continental approach required that notification be given to each individual ship, which could be captured only on a second attempt to break blockade. The right of capture of a ship for breach of blockade applied to the region of sea and harbour actually held by the belligerent force.[212] Under the Anglo-American approach, notice could be by simple fact accompanied by a declaration of an officer of the fleet, or by formal declaration to the neutral powers.[213] The Anglo-American approach linked the

[205] For the rejection of paper blockades see *Juffrow Maria Schroeder (Greenwold)* (1800) 3 C Rob 147; 165 ER 417.

[206] *Kent's Commentary* (n 173) 342.

[207] Hall (8th edn, n 51) 854–5. It was this more lenient approach to effectiveness that appeared to give rise to the largely British practice of 'pacific blockade', advanced as a means short of war that left the shipping of third States undisturbed. See C Parry, 'British Practice in Some Nineteenth Century Pacific Blockades' (1938) 8 ZaöRV 672, 683–4.

[208] *Kent's Commentary* (n 173) 343.

[209] J Westlake, 'Commercial Blockade' in L Oppenheim (ed) *The Collected Papers of John Westlake on Public International Law* (CUP 1914) 312, 336.

[210] Wheaton (8th edn) §512; Convention of St Petersburg (Great Britain-Russia) (signed 17 June 1801) 56 CTS 105. A similar approach is taken in *Kent's Commentary* (n 173) 341.

[211] Moore, *Digest* VII 794–5.

[212] Hautefeuille (n 171) II 239.

[213] R Phillimore, *Commentaries upon International Law* III (T & JW Johnson 1854–1857) 293.

question of breach to the ship's knowledge of the blockade and its intent to evade it. There had to be actual or constructive knowledge. To sail for a blockaded port with knowledge of the blockade, accompanied by the intent to evade it, constituted breach.[214] A ship breaching a blockade, or with the intention of doing so, could be captured at any stage on its journey, including the return voyage.[215]

v. Unneutral service

The concept of unneutral service is often described as an analogue of contraband, which deals with the acts of neutral vessels that render assistance to a belligerent that is so significant as to amount to colouring the neutral vessel with enemy character. The concept began to be isolated as distinct from contraband in nineteenth century prize cases, initially to cover the situation of the transport of belligerent troops and dispatches relating to the operation of war, which had previously been considered under the category of contraband. The foundations of the concept, however, may be seen in the Rule of 1756 and the earlier fundamental distinction between trade *with* a belligerent and carrying trade *for*, or on behalf of, a belligerent. Neutral traders who were engaged in colonial trade were engaging in the latter and becoming part of the belligerent war effort.[216]

The carriage of combatants on neutral vessels was one example of unneutral service. *The Carolina* concerned a Swedish vessel transporting French troops to Alexandria. The vessel was captured after the troops had been conveyed to their destination. It was held that, had the vessel had been taken *in delicto*, it would have been subject to condemnation due to the nature of its conveyance.[217] In *The Friendship*, a neutral American ship was captured voyaging from Baltimore to Bordeaux with French mariners aboard. Sir William Scott stated that the essential question was whether the vessel was in fact neutral carrying on an 'innoxious commerce', or had assumed the character of a 'transport vessel engaged in the immediate military service of the enemy.'[218] The conduct of the vessel meant it was the latter:

> It is the case of a vessel letting herself out in a distinct manner, under a contract with the enemy's Government, to convey a number of persons, described as being in the service of the enemy, with their military character travelling with them, and to restore them to their own country in that character.[219]

[214] *The Columbia (Weeks)* (1799) 1 C Rob 154, 156; 165 ER 132, 132; *Yeaton v Fry* 5 Cranch 335; *The Nereide* 9 Cranch 440. In the case of a blockade *de facto*, the lack of knowledge of the blockade meant it was not an offence for a neutral ship to sail to a blockaded port.

[215] Wheaton (8th edn) §523.

[216] N Hill, 'The Origin of the Law of Unneutral Service' (1929) 23 AJIL 56, 59.

[217] *The Carolina (Nordquist)* (1802) 4 C Rob 256, 165 ER 604.

[218] *The Friendship (Collard)* (1807) 6 C Rob 420; 165 ER 985, 986.

[219] Ibid 988.

The consequence of capture was the condemnation of the vessel.[220]

The other key aspect of unneutral service was the conveyance of official dispatches of a government. Diplomatic dispatches from an ambassador in a neutral country were distinguished from military dispatches; the former were immune from seizure and to carry them was an innocent act.[221] The principle that carriage of dispatches was distinct from the concept of contraband was established in *The Constitution* and followed explicitly in *The Atalanta,* in which it was noted that the consequence of such service were 'infinitely beyond the effect of any contraband that can be conveyed.'[222] The rationale for punishing the conveyance of despatches was the same that existed under the Rule of 1756, namely, to prevent a neutral ship from assuming the duties on behalf of a belligerent.[223] Yet one consequence of *The Atalanta* was that a fraudulent intention had to be established, as well as the fact of carriage itself. Like the carriage of combatants, the penalty for carriage of despatches was the forfeiture of the ship.[224]

Although an extrapolation from basic principles that was developed primarily by the British prize court, the concept of unneutral service gathered considerable acceptance. Those in favour of greater restrictions on contraband were generally in favour of the concept of unneutral service. Thus the motion of the Institute of International Law on the regulation of contraband proposed by Rikard Kleen also regulated the concept of 'transport service.'[225]

c. Neutral Duties Towards Belligerents

By the end of the nineteenth century the law of neutrality became refashioned as a self-standing corpus of obligations. By the end of the Franco-Prussian War, neutrality had shifted from a permissive regime to a body of rules that understood the maintenance of neutral status as dependent on a neutral's own ability to police and regulate the acts of those within its jurisdiction, and to treat belligerents on the basis of impartiality.

The importance of the animating concept of impartiality to neutrality during the nineteenth century is evident in the practice of the period. Impartiality appeared to function in two distinct ways. First, it operated to guarantee an equal application of rules of neutrality concerned with abstention and prevention.

[220] The same result was reached in the case of *The Orozembo (Brewster)* (1807) 6 C Rob 430, 165 ER 988.

[221] *The Caroline (Doah)* (1808) 6 C Rob 461; 165 ER 999. Sir William Scott drew a distinction with the carrying of dispatches between a colony and its mother country.

[222] *The Atalanta (Klein)* (1808) 6 Rob 440, 455; 165 ER 991, 997.

[223] Ibid 455; 997.

[224] Ibid 458; 998.

[225] 'International Regulation of Contraband of War' in J B Scott (ed) *Resolutions on the Institute of International Law Dealing with the Law of Nations* (OUP 1916) 129, sections 6–8.

Secondly, it operated as a governing principle of passive non-interference in those matters which the neutral State chose not to regulate.

i. Impartiality as equality

At the time of the United States' declaration of neutrality in 1793, 'for every treaty stipulating strict impartiality as the cornerstone of neutral conduct, there were several others which provided that in case one of the parties should be at war, the other should accord it the sort of assistance which characterised benevolent neutrality.'[226] This position changed during the course of the following century. During the Franco-Prussian War, in response to the suggestion that Great Britain could adopt a position of 'benevolent neutrality' favourable to Germany, the British Foreign Secretary Earl Granville responded that:

> ...it seems hardly to admit of doubt that neutrality, when it once departs from strict impartiality, runs the risk of altering its essence, and that the moment a neutral allows his proceedings to be biassed [sic] by predilection for one of two belligerents he ceases to be a neutral. The idea, therefore, of benevolent neutrality can mean little less than the extinction of neutrality.[227]

As noted above, it had previously been common for one State to supply another with troops pursuant to treaty. This practice was not regarded as a deviation from neutrality but simply as a different species of status, namely 'imperfect' or 'conventional' neutrality.[228] In the nineteenth century this conduct was widely viewed as a violation of neutrality.[229] This may be illustrated by examining the different versions of Wheaton's classic text, *Elements of International Law*. In his original text of 1836, Wheaton had distinguished between perfect and imperfect neutrality and argued that the fulfilment of treaty obligations did not result in a forfeiture of neutrality, 'nor render [the neutral] the enemy of the other belligerent nation, because it does not render him the general associate of its enemy.'[230] By 1866, the text states that the position has been modified by practice:

> the progress of modern times has been towards insisting on entire and impartial neutrality. A belligerent would be justified in treating any State as an enemy throughout, which rendered any aid to its enemy, whether in pursuance of treaty obligations or not, or which gave or withheld belligerent privileges unequally.[231]

226 Hyneman (n 132) 285.

227 61 BFSP 759–60.

228 *Smith's International Law* (n 204) 294.

229 See for example, Kleen (n 159) I 109: 'Est nulle la prétendue neutralité dite imparfaite ou limitée et qui comporterait une somme moins grande de devoirs à remplir, soit pour les neutres, soit pour les belligérants.'

230 Wheaton (1st edn Carey, Lea and Blanchard, Philadelphia 1836) §517. Wheaton earlier distinguishes between 'natural, or perfect neutrality' and 'imperfect, qualified or conventional neutrality' (509). For Wheaton, 'natural neutrality' is 'that which every sovereign State has a right, independent of positive compact, to observe in respect to the wars in which other States may be engaged.'

231 Wheaton (8th edn) §518.

By the end of the nineteenth century, the trend was towards 'perfect neutrality' that did not admit departure from impartiality of conduct towards the belligerents, even on the basis of a pre-existing treaty obligation. This obligation was recognized and enforced in the Boer War.[232] Smith dates the final British example of military assistance being furnished to one belligerent pursuant to treaty to 1826.[233] The preponderance of opinion is that this practice is now extinct.[234]

ii. Impartiality as non-interference

In the nineteenth century, not only was the neutral State required to abstain from conduct previously available to it; it was also required actively to prevent certain activity from taking place within its jurisdiction. In matters the neutral State was required to prohibit and to prevent, the neutral was required to discharge its obligations of impartiality and to treat the belligerents on the basis of equality. There was certain conduct that the neutral State was not required to regulate, however, concerning its own and its citizens' right of commerce. In these matters, the principle of impartiality meant something slightly different.

Impartiality could mean the equal withholding of privileges to both belligerents; but it could also mean passive equal treatment on the basis of *laissez-faire* principles. In the aspects of conduct it was not required to prohibit or prevent, the neutral State was left certain regulatory space with regard to economic matters. Impartiality applied to this sphere meant the withdrawal of privileges and restrictions in order to permit the open expression of the 'natural right' of commerce. One sees here the key influence of Vattel's understanding of the natural order of commerce, which it was the duty of international law to protect and preserve from reason of State.[235] This right of commerce had to operate impartially. Travers Twiss argued that a belligerent State 'may justly expect that a Neutral Nation will not prohibit any trade within its ports, whenever such prohibition would clearly work a greater prejudice to one Belligerent than to the other, and so be indirectly an act of favour to the latter.'[236] This was thus an acknowledgement that, in practice, what was impartial in formal terms could have an inequitable effect:

> For instance, a war may arise between the two countries, one of which in time of peace exports arms and imports provisions, whilst the other exports provisions and imports arms; in other words, between two countries, one of which is highly advanced in manufacturing industry, whilst the other is strictly agricultural. It is

[232] T Baty, *International Law in South Africa* (Stevens and Haynes 1900) 69–77.
[233] *Smith's International Law* (n 204) 295.
[234] See Phillimore III (n 213) 186–7; Grewe (n 13) 535; Holland (n 14) 403; 457. Against: *Kent's Commentary* (n 173) 302. Lawrence states that an example of the practice comes 'very near the border between the permitted and the forbidden' (Lawrence (1st edn) 521).
[235] For Vattel's influence in nineteenth century international law see Jouannet (n 77) 110–12.
[236] Twiss (n 146) 472.

> obvious that a Nation will not act with impartiality towards both Belligerents, if it should prohibit the exportation of arms and allow the exportation of provisions.[237]

The most prudent course of conduct in this instance was for the neutral State to adhere to the *courant normal*: to maintain, or at least not to disturb, the flow of trade that pre-existed the outbreak of hostilities; to do nothing to modify the balance of trade as a result of the war.[238] This was a reflection of natural order. According to this approach, Twiss notes, 'the maintenance of an order of things which existed prior to the war, against which no complaint was raised in time of peace by any other Nation, cannot expose a Neutral Nation to any imputation of bad faith towards either of two Belligerent parties.'[239] This would preserve the rights of commerce from interference by the belligerent's more powerful right of self defence.

Certain conduct was in the course of becoming subject to the duty of abstention but for a large part of the nineteenth century remained a subject of sovereign discretion. One example concerns the rules placed on belligerents' entry and exit from neutral ports. The rules on the entry and exit of belligerent ships from neutral ports remained largely a matter of sovereign discretion. The neutral's discretion to regulate sailings of ships of rival belligerents in the same neutral port goes back to 1605, at least in England.[240] Britain imposed a 'twenty-four hours' rule governing the departure of opposing belligerent warships from neutral harbours, but other States adopted different rules on the issue.[241] In 1898 the *Institut de droit international* set down rules for entry and exit from neutral ports, but the issue continued to be viewed as within the power of the neutral's discretion at the time of the Russo-Japanese War.[242]

A further example relates to the provisions that belligerent ships could take on in neutral ports. The neutral could choose impartially to impose particular restrictions on the provisioning of ships. Coal when carried by a neutral ship to a belligerent port was a matter of contraband control that the neutral State was not required to regulate. However, the fuelling of belligerents in neutral ports, although generally permissible throughout the nineteenth century, was on the boundary between action it had the power to regulate on the basis of impartiality and conduct it was required to prohibit on the basis of the duty of prevention. In

[237] Ibid 473. [238] To similar effect Westlake (n 199) 382.

[239] Twiss (n 146) 473–4; Lorimer (n 150) 176.

[240] Marsden, *Documents* I, 353, 357–8: 'That the ship of warre which came in firste bee suffred to departe a Tyde or two before thither which came in laste, and that for soe long tyme they shall staye and detaine any ship of warre that would offer to pursue another out of any our Ports immediatelie.'

[241] McNair, *International Law Opinions* III 156–8; Lawrence (n 183) 123.

[242] A S Hershey, 'Some Questions of International Law Arising from the Russo-Japanese War III' (1904) 16 TGB 452, 457. 'Status of Ships and their Crews in Foreign Ports in Time of Peace and in Time of War' in J B Scott (ed) *Resolutions of the Institute of International Law Dealing with the Law of Nations* (OUP 1916) 143.

the Russo-Japanese War, Britain's practice was to permit the belligerent ship to take on only as much coal as was necessary to reach the nearest port of their own country, and no two supplies of coal for the vessel were to be granted in intervals shorter than three months.[243]

iii. Abstention: obligations of result

Higgins notes that '[i]n considering the growth of the law of neutrality it will be found that territorial sovereignty is at the same time a source of neutral responsibility as well as its measure.'[244] The neutral State was limited in its responsibility to matters occurring on its own territory, and was not responsible for actions taken by its citizens beyond the three-mile limit from its territory. While this distinction appears doctrinally straightforward, in practice what was required of the State itself within its territory was a matter of contestation, particularly concerning whether it was required to restrain its citizens from engaging in certain actions, particularly concerning the carriage of contraband. Indeed, in relation to the obligations of abstention and prevention, the distinction between neutral States and neutral individuals is paramount. There were a number of restrictions constituting obligations of result placed upon the neutral State deriving from the duty of abstention from all acts that would involve the neutral in hostilities.

(i) Prohibition on the supply of arms and warships

The neutral State was under an obligation not directly to supply arms and munitions of war to a belligerent party.[245] Yet it was not required to restrain its citizens from carrying arms and other munitions of war to belligerents, which were defined as absolute contraband by all States. It was for belligerents to police the private trade in weapons by means of contraband control.

The neutral State was under a general obligation not to sell warships to belligerents. Unlike the situation of arms and other munitions of war, the neutral State was under an obligation to prevent its citizens from selling and fitting out warships in neutral ports; unlike contraband, which the belligerent had the right to control, the neutral State was under an obligation to prevent the export of warships that were to be put to use in hostilities.

(ii) Prohibition on the supply of combatants

The neutral State was under an obligation not to supply troops to belligerents. Whereas previously the furnishing of troops had been permissible pursuant to

243 Lawrence (n 183) 124.

244 A P Higgins, 'International Law and the Growth of the Empire, 1793-1870' in J H Rose et al (eds) *The Cambridge History of the British Empire: Volume II: The Growth of the New Empire 1783–1870* (CUP 1940) 842, 860.

245 Lawrence (1st edn) 520–1. Lawrence accepts that the preferable policy is for complete abstention but then qualifies this view through discussion of a number of exceptions. He notes, for example, that it may be acceptable for the government to continue to sell old arms and stores from its arsenals (520).

treaty, 'perfect neutrality' rendered this illegal; the neutral State was required to abstain from all forms of military support to a belligerent. As with the carriage of contraband, however, the neutral State was not required to police the activities of its neutral citizens in acting as troop transports, which was regulated by the concept of unneutral service.

(iii) Prohibition on the provision of loans

The neutral State was prohibited from issuing loans to belligerents.[246] Whether the neutral State was required to prohibit its citizens from loaning money to belligerents was more uncertain. The English courts and a number of international writers took the view that international law prohibited loans by neutral individuals.[247] British authors disagreed with this analysis. Hall said that to impose an obligation on neutral governments to police loans by their citizens would go against the fundamental principle that States are not responsible for the commercial acts of their citizens.[248] Lawrence disagreed sharply with this analysis and suggested that it betrayed an ignorance of the distinction between neutral governments and individuals; the neutral individual 'commits no breach of the common law of nations by lending, and his government is under no obligation to attempt the impossible task of preventing him.'[249] To attempt to prevent such commercial transactions would be possible only by 'an amount of espionage and interference which would outrage human nature and render all trade impossible.'[250] No war could take place 'without a free resort by the combatant powers to neutral money markets.'[251] The view from the continent was stricter and generally regarded the provision of loans as impermissible.[252] By the close of the nineteenth century, it appears that there was a general consensus that, in the words of Phillimore, '[a] nation which furnishes aid, whether of men or money, to both belligerents may be *impartial*, but certainly is not *neutral*.'[253]

iv. Prevention—obligations of conduct

The obligations on neutral States were not solely those of abstention from certain conduct previously available to it. In the nineteenth century it became generally accepted that a State was 'responsible for whatever is done within its jurisdiction, for it must be *presumed* to be capable of preventing or punishing offences committed within its boundaries.'[254] Duties of prevention required the neutral State to restrain the activities of its citizens with regard to certain conduct occurring on

[246] Phillimore III (n 213) 193–5; Lawrence (1st edn) 520; Westlake, *International Law* II 217.

[247] *De Wutz v Hendricks* (1824) 2 Bing 314; Phillimore III (n 213) 193–5; H W Halleck, *International Law* (H H Bancroft and Company 1861) 526; S Baker, *Halleck's International Law, or Rules Regulating the Intercourse of States in Peace and War* II (Kegan Paul and Co 1878) 196–7.

[248] Hall (4th edn) 619–20. [249] Lawrence (1st edn) 523. [250] Ibid 523. [251] Ibid.

[252] J C Bluntschli, *Le Droit International codifié* (M C Lardy (tr)) (2nd edn, Guillaumin 1874) §768.

[253] Phillimore III (n 213) 193 (emphasis in original).

[254] Ibid 191. Emphasis in original.

neutral and belligerent territory, as well as to prevent certain belligerent conduct from occurring on neutral territory.

(i) Prevention of the levying of troops, the enlistment of troops, and the acceptance of letters of marque

It was the neutral's duty to prohibit the levy of troops within its jurisdiction. Towards the end of the nineteenth century this prohibition transformed from a regulatory power to be exercised impartiality to an absolute prohibition. The traditional view was that a belligerent could not levy troops on neutral territory without consent, but that the neutral could choose to grant this request as long as it did so impartially.[255] Writing in 1874, however, Hall accepted that the prohibition on levying of troops 'is now fully recognised as the foundation of a duty.'[256] In 1904, upon the outbreak of the Russo-Japanese War, Hershey argued that the levying of troops within a neutral State 'is distinctly forbidden in modern times by the law of nations, and the failure to prevent these things would constitute a serious breach of neutrality.'[257]

The neutral State must also prohibit the enlistment of neutral subjects in armies abroad. This duty is distinct from the duty of the State not itself to furnish troops. This was a subject that was increasingly regulated by domestic legislation. In 1818, the United States passed its Foreign Enlistment Act prohibiting the enlistment of its subjects in the armies of belligerent States. The United Kingdom followed suit in 1819.[258] The difficulties of enforcing the 1819 Act led to the appointment in 1867 of a panel of commissioners to consider revisions to the 1819 legislation.[259] The report recommended the amendment of the 1819 legislation to include a prohibition on the building, equipping, fitting out, arming, or dispatch of any ship with intent or knowledge that the ship will be employed in the service of a foreign power, to regulate the obligation to prevent hostile expeditions from neutral territory (a key issue in the American Civil War).[260] The legislation was amended in 1870.[261] Continental States did not immediately follow a

[255] Ibid 187.

[256] W E Hall, *The Rights and Duties of Neutrals* (Longmans, Green & Co 1874) 55.

[257] A S Hershey, 'Some Questions of International Law Arising from the Russo-Japanese War III' (1904) 16 TGB 452, 454.

[258] For debate on the 1819 Act, see Parl Deb 40 (1819) 1379 (HL).

[259] *Report of the Neutrality Laws Commissioners together with An Appendix containing Reports from Foreign States and Other Documents* (HMSO 1868). It seems that Liverpool shipowners themselves supported amendments to the Foreign Enlistment Act. Annex VII: 'Copy of a Memorial from certain Shipowners of Liverpool to the Secretary of State for Foreign Affairs, suggesting an alteration in the Foreign Enlistment Act'.

[260] Ibid 5. The proposal was not accepted unanimously. See the dissent issued by one of the commissioners, Vernon Harcourt.

[261] 1870 Act. The 1870 Act applied to all subjects of the British Crown and its provisions extended to all British dominions.

similar approach to the domestic regulation of foreign enlistment.[262] However, by the end of the century, a considerable number of States imposed domestic restrictions on either the recruitment or enlistment of troops within neutral jurisdiction in order to comply with the international obligation.[263] By the end of the century it was clearly recognized in general international law that a State was required to prevent the departure of its citizens to join the forces of belligerents fighting abroad, and in 1876 the Russian government was accused of breaching neutrality in permitting a large number of Russian volunteers to join Serbian forces in hostilities against the Ottoman Empire.[264]

A correlative duty was a prohibition on the neutral State to prevent its citizens from accepting letters of marque from belligerents.[265] The prohibition on the acceptance of letters of marque was part of the development of a general shift towards an increasingly rigorous understanding of territorial inviolability and had taken root in America; however, the prohibition on privateering of the Declaration of Paris led to the practice's rapid decline and eventual desuetude.[266]

(ii) Prevention of passage of troops through neutral territory

The requirement to police and prevent belligerent activity in neutral territory grew throughout the nineteenth century. This can be divided into the prevention of passage across neutral territory and belligerent activities in neutral territory. Some writers viewed passage as a grant to be exercised impartially.[267] By the end of the century, however, the nature of the obligation appeared to have tightened, such that the grant of passage even on the basis of impartiality was viewed as a non-neutral act.[268] The right of innocent passage through a neutral State's territorial sea seemed to have been viewed as an exception.[269]

(iii) Belligerent hostilities and activities in neutral jurisdiction

As well as being under an obligation to prevent passage, there was a clear and long-standing obligation on neutral States to ensure that no hostilities took place in, or were prepared from, neutral jurisdiction.[270] Proclamations of neutrality at the commencement of hostilities frequently recited the prohibition on belligerent use of neutral territory as a staging ground or place of resort for warlike purposes.[271]

[262] See for example, the survey of State practice in *Report of the Neutrality Laws Commissioners* Appendix IV.

[263] Thomson (n 22) 80–1.

[264] Lawrence (1st edn) 533.

[265] Hall (3rd edn) 622.

[266] Lawrence (1st edn) 534.

[267] Wheaton (8th edn) §427; Phillimore III (n 213) 195; Twiss (n 146) 443.

[268] Hall (n 51) 52–3; Hall (4th edn) 624; Holland (n 14) 456.

[269] Twiss (n 146) 445.

[270] Hall (4th edn) 626; Lawrence (n 183) 120–1. The obligation had been set out clearly by Sir William Scott in *Twee Gebroeders (No 1) (Alberts)* 3 C Rob 162, 164; 165 ER 422, 423.

[271] McNair, *International Law Opinions* III, 156–8.

A related requirement was to disarm and intern belligerent troops found in neutral territory. This rule was enforced during the Franco-Prussian War of 1870, when Switzerland interned French ships seeking to pass through Swiss territory.[272] The Second Hague Convention of 1899, on the laws and customs of war on land, codified this requirement to intern troops of belligerents found in neutral territory.[273] Pursuant to the treaty, the neutral State could authorize passage through its territory of wounded or sick members from the forces of belligerents, on the condition that the trains bringing them carried neither combatants nor war material.[274] By the turn of the century, the belligerent was generally forbidden to bring prizes into neutral ports.[275]

(iv) Fitting out of warlike expeditions in neutral jurisdiction

The most controversial extension of neutral duty in the nineteenth century concerned the prevention of warlike expeditions prepared in neutral territory. The boundaries between the fitting out of a ship for a warlike expedition and the export of a warship as contraband raised difficult questions about the appropriate boundaries of neutral duty. The long-standing approach had been the view expressed by Justice Story in *The Santissima Trinidad*: the sale of warships was a matter of 'commercial adventure' that the neutral State was not required to police or prevent but which belligerents could intercept as a measure of contraband control.[276] Whether the neutral State had duties to prevent the building of warships in neutral territory, however, became a matter of some urgency during the course of the American Civil War.

At issue was the building and fitting out of warships in British ports, which were used to destructive effect in the hostilities. A number of the cases of alleged misconduct on the part of Britain became known as the *Alabama* claims.[277] The *Alabama* was a ship built in Liverpool that was launched in May 1862. The US demanded compensation from Britain for failing to prevent the *Alabama* and other commerce-raiders from being fitted out to sail against ships of the union. At the time of its departure from British waters, the *Alabama* was not fitted out for warlike purposes. Unarmed, she sailed for the Azores where she was met by two ships, the *Bahama* and the *Agrippina,* which provided the *Alabama* with crews, coal, and military supplies. The *Alabama* then received a commission as a Confederate cruiser.

[272] Grewe (n 13) 536–7.

[273] Convention with Respect to the Laws and Customs of War on Land (signed 29 July 1899, entered into force 4 September 1900) 187 CTS 429, art 57.

[274] Ibid, art 59.

[275] Holland (n 14) 467. The earlier view of Twiss was that, absent a contrary view set out by the neutral, the belligerent was entitled to bring prizes into neutral ports: Twiss (n 146) 451.

[276] *The Santissima Trinidad* (1822) 7 Wheaton 283, 300. Support for this general view may be found in Hall (4th edn) 634–5.

[277] On the arbitration see A Cook, *The Alabama Claims: American Politics and Anglo-American Relations, 1865–1872* (Cornell University Press 1975). For background to the arbitration see generally T Bingham, 'The Alabama Claims Arbitration' (2005) 54 ICLQ 1.

The US protested to the British government that ships intended for warlike purposes against a belligerent had to be prevented. The US argued that the *Alabama* was intended for commerce raiding against union shipping; that the UK was aware of this intention; and that to permit vessels with such an intention to leave the jurisdiction was a violation of neutral duty.[278] The United Kingdom disputed the US interpretation of neutral duty. It claimed the neutral was liable only when the ship was in such a state of readiness that it could be viewed as a hostile expedition when leaving neutral jurisdiction.[279] Its view appeared to be that a ship adapted for war was an article of contraband trade unless it left the neutral port in a condition to commence hostilities when it passed beyond neutral jurisdiction.[280] At the time of the *Alabama*'s departure from Liverpool, the UK contended that it was under no obligation to prevent the *Alabama's* departure, since it was unarmed when it left neutral jurisdiction.

After protracted negotiation, it was agreed in the Treaty of Washington of 1871 that the question of Great Britain's responsibility should be submitted to arbitration.[281] The Treaty provided that the tribunal was to apply a series of rules, in addition to consistent principles of international law, in deciding the dispute, as follows:

> *Rules*
>
> A neutral Government is bound –
>
> First, to use due diligence to prevent the fitting out, arming or equipping, within its jurisdiction, of any vessel which it has reasonable ground to believe is intended to cruise or to carry on war against a Power with which it is at peace; and also to use like diligence to prevent the departure from its jurisdiction of any vessel intended to cruise or carry on war as above, such vessel having been specially adapted, in whole or in part, within such jurisdiction, to war-like use.
>
> Secondly, not to permit or suffer either belligerent to make use of its ports or waters as the base of naval operations against the other, or for the purpose of the renewal or augmentation of military supplies or arms, or the recruitment of men.
>
> Thirdly, to exercise due diligence in its own ports and waters, and, as to all persons within its jurisdiction, to prevent any violation of the foregoing obligations and duties.[282]

The Treaty explicitly stated that Great Britain did not accept these rules as statements of existing law but would apply them for purposes of the arbitration.[283] It

[278] Wheaton (8th edn) §562–3.
[279] Holland (n 14) 475. [280] Lawrence (1st edn) 543.
[281] Treaty Between Great Britain and the United States of America, for the amicable settlement of all causes of difference between the two Countries signed 8 May 1871 (1870–1871) 61 BFSP 40.
[282] Ibid, art 6. [283] Ibid.

further provided that Great Britain and the United States would apply the rules between themselves in future, and bring them to the knowledge of other maritime powers and invite them to accede to them.[284]

The tribunal issued its decision in September 1872. In relation to the *Alabama*, it found that Great Britain had failed to exercise due diligence and had thereby violated the first and the third rules of the Treaty. In relation to the *Florida*, Great Britain had violated all three rules of the Treaty. And in the case of the *Shenandoah*, it violated the second and third rules.[285] Great Britain was ordered to pay to the United States $15,500,000 in gold (roughly equivalent to £3,000,000).[286]

How far the rules of the Treaty of Washington reflected customary international law, and the correctness of their interpretation in the *Alabama*, was a matter of immediate and obvious controversy. Much turned on what 'due diligence' required. The US approach was that diligence was commensurate with the emergency faced or the 'magnitude of the results of negligence.' The British argued that due diligence was a shifting standard dependent on the nature of the obligation itself.[287] The Tribunal appeared to accept the American approach; it found that due diligence 'ought to be exercised by neutral governments in exact proportion to the risks to which either of the belligerents may be exposed, from a failure to fulfil the obligations of neutrality on their part.'[288] Although the Tribunal found that due diligence was a shifting standard, dependent on the risk to which a belligerent was exposed, the neutral State's available means of redress was not a factor in determining whether the obligation was discharged. It noted that Great Britain 'cannot justify itself for a failure in due diligence on the plea of insufficiency of the legal means of action which it possessed.'[289]

This interpretation attracted strong criticism. For example, Lawrence claimed that it 'destroys that impartiality which is the essence of neutral duty.'[290] Regardless of the precise meaning to be given to the term 'due diligence', however, the extension of responsibility to encompass this area was welcomed, particularly by a number of continental jurists.[291] In 1875, the *Institut de droit International* adopted the three

[284] Ibid.

[285] *Alabama Claims of the United States of America against Great Britain* 29 RIAA 125.

[286] Ibid 134. For UK legal opinions on the case, see McNair, *International Law Opinions* III, 171–87. On the arbitration see (from a British perspective) M Bernard, *An Historical Account of the Neutrality of Great Britain during the American Civil War* (Longman's, Green, Reader, and Dyer 1870) chapter 14; F W Hackett, *Reminiscences of the Geneva Tribunal of Arbitration* (Houghton Mifflin, 1911). The British appointee, Alexander Cockburn, dissented. The full text of his dissent may be found in FO 881/2085.

[287] The arguments are contained in FO 881/2087.

[288] *Alabama Claims* (n 285) 129.

[289] Ibid 131.

[290] Lawrence (1st edn) 539–40. Lawrence proposed that the relevant standard should instead be the 'kind and amount of diligence which a strong and careful government would use to put down smuggling.' See also the criticism of Lorimer (n 150) 157–63.

[291] J C Bluntschli, 'Opinion Impartialle sur la Question de l'Alabama et sur la Manière de la Résoudre' (1870) 2 RDILC 452; C Calvo, 'Examen des Trois Règles de droit international proposées dans le Traité de Washington' (1874) 6 RDILC 453. A notable dissenting voice is Lorimer (n 150) 157–63.

rules in modified form.[292] Hall considered that a rule prohibiting the outfit and construction of war ships was 'in the course of growth.' He noted that, 'although it is adopted by the most important maritime Powers, it is not yet old enough or quite wide enough to have become compulsory on those Nations which have not yet signified their voluntary adherence to it.' In the meantime, while the rule was developing, Hall stated that a neutral State could build and arm a ship to belligerent order, and deliver it to a belligerent outside neutral territory ready to receive a fighting crew.[293] Lawrence in 1895 considered that 'the question is still far from settlement' but admitted that at the time of the arbitral award, 'old principles have been thoroughly discredited and the maritime Powers have come to no agreement upon new ones.'[294]

This was the case in the Russo-Japanese War of 1904–1905. Upon the accusation that Germany had failed to prevent the sale to Russia of transatlantic steamers and torpedo boats, German Chancellor von Bülow is reported to have remarked that such sales were permissible under international law.[295] Yet there was little consensus as to what criterion divided permissible trading from action that the State was required to prevent. Surveying that practice Lawrence distinguished between a mere contraband article and a ship fitted out for warfare. The distinction he posited was one between 'mere trading' and 'something akin to active participation.'[296] The threshold was crossed from one to the other when neutral territory was used either as the 'starting-point of expeditions' or as a 'base of operations.'[297] The *locus classicus* of a 'starting-point of expeditions' was the construction and fitting out of a warship in neutral territory. The concept of a 'base of operations' was somewhat more elastic.

(v) The use of a base of naval operations in neutral territory

The concept of a base of operations was reflected in the second rule of the Treaty of Washington. Unlike the duty to prevent the launching of hostile expeditions, the base of operations principle addressed the use by belligerents of depots in neutral territory to restock and refuel naval stores and equipment.

There had existed a long-standing duty not to increase the war-making ability of belligerent ships in neutral jurisdiction. As Lawrence notes, '[l]ong before 1865 it had been recognised that a belligerent vessel ought not to leave a neutral port a more efficient fighting-machine than she entered it.'[298] Unlike the duty to prevent warlike expeditions, it is the frequent use of neutral territory as a 'base' that constitutes a violation of the obligation.[299]

292 'International Duties of States – Rules of Washington' in J B Scott (ed) *Resolutions of the Institute of International Law Dealing with the Law of Nations* (OUP 1916) 12.

293 Hall (4th edn) 639.

294 Lawrence (1st edn) 549.

295 A S Hershey, 'Some Questions of International Law Arising from the Russo-Japanese War IV' (1904) 16 TGB 538, 539.

296 Lawrence (n 183) 181. See also Hershey (n 295) 540.

297 Lawrence (n 183) 181.

298 Lawrence (1st edn) 531.

299 Lawrence (1st edn) 504–5.

During the *Alabama* arbitration Great Britain was found to have violated the second and third rules of the Treaty of Washington in the case of the *Shenandoah.* The *Shenandoah* was a confederate cruiser which entered the port of Melbourne in need of provisions, repairs, and coal. The ship was refitted and provisioned in Melbourne and then went on to attack shipping at the Cape of Good Horn. It was claimed by the United States that the *Shenandoah* had converted Melbourne into a base of operations for belligerent use and that Great Britain had thereby failed in its neutral obligation. The Tribunal found that Great Britain had indeed failed to discharge the obligations stemming from rules two and three of the Treaty of Washington and was thereby responsible for all acts committed by the *Shenandoah* after its departure from Melbourne in February 1865.[300] This interpretation of the base of operations principle has been criticized on the basis that it is repeated use, and not a single instance of supply, as was the case with the *Shenandoah,* that characterizes the existence of a base of operations.[301]

d. The Right to Remain Neutral and Neutral Rights towards Belligerents

The neutral State's ability to remain inviolable was initially quite limited, as States could simply exchange a State's neutrality for belligerency through a declaration of war. A termination of neutrality by declaration of war thus did not necessarily violate international law—which would have been the case if neutrality were seen as a legal right. As Quincy Wright points out, according to leading publicists of the nineteenth century:

> Neutrality was neither a right nor a duty: If war exists, non-participants are neutral until they make war on some other State or some other State makes war on them, but in the absence of a special treaty establishing a status of permanent neutrality or prohibiting war under the circumstances, there is no legal obstacle to the occurrence of either of these events. Thus, in the absence of special treaty, States shall have no right to remain neutral nor are they under any duty to remain neutral.[302]

Some authors in the nineteenth century, however, had suggested that States possessed the 'right to remain neutral'.[303] That is, in contrast to the view that a belligerent could declare war on a neutral State, thereby transforming its status from

[300] *Alabama Claims* (n 285) 132. [301] Hall (3rd edn) 628–9.

[302] Q Wright 'Project of the American Institute of International Law on Maritime Neutrality (No 26)' (1927) 21 AJIL 127, 128.

[303] See, for example, Ortolan, *Règles internationales et diplomatie de la mer* 77; Hautefeuille, *Des droits et des devoirs des nations neutres* 1: 174–5; Halleck, *Elements of International Law* 231; Wheaton (8th edn) §426.

neutral to belligerent at will. The view that neutrality itself, as a status, could be perceived as a 'right' that belligerents violated by attacking neutral States, was one which was eventually incorporated into the Hague Conventions.

Alongside an emerging acceptance that every State had the 'right' to neutrality as a status, the view also developed that, alongside the right to remain neutral, neutral States themselves possessed various rights as corollaries to duties extended towards belligerents. These rights were the continuation of rights that all States were said to possess in peacetime deriving from sovereignty and independence, as modified by the exigencies of war, and were primarily the right to territorial inviolability and the right to trade.[304] The acknowledgement that all States possessed certain rights reflected the emergence of a liberal international law focused on negative co-existence.[305]

The acknowledgement that neutrals had certain rights stemming from their status as neutrals was discussed at the Second Hague Peace Conference and eventually resulted in the inclusion of certain neutral rights in the two Hague Conventions relating to neutrality. At the Conference, France had submitted a text that proceeded from the perspective of the duties of a neutral State. In response to the draft, the Belgian delegate noted that it was important 'to call attention to the fact that neutrals not only have duties but that they also have rights.'[306] There was therefore a need to appreciate that the issue was not confined to the neutral's duty of prevention: 'the obligations of neutrals in this regard flow from an inhibition of general application which logically concerns belligerents primarily before affecting neutrals.'[307] Belgium therefore requested the inclusion of the statement that 'the territory of neutral States is inviolable.'[308] A report of the third commission stated that:

> The starting-point of the regulations ought to be the sovereignty of the neutral State, which cannot be affected by the mere fact that a war exists in which it does not intend to participate. Its sovereignty should be respected by the belligerents, who cannot implicate it in the war or molest it with acts of hostility.[309]

The report went on to emphasize that the obligation contained in Article 1 of Hague Convention XIII was an obligation to respect another State's sovereignty, and therefore did not stem from the existence of war: 'The principle which it is proper to affirm at the outset is the obligation upon belligerents to respect the

[304] Hautefeuille, *Des droits et des devoirs des nations neutres* 1:247–50.

[305] Jouannet (n 77) 124–31.

[306] *Hague Conference Proceedings* vol III 174. The Belgian delegate continued: 'Etrangers aux hostilités (les neutres) ont le droit primordial d'exiger qu'on ne les y mèle ni directement, ni indirectement.' ('Being themselves strangers to the hostilities they have the primordial right to demand that they not be implicated in them directly or indirectly.')

[307] Ibid. [308] Ibid. [309] *Hague Conference Proceedings* vol I 278, 290.

sovereign rights of neutral States. This obligation is not a consequence of the war any more than the right of the State to inviolability of its territory is a consequence of its neutrality. The obligation and the right are inherent in the very existence of States.'[310] Neutral territory was inviolable because sovereign territory was inviolable, not because of the special character of the status of neutrality.[311] A belligerent could no longer refuse to recognize a neutral's territorial inviolability; according to James Brown Scott, the position under the Hague Conventions is that '[n]eutrality is a recognised status which the belligerent is forced to recognise.'[312]

At the time, this may have been progressive development that did not yet reflect customary international law. In the first edition of Oppenheim's *International Law*, published in 1906 prior to the Second Hague Conference, it was suggested that 'just as third States have no duty to remain neutral in a war, so they have no right to demand to remain neutral.'[313] Following Germany's violation of Belgium's neutrality in 1914, however, this view was challenged as no longer reflective of international law.[314] By the third edition of *Oppenheim's International Law*, published in 1921 and edited by Roxburgh, the view had changed:

> the Law of Nations in its present development objects to a would-be neutral State being forced into war, and a belligerent who refuses to recognise it as neutral violates International Law, although not neutrality.[315]

The Hague Conventions state that belligerents are under an obligation to respect the territory of neutral States. Article 1 of Hague Convention V states the general principle: 'The territory of neutral Powers is inviolable.'[316] According to Article 1 of Hague Convention XIII, 'belligerents are bound to respect the sovereign rights of neutral Powers and to abstain, in neutral territory or neutral waters, from any act which would, if knowingly permitted by any Power, constitute a violation of

[310] Ibid 290.

[311] Hyde suggests that the rule of the inviolability of sovereign territory derives from the principle that no act should be committed in derogation of a State's sovereignty rather than from the character of neutrality. Hyde 'Duties of States in Naval War' 508.

[312] J B Scott *The Hague Peace Conferences of 1899 and 1907: Volume I* (John Hopkins, Baltimore 1097) 543–4; see also A S de Bustamente, 'The Hague Convention Concerning the Rights and Duties of Neutral Powers and Persons in Land Warfare' (1908) 2 AJIL 95.

[313] L Oppenheim *International Law* (Longmans, Green and Co, London 1906) 322. Oppenheim further suggested that it was purely a question of policy, and not of law, whether a State retained its neutrality (ibid 317).

[314] See C de Visscher, 'De la Belligérance dans ses Rapports avec la Violation de la Neutralité' (1916) 2 PW 93, 100; the opposing view is expressed in 'The Hague Conventions and the Neutrality of Belgium and Luxemburg' (1915) 9 AJIL 959 and J D Falconbridge, 'The Right of a Belligerent to Make War Upon a Neutral' (1918) 4 TGS 204.

[315] R F Roxburgh (ed) *Oppenheim's International Law* (3rd edn Longmans, Green and Co, London 1921) 406.

[316] HC V art 1.

neutrality.'[317] According to Articles 2 to 4 of Hague Convention V, belligerents are prohibited from taking certain actions on neutral territory.[318] Similarly, Article 2 of Hague Convention XIII provides that any belligerent act of hostility committed in the territorial waters of a neutral Power constitutes a violation of neutrality.[319] Articles 4 and 5 of Hague Convention XIII prohibit a belligerent from setting up a prize court in neutral territory, or from using neutral territory as a base of operations, respectively.[320] Article 18 of Hague Convention XIII provides that belligerent warships may not make use of neutral ports, roadsteads or territorial waters to increase supplies of war material or their armament or for completing their crews.[321]

The approach of the Hague Conventions, therefore, is significant. Instead of approaching the question from the perspective solely of neutral duty, the emphasis is on the interlocking duties on belligerents not to violate the right of neutrals to inviolability, as well as the neutral State's duties of prevention and abstention. Thus in Hague Convention V, while a belligerent is under a duty, under Articles 2 and 3, not to take certain action in neutral territory, the neutral State is under an obligation not to allow any of those belligerent actions to occur on its territory.[322] As de Bustamente notes:

> Instead of saying, for example, that the neutral must prevent the passage across its territory of the belligerent army, it is now held that the combatants must refrain from crossing neutral territory with their armies. This is not simply a different form of expression, but a radical change in the situation of both, and therefore in their international responsibility.[323]

The Hague Conventions represented a shift away from the position that a neutral State's status could be changed by a belligerent's declaration of war on it, or by a physical attack on the neutral State; authors who continued to adhere to this position following the outbreak of the First World War began to receive strong criticism.[324] The protection afforded to a State by Article 2(4) of the UN Charter

317 HC XIII art 1.

318 Article 2, for example, provides that 'Belligerents are forbidden to move troops or convoys of either munitions of war or supplies across the territory of a neutral Power.'

319 HC XIII art 2. According to Article 10, however, '[t]he neutrality of a State is not affected by the mere passage through its territorial waters of war-ships or prizes belonging to belligerents.'

320 HC XIII art 4; HC XIII art 5. However, the prohibition on the establishment of a prize court in neutral territory has 'long been the law of nations.' Hyde (n 311) 509.

321 HC XIII art 18. 322 HC V art 5.

323 A S de Bustamente, 'The Hague Convention Concerning the Rights and Duties of Neutral Powers and Persons in Land Warfare' (1908) 2 AJIL 95, 97. See also S W D Rowson, 'Modern Blockade: Some Legal Aspects' (1946) 23 BYBIL 346, 347: '[i]t is a comparatively modern notion that neutrals have rights against belligerents, who are under corresponding duties to neutrals.'

324 See, for example, as a notable proponent of Oppenheim's position, J D Falconbridge 'The Right of a Belligerent to Make War on a Neutral' (1918) 4 TGS 204.

meant a further level of protection for the neutral State and further strengthened the concept of neutral rights.

5. Conclusion

The history of neutrality reveals the shifting contours of the concept. Neutrality emerged as a loose collection of rules relating to maritime commerce, in large part driven by the demands of merchants. Only much later did neutrality begin to take shape as a coherent body of rules, constructed to manage the tensions between commercial society and belligerent necessity.

Indeed, it was in the nineteenth century that the law of neutrality experienced its 'golden age.'[325] It was a period of steady advance in the acceptance of neutrality as a legal status with detailed rights and duties, and alongside these developments emerged the institutional view of neutrality that no longer permitted States to dispose contractually of their neutral rights and obligations. However, the law of neutrality reached its highest pitch of development at the beginning of the twentieth century—a century which would challenge the body of neutral rights and duties and the very existence of neutrality as a legal institution.

The law of neutrality had frequently throughout history been identified with the concept of impartiality; a common view was that 'the character of neutrality was, that nothing should be granted to one party which was not allowed to the other.'[326]

[325] C de Visscher *Theory and Reality in Public International Law* (P E Corbett (tr)) (PUP, Princeton 1957) 297.

[326] (1819) 40 Parl Deb (HL) 1379 (Lord Bathurst). Lord Holland argued that 'impartiality constituted neutrality' (1391).

Bibliography

1. Books and monographs

T Baty *International Law in South Africa* (Stevens and Haynes, London 1900).

T Becker *Terrorism and The State: Rethinking the Rules of State Responsibility* (Hart, Oxford 2006).

G Best *War and Law Since 1945* (Clarendon Press, Oxford 1994).

H Blix *Sovereignty, Aggression and Neutrality* (Dag Hammarskjöld Foundation, Sweden 1970).

M Bothe, K J Partsch and W A Solf (eds) *New Rules for Victims of Armed Conflicts: Commentary on the Two 1977 Protocols Additional to the Geneva Conventions of 1949* (Martinus Nijhoff, The Hague 1982).

D W Bowett *Self-Defence in International Law* (Manchester UP, Manchester 1958).

D W Bowett *United Nations Forces: A Legal Study of United Nations Practice* (Stevens & Sons, London 1964).

O Bring *Neutralitetens uppgång och fall—eller den kollektiva säkerhetens historia (Atlantis, Stockholm 2008).*

I Brownlie *International Law and the Use of Force by States* (Clarendon Press, Oxford 1963).

M Byers *Custom, Power and the Power of Rules* (CUP, Cambridge 1999).

M W Cagle and F A Manson *The Sea War in Korea* (United States Naval Institute, Annapolis 1957).

A Carty and R A Smith (eds) *Sir Gerald Fitzmaurice and the World Crisis: A Legal Adviser in the Foreign Office, 1932–1945* (Kluwer Law International, The Hague 2000).

E Castrén *The Present Law of War and Neutrality* (Suomalaisen Tiedeakatemia Toimitsuksia, Helsinki 1954).

B Cheng *General Principles of Law as applied by International Courts and Tribunals* (Grotius Publications, Cambridge 1987).

S Chesterman *Just War or Just Peace: Humanitarian Intervention and International Law* (OUP, Oxford 2000).

C Chinkin *Third Parties in International Law* (Clarendon Press, Oxford 1993).

O Corten *Le droit contre la guerre: l'interdiction du recours à la force en droit international contemporain* (Pedone, Paris 2003).

J Crawford *The Creation of States in International Law* (2nd edn OUP, Oxford 2006).

I H Daalder and M E O'Hanlon *Winning Ugly: NATO's War to Save Kosovo* (Brookings, Washington DC 2000).

F Deák and P Jessup (eds) *A Collection of Neutrality Laws, Regulations and Treaties of Various Countries I* (Greenport Press, Westport 1974).

R Divine *The Reluctant Belligerent: American Entry Into World War II* (Wiley, New York 1965).

Y Dinstein *War, Aggression and Self-Defence* (4th edn CUP, Cambridge 2005).

Y Dinstein *The International Law of Belligerent Occupation* (CUP, Cambridge 2009).

Y Dinstein *The Conduct of Hostilities under the Law of International Armed Conflict* (2nd edn CUP, Cambridge 2010).
J M Farrall *United Nations Sanctions and the Rule of Law* (CUP, Cambridge 2007).
E H Feilchenfeld *The International Economic Law of Belligerent Occupation* (Carnegie Endowment for International Peace, Washington 1942).
R Fisk *In Time of War: Ireland, Ulster and the Price of Neutrality 1939–1945* (Paladin, London 1983).
T M Franck *Recourse to Force: State Action Against Threats and Armed Attacks* (CUP, Cambridge 2002).
J Gardam *Necessity, Proportionality and the Use of Force by States* (CUP, Cambridge 2004).
J W Garner *International Law and the World War* (Longmans, Green and Co, London 1920).
G von Glahn *The Occupation of Enemy Territory: A Commentary on the Law and Practice of Belligerent Occupation* (University of Minnesota Press, Minneapolis 1957).
L M Goodrich and A P Simons *The United Nations and the Maintenance of International Peace and Security* (Greenwood Press, Westport 1955).
L M Goodrich et al *Charter of the United Nations: Commentary and Documents* (3rd edn Columbia UP, New York 1969).
C Gray *International Law and the Use of Force* (3rd edn OUP, Oxford 2008).
L C Green *The Contemporary Law of Armed Conflict* (3rd edn, Manchester UP, Manchester 2008).
M Greenspan *The Modern Law of Land Warfare* (University of California Press, Berkeley 1959).
W Grewe, *The Epochs of International Law* (M Byers (ed and tr)) (Walter de Grutyer 2000).
F Grob *The Relativity of War and Peace: A Study in Law, History and Politics* (Yale University Press, New Haven 1949).
W E Hall *The Rights and Duties of Neutrals* (Longmans, Green and Co, London 1874).
W E Hall (A P Higgins (ed)) *International Law: A Treatise* (8th edn Clarendon Press, Oxford 1924).
W H von Heinegg (ed) *Methods and Means of Combat in Naval Warfare: Report & Commentaries of the Round-Table of Experts on International Humanitarian Law Applicable to Armed Conflicts at Sea* (Bochumer Schriften 8, Universitätsverlag Brockmeyer, Bochum 1992).
J-M Henckaerts and L Doswald-Beck (eds) *Customary International Humanitarian Law* vol I (CUP, Cambridge 2005).
A P Higgins *The Hague Peace Conferences and Other International Conferences Concerning the Laws and Usages of War: Texts of Conventions With Commentaries* (Cambridge University Press, Cambridge 1909).
R Higgins, *United Nations Peacekeeping 1946–1967: Documents and Commentary* vol II (OUP, Oxford 1970).
R Higgins *Problems and Process: International Law and How We Use It* (OUP, Oxford 1994).
W I Hull *The Two Hague Conferences And Their Contributions to International Law* (Ginn & Company, Boston 1908).
H Kelsen *Collective Security and International Law* (US Government Printing Office, Washington DC 1955).
H Kelsen (R W Tucker (ed)) *Principles of International Law* (2nd edn Holt, Rinehart and Winston, New York 1967).
D Kimel *From Promise to Contract: Towards a Liberal Theory of Contract* (Hart, Oxford 2003).

G R Kleinfeld and L A Tambs *Hitler's Spanish Legion: The Blue Division in Russia* (Southern Illinois University Press, London 1979).
J Köpfer Die *Neutralität im Wandel der Erscheinungsformen militärischer Auseinandersetzungen* (München 1975)
E Lauterpacht et al (eds) *The Kuwait Crisis: Basic Documents* (Cambridge International Documents Series I, Grotius, Cambridge 1991).
T J Lawrence *The Principles of International Law* (2nd edn Macmillan, London 1895).
T J Lawrence *The Principles of International Law* (5th edn D C Heath and Co, Boston 1910).
T J Lawrence, *War and Neutrality in the Far East* (Macmillan and Co 1904)
R Lemkin *Axis Rule in Occupied Europe* (Carnegie Endowment for International Peace, Washington 1944).
H S Levie *The Code of International Armed Conflict* vol II (Oceana Publications, London 1986).
J Lorimer *Institutes of the Law of Nations: A Treatise of the Jural Relations of Separate Political Communities: Volume II* (William Blackwood and Sons, Edinburgh 1884).
V Lowe *International Law* (OUP, Oxford 2007).
W Lowrie and M St Clair Clarke (eds) *American State Papers: Documents, Legislative and Executive, of the Congress of the United States, from the First Session of the First to the Second Session of the Twenty-Second Congress, Inclusive* vol I (Gales and Seaton, Washington 1833).
H Mahajan *Arms Transfer to India, Pakistan and the Third World* (Young Asia Publications, New Delhi 1981).
A D McNair (ed) *International Law Opinions* vol III (CUP, Cambridge 1956).
A D McNair and A Watts *The Legal Effects of War* (4th edn CUP, Cambridge 1966).
N Melzer *Targeted Killing in International Law* (OUP, Oxford 2008).
N Melzer *Interpretative Guidance on the Notion of Direct Participation in Hostilities under International Humanitarian Law* (ICRC 2009).
H Meyrowitz *Le principe de l'égalité des belligérants devant le droit de la guerre* (Éditions A Pedone, Paris 1970).
A Montefiore (ed) *Neutrality and Impartiality: The University and Political Commitment* (CUP, Cambridge 1975).
J B Moore *History and Digest of the International Arbitrations to which the United States has been a Party* vol I (Government Printing Office, Washington DC 1898).
J B Moore *Digest of International Law* vol VII (US Government Printing Office, Washington DC 1907).
S Neff *The Rights and Duties of Neutrals* (Manchester UP, Manchester 2000).
S Neff *War and the Law of Nations: A General History* (CUP, Cambridge 2005).
P J Noel Baker *The Present Juridical Status of the British Dominions in International Law* (Longmans, Green and Co, London 1929).
E Nys *Le droit international, les principes, les théories, les faits* vol II (1st edn, A Castaigne, Brussels 1906).
D P O'Connell *International Law: Volume 1* (2nd edn Stevens & Sons, London 1970)
D P O'Connell *The Influence of Law on Seapower* (Manchester UP, Manchester 1975).
D P O'Connell (I A Shearer (ed)) *The International Law of the Sea: Volume II* (Clarendon Press, Oxford 1984).
P Okowa *State Responsibility for Transboundary Air Pollution in International Law* (OUP, Oxford 2000).
L Oppenheim *International Law—A Treatise* vol II (1st edn Longmans, London 1906).
L Oppenheim (H Lauterpacht (ed)) *International Law—A Treatise* vol II (7th edn Longmans, London 1952).

L Oppenheim (R F Roxburg (ed)) *International Law—A Treatise* vol II (3rd edn Longmans, London 1921).
N Ørvik *The Decline of Neutrality 1914–1941* (2nd edn Frank Cass, London 1971).
J Pauwelyn *Conflict of Norms in Public International Law: How WTO Law Relates to other Rules of International Law* (CUP, Cambridge 2003).
J S Pictet (ed) *Commentary I: Geneva Convention for the Amelioration of the Condition of the Wounded and Sick in Armed Forces in the Field* (ICRC, Geneva 1952) 32.
J S Pictet (ed) *Commentary IV: Geneva Convention Relative to the Protection of Civilian Persons in Time of War* (ICRC, Geneva 1958).
E Rauch *The Protocol Additional to the Geneva Conventions for the Protection of Victims of International Armed Conflicts and the United Nations Convention on the Law of the Sea: Repercussions on the Law of Naval Warfare* (Duncker & Humblot, Berlin 1984).
J Raz *The Morality of Freedom* (Clarendon Press, Oxford 1986).
A Roberts and D Zaum *Selective Security: War and the United Nations Security Council since 1945* (Adelphi Paper 395, Routledge, Abingdon 2008).
J F L Ross *Neutrality and International Sanctions: Sweden, Switzerland and Collective Security* (Praeger, New York 1989).
T C Salmon *Unneutral Ireland: An Ambivalent and Unique Security Policy* (Clarendon Press, Oxford 1989).
Y Sandoz et al (eds) *Commentary on the Additional Protocols of 8 June 1977 to the Geneva Conventions of 12 August 1949* (Martinus Nijhoff, Geneva 1987).
D Sarooshi *The United Nations and the Development of Collective Security: The Delegation by the UN Security Council of its Chapter VII Powers* (Clarendon Press, Oxford 1999).
O Schachter *International Law in Theory and Practice* (Martinus Nijhoff, Dordrecht 1991).
C Schmitt *The* Nomos *of the Earth in the International Law of the* Jus Publicum Europaeum (G L Ulmen (tr)) (Telos Press, New York 2003).
G Schwarzenberger *International Law as Applied by International Courts and Tribunals* vol II (Stevens & Sons, London 1968).
J B Scott *The Hague Peace Conferences of 1899 and 1907: Volume I* (Johns Hopkins, Baltimore 1909).
J B Scott (ed) *Resolutions of the Institute of International Law* (Carnegie Endowment of International Peace, Washington D C 1916).
F Seyersted *United Nations Forces in the Law of Peace and War* (A W Sijthoff, Leiden 1966).
M N Shaw *International Law* (6th edn CUP, Cambridge 2008).
I A Shearer *Starke's International Law* (11th edn Butterworths, London 1994).
G Simpson *Great Powers and Outlaw States: Unequal Sovereigns in the International Legal Order* (CUP, Cambridge 2004).
H A Smith (ed) *Great Britain and the Law of Nations: Volume I—States* (P S King & Son, London 1932).
J M Spaight *Air Power and War Rights* (3rd edn Longmans, Green and Co, London 1947).
Stockholm International Peace Research Institute (SIPRI) (F T Blackaby et al) (eds) *The Arms Trade with the Third World* (Almqvist & Wiksell, Stockholm 1971).
J Stone, *Legal Controls of International Conflict* (Maitland Publications, Sydney 1959).
N Stürchler *The Threat of Force in International Law* (CUP, Cambridge 2007).
S Takahashi *International Law Applied to the Russo-Japanese War* (Banks Law Publishing, New York 1908).
S Talmon *Recognition of Governments in International Law: With Particular Reference to Governments in Exile* (Clarendon Press, Oxford 1998)
R W Tucker *The Law of War and Neutrality at Sea* (US Government Printing Office, Washington 1957).

T Twiss *The Law of Nations Considered as Independent Political Communities: On the Rights and Duties of Nations in Time of War* (2nd edn Clarendon Press, Oxford 1875).
E de Vattel *The Law of Nations* (J Chitty (tr)) (T & J Johnson & Co, Philadephia 1863).
J H W Verzijl *International Law in Historical Perspective: Part IX-B The Law of Neutrality* (Sijthoff & Noordhoff, Alphen Aan Den Rijn 1979).
C de Visscher *Theory and Reality in Public International Law* (P E Corbett (tr)) (PUP, Princeton 1957).
J Westlake *International Law* (CUP, Cambridge 1907).
E de Wet *The Chapter VII Powers of the United Nations Security Council* (Hart, Oxford 2004).
H Wheaton *Elements of International Law* (Carey, Lea and Blanchard, Philadelphia 1836).
H Wheaton (R H Dana (ed)) *Elements of International Law* (8th edn Little, Brown, Boston 1866).
C F Wicker *Neutralisation* (OUP, London 1911)
Z Yihdego *The Arms Trade and International Law* (Hart, Oxford 2007).

2. Articles

L M Alexander 'International Straits' in H B Robertson Jr (ed) *The Law of Naval Operations* (International Law Studies 64, US Naval War College, Newport 1991) 91.
C D Allin 'The Neutrality of British Dominions' (1922) 20 Mich LR 819.
C D Allin 'Proposals for the Neutrality of the British Colonies' (1922) 37 PSQ 415.
C F Amerasinghe 'The Charter *Travaux Préparatoires* and United Nations Powers to Use Armed Force' (1966) 4 CYIL 81.
S Amin 'The Iran-Iraq War: Legal Implications' (1982) 6 MP 193.
Anonymous 'The Hague Conventions and the Neutrality of Belgium and Luxemburg' (1915) 9 AJIL 959.
Anonymous 'The Sale of Munitions of War' (1915) 9 AJIL 927.
Anonymous 'The Present Position of "Neutral" States (1947) 1 ILQ 212.
Anonymous 'The Security Council and the Suez Canal' (1952) 1 ICLQ 85.
Anonymous 'International Law and Military Operations Against Insurgents in Neutral Territory' (1968) 68 Col LR 1127.
Y Arai-Takahashi 'Disentangling Legal Quagmires: The Legal Characterisation of the Armed Conflicts in Afghanistan Since 6/7 October 2001 and the Question of Prisoner of War Status' (2002) 5 YBIHL 61.
J Astley III and M N Schmitt 'The Law of the Sea and Naval Operations' (1997) 42 AFLR 119.
S D Bailey 'Cease-Fires, Truces, and Armistices in the Practice of the UN Security Council' (1977) 71 AJIL 461.
T Baty 'Abuse of Terms: "Recognition"; "War"' (1936) 30 AJIL 377.
I Baudisch 'Case Note' (2006) 100 AJIL 911.
R R Baxter 'So-Called "Unprivileged Belligerency": Spies, Guerillas, and Saboteurs' (1951) 28 BYBIL 323.
R R Baxter 'Passage of Ships Through International Waterways in Time of War' (1954) 31 BYBIL 187.
R R Baxter 'The Legal Consequences of the Unlawful Use of Force Under the Charter' (1968) 62 PAS 68.
M A Becker 'The Shifting Public Order of the Oceans: Freedom of Navigation and the Interdiction of Ships at Sea' (2005) 46 HILJ 131.

D J Bederman 'The Feigned Demise of Prize' (1995) 9 EILR 31.
C Bell 'Peace Agreements: Their Nature and Legal Status' (2006) 100 AJIL 373.
M Berdal 'The Security Council and Peacekeeping' in V Lowe et al (eds) *The United Nations Security Council and War: The Evolution of Thought and Practice since 1945* (OUP, Oxford 2008) 175.
F Berman 'The Authorisation Model: Resolution 678 and Its Effects' in D Malone (ed) *The UN Security Council: From the Cold War to the 21st Century* (Boulder, Lynne Rienner 2004) 153.
N Berman 'Privileging Combat? Contemporary Conflict and the Legal Construction of War' (2004–2005) 43 CJTL 1.
R Bernhardt 'Article 103' in B Simma et al (eds) *The Charter of the United Nations: A Commentary* (2nd edn OUP, Oxford 2002) 1292.
N Bhuta 'States of Exception: Regulating Targeted Killing in a "Global Civil War"' in P Alston and E MacDonald (eds) *Human Rights, Intervention and the Use of Force* (OUP, Oxford 2008) 243.
J P Bialke 'United Nations Peace Operations: Applicable Norms and the Application of the Law of Armed Conflict' (2001) 50 AFLR 1.
R Bierzanek 'Commentary to the 1923 Hague Rules for Aerial Warfare' in N Ronzitti (ed) *The Law of Naval Warfare: A Collection of Agreements and Documents with Commentaries* (Martinus Nijhoff, Dordrecht 1988) 396.
R Bindschedler 'Neutrality, Concept and General Rules' in R Bernhardt (ed) *Encyclopedia of Public International Law: Volume III* (Elsevier, Amsterdam 1997) 549.
T Bingham 'The Alabama Claims Arbitration' (2005) 54 ICLQ 1.
W R Bisschop 'The *Altmark*' (1940) 26 TGS 67.
H Blix 'When are the Laws of War and Neutrality Applicable?' (1976) 32 REDI 125.
B A Boczek 'Permanent Neutrality and Collective Security: The Case of Switzerland and the United Nations Sanctions Against Southern Rhodesia' (1969) 1CWRJIL 73.
B A Boczek 'Law of Warfare at Sea and Neutrality: Lessons from the Gulf War' (1989) 20 ODIL 239.
B A Boczek 'Peaceful Purposes of the United Nations Convention on the Law of the Sea' (1989) 20 ODIL 359.
E M Borchard 'Restatement of the Law of Neutrality in Maritime War' (1928) 22 AJIL 614.
E Borchard 'Neutrality' (1938) 48 YLJ 37.
E Borchard 'The Attorney General's Opinion on the Exchange of Destroyers for Naval Bases' (1940) 34 AJIL 690.
E Borchard 'Was Norway Delinquent in the Case of the Altmark?'(1940) 34 AJIL 289.
M Bothe 'Commentary on the 1977 Additional Protocol I' in N Ronzitti (ed) *The Law of Naval Warfare: A Collection of Agreements and Documents with Commentaries* (Martinus Nijhoff, Dordrecht 1988) 760.
M Bothe 'Neutrality in Naval Warfare: What is Left of Traditional International Law?' in A J M Delissen and G J Tanja (eds) *Humanitarian Law of Armed Conflict: Challenges Ahead: Essays in Honour of Frits Kalshoven* (Martinus Nijhoff, Dordrecht 1991) 387.
M Bothe 'Neutrality at Sea' in I F Dekker and H H G Post (eds) *The Gulf War of 1980–1988* (Martinus Nijhoff, Dordrecht 1992) 205.
M Bothe 'Comments' in H H G Post (ed) *International Economic Law and Armed Conflict* (Martinus Nijhoff, Dordrecht 1994) 35.
M Bothe 'The Law of Neutrality' in D Fleck (ed) *The Handbook of International Humanitarian Law* (2nd edn OUP, Oxford 2008) 571.
J Boulden 'Mandates Matter: An Exploration of Impartiality in United Nations Operations' (2005) 11 GG 147.

K Boustany 'Brocklebank: a Questionable Decision of the Court Martial Appeal Court of Canada' (1998) 1 YIHL 371.
J L Brierly 'Sanctions' (1931) 17 TGS 67.
H W Briggs 'Neglected Aspects of the Destroyer Deal' (1940) 34 AJIL 569.
O Bring 'Commentary on the 1938 Stockholm Declaration' in N Ronzitti (ed) *The Law of Naval Warfare: A Collection of Agreements and Documents* (Martinus Nijhoff, Dordrecht 1988) 839.
O Bring 'Comments' in I F Dekker and H H G Post (eds) *The Gulf War of 1980–1988* (Martinus Nijhoff, Dordrecht 1992) 243.
N Brown 'Panel III Commentary – Maritime and Coalition Operations' in F L Borch and P S Wilson (eds) *International Law and the War on Terror* (International Law Studies 79, US Naval War College, Newport 2003) 303.
T D Brown Jr 'World War Prize Law Applied in a Limited War Situation: Egyptian Restrictions on Neutral Shipping with Israel' (1965–1966) 50 Minn LR 849.
I Brownlie 'Volunteers and the Law of War and Neutrality' (1956) 5 ICLQ 570.
I Brownlie 'Review of S R Chowdhury, *Military Alliances and Neutrality in War and Peace*' (1968) 16 ICLQ 832.
I Brownlie and C J Apperley 'Kosovo Crisis Inquiry: Memorandum on the International Law Aspects' (2000) 49 ICLQ 878.
F Bugnion 'Guerre juste, guerre d'aggression et droit international humanitaire' (2002) 84 IRRC 523.
H Bull 'The Grotian Conception of International Society' in K Anderson and A Hurrell (eds) *Hedley Bull on International Society* (Macmillan, Basingstoke 2000) 95.
H Burmester 'The Recruitment and Use of Mercenaries in Armed Conflict' (1978) 72 AJIL 37.
A S de Bustamente 'The Hague Convention Concerning the Rights and Duties of Neutral Powers and Persons in Land Warfare' (1908) 2 AJIL 95.
N Butler 'From Collective Defence to Peace Enforcement' in A Schnabel and R Thakur (eds) *Kosovo and the Challenge of Humanitarian Intervention* (United Nations University Press, Tokyo 2000) 273.
E Cannizzaro 'Contextualising Proportionality: *Jus ad Bellum* and *Jus in Bello* in the Lebanese War' (2006) 88 IRRC 779.
G E Carlisle 'The Interrelationship of International Law and United States Naval Operations in Southeast Asia' (1967–1968) 22 JAGJ 8.
L Caruana and H Rockoff 'A Wolfram in Sheep's Clothing: Economic Warfare in Spain, 1940-1944' (2003) 63 JEH 100.
J Carver and J Hulsmann 'The Role of Article 50 of the UN Charter in the Search for International Peace and Security' (2000) 49 ICLQ 528.
A Cavaglieri 'Belligeranza, Neutralità e Posizioni Giuridiche Intermedie' (1919) 13 RDI 58.
S Chesterman 'Neutrality and its Discontents' (Swiss Security Policy Hearings 2009) < http://www.sipol09.ethz.ch/Transkriptionen/Ausland/Prof.-Simon-Chesterman> accessed 12 December 2009.
C Chinkin 'The Legality of NATO's Action in the Former Republic of Yugoslavia (FRY) under International Law' (2000) 49 ICLQ 910.
B A Clark 'Recent Evolutionary Trends Concerning Naval Interdiction of Seaborne Commerce as a Viable Sanctioning Device' (1972–1973) 27 JAGJ 160.
H McD Clokie 'The British Dominions and Neutrality' (1940) 34 APSR 737.
G S Corn 'Making the Case for Conflict Bifurcation in Afghanistan: Transnational Armed Conflict, al Qaida and the Limits of the Associated Militia Concept' in M N Schmitt (ed) *The War in Afghanistan: A Legal Analysis* (International Law Studies 85, US Naval War College, Newport 2009) 181.

O Corten 'Les arguments avancés par la Belgique pour justifier son soutien aux Etats-Unis dans le cadre de la guerre contre l'Irak' (2005) 38 RBDI 417.

P Cronin 'Panel III Commentary – Maritime and Coalition Operations' in F L Borch and P S Wilson (eds) *International Law and the War on Terror* (International Law Studies 79, US Naval War College, Newport 2003) 301.

W Czapliński and G Danilenko 'Conflicts of Norms in International Law' (1990) 21 NYIL 3.

J G Dalton 'The Influence of Law on Seapower in Desert Shield/Desert Storm' (1993) 41 Naval LR 27.

E David 'La guerre du Golfe et le droit international' (1987) 23 RBDI 153.

G Dehn 'The Effect of the United Nations Charter on the Development of International Law with Special Reference to the Status on Neutrality and the Hague and Geneva Conventions' in International Law Association Report of the Forty-First Conference (Cambridge 1946) (International Law Association, Cambridge 1946) 39.

D Detwiler 'Spain and the Axis in World War II' (1971) 33 JOP 36.

S Dinitz 'The Legal Aspects of the Egyptian Blockade of the Suez Canal' (1956–1957) 45 Geo LJ 169.

Y Dinstein 'The Laws of Neutrality' (1984) 14 IYHR 80.

Y Dinstein 'Legitimate Military Objectives Under the Current *Jus in Bello*' in A E Wall (ed) *Legal and Ethical Lessons of NATO's Kosovo Campaign* (International Law Studies 78, US Naval War College, Newport 2002) 139.

Y Dinstein 'The Interaction Between Customary International Law and Treaties' (2006) 322 RCADI 243.

Y Dinstein 'Distinction and Loss of Civilian Protection in International Armed Conflicts' in M D Carsten (ed) *International Law and Military Operations* (International Law Studies 84, US Naval War College, Newport 2008) 183.

K Dörmann 'The Legal Situation of "Unlawful/Unprivileged Combatants"' (2003) 85 IRRC 45.

L Doswald-Beck, 'The International Law of Naval Armed Conflicts: the Need for Reform' (1986–1987) 7 IYIL 251.

L Dubouis 'L'embargo dans la pratique contemporaine' (1967) 13 AFDI 99.

K Duff 'Spain Between the Allies and the Axis' in A Toynbee and V M Toynbee (eds) *Survey of International Affairs 1939–1946: the War and the Neutrals* (OUP, London 1956) 256.

C Eagleton 'The Attempt to Define War' (1932–1933) 15 Int Conc 233.

C Eagleton 'The Duty of Impartiality on the Part of a Neutral' (1940) 34 AJIL 99.

M Evans 'The Restoration of Diplomatic Relations between Argentina and the United Kingdom' (1991) 40 ICLQ 473.

J D Falconbridge 'The Right of a Belligerent to Make War Upon a Neutral' (1918) 4 TGS 204.

B Fassbender 'The United Nations Charter as Constitution of the International Community' (1998) 36 CJTL 529.

W J Fenrick 'Legal Aspects of the Falklands Naval Conflict' (1985) 24 RDPM 243.

W J Fenrick 'The Exclusion Zone Device in the Law of Naval Warfare' (1986) 24 CYIL 91.

W J Fenrick 'Intervention' (1987) 26 RDPM 137.

C G Fenwick 'War Without a Declaration' (1937) 31 AJIL 694.

C G Fenwick '"The Old Order Changeth, Yielding Place to New"' (1953) 47 AJIL 84.

C G Fenwick 'Is Neutrality Still a Term of Present Law?' (1969) 63 AJIL 100.

L E Fielding 'Maritime Interception: Centrepiece of Economic Sanctions in the New World Order' (1992–1993) 53 *Louisiana LR* 1191.

J E Fink 'The Gulf of Aqaba and the Strait of Tiran: The Practice of "Freedom of Navigation" After the Egyptian-Israeli Peace Treaty' (1995) 42 Nav LR 121.
G G Fitzmaurice 'Some Aspects of Modern Contraband Control and the Law of Prize' (1945) 22 BYBIL 73.
G Fitzmaurice 'The General Principles of International Law Considered from the Standpoint of the Rule of Law' (1957-II) 92 RCADI 1, 7.
D Flint 'Neutrality and the Iraqui-Iran War' (1984) AILN 47.
T M Franck and F Patel 'UN Police Action in Lieu of War: "The Old Order Changeth"' (1991) 85 AJIL 63.
T M Franck 'On Proportionality of Countermeasures in International Law' (2008) 102 AJIL 715.
H Freudenschuß 'Between Unilateralism and Collective Security: Authorisations of the Use of Force by the UN Security Council' (1994) 5 EJIL 492.
W Friedmann 'The Growth of State Control over the Individual and its Effect upon the Rules of International State Responsibility' (1938) 19 BYBIL 118.
J A Frowein 'Legal Consequences for International Law Enforcement in Case of Security Council Inaction' in J Delbrück (ed) *The Future of International Law Enforcement: New Scenarios—New Law?* (Duncker & Humblot, Berlin 1993) 111.
J A Frowein 'Reactions by Not Directly Affected States to Breaches of Public International Law' (1994) 248 RCADI 345.
J A Frowein and N Krisch 'Article 2(5)' in B Simma et al (eds) *The Charter of the United Nations: A Commentary* (2nd edn OUP, Oxford 2002) 136.
J A Frowein and N Krisch 'Article 39' in B Simma et al (ed) *The Charter of the United Nations: A Commentary* (2nd edn OUP, Oxford 2002) 717.
J A Frowein and N Krisch 'Article 43' in B Simma et al (eds) *The Charter of the United Nations: A Commentary* vol 1 (2nd edn OUP, Oxford 2002) 760.
J G Gardam 'Proportionality and Force in International Law' (1993) 87 AJIL 391.
J G Gardam 'A Role for Proportionality in the War on Terror' (2005) 74 NJIL 3.
J W Garner 'Some True and False Conceptions Regarding the Duty of Neutrals in Respect to the Sale and Exportation of Arms and Munitions to Belligerents' (1916) 10 PAS 18.
J W Garner 'Proposed Rules for the Regulation of Aerial Warfare' (1924) 18 AJIL 56.
C Garraway 'The Use and Abuse of Military Manuals' (2004) 7 YIHL 425.
C Garraway 'To Kill or Not to Kill? – Dilemmas on the Use of Force' (2010) 14 JCSL 499.
H-P Gasser 'Protection of the Civilian Population' in D Fleck (ed) *The Handbook of International Humanitarian Law* (2nd edn OUP, Oxford 2008) 237.
P Gautier 'General Participation Clause (Clausula si omnes)' IV *MPEPIL* (2006) 368.
G Ginsburgs 'The Soviet Union as a Neutral 1939-1941' (1958) 10 *Soviet Studies* 12.
G Ginsburgs 'The Soviet Union, the Neutrals and International Law in World War II' (1962) 11 ICLQ 171.
A Gioia 'Neutrality and Non-Belligerency' in H H G Post (ed) *International Economic Law and Armed Conflict* (Martinus Nijhoff, Dordrecht 1994) 51.
A Gioia 'Neutrality in Air Warfare' in N Ronzitti and G Venturini (eds) *The Law of Air Warfare: Contemporary Issues* (Eleven International Publishing, Utrecht 2006) 181.
A Gioia and N Ronzitti 'The Law of Neutrality: Third States' Commercial Rights and Duties' in I F Dekker and H H G Post (eds) *The Gulf War of 1980–1988* (Martinus Nijhoff, Dordrecht 1992) 221.
R Goodman 'The Detention of Civilians in Armed Conflict' (2009) 103 AJIL 48.
V Gowlland-Debbas 'Security Council Enforcement Action and Issues of State Responsibility' (1994) 43 ICLQ 55.

V Gowlland-Debbas 'The Functions of the United Nations Security Council in the International Legal System' in M Byers (ed) *The Role of Law in International Politics: Essays in International Relations and International Law* (OUP, Oxford 2000) 277.
C Gray 'The British Position with Regard to the Gulf Conflict' (1988) 37 ICLQ 420.
C Gray 'The British Position with Regard to the Gulf Conflict (Iran-Iraq): Part 2' (1991) 40 ICLQ 464.
C Gray, 'After the Ceasefire: Iraq, the Security Council and the Use of Force' (1994) 65 BYBIL 135.
C Gray 'The Eritrea/Ethiopia Claims Commission Oversteps its Boundaries: A Partial Award?' (2006) 17 EJIL 699.
C Gray 'The Charter Limitations on the Use of Force: Theory and Practice' in V Lowe et al (eds) *The United Nations Security Council and War: The Evolution of Thought and Practice Since 1945* (OUP, Oxford 2008) 86.
L C Green 'The Nature of the "War" in Korea' (1951) 4 ILQ 462.
J A Green 'The Oil Platforms Case: An Error in Judgment?' (2004) 9 JCSL 357.
C Greenwood 'The Relationship Between *Ius ad Bellum* and *Ius in Bello*' (1983) 9 RIS 221.
C Greenwood 'The Concept of War in International Law' (1987) 36 ICLQ 283.
C Greenwood 'Remarks' (1988) 82 PAS 146.
C Greenwood 'Self-Defence and the Conduct of International Armed Conflict' in Y Dinstein (ed) *International Law in a Time of Perplexity: Essays in Honour of Shabtai Rosenne* (Martinus Nijhoff, Dordrecht 1989) 273.
C Greenwood 'Comments' in I F Dekker and H H G Post (eds) *The Gulf War of 1980–1988* (Martinus Nijhoff, Dordrecht 1992) 212.
C Greenwood 'New World Order or Old? The Invasion of Kuwait and the Rule of Law' (1992) 55 MLR 153.
C Greenwood 'The Effects of the United Nations Charter on the Law of Naval Warfare' in W H von Heinegg (ed) *Visit, Search, Diversion and Capture: the Effect of the United Nations Charter on the Law of Naval Warfare* (Bochumer Shriften Band 24, Universitätsverlag Brockmayer, Bochum 1995) 133.
C Greenwood 'Protection of Peacekeepers: The Legal Regime' (1996) 7 DJCIL 185.
C Greenwood 'International Humanitarian Law and United Nations Military Operations' (1998) 1 YBIHL 3.
C Greenwood 'Remarks' in A E Wall (ed) *Legal and Ethical Lessons of NATO's Kosovo Campaign* (International Law Studies 78, US Naval War College, Newport 2002) 127.
C Greenwood 'The Applicability of International Humanitarian Law and the Law of Neutrality to the Kosovo Campaign' in A E Wall (ed) *Legal and Ethical Lessons of NATO's Kosovo Campaign* (International Law Studies 78, US Naval War College, Newport 2003) 35.
C Greenwood 'Scope of Application of Humanitarian Law' in D Fleck (ed) *The Handbook of International Humanitarian Law* (2nd edn OUP, Oxford 2008) 45.
C N Gregory 'Neutrality and the Sale of Arms' (1916) 10 AJIL 543.
L Gross 'Passage Through the Suez Canal of Israeli-Bound Cargo and Israeli Ships' (1957) 51 AJIL 530.
G Hägglöf 'A Test of Neutrality: Sweden in the Second World War' (1960) 36 IA 153.
J W Halderman 'Legal Basis for United Nations Armed Forces' (1962) 56 AJIL 971.
'Commentary' (Remarks of T Halkiopoulos) (1987–1988) 14 SJILC 581.
F Hampson 'Belligerent Reprisals and the 1977 Protocols to the Geneva Conventions of 1949' (1988) 37 ICLQ 818.
L Heffeman and A Whelan 'Ireland, the United Nations and the Gulf Conflict: Legal Aspects' (1991) 3 ISIA 115.

G J F van Hegelsom 'Methods and Means of Combat in Naval Warfare' in W H von Heinegg (ed) *Methods and Means of Combat in Naval Warfare: Report & Commentaries of the Round-Table of Experts on International Humanitarian Law Applicable to Armed Conflicts at Sea* (Bochumer Schriften Band 8, Universitätsverlag Brockmeyer, Bochum 1992) 1.

W H von Heinegg 'Visit, Search, Diversion and Capture in Naval Warfare: Part II, Developments Since 1945' (1992) 30 CYIL 89.

W H von Heinegg 'The Current State of International Prize Law' in H H G Post (ed) *International Economic Law and Armed Conflict* (Martinus Nijhoff, Dordrecht 1994) 5.

W H von Heinegg 'The Law of Naval Warfare and International Straits' in L C Green and M N Schmitt (eds) *The Law of Armed Conflict: Into the Next Millennium* (International Law Studies 71, US Naval War College, Newport 1998) 263.

W H von Heinegg 'Naval Blockade' in M N Schmitt and A R Thomas (eds) *International Law Across the Spectrum of Conflict: Essays in Honour of Professor L C Green on the Occasion of his Eightieth Birthday* (International Law Studies 75, US Naval War College, Newport 2000) 203.

W H von Heinegg, 'Factors in War to Peace Transitions' (2003–2004) 27 HJLPP 843.

W H von Heinegg 'The United Nations Convention on the Law of the Sea and Maritime Security Operations' (2005) 48 GYIL 151.

W H von Heinegg 'Current Legal Issues in Maritime Operations: Maritime Interception Operations in the Global War on Terrorism, Exclusion Zones, Hospital Ships and Maritime Neutrality' in R B Jaques (ed) *Issues in International Law and Military Operations* (International Law Studies 80, US Naval War College, Newport 2006) 207.

W H von Heinegg 'The Current State of the Law of Naval Warfare: A Fresh Look at the *San Remo Manual*' in A M Helm (ed) *The Law of War in the 21st Century: Weaponry and the Use of Force* (International Law Studies 82, US Naval War College, Newport 2006) 269.

W H von Heinegg '"Benevolent" Third States in International Armed Conflicts: The Myth of the Irrelevance of the Law of Neutrality' in M N Schmitt and J Pejic (eds) *International Law and Armed Conflict: Exploring the Faultlines* (Martinus Nijhoff, Leiden 2007) 543.

W H von Heinegg 'The Law of Armed Conflict at Sea' in D Fleck (ed) *The Handbook of International Humanitarian Law* (2nd edn OUP, Oxford 2008) 475.

W H von Heinegg 'Manoeuvring in Rough Waters: The UK Manual of the Law of Armed Conflict and the Law of Naval Warfare' in A Fischer-Lescano et al (eds) *Frieden in Freiheit: Festschrift für Michael Bothe zum 70. Geburtstag* (Nomos Verlag, Baden-Baden 2008) 427.

W H von Heinegg 'International Economic Relations and Armed Conflict' in A de Guttry, H H G Post and G Venurini (eds) *The 1998–2000 War Between Eritrea and Ethiopia: An International Legal Perspective* (TMC Asser Press, The Hague 2009) 371.

W H von Heinegg and M Donner 'New Developments in the Protection of the Natural Environment in Naval Armed Conflicts' (1994) 37 GYIL 281.

E Hernàndez-Sandioca and E Moradiellos 'Spain and and the Second World War 1939–1945' in N Wylie (ed) *European Neutrals and Non-Belligerents During the Second World War* (CUP, Cambridge 2002) 246.

A S Hershey 'Some Questions of International Law Arising from the Russo-Japanese War I: Failure to Declare War and Alleged Violation of Korean Neutrality' (1904) 16 GB 306.

A S Hershey 'Some Questions of International Law Arising from the Russo-Japanese War II: The Hay Note and Chinese Neutrality' (1904) 16 GB 375.

J A Hessbruegge 'The Historical Development of the Doctrines of Attribution and Due Diligence in International Law' (2004) 36 NYUJILP 265.

F C Hicks 'The Equality of States and the Hague Conferences' (1908) 2 AJIL 530.
R Higgins 'Legal Limits to the Use of Force by Sovereign States: United Nations Practice' (1961) 37 BYBIL 269.
R Higgins, 'The June War: the United Nations and Legal Background' (1968) 3 JCH 253.
R Higgins 'The New United Nations and the Former Yugoslavia' (1993) 69 IA 465.
S E Hilton 'Argentine Neutrality, September, 1939 – June, 1940: A Re-Examination' (1966) 22 The Americas 227.
A H Hudson 'Effect on Commercial law of Non-Declaration of War' in P Rowe (ed) *The Gulf War of 1990 in International and English Law* (Routledge, London 1993) 333.
D R Humphrey 'Belligerent Interdiction of Neutral Shipping in International Armed Conflict' (1997) 2 JCSL 23.
A Hurrell 'Collective Security and International Order Revisited' (1992) 11 *Int Relations* 37.
S Hurwitz 'Was Denmark at War?' (1945) 16 NT 49.
C C Hyde 'The Hague Convention Respecting the Rights and Duties of Neutral Powers in Naval War' (1908) 2 AJIL 507.
C C Hyde 'The *City of Flint*' (1940) 34 AJIL 89.
K Ipsen 'Combatants and Non-Combatants' in D Fleck (ed) *The Handbook of International Humanitarian Law* (2nd edn OUP, Oxford 2008) 79.
R H Jackson 'Address by Robert H Jackson, Attorney General of the United States, Inter-American Bar Association, Havana, Cuba, March 27, 1941' (1941) 35 AJIL 348.
M Janis 'Neutrality' in H B Robertson Jr (ed) *The Law of Naval Operations* (International Law Studies 64, US Naval War College, Newport 1991) 148.
M Jenkins 'Air Attacks on Neutral Shipping in the Persian Gulf: The Legality of the Iraqi Exclusion Zone and Iranian Reprisals' (1985) 8 BCICLR 517.
R Y Jennings 'The Caroline and Mcleod Cases' (1938) 32 AJIL 82.
R Y Jennings 'Government in Commission' (1946) 23 BYBIL 112.
P Jessup 'Should International Law Recognise an Intermediate Status Between Peace and War?' (1954) 48 AJIL 98.
P Joenniemi 'Models of Neutrality: The Traditional and Modern' (1988) 23 CC 53.
D Jinks 'Protective Parity and the Laws of War' (2003–2004) 79 NDLR 1493.
T D Jones 'The International Law of Maritime Blockade – A Measure of Naval Economic Interdiction' (1983) 26 How LJ 759.
J Kammerhofer 'Oil's Well that Ends Well? Critical Reflections on the Merits Judgement in the *Oil Platforms* Case'(2004) 17 LJIL 695.
E Karsh 'International Co-operation and Neutrality' (1988) 25 JPR 57.
J E Kastenberg 'Non-Intervention and Neutrality in Cyberspace: An Emerging Principle in the National Practice of International Law' (2009) 64 AFLR 43.
S Kaye 'Freedom of Navigation in a Post 9/11 World: Security and Creeping Jurisdiction' in D Freestone, R Barnes and D M Ong (eds) *The Law of the Sea: Progress and Prospects* (OUP, Oxford 2006) 347.
D Kennedy 'International Law and the Nineteenth Century: History of an Illusion' (1997–1998) 17 QLR 99.
D Kimel 'Neutrality, Autonomy and Freedom of Contract' (2001) 21 OJLS 473.
H Kirchoff 'Denmark, September 1939-April 1940' in N Wylie (ed) *European Neutrals and Non-Belligerents in the Second World War* (CUP, Cambridge 2002) 34.
F L Kirgis 'NATO Interdiction of Oil Tankers' *ASIL Insights* (April 1999) <http://www.asil.org/insigh33.cfm> accessed 10 December 2009.
A Kiss (ed) *Répertoire de la pratique française en matière de droit international public vol VI* (Éditions CNRS, Paris 1969).

R Kolb 'Does Article 103 of the Charter of the United Nations Apply only to Decisions or also to Authorisations Adopted by the Security Council?' (2004) 64 ZaöRV 21.

T Komarnicki 'The Place of Neutrality in the Modern System of International Law' (1952–I) 80 RCADI 399.

T Komarnicki 'The Problem of Neutrality under the United Nations Charter' (1953) 38 TGS 77.

D Kritsiotis 'The Kosovo Crisis and NATO's Application of Armed Force against the Federal Republic of Yugoslavia' (2000) 49 ICLQ 330.

D Kritsiotis 'Topographies of Force' in M N Schmitt and J Pejic (eds) *International Law and Armed Conflict: Exploring the Faultlines* (Maritnus Nijhoff, Leiden 2007) 29.

J L Kunz 'Neutrality and the European War 1939-1940' (1941) 39 Mich LR 719.

J L Kunz 'British Prize Cases, 1939-1941' (1942) 36 AJIL 204.

J L Kunz 'The Position of Argentina' (1944) 38 AJIL 436.

J L Kunz 'The Geneva Conventions of August 12, 1949' in G A Lipsky (ed) *Law and Politics in the World Community: Essays on Hans Kelsen's Pure Theory and Related Problems in International Law* (University of California Press, Berkeley 1953) 283.

J L Kunz 'The Laws of War' (1956) 50 AJIL 313.

E Kussbach 'L'évolution de la notion de neutralité dans les conflits armés actuels: rapport général' (1978) 17 RDPM 19.

E Kussbach 'Le protocole additionnel I et les états neutres' (1980) 62 IRRC 231.

P J Kuyper 'Community Sanctions Against Argentina: Lawfulness under Community and International Law' in D O'Keeffe and H G Schermers (eds) *Essays in European Law and Integration* (Kluwer, Deventer 1982) 141.

P J Kwast 'Maritime Interdiction of Weapons of Mass Destruction in an International Legal Perspective' (2007) 38 NYIL 163.

R Lagoni 'Remarks' (1988) 82 PAS 161.

J F Lalive 'International Organisation and Neutrality' (1947) 24 BYBIL 73.

E Lauterpacht 'The Legal Irrelevance of the "State of War"' (1968) 62 PAS 58.

E Lauterpacht 'The Legal Irrelevance of the "State of War"' (1968) 62 PAS 58.

H Lauterpacht '"Resort to War" and the Interpretation of the Covenant During the Manchurian Dispute' (1934) 28 AJIL 43.

H Lauterpacht 'The Problem of the Revision of the Law of War' (1952) 29 BYBIL 360.

H Lauterpacht 'The Limits of the Operation of the Law of War' (1953) 30 BYBIL 206.

H Lauterpacht 'Memorandum on the Principles of International Law Governing the Question of Aid to the Allies by the United States, 15 January 1941' in E Lauterpacht (ed) *International Law: Being the Collected Papers of Hersch Lauterpacht* vol V (CUP, Cambridge 2004) 645.

H Lauterpacht 'The Future of Neutrality, December 1941' in E Lauterpacht (ed) *International Law: Being the Collected Papers of Hersch Lauterpacht* vol V (CUP, Cambridge 2004) 675.

R Leckow 'The Iran-Iraq Conflict in the Gulf: The Law of War Zones' (1988) 37 ICLQ 629.

P Leroy 'L'affaire de l'« Attiliò Regolo » et autres navires' (1965) 11 AFDI 278.

H Levie 'The Nature and Scope of the Armistice Agreement' (1956) 50 AJIL 880.

R Liivoja 'The Scope of the Supremacy Clause of the United Nations Charter' (2008) 57 ICLQ 583.

V Lowe 'The Impact of the Law of the Sea on Naval Warfare' (1987–1988) 14 SJILC 657.

A V Lowe 'The Laws of War at Sea and the 1958 and 1982 Conventions' (1988) 12 MP 286.

A V Lowe 'Self-Defence at Sea' in W E Butler (ed) *The Non-Use of Force in International Law* (Martinus Nijhoff, Dordrecht 1989) 185.

A V Lowe 'The Commander's Handbook on the Law of Naval Operations and the Contemporary Law of the Sea' in H B Robertson Jr (ed) *The Law of Naval Operations* (International Law Studies 64, US Naval War College, Newport 1991) 109.
A V Lowe 'United Kingdom: Commentary' in A De Guttry and N Ronzitti (eds) *The Iran-Iraq War (1980–1988) and the Law of Naval Warfare* (Grotius Publications, Cambridge 1993) 241.
V Lowe 'International Legal Issues Arising in the Kosovo Crisis' (2000) 49 ICLQ 934.
E C Luck 'A Council for All Seasons: The Creation of the Security Council and its Relevance Today' in V Lowe et al (eds) *The United Nations Security Council and War: The Evolution of Thought and Practice since 1945* (OUP, Oxford 2008) 61.
N Lupi 'Report of the Enquiry Commission on the Behaviour of Italian Peace-keeping Troops in Somalia' (1998) 1 YIHL 375.
S Lyons 'Naval Operations in the Gulf' in P Rowe (ed) *The Gulf War in International and English Law* (Routledge, London 1993) 155.
B MacChesney 'The Altmark Incident and Modern Warfare – "Innocent Passage" in Wartime and the Right of Belligerents to Use Force to Redress Neutrality Violations' (1957–1958) 52 *Northwestern ULR* 320.
S Mahmoudi 'Passage of Warships Through the Strait of Hormuz' (1991) 15 MP 338.
A Mayama 'The Influence of the Straits Transit Regime on the Law of Neutrality at Sea' (1995) 26 ODIL 1.
M S McDougal 'Peace and War: Factual Continuum with Multiple Legal Consequences' (1955) 49 AJIL 63.
R McLaughlin 'United Nations Mandated Naval Interdiction Operations in the Territorial Sea?' (2002) 51 ICLQ 249.
A D McNair 'The Legal Meaning of War, and the Relation of War to Reprisals' (1925) 11 TGS 29.
R McNamara 'Britain, Nasser and the Outbreak of the Six Day War' (2000) 35 JCH 619.
F Mehr, 'Neutrality in the Gulf War' (1989) 20 ODIL 105.
F Messineo 'The House of Lords in *Al-Jedda* and Public International Law: Attribution of Conduct to UN-Authorised Forces and the Power of the Security to Displace Human Rights' (2009) 56 NILR 35.
H Meyrowitz 'Le Protocole Additionnel I aux Conventions de Genève de 1949 et le droit de la guerre maritime' (1985) 89 RGDIP 243.
H Meyrowitz 'La guerre du Golfe et le droit des conflits armés' (1992) 96 RGDIP 551.
M Milanović 'Norm Conflict in International Law: Whither Human Rights?' (2009) 20 DJCIL 69.
M Milanović 'A Norm Conflict Perspective on the Relationship Between International Humanitarian Law and Human Rights Law' (2010) 14 JCSL 459.
B Møller 'The Nordic Countries: Whither the West's Conscience?' in A Schnabel and R Thakur (eds) *Kosovo and the Challenge of Humanitarian Intervention* (United Nations University Press, Tokyo 2000) 151.
D Momtaz 'Iran: Commentary' in A De Guttry and N Ronzitti (eds) *The Iran-Iraq War (1980–1988) and the Law of Naval Warfare* (Grotius Publications, Cambridge 1993) 19.
J N Moore 'Legal Dimensions of the Decision to Intercede in Cambodia' (1971) 65 AJIL 38.
J N Moore 'The Regime of Straits and the Third United Nations Conference on the Law of the Sea' (1980) 74 AJIL 77.
W C Morey 'The Sale of Munitions of War' (1916) 10 AJIL 467.
H J Morgenthau 'The End of Switzerland's "Differential" Neutrality' (1938) 32 AJIL 558
E P J Myjer and N D White 'The Twin Towers Attack: an Unlimited Right to Self-Defence?' (2002) 7 JCSL 5.

S Neff 'Prerogatives of Violence: In Search of the Conceptual Foundations of Belligerents' Rights' (1997) 38 GYIL 41.
P M Norton 'Between the Ideology and the Reality: The Shadow of the Law of Neutrality' (1976) 17 HILJ 249.
D P O'Connell 'International Law and Contemporary Naval Operations' (1970) 44 BYBIL 19.
M E O'Connell 'Defining Armed Conflict' (2008) 13 JCSL 393.
A Orakhelashvili 'The Legal Basis of the United Nations Peace-Keeping Operations' (2002–2003) 43 VJIL 485.
A Orakhelashvili 'The Post-War Settlement in Iraq: the UN Security Council Resolution 1483 (2003) and General International Law' (2003) 8 JCSL 307.
A Orakhelashvili 'The Impact of Peremptory Norms on the Interpretation and Application of United Nations Security Council Resolutions' (2005) 16 EJIL 59.
A Orakhelashvili 'The Power of the UN Security Council to Determine the Existence of a "Threat to the Peace"' (2006) 1 Irish YIL 61.
A Orakhelashvili 'Overlap and Convergence: The Interaction Between *Jus ad Bellum* and *Jus in Bello*' (2007) 12 JCSL 157.
K O'Rourke 'Panel III Commentary – Maritime and Coalition Operations' in F L Borch and P S Wilson (eds) *International Law and the War on Terror* (International Law Studies 79, US Naval War College, Newport 2003) 297.
B H Oxman 'The Regime of Warships Under the United Nations Convention on the Law of the Sea' (1984) 24 VJIL 809.
N J Padelford 'The New Scandinavian Neutrality Rules' (1938) 32 AJIL 789.
N J Padelford 'The United Nations and Korea: A Political Résumé' (1951) 5 IO 685.
W H Parks 'Air War and the Law of War' (1990) 32 AFLR 1.
J J Paust and A P Blaustein 'The Arab Oil Weapon: A Threat to International Peace' (1974) 68 AJIL 410.
A K Pavithran 'The Indo-Pakistan War of 1971' (1972) 3 East JIL 247.
D L Peace 'Major Maritime Events in the Persian Gulf Between 1984 and 1991: A Juridical Analysis' (1990–1991) 31 VJIL 545.
J Peck 'The UN and the Laws of War: How can the World's Peacekeepers be Held Accountable?' (1995) 21 SJILC 283.
J-G Perron 'Panel III Commentary – Maritime and Coalition Operations' in F L Borch and P S Wilson (eds) *International Law and the War on Terror* (International Law Studies 79, US Naval War College, Newport 2003) 309.
G C Petrochilos 'The Relevance of the Concepts of War and Armed Conflict to the Law of Neutrality' (1998) 31 VJTL 575.
R Pisillo-Mazzeschi 'The Due Diligence Rule and the Nature of International Responsibility of States' (1992) 35 GYIL 9.
G P Politakis 'Waging War at Sea: the Legality of War Zones' (1991) 38 NILR 125.
G P Politakis 'Variations on a Myth: Neutrality and the Arms Trade' (1992) 35 GYIL 435.
G P Politakis 'From Action Stations to Action: US Naval Deployment, "Non-Belligerency," and "Defensive Reprisals" in the Final Year of the Iran-Iraq War' (1994) 25 ODIL 31.
G P Politakis 'UN-Mandated Naval Operations and the Notion of Pacific Blockade: Comments on Some Recent Developments' (1994) 6 AJICL 173.
H H G Post 'Some Curiosities in the Sources of the Law of Armed Conflict Conceived in a General International Legal Perspective' (1994) 25 NYIL 83.
L Preuss 'Some Effects of Governmental Controls on Neutral Duties' (1937) 31 PAS 108.
L Preuss 'The Concepts of Neutrality and Non-Belligerency' (1941) 218 AAAPSS 97.
J de Preux 'The Geneva Conventions and Reciprocity' (1985) 244 IRRC 25.

D Raab '"Armed Attack" After the *Oil Platforms* Case' (2004) 17 LJIL 719.

A Randelzhofer 'Article 2(4)' in B Simma et al (eds) *The Charter of the United Nations: A Commentary I* (2nd edn OUP, Oxford 2002) 112.

E Rauch 'Le droit contemporain de la guerre maritime: quelques problèmes créés par le Protocole additionnel I de 1977' (1985) 89 RGDIP 958.

W M Reisman 'The Regime of Straits and National Security: an Appraisal of International Law Making' (1980) 74 AJIL 48.

W M Reisman and W K Lietzau 'Moving International Law from Theory to Practice: The Role of Military Manuals in Effectuating the Law of Armed Conflict' in H B Robertson Jr (ed) *The Law of Naval Operations* (International Law Studies 64, US Naval War College, Newport 1991) 1.

J A Roach 'Missiles on Target: Targeting and Defence Zones in the Tanker War' (1990/1991) 31 VJIL 593.

A Roberts 'What is a Military Occupation?' (1984) 55 BYBIL 249.

A Roberts 'The United Nations and International Security' (1993) 35 *Survival* 3.

A Roberts 'The Laws of War in the 1990-91 Gulf Conflict' (1993/1994) 18 IS 124.

A Roberts 'From San Francisco to Sarajevo: The UN and the Use of Force' (1995) 37 *Survival* 7.

A Roberts 'Counterterrorism and the Laws of War: A Critique of the US Approach' (Address at The Brookings Institution, 11 March 2002) <http://www.brookings.edu/events/2002/0311terrorism.aspx> accessed 21 January 2007.

A Roberts 'The Laws of War in the War on Terror' in F L Borch and P S Wilson (eds) *International Law and the War on Terror* (International Law Studies 79, US Naval War College, Newport 2003) 175.

A Roberts 'Transformative Military Occupation: Applying the Laws of War and Human Rights' (2006) 100 AJIL 580.

A Roberts 'The Equal Application of the Law of War: a Principle under Pressure' (2008) 90 IRRC 931.

A Roberts 'Afghanistan and International Security' in M N Schmitt (ed) *The War in Afghanistan: A Legal Analysis* (International Law Studies 85, US Naval War College, Newport 2009) 3.

H B Robertson Jr 'Commentary' (1987–1988) 14 SJILC 581.

H B Robertson Jr 'The "New" Law of the Sea and the Law of Armed Conflict at Sea' (Newport Paper 3, US Naval War College, Newport 1992).

H B Robertson Jr 'Theatre of Operations in Naval Warfare: Different Maritime Areas' in W H von Heinegg (ed) *Regions of Operations of Naval Warfare: Reports and Commentaries of the Round-Table of Experts on International Humanitarian Law Applicable to Armed Conflicts at Sea* (Bochumer Schriften Band 25, Universitätsverlag Brockmeyer, Bochum 1995), 1.

H B Robertson Jr 'The Principle of the Military Objective in the Law of Armed Conflict' (1997–1998) 8 USAFAJLS 35.

N Ronzitti 'International Supply of Conventional Armaments: Legal Aspects and Implications of the United Nations General Assembly Resolution 42/75 I' (1991) 26 *Int Spectator* 69.

N Ronzitti 'Le droit humanitaire applicable aux conflits armés en mer' (1994) 248 RCADI 9.

N Ronzitti 'Commentary' in A Wall (ed) *Legal and Ethical Lessons of NATO's Kosovo Campaign* (International Law Studies 78, US Naval War College, Newport 2003) 113.

N Ronzitti 'Italy's Non-Belligerency During the Iraqi War' in M Ragazzi (ed) *International Responsibility Today: Essays in Memory of Oscar Schachter* (Martinus Nijhoff, Leiden 2005) 197.

N Ronzitti 'The Codification of Air Warfare' in N Ronzitti and G Venturini (eds) *The Law of Air Warfare: Contemporary Issues* (Eleven International Publishing, Utrecht 2006) 3.

N Ronzitti 'US Military Bases in Italy: In Keeping with International Law? Still Needed?' (2008) 43 *Int Spectator* 79.

A Ross 'Denmark's Legal Status During the Occupation' (1949) 1 *Jus Gentium* 3.

E V Rostow 'Until What? Enforcement Actions of Collective Self-Defence?' (1991) 85 AJIL 506.

S W D Rowson 'Modern Blockade: Some Legal Aspects' (1946) 23 BYBIL 346

S W D Rowson 'Prize Law During the Second World War' (1947) 24 BYBIL 160.

H Rumpf 'Is a Definition of War Necessary?' (1938) 18 BULR 686.

W Sadurski 'Neutrality of Law Towards Religion' (1989–1990) 12 Syd LR 420.

W Sadurski 'Joseph Raz on Liberal Neutrality and the Harm Principle' (1990) 10 OJLS 122.

G Scelle 'Jus in Bello, Jus ad Bellum' in *Varia Juris Gentium: Liber Amicorum Presented to J P A François* (A W Sitjhoff, Leiden 1959) 292.

D Scheffer 'The Security Council and International Law on Military Occupations' in V Lowe et al (eds) *The United Nations Security Council and War: The Evolution of Thought and Practice since 1945* (OUP, Oxford 2008) 580.

D Schindler 'The Different Types of Armed Conflicts According to the Geneva Conventions and Protocols' (1979) 163 RCADI 131.

D Schindler 'State of War, Belligerency, Armed Conflict' in A Cassese (ed) *The New Humanitarian Law of Armed Conflict* (Editoriale Scientifica, Napoli 1979) 1.

D Schindler 'United Nations Forces and International Humanitarian Law' in C Swinarski (ed) *Studies and Essays on International Humanitarian Law* (Martinus Nijhoff, The Hague 1984) 521.

D Schindler 'Commentary on the 1907 Hague Convention XIII Concerning the Rights and Duties of Neutral Powers in Naval War' in N Ronzitti (ed) *The Law of Naval Warfare: A Collection of Agreements and Documents with Commentaries* (Martinus Nijhoff, Dordrecht 1988) 193.

D Schindler 'Transformations in the Law of Neutrality Since 1945' in A J M Delissen and G J Tanja (eds) *Humanitarian Law of Armed Conflict: Challenges Ahead* (Martinus Nijhoff, Dordrecht 1991) 367.

M N Schmitt 'Aerial Blockades in Historical, Legal and Practical Perspective' (1991) 2 USAFAJLS 21.

M N Schmitt '"Change Direction" 2006: Israeli Operations in Lebanon and the International Law of Self-Defence' in M D Carsten (ed) *International Law and Military Operations* (International Law Studies 84, US Naval War College, Newport 2008) 265.

N Schultz 'Was the War on Iraq Illegal? The German Federal Administrative Court's Judgement of 21st June 2005' (2006) 7 Ger LJ 25.

G Schwarzenberger 'The "Aid Britain" Bill and the Law of Neutrality' (1941) 27 TGS 1.

G Schwarzenberger '*Jus Pacis ac Belli?* Prolegomena to a Sociology of International Law' (1943) 37 AJIL 460.

G Schwarzenberger 'Report on Some Aspects of the Principle of Self-Defence in the Charter of the United Nations and the Topics Covered by the Dubrovnik Resolution' in International Law Association Report of the Forty-Eighth Conference (New York, 1958) (International Law Association, New York 1958) 550.

I F I Shihata 'Destination Embargo of Arab Oil: Its Legality Under International Law' (1974) 68 AJIL 591.

D Shraga 'The United Nations as an Actor Bound by International Humanitarian Law' (1998) 5 IP 64.

K Skubiszewski 'Use of Force by States. Collective Security. Law of War and Neutrality' in M Sørensen (ed) *Manual of Public International Law* (Macmillan, London 1968) 739.
R Sloane 'The Cost of Conflation: Preserving the Dualism of *Jus ad Bellum* and *Jus in Bello* in the Contemporary Law of War' (2009) 34 YJIL 47.
H A Smith 'The Government of Occupied Territory' (1944) 21 BYBIL 151.
W A Solf 'Intervention' (1987) 26 RDPM 149.
H A Steiner 'Italian War and Neutrality Legislation' (1939) 33 AJIL 151.
D G Stephens 'The Impact of the 1982 Law of the Sea Convention on the Conduct of Peacetime Naval/Military Operations' (1998–1999) 29 *Cal Western ILJ* 283.
D Stephens 'The Legal Efficacy of Freedom of Navigation Assertions' in R B Jacques (ed) *Issues in International Law and Military Operations* (International Law Studies 80, US Naval War College, Newport 2000) 235.
D G Stephens 'Law of Naval Warfare and Zones' in R Jaques (ed) *Maritime Operational Zones* (US Naval War College, Newport 2006) 4/1.
A Stewart 'The British Government and the South African Neutrality Crisis, 1938-39' (2008) 123 EH Rev 947.
E C Stowell 'The Juridical Significance of World War II' (1944) 38 AJIL 106.
S P Subedi 'Neutrality in a Changing World: European Neutral States and the European Community' (1993) 42 ICLQ 238.
F B Swayze 'Traditional Principles of Blockade in Modern Practice: United States Mining of Internal and Territorial Waters of North Vietnam' (1977) 29 JAGJ 143.
P C Szasz 'UN Forces and International Humanitarian Law' in M N Schmitt (ed) *International Law Across the Spectrum of Conflict: Essays in Honour of Professor L C Green on the Occasion of his Eightieth Birthday* (International Law Studies 75, US Naval War College, Newport 2000) 507.
W Taft IV 'Self-Defence and the *Oil Platforms* Decision' (2004) 29 YJIL 295.
S Talmon 'The Constitutive Versus the Declaratory Theory of Recognition: *Tertium non Datur?*' (2005) 75 BYBIL 101.
C Tams 'The Use of Force Against Terrorists' (2009) 20 EJIL 359.
H J Taubenfeld 'International Armed Forces and the Rules of War' (1951) 45 AJIL 671.
H J Taubenfeld, 'International Actions and Neutrality' (1953) 47 AJIL 377.
J-M Thouvenin 'Circumstances Precluding Wrongfulness in the ILC Articles on State Responsibility: Self-Defence' in J Crawford, A Pellet and S Olleson (eds) *The Law of International Responsibility* (OUP, Oxford 2010) 455.
D Thürer 'UN Enforcement Measures and Neutrality: The Case of Switzerland' (1992) 30 AV 63.
B D Tittemore 'Belligerents in Blue Helmets: Applying International Humanitarian Law to United Nations Peace Operations' (1997) 33 SJIL 61.
J Trappe 'On the Jurisdiction of the Egyptian Prize Court, 1948-1960' (1959–60) 15–16 REDI 60.
K Trapp 'Back to Basics: Necessity, Proportionality, and the Right of Self-Defence against Non-State Terrorist Actors' (2007) 56 ICLQ 141.
R W Tucker 'The Interpretation of War under Current International Law' (1951) 4 ILQ 11.
J S Tulchin 'The Argentine Proposal for Non-Belligerency, April 1940' (1969) 11 Journal of Inter-American Studies 571.
B Urquhart 'Remarks' (1993) 87 PAS 284.
D Vagts 'Switzerland, International Law and World War II' (1997) 91 AJIL 466
A Vandenbosch 'Neutrality and Problems of Peaceful Change' (1936) 30 PAS 129.
A Verdross 'Règles générales du droit international de la paix' (1929) 30 RCADI 279.

A Verdross 'General International Law and the United Nations Charter' (1954) 30 IA 342.
J G Verplaetse, 'The *ius in bello* and Military Operations in Korea 1950-1953' (1963) 23 ZaöRV 679.
M Virally 'Le principe de réciprocité dans le droit international contemporain' (1967) 122 RCADI 3.
C de Visscher 'De la belligérance dans ses rapports avec la violation de la neutralité' (1916) 2 PW 93.
S Vité 'Typology of Armed Conflicts in International Humanitarian Law: Legal Concepts and Actual Situations' (2009) 91 IRRC 69.
M Voelckel 'Faut-il encore déclarer la guerre?' (1991) 37 AFDI 7.
C H M Waldock 'The Release of the *Altmark's* Prisoners' (1947) 24 BYBIL 216.
C H M Waldock 'The Regulation of the Use of Force by Individual States in International Law' (1952) 81 RCADI 451.
W L Walker 'Recognition of Belligerency and Grant of Belligerent Rights' (1937) 23 TGS 177.
G K Walker 'Information Warfare and Neutrality' (2000) 33 VJTL 1079.
G K Walker *The Tanker War 1980–1988: Law and Policy* (International Law Studies 74, US Naval War College, Newport 2000).
G Walker 'Application of the Law of Armed Conflict During Operation Allied Force: Maritime Interdiction and Prisoner of War Issues' in A E Wall (ed) *Legal and Ethical Lessons of NATO's Kosovo Campaign* (International Law Studies 78, US Naval War College, Newport 2003) 85.
C Warbrick 'The Invasion of Kuwait by Iraq' (1991) 40 ICLQ 965.
G Warner 'Review Article: Nixon, Kissinger and the Breakup of Pakistan, 1971' (2005) 81 IA 1097.
K Watkin 'Combatants, Unprivileged Belligerents and Conflicts in the 21st Century' (2003) 69 IDFLR 73.
M Weller 'Peace-Keeping and Peace Enforcement in the Republic of Bosnia and Herzegovina' (1996) 56 ZaöRV 70.
D L Wheeler 'The Price of Neutrality: Portugal, the Wolfram Question, and World War II(II)' (1986) 23(2) *Luso-Brasilian Review* 97.
D L Wheeler 'The Price of Neutrality: Portugal, the Wolfram Question, and World War II' (1986) 23(1) *Luso-Brasilian Review* 107.
N D White and A Abass 'Countermeasures and Sanctions' in M D Evans (ed) *International Law* (2nd edn OUP, Oxford 2006) 509.
W L Williams 'Neutrality in Modern Armed Conflicts: A Survey of the Developing Law' (1980) 90 Mil LR 9.
S Wills 'Military Interventions on Behalf of Vulnerable Populations: the Legal Responsibilities of States and International Organisations Engaged in Peace Support Operations' (2004) 9 JCSL 387.
S Wills 'Occupation Law and Multi-National Operations: Problems and Perspectives' (2006) 77 BYBIL 256.
R Wolfrum 'Reflagging and Escort Operations in the Persian Gulf: an International Law Perspective' (1988–1989) 29 VJIL 387.
R Wolfrum 'Military Activities on the High Seas: What are the Impacts of the UN Convention on the Law of the Sea?' in L C Green and M N Schmitt (eds) *The Law of Armed Conflict: Into the Next Millennium* (International Law Studies 71, US Naval War College, Newport 1998) 501.
M Wood 'The Interpretation of Security Council Resolutions' (1998) 2 MPYBUNL 73.

M Wood 'The UN Security Council and International Law: The Legal Framework of the Security Council' (Hersch Lauterpacht Memorial Lectures, University of Cambridge 2006) (7 November 2006) 19 <http://www.lcil.cam.ac.uk/Media/lectures/pdf/2006_hersch_lecture_1.pdf> accessed 20 December 2006.
Q Wright 'The Outlawry of War' (1925) 19 AJIL 76.
Q Wright 'Project of the American Institute of International Law on Maritime Neutrality (No 26)' (1927) 21 AJIL 127.
Q Wright 'Neutrality and Neutral Rights Following the Pact of Paris for the Renunciation of War' (1930) 24 PAS 79.
Q Wright 'When Does War Exist?' (1932) 26 AJIL 362.
Q Wright, 'The Test of Aggression in the Italo-Ethiopian War' (1936) 30 AJIL 45.
Q Wright 'The Present Status of Neutrality' (1940) 34 AJIL 391.
Q Wright 'The Transfer of Destroyers to Great Britain' (1940) 34 AJIL 680.
Q Wright 'The Outlawry of War and the Law of War' (1953) 47 AJIL 365.
Q Wright 'How Hostilities have Ended: Peace Treaties and Alternatives' (1970) 392 *Annals of the American Academy of Political and Social Science* 51.
K Zemanek 'Neutrality in Land Warfare' in R Bernhardt (ed) *Encyclopedia of Public International Law: Volume III* (Elsevier, Amsterdam 1997) 555.
A Zimmermann 'The Second Lebanon War: *Jus ad Bellum, Jus in Bello* and the Issue of Proportionality' (2007) 11 MPYBUNL 99.

3. Newspapers and broadcasts

J W Finney 'US Seeks to Hold a Neutral Stance' *New York Times* (New York, 6 June 1967) 1.
'Israel Claims Land and Air Successes as Britain and US Declare Neutrality' *Guardian* (London 6 June 1967) <http://www.guardian.co.uk/fromthearchive/story/0,,1680910,00.html> accessed 3 March 2007.
SWB (1971) Part 1 Second Series SU/3864 (14 December 1971) (SU/3864/A3/2).
'Bonn Bids US Halt Arms to Israel via Germany' *New York Times* (New York, 25 October 1973) 20.
L Gelb 'US Jets for Israel Took Route Around Some Allies' *New York Times* (New York, 25 October 1973) 1.
H Smith 'Moscow Exhibits Tension, But No Intent to Intervene' *New York Times* (New York, 26 October 1973) 1.
A Shuster 'Europeans Irked by US Complaint' *New York Times* (New York, 30 October 1973) 14.
R Koven 'French Jets Delivered to Iraqis' *Washington Post* (Washington DC 2 February 1981).
'Iran Calls Kuwaiti Attitude on Seized Ship Provocative' *AP* (5 May 1981).
M Tran 'China Role in War Worries US/Reagan Administration Calls on Peking to Confirm Neutrality in Iran-Iraq Conflict' *Guardian* (London 27 August 1986).
'Rafsanjani News Conference Iran's Neutrality; Iraqi planes; Relations with USA' SWB (London, 5 February 1991).
'War in the Gulf; India Says It Will Withdraw US Planes' Refueling Right' *New York Times* (New York, 18 February 1991).
'War in the Gulf; Refueling of Jets in India to Stop' *New York Times* (New York, 20 February 1991).
J Gettleman, 'Ethiopia Hits Somali Targets, Declaring War' *New York Times* (New York 25 December 2006) <http://www.nytimes.com/2006/12/25/world/africa/25somalia.html?

ex=1324702800&en=76137f5021bdfbb8&ei=5088&partner=rssnyt&emc=rss> accessed 26 December 2006.

'US Volunteers Join Kosovo Rebels' *BBC News* (London 20 April 1999) < http://news.bbc.co.uk/1/hi/world/europe/323739.stm> accessed 27 January 2007.

'Russia to Ignore NATO Embargo' *BBC News* (London, 25 April 1999) < http://news.bbc.co.uk/1/hi/world/europe/327498.stm> accessed 9 December 2009.

'Turning Off Serbia's Oil Supply' *BBC News* (London 29 April 1999) < http://news.bbc.co.uk/1/hi/world/europe/330589.stm> accessed 9 December 2009.

S Castle 'War in the Balkans: Embargo – NATO Sidesteps Oil Stand-off With Russia' *The Independent* (London 1 May 1999) < http://www.independent.co.uk/news/war-in-the-balkans-embargo—nato-sidesteps-oil-standoff-with-russia-1090613.html?cmp=ilc-n> accessed 9 December 2009.

'Weapons Ship Mystery Deepens' *BBC News* (London 10 January 2002) <http://news.bbc.co.uk/1/hi/world/middle_east/1753233.stm> accessed 20 July 2009.

'Israel Imposes Lebanon Blockade' *BBC News* (London 13 July 2006) < http://news.bbc.co.uk/1/hi/5175160.stm> accessed 10 June 2008.

H M Fattah and S Erlanger 'Israel Blockades Lebanon; Wide Strikes by Hezbollah' *New York Times* (New York 14 July 2006) < http://www.nytimes.com/2006/07/14/world/middleeast/14mideast.html> (accessed 12 November 2006).

'Israel Declares Ceasefire in Gaza' *BBC News* (London 18 January 2009) <http://news.bbc.co.uk/1/hi/world/middle_east/7835794.stm> accessed 18 January 2009.

T Buck, D Dombey and D Strauss 'Israel Condemned After Flotilla Attack' *Financial Times* (London 31 May 2010) < http://www.ft.com/cms/s/0/b09c57f6-6c80-11df-91c8-00144feab49a.html?ftcamp=rss> accessed 2 June 2010.

'Deaths as Israeli Forces Storm Gaza Aid Ship' *BBC News* (London 31 May 2010) <http://www.bbc.co.uk/news/10195838> accessed 1 June 2010.

C Lynch 'Israel's Flotilla Raid Revives Questions of International Law' *Washington Post* (Washington DC 1 June 2010) < http://www.washingtonpost.com/wp-dyn/content/article/2010/06/01/AR2010060102934.html?hpid=topnews> accessed 2 June 2010.

A Hirsch 'Was the Gaza Flotilla Raid Legal?' *Guardian* (London 1 June 2010) <http://www.guardian.co.uk/law/afua-hirsch-law-blog/2010/jun/01/gaza-freedom-flotilla-international-law> accessed 2 June 2010.

A Pfeffer and A Harel 'IDF Preparing for Forceful Interception of Libya-sponsored Aid Ship Bound for Gaza' *Haaretz* (Tel Aviv 13 July 2010) < http://www.haaretz.com/print-edition/news/idf-preparing-for-forceful-interception-of-libya-sponsored-aid-ship-bound-for-gaza-1.301557> accessed 14 July 2010.

B Ravid 'Foreign Ministry Advises IDF: Don't Stop Gadhafi Ship Until it Approaches Gaza Waters' *Haaretz* (Tel Aviv 13 July 2010) < http://www.haaretz.com/print-edition/news/foreign-ministry-advises-idf-don-t-stop-gadhafi-ship-until-it-approaches-gaza-waters-1.301561> accessed 14 July 2010.

4. Reports, conference papers and Conference Proceedings

1. Non-Governmental Organizations

(a) International Law Association

British Maritime Law Committee 'Report' in International Law Association Report of the Twenty-Ninth Conference (Portsmouth, 1920) (International Law Association, Portsmouth 1920) 165.

Neutrality Committee 'Report of the Neutrality Committee' in International Law Association Report of the Thirty-Seventh Conference (International Law Association, Oxford 1932) 159.

Committee on Maritime Neutrality 'Final Report' International Law Association Report of the Sixty-Eighth Conference (Taipei 1998) (International Law Association, Taipei 1998) 496.

Committee on the Use of Force 'Initial Report on the Meaning of Armed Conflict in International Law' International Law Association Report of the Seventy-Third Conference (Rio de Janeiro, 2008) (International Law Association, 2008) 814.

Committee on the Use of Force 'Draft Final Report on the Meaning of Armed Conflict in International Law' (The Hague 2010) (International Law Association, 2010) 1 < http://www.ila-hq.org/en/committees/draft-committee-reports-the-hague-2010.cfm> accessed 15 August 2010.

(b) Institute of International Law

Institut de droit international 'Les lois de la guerre sur terre. Manuel publié par l'Institut de droit international' (1881–1882) 5 *Annuaire* 157.

(c) International Commission of Jurists

'General Report of the Commission of Jurists at The Hague Part II: Rules of Aerial Warfare' (1923) 17 AJILS 245.

(d) Other

Conference of Government Experts on the Reaffirmation and Development of International Humanitarian Law Applicable in Armed Conflicts: Second Session 3 May -3 June 1972: Report on the Work of the Conference Volume I (ICRC, Geneva 1972).

Official Records of the Diplomatic Conference on the Reaffirmation and Development of International Humanitarian Law Applicable in Armed Conflicts, Geneva 1974–1977: Vol III (Federal Political Department, Berne 1978) (CDDH/45).

Official Records of the Diplomatic Conference on the Reaffirmation and Development of International Humanitarian Law Applicable in Armed Conflicts, Geneva 1974–1977: Volume VI (Federal Political Department, Bern 1978) (CDDH/SR.42).

Official Records of the Diplomatic Conference on the Reaffirmation and Development of International Humanitarian Law Applicable in Armed Conflicts, Geneva 1974–1977: Vol XI (Federal Political Department, Berne 1978) (CDDH/II/SR.20).

'The Chatham House Principles of International Law on the Use of Force in Self-Defence' (2006) 55 ICLQ 963.

'Committee on Study of Legal Problems of the United Nations "Should the Laws of War Apply to United Nations Enforcement Action?"' (1952) 46 PAS 216, 220.

'Committee for the Protection of Human Life in Armed Conflicts: Law of Naval Warfare' 26 (1988) RDPM 11, 49–50.

The Proceedings of the Hague Peace Conferences: Translation of the Official Texts—The Conference of 1907 5 vols (OUP, New York 1920–1921).

Harvard Research on International Law 'Harvard Draft Convention on Rights and Duties of Neutral States in Naval and Aerial War' (1939) AJILS 167.

Harvard Research on International Law 'Draft Convention on Rights and Duties of States in Case of Aggression' (1939) 33 AJILS 819.

Harvard Program on Humanitarian Policy and Conflict Research *Manual on International Law Applicable to Air and Missile Warfare* (Harvard, 2009).

Institute of International Humanitarian Law *San Remo Manual on International Law Applicable to Armed Conflicts at Sea* (San Remo, 1994).

Human Rights Watch *White Flag Deaths: Killings of Palestinian Civilians During Operation Cast Lead* (August 2009) 51 <http://www.hrw.org/en/reports/2009/08/13/white-flag-deaths> accessed 2 September 2009.

Independent International Fact-Finding Mission on the Conflict in Georgia *Report: Volume II* (September 2009) 229 <http://www.ceiig.ch/Report.html> accessed 3 November 2009.

2. States

(a) Australia

Australian Law Reform Commission 'Criminal Admiralty Jurisdiction and Prize' (ALRC Report 48, Canberra 1990).

(b) European Union

Commission (EC) 'Protection of the Environment in Times of Armed Conflict: Report Established by a Study Group (Bothe, Cassese, Kalshoven, Kiss, Salmon and Simmonds)' (1984).

(c) Switzerland

Switzerland Federal Department of Foreign Affairs 'White Paper on Neutrality: Annex to the Report on Swiss Foreign Policy for the Nineties' (29 November 1993) < http://www.eda.admin.ch/etc/medialib/downloads/edazen/topics/intla/cintla.Par.0027.File.tmp/White_Paper_on_Neutrality.en.pdf> accessed 20 August 2007.

Switzerland Federal Department of Foreign Affairs 'Swiss Neutrality in Practice Current Aspects: Report of the Interdepartmental Working Group of 30 August 2000' (30 August 2000) <http://www.eda.admin.ch/eda/en/home/topics/intla/cintla/ref_neutr.html> accessed 21 December 2006.

Swiss Federal Department of Foreign Affairs 'Neutrality under Scrutiny in the Iraq Conflict: Summary of Switzerland's Neutrality Policy during the Iraq Conflict' (2 December 2005) <http://www.eda.admin.ch/eda/en/home/topics/intla/cintla/ref_neutr.html> accessed 21 January 2007.

(d) UK

Select Committee on the Constitution 'Waging War: Parliament's Role and Responsibility: Volume I' HL (2005–2006).

(e) US

'United States: Secretary of Defence Report (Weinberger Report) to the Congress on Security Arrangements in the Persian Gulf' (1987) 26 ILM 1433.

'United States: Department of Defence Report to Congress on the Conduct of the Persian Gulf War - Appendix on The Role of the Law of War' (1992) 31 ILM 612.

5. Military Handbooks and Manuals

1. Australia

Australia *Law of Armed Conflict Commander's Guide* (ADFP 37 Supp 1—Interim Edition (1994)).

Australia *Operations Law for RAAF Commanders* (AAP 1003) (2nd edn 2004).

2. Canada

Canada JAG *Law of Armed Conflict at the Operational and Tactical Levels* (2nd edn 2003).

3. France

France Ministry of Defence *Manuel de droit des conflits armés* (Ministère de la Defense, Paris 2001).

4. Germany

Germany Federal Ministry of Defence *Humanitarian Law in Armed Conflict Manual* (English Edition) (Triservice Manual ZDv 15/2) (1992).

5. Italy

Italy *Elementary Rules of Armed Conflict Manual (Regole Elementari di Diritto di Guerra)* (1991).

6. New Zealand

New Zealand Directorate of Legal Services *Interim Law of Armed Conflict Manual* (DM 112) (1992).

7. Sweden

Sweden *International Humanitarian Law in Armed Conflict with Reference to the Swedish Total Defence System* (1991).

8. UK

UK Ministry of Defence *Manual of the Law of Armed Conflict* (OUP, Oxford 2004).

UK *The Law of War on Land, being Part III of the Manual of Military Law* (HMSO, London 1958).

9. US

US *Operational Law Handbook* (2009).

US Department of the Navy *Naval Commander's Handbook* (NWP 1-14M) (2007).

US Department of the Navy *Law of Naval Warfare Manual* (NWIP 10–2) (1955).

US Department of the Army *The Law of Land Warfare* (FM 27–10) (US War Office, Washington DC 1956).

6. Treaties

Declaration of Paris (signed 16 April 1856) 115 CTS 1.

Treaty for an Amicable Settlement of All Causes of Differences between the United States and Great Britain (adopted 8 May 1871, entered into force 17 June 1871) 143 CTS 145.

Hague Convention II with Respect to the Laws and Customs of War on Land and its Annex: Regulations concerning the Laws and Customs of War on Land (signed 29 July 1899, entered into force 4 September 1900) 187 CTS 429.

Convention III Relative to the Opening of Hostilities (adopted 18 October 1907, entered into force 26 January 1910) 205 CTS 264 (HC III).

Hague Convention V Respecting the Rights and Duties of Neutral Powers and Persons in Case of War on Land (signed 18 October 1907, entered into force 26 January 1910) 205 CTS 299 (HC V).

Hague Convention XIII Concerning the Rights and Duties of Neutral Powers in Naval War (signed 18 October 1907, entered into force 26 January 1910) 205 CTS 395 (HC XIII).

Declaration Concerning the Laws of Naval War (signed 26 February 1909) 208 CTS 338.

Protocol for the Prohibition of the Use in War of Asphyxiating, Poisonous or Other Gases, and of Bacteriological Methods of Warfare (signed 17 June 1925, entered into force 8 February 1928) 94 LNTS 65.
Convention on Maritime Neutrality (Signed on 20 February 1928, entered into Force 12 January 1931) 135 LNTS 187.
Treaty Providing for the Renunciation of War as an Instrument of National Policy (adopted 27 August 1928, entered into force 24 July 1929) 94 LNTS 57.
Declaration Regarding Similar Rules of Neutrality (signed 27 May 1938) 188 LNTS 294.
United Nations Charter (adopted 26 June 1945, entered into force 24 October 1945) 1 UNTS xvi.
Geneva Convention I for the Amelioration of the Condition of the Wounded and Sick in Armed Forces in the Field (adopted 12 August 1949, entered into force 21 October 1950) 75 UNTS 31 (GC I).
Geneva Convention II for the Amelioration of the Condition of Wounded, Sick and Shipwrecked Members of Armed Forces at Sea (adopted 12 August 1949, entered into force 21 October 1950) 75 UNTS 85 (GC II).
Geneva Convention III Relative to the Treatment of Prisoners of War (adopted 12 August 1949, entered into force 21 October 1950) 75 UNTS 135 (GC III).
Geneva Convention IV Relative to the Protection of Civilian Persons in Time of War (adopted 12 August 1949, entered into force 21 October 1950) 75 UNTS 287 (GC IV).
General Armistice Agreement Between Israel and Egypt (1949) 42 UNTS 251.
General Armistice Agreement Between Israel and Lebanon (1949) 42 UNTS 287.
General Armistice Agreement Between Israel and Jordan (1949) 42 UNTS 303.
General Armistice Agreement Between Israel and Syria (1949) 42 UNTS 327.
Convention on the Territorial Sea and the Contiguous Zone (adopted 29 April 1958, entered into force 10 September 1964) 516 UNTS 205.
The Antarctic Treaty (adopted 1 December 1959, entered into force 23 June 1961) 402 UNTS 71.
Vienna Convention on the Law of Treaties (adopted 23 May 1969, entered into force 27 January 1980) 1155 UNTS 331.
Geneva Protocol I Additional to the Geneva Conventions of 12 August 1949, and Relating to the Protection of Victims of International Armed Conflicts (adopted 8 June 1977, entered into force 7 December 1978) 1125 UNTS 3.
United Nations Convention on the Law of the Sea (adopted 10 December 1982, entered into force 16 November 1994) 1833 UNTS 3 (LOSC).

7. United Nations Documents

1. International Law Commission

ILC Yearbook of the International Law Commission (1949) YBILC (1949) 51.
ILC Yearbook of the International Law Commission (1979) Volume II
ILC Yearbook of the International Law Commission (1980) Volume II
ILC 'Report of the International Law Commission on the Work of its 32nd Session' (5th May–25th July 1980) UN Doc A/35/10.
ILC 'Second Report on State Responsibility by Mr James Crawford, Special Rapporteur: Addendum' (30 April 1999) UN Doc A/CN.4/498, Add.2.
ILC 'Report of the International Law Commission on the Work of its 53rd Session' (23 April–10 August 2001) UN Doc A/56/10.

ILC 'The Effect of Armed Conflict on Treaties: An Examination of Practice and Doctrine: Memorandum by the Secretariat' (1 February 2005) UN Doc A/CN.4/550.
ILC 'First Report on the Effect of Armed Conflict on Treaties by Mr Ian Brownlie, Special Rapporteur' (25 April 2005) UN Doc A/CN.4/552.
ILC 'Fragmentation of International Law: Report of the Study Group of the International Law Commission' (13 April 2006) UN Doc A/CN.4/L.682.

2. UN Secretary-General

'An Agenda for Peace: Preventive Diplomacy, Peacemaking and Peace-Keeping' (17 June 1992) UN Doc A/47/277.
'Further Report of the Secretary-General Pursuant to Security Council Resolution 721' (5 January 1992) UN Doc S/23363.
'Supplement to An Agenda for Peace: Position Paper of the Secretary-General on the Occasion of the Fiftieth Anniversary of the United Nations' (25 January 1995) UN Doc A/50/60-S/1995/1.
'UN Secretary-General's Bulletin: Observance by United Nations Forces of International Humanitarian Law' (6 August 1999) UN Doc ST/SGB/1999/13.
'Report of the Panel on United Nations Peace Operations' (21 August 2000) UN Doc A/55/305-S/2000/809.
'Report of the Secretary-General on the Implementation of Security Council Resolution 1701 (2006)' (28 June 2007) UN Doc S/2007/392.

3. UN Security Council

(a) Resolutions

UNSC Res 82 (25 June 1950) UN Doc S/1501.
UNSC Res 83 (27 June 1950) UN Doc S/1511.
UNSC Res 84 (7 July 1950) UN Doc S/1588.
UNSC Res 95 (1 September 1951) UN Doc S/2322.
UNSC Res 161 (21 February 1961) UN Doc S/4741.
UNSC Res 232 (16 December 1966) SCOR Resolutions and Decisions 7.
UNSC Res 502 (3 April 1982) SCOR Resolutions and Decisions 15.
UNSC Res 540 (31 October 1983) SCOR Resolutions and Decisions 6.
UNSC Res 552 (1 June 1984) SCOR Resolutions and Decisions 15.
UNSC Res 612 (9 May 1988) SCOR Resolutions and Decisions 10.
UNSC Res 660 (2 August 1990) SCOR Resolutions and Decisions 19.
UNSC Res 661 (6 August 1990) SCOR Resolutions and Decisions 19.
UNSC Res 665 (25 August 1990) SCOR Resolutions and Decisions 21.
UNSC Res 670 (25 September 1990) SCOR Resolutions and Decisions 24.
UNSC Res 678 (29 November 1990) SCOR Resolutions and Decisions 27.
UNSC Res 687 (3 April 1991) SCOR Resolutions and Decisions 11.
UNSC Res 713 (25 September 1991) SCOR Resolutions and Decisions 42.
UNSC Res 727 (8 January 1992) SCOR Resolutions and Decisions 7.
UNSC Res 787 (16 November 1992) UN Doc S/RES/787.
UNSC Res 820 (17 April 1993) UN Doc S/RES/820.
UNSC Res 940 (31 July 1994) UN Doc S/RES/940.
UNSC Res 1160 (31 March 1998) UN Doc S/RES/1160.
UNSC Res 1199 (23 September 1998) UN Doc S/RES/1199.
UNSC Res 1264 (15 September 1999) UN Doc S/RES/1264.
UNSC Res 1296 (19 April 2000) UN Doc S/RES/1296.
UNSC Res 1483 (22 May 2003) UN Doc S/RES/1483

UNSC Res 1484 (30 May 2003) UN Doc S/RES/1484.
UNSC Res 1528 (27 February 2004) UN Doc S/RES/1528.
UNSC Res 1529 (29 February 2004) UN Doc S/RES/1529.
UNSC Res 1776 (19 September 2007) UN Doc S/RES/1776.

(b) Letters

UNSC 'Letter dated 5 May 1970 from the Permanent Representative of the United States of America to the United Nations addressed to the President of the Security Council' (5 May 1970) UN Doc S/9781.

UNSC 'Letter Dated 8 May 1972 from the Permanent Representative of the United States to the United Nations Addressed to the President of the Security Council' (9 May 1972) UN Doc S/10631.

UNSC 'Letter dated 21 October 1980 from the Charge d'affaires of the Permanent Mission of Iran to the United Nations addressed to the Secretary-General' (22 October 1980) UN Doc S/14226.

UNSC 'Note Verbale dated 1 March 1982 from the Permanent Mission of France to the United Nations addressed to the Security Council: Annex Declaration by the French Republic Concerning the Neutrality of Malta' (3 March 1982) UN Doc S/14892.

UNSC 'Letter dated 28 April 1982 from the Permanent Representative of the United Kingdom of Great Britain and Northern Ireland to the United Nations addressed to the President of the Security Council' (28 April 1982) UN Doc S/15006.

UNSC 'Letter Dated 25 May 1984 from the Permanent Representative of the Islamic Republic of Iran to the United Nations Addressed to the Secretary-General' (25 May 1984) UN Doc S/16585.

UNSC 'Letter dated 10 July 1985 from the Permanent Representative of Kuwait to the United Nations Addressed to the Secretary-General' (11 July 1985) UN Doc S/17335.

UNSC 'Letter dated 19 July 1985 from the Permanent Representative of the Islamic Republic of Iran to the United Nations Addressed to the Secretary-General' (22 July 1985) UN Doc S/17348.

UNSC 'Annex to the Letter dated 20 September 1985 from the Permanent Representative of Kuwait to the United Nations Addressed to the Secretary-General' (20 September 1985) UN Doc S/17482.

UNSC 'Letter dated 25 September 1985 from the Permanent Representative of the Islamic Republic of Iran to the United Nations Addressed to the Secretary-General' (25 September 1985) UN Doc S/17496.

UNSC 'Letter Dated 5 January 1987 From the Charge d'affaires A I of the Permanent Mission of the Islamic Republic of Iran to the United Nations Addressed to the Secretary-General' (5 January 1987) UN Doc S/18557.

UNSC 'Letter Dated 12 January 1987 From the Charge d'affaires A I of the Permanent Mission of Kuwait to the United Nations Addressed to the Secretary-General' (12 January 1987) UN Doc S/18582.

UNSC 'Letter Dated 9 April 1987 from the Permanent Representative of the Islamic of Iran to the United Nations Addressed to the Secretary-General' (10 April 1987) UN Doc S/18794.

UNSC 'Letter Dated 29 July 1987 From the Charge d'affaires A I of the Permanent Mission of Kuwait to the United Nations Addressed to the Secretary-General' (29 July 1987) UN Doc S/19005.

UNSC 'Letter Dated 14 August 1987 from the Permanent Representative of the Islamic Republic of Iran to the United Nations Addressed to the Secretary-General' (14 August 1987) UN Doc S/19041.

UNSC 'Letter Dated 1 September 1987 from the Permanent Representative of Kuwait to the United Nations Addressed to the Secretary-General' (1 September 1987) UN Doc S/19093.

UNSC 'Letter Dated 16 October 1987 from the Permanent Representative of Kuwait to the United Nations Addressed to the Secretary-General' (16 October 1987) UN Doc S/19215.

UNSC 'Letter Dated 22 October 1987 from the Permanent Representative of Kuwait to the United Nations Addressed to the Secretary-General' (22 October 1987) UN Doc S/19227.

UNSC 'Letter Dated 6 January 1988 from the Charge d'affaires A I of the Permanent Mission of the Islamic Republic of Iran to the United Nations Addressed to the Secretary-General' (7 January 1988) UN Doc S/19409.

UNSC 'Letter Dated 11 January 1988 from the Charge d'affaires A I of the Permanent Mission of Kuwait to the United Nations Addressed to the Security Council' (11 January 1988) UN Doc S/19417.

UNSC 'Letter Dated 18 April 1988 from the Acting Permanent Representative of the Islamic Republic of Iran to the United Nations Addressed to the Secretary-General' (18 April 1988) UN Doc S/19797.

UNSC 'Letter Dated 20 April 1988 from the Permanent Representative of Kuwait to the United Nations Addressed to the Secretary-General' (20 April 1988) UN Doc S/19811.

UNSC 'Letter Dated 26 April 1988 from the Acting Permanent Representative of the Islamic Republic of Iran to the United Nations Addressed to the Secretary-General' (26 April 1988) UN Doc S/19841.

UNSC 'Letter Dated 28 April 1988 From the Permanent Representative of Kuwait to the United Nations Addressed to the Secretary-General' (24 April 1988) UN Doc S/19849.

UNSC 'Letter Dated 4 May 1988 from the Charge d'affaires A I of the Permanent Mission of the Islamic Republic of Iran to the United Nations Addressed to the Secretary-General' (5 May 1988) UN Doc S/19865.

UNSC 'Letter Dated 9 May 1988 from the Permanent Representative of Kuwait to the United Nations Addressed to the Secretary-General' (9 May 1988) S/19872.

UNSC 'Letter Dated 29 June 1988 From the Acting Permanent Representative of the Islamic Republic of Iran to the United Nations Addressed to the Secretary-General' (29 June 1988) UN Doc S/19971.

UNSC 'Letter dated 7 July 1988 from the Acting Permanent Representative of the Islamic Republic of Iran to the United Nations addressed to the Secretary-General' (11 July 1988) UN Doc S/20003.

UNSC 'Note Verbale dated 7 July 1988 from the Interests Section of the Islamic Republic of Iran in Washington addressed to the Embassy of Algeria in Washington' (15 March 1989) UN Doc S/20525.

UNSC 'Annex: Note Verbale dated 7 July 1988 from the Interests Section of the Islamic Republic of Iran in Washington addressed to the Embassy of Algeria in Washington' (15 March 1989) UN Doc S/20525.

UNSC 'Letter Dated 11 July 1988 From the Charge d'affaires A I of the Permanent Mission of Saudi Arabia to the United Nations Addressed to the Secretary-General' (11 July 1988) UN Doc S/20007.

UNSC 'Letter Dated 14 July 1988 from the Permanent Representative of Kuwait to the United Nations Addressed to the Secretary-General' (14 July 1988) UN Doc S/20015.

UNSC 'Letter dated 15 March 1989 from the Charge d'affaires A I of the Permanent Mission of the Islamic Republic of Iran to the United Nations Addressed to the Secretary-General' (15 March 1989) UN Doc S/20525.

UNSC 'Letter dated 26 July 1989 from the Permanent Representative of the Lao People's Democratic Republic to the United Nations addressed to the Security Council' (26 July 1989) UN Doc S/20751.

UNSC 'Letter Dated 12 August 1990 from the Permanent Representative of Kuwait to the United Nations Addressed to the President of the Security Council' (13 August 1990) UN Doc S/21498.

UNSC 'Letter Dated 15 August 1990 from the Permanent Representative of the Libyan Arab Jamahiriya to the United Nations Addressed to the Secretary-General' (16 August 1990) UN Doc S/21529.

UNSC 'Letter Dated 16 August 1990 from the Charge d'affaires A I of the United States Mission to the United Nations Addressed to the Security Council, 16 August 1990' (16 August 1990) UN Doc S/21537.

UNSC 'Letter Dated 20 August 1990 From the Permanent Representative of Jordan to the United Nations Addressed to the Secretary-General' (20 August 1990) UN Doc S/21571.

UNSC 'Note Verbale Dated 19 August 1990 From the Charge d'affaires A I of the Permanent Mission of the Sudan to the United Nations Addressed to the President of the Security Council' (21 August 1990) UN Doc S/21574.

UNSC 'Letter Dated 23 October 1990 From the Permanent Representative of the Islamic Republic of Iran to the United Nations Addressed to the Secretary-General' (24 October 1990) UN Doc S/21902.

UNSC 'Letter Dated 23 October 1990 From the Permanent Representative of the Islamic Republic of Iran to the United Nations Addressed to the Secretary-General' (24 October 1990) UN Doc S/21903.

UNSC 'Letter Dated 23 October 1990 From the Permanent Representative of the Islamic Republic of Iran to the United Nations Addressed to the Secretary-General' (24 October 1990) UN Doc S/21904.

UNSC 'Letter from the Permanent Representative of the Islamic Republic of Iran to the United Nations addressed to the Secretary-General' (28 January 1991) UN Doc S/22163.

UNSC 'Letter dated 11 November 1998 from the Permanent Representative of Djibouti to the United Nations addressed to the President of the Security Council' (11 November 1998) UN Doc S/1998/1062.

UNSC 'Letter dated 19 November 1998 from the Permanent Representative of Eritrea to the United Nations addressed to the President of the Security Council' (19 November 1998) UN Doc S/1998/1097.

UNSC 'Letter dated 20 November 1998 from the Permanent Representative of Djibouti to the United Nations addressed to the President of the Security Council' (20 November 1998) UN Doc S/1998/1107.

UNSC 'Letter dated 7 October 2001 from the Permanent Representative of the United States of America to the United Nations addressed to the President of the Security Council' (7 October 2001) UN Doc S/2001/946.

(c) Meeting Records

UN Verbatim Record (4 August 1949) SCOR Resolutions and Decisions 26.

UNSC Verbatim Record (7 September 1950) SCOR Resolutions and Decisions 9.

UNSC Verbatim Record (25 February 1979) SCOR Resolutions and Decisions 9.

UNSC Verbatim Record (25 May 1984) UN Doc S/PV.2541.

UNSC Verbatim Record (25 May 1984) UN Doc S/PV.2542.

UNSC Verbatim Record (29 May 1984) UN Doc S/PV.2543.

UNSC Verbatim Record (30 May 1984) UN Doc S/PV.2545.

UNSC Verbatim Record (1 June 1984) UN Doc S/PV.2546.

UNSC Verbatim Record (29 November 1990) UN Doc S/PV.2963 33.

UNSC Verbatim Record (31 March 1998) UN Doc S/PV.3868 10.

UNSC Verbatim Record (19 September 2007) UN Doc S/PV.5744.

4. UN General Assembly

UNGA Res 2625 (XXV) 'Annex: Declaration on Principles of International Law concerning Friendly Relations and Co-operation among States in Accordance with the Charter of the United Nations' (24 October 1970) UN Doc A/8028.

UNGA Res 3314 (XXIX) 'Annex: Definition of Aggression' (14 December 1974) UN Doc A/9890.

UNGA 'Annex: Draft Model Agreement Between the United Nations and Member States Contributing Personnel and Equipment to the United Nations Peace-Keeping Operations' (23 May 1991) UN Doc A/46/185.

UNGA Res 46/182 (19 December 1991) UN Doc A/RES/46/182.

UNGA 'Report of the Special Committee on the Charter of the United Nations and on the Strengthening of the Role of the Organisation: Implementation of the Provisions of the Charter of the United Nations related to Assistance to Third States affected by the Application of Sanctions under Chapter VII of the Charter' (22 August 1995) UN Doc A/50/361.

5. UN Department of Peace Keeping Operations

UNDPKO *United Nations Peacekeeping Operations: Principles and Guidelines* (2008) <http://pbpu.unlb.org/pbps/Library/Capstone_Doctrine_ENG.pdf> access 21 January 2009.

6. UN Human Rights Council

UNHRC 'Human Rights in Palestine and other Occupied Arab Territories: Report of the United Nations Fact-Finding Mission on the Gaza Conflict' (25 September 2009) UN Doc A/HRC/12/48.

UNHRC 'Report of the Commission of Inquiry on Lebanon Pursuant to Human Rights Council Resolution S-2/1' (23 November 2006) UN Doc A/HRC/3/2.

Index